THE CAMBRIDGE COMPANIO
MODERN AMERICAN POETI

The Cambridge Companion to Modern American Poetry comprises original essays by nineteen distinguished scholars. It offers a critical overview of major and emerging American poets of the twentieth century in addition to critical accounts of the representative schools, movements, regional settings, archival resources, and critical reception that define modern American poetry. The *Companion* stretches the narrow term of "literary modernism," which encompasses works published from approximately 1890 to 1945, to include a more capacious and usable account of American poetry's evolution from the twentieth century to the present. The essays collected here seek to account for modern American verse against the contexts of broad political, social, and cultural fields and forces. This volume gathers together major voices that represent the best in contemporary critical approaches and methods.

Walter Kalaidjian is professor and chair of the department of English at Emory University. He is the author of *The Edge of Modernism: American Poetry and the Traumatic Past* and editor of *The Cambridge Companion to American Modernism*.

A complete list of books in the series is at the back of this book.

THE CAMBRIDGE
COMPANION TO

MODERN AMERICAN POETRY

THE CAMBRIDGE COMPANION TO

MODERN AMERICAN POETRY

Edited by

WALTER KALAIDJIAN
Emory University

CAMBRIDGE
UNIVERSITY PRESS

32 Avenue of the Americas, New York, NY 10013-2473, USA

Cambridge University Press is part of the University of Cambridge.

It furthers the University's mission by disseminating knowledge in the pursuit of
education, learning, and research at the highest international levels of excellence.

www.cambridge.org
Information on this title: www.cambridge.org/9781107683280

© Cambridge University Press 2015

First published 2015

Printed in Great Britain by Clays Ltd, St Ives plc

A catalog record for this publication is available from the British Library.

Library of Congress Cataloging in Publication data
The Cambridge companion to modern American poetry / [edited by]
Walter Kalaidjian, Emory University.
pages   cm. – (Cambridge companions to literature)
Includes bibliographical references and index.
ISBN 978-1-107-04036-6 (hardback) – ISBN 978-1-107-68328-0 (paperback)
1. American poetry – 20th century – History and criticism.   2. Literature and
society – United States – History – 20th century.   3. Modernism (Literature) – United
States.   I. Kalaidjian, Walter B., 1952– editor.
PS323.5.C28   2015
811'.509–dc23   2014025978

ISBN 978-1-107-04036-6 Hardback
ISBN 978-1-107-68328-0 Paperback

CONTENTS

CONTENTS

FIGURES

NOTES ON CONTRIBUTORS

BARTHOLOMEW BRINKMAN is Assistant Professor of English at Framingham State University, where he specializes in modern American poetry, print culture, cultural studies, and digital humanities. He is currently completing a book project on poetic modernism in the culture of mass print and coedits with Cary Nelson the Modern American Poetry Site.

EDWARD BRUNNER is Professor of English at Southern Illinois University, Carbondale. His most recent study is *Cold War Poetry* (2001). He teaches courses in modern poetry, popular culture, and graphic novels.

STEPHEN BURT is Professor of English at Harvard and the author of several books of criticism and poetry, among them *The Forms of Youth: Twentieth-Century Poetry and Adolescence* (2013) and, with David Mikics, *The Art of the Sonnet* (2011).

MARIA DAMON is Professor and Chair of the Department of Humanities and Media Studies at the Pratt Institute of Art. She is the author of *The Dark End of the Street: Margins in American Vanguard Poetry* (1993) and *Postliterary America: From Bagel Shop Jazz to Micropoetries* (2011) and the coeditor, with Ira Livingston, of *Poetry and Cultural Studies: A Reader* (2009).

ANNE DAY DEWEY teaches American literature at Saint Louis University's Madrid campus. Her work on twentieth-century poetry includes *Beyond* Maximus: *The Construction of Public Voice in Black Mountain Poetry* (2007); *The Collected Poems of Denise Levertov*, coedited with Paul Lacey (2013); and *Among Friends: Engendering the Social Site of Poetry* (2013), essays on friendship, gender, and poetry coedited with Libbie Rifkin.

RACHEL BLAU DUPLESSIS is the author of the long poem *Drafts*, spanning 1986 to 2012 (2013). She has written six critical books (from Cambridge, Iowa, and Alabama University Presses), coedited several anthologies, and published numerous articles on gender and poetics. DuPlessis edited *The Selected Letters of George*

Oppen (1990), coedited *The Objectivist Nexus* (1999), and has written extensively on objectivist poets. She is Professor Emerita at Temple University.

ALAN GOLDING teaches poetry and poetics at the University of Louisville. He is the author of *From Outlaw to Classic: Canons in American Poetry* (1995) and of numerous essays on modernist and contemporary poetry. His current projects include *Writing the New into History: Poetic Form and Social Formations in American Poetry*, under contract with the University of Alabama Press, and *"Isn't the Avant-Garde Always Pedagogical,"* a book on experimental poetics and / as pedagogy.

KAPLAN HARRIS is Associate Professor of English at St. Bonaventure University. His recent work can be found in *American Literature, Contemporary Literature, Paideuma, Postmodern Culture, Sagetrieb,* and *Poetry* magazine, and he is finishing a book on poetry and activism in the wake of the New Left. He edited, with Rod Smith and Peter Baker, *The Selected Letters of Robert Creeley* (2014).

YUNTE HUANG is Professor of English at the University of California, Santa Barbara. He is the author of *Transpacific Displacement* (2003), *Transpacific Imaginations* (2008), and others. His most recent book, *Charlie Chan: The Untold Story of the Honorable Detective and His Rendezvous with American History* (2010), won the Edgar Award and was a finalist for the National Book Critics Circle Award.

WALTER KALAIDJIAN is Professor and Chair of the English department of Emory University. He is the author of *Languages of Liberation: The Social Text in Contemporary American Poetry* (1989), *American Culture Between the Wars: Revisionary Modernism and Postmodern Critique* (1993), and *The Edge of Modernism: American Poetry and the Traumatic Past* (2005). In addition, he is the editor of *The Cambridge Companion to American Modernism* (2005).

EVAN KINDLEY is Visiting Assistant Professor at Claremont McKenna College. He is currently at work on a book manuscript entitled *Critics and Connoisseurs: Poet-Critics and the Administration of Modernism* and a critical biography of Hugh Kenner.

JANET MCADAMS won the American Book Award for her first poetry collection, *The Island of Lost Luggage* (2000). She is the author of a second collection, *Feral* (2007), and a novel, *Red Weather* (2012). She teaches at Kenyon College and, in 2005, founded the award-winning Earthworks Indigenous Poetry Series for Salt Publishing, UK.

CARY NELSON is Jubilee Professor of Liberal Arts and Sciences at the University of Illinois at Urbana-Champaign and formerly served as president of the American Association of University Professors. His many authored and edited books include *Repression and Recovery: Modern American Poetry and the Politics of Cultural Memory, 1910–1945* (1989); *Manifesto of a Tenured Radical* (1997); *Revolutionary Memory: Recovering the Poetry of the American Left* (2001); and *No University Is an Island: Saving Academic Freedom* (2010).

JOHN TIMBERMAN NEWCOMB is Professor of English at the University of Illinois at Urbana-Champaign. He has published three books on American poetry: *Wallace Stevens and Literary Canons* (1992), *Would Poetry Disappear? American Verse and the Crisis of Modernity* (2004), and *How Did Poetry Survive? The Making of Modern American Verse* (2012).

KIERAN QUINLAN is Professor of English at the University of Alabama at Birmingham. His books to date are *John Crowe Ransom's Secular Faith* (1989); *Walker Percy, the Last Catholic Novelist* (1996, 1998); and *Strange Kin: Ireland and the American South* (2005). He has just completed a study of Seamus Heaney and the decline of Irish Catholicism.

EVIE SHOCKLEY is Associate Professor of English at Rutgers University. She is the author of *Renegade Poetics: Black Aesthetics and Formal Innovation in African American Poetry* (2011), a critical study, as well as two books of poetry: *the new black* (2012), winner of the 2012 Hurston/Wright Legacy Award in Poetry, and *a half-red sea* (2006).

JAMES SMETHURST teaches Afro-American studies at the University of Massachusetts Amherst. He is the author of *The New Red Negro: The Literary Left and African American Poetry, 1930–1946* (1999); *The Black Arts Movement: Literary Nationalism in the 1960s and 1970s* (2005); and *The African American Roots of Modernism* (2011). He coedited *Left of the Color Line* (2003), *Radicalism in the South since Reconstruction* (2010), and *SOS – Calling All Black People: A Black Arts Reader* (2014).

MICHAEL THURSTON is Professor of English and Director of the American Studies Program at Smith College. He teaches courses on twentieth-century poetry in English, modernism, American literature, and American studies and has published numerous essays and reviews and three books: *Making Something Happen: American Political Poetry between the World Wars* (2001), *The Underworld in Twentieth-Century Poetry: From Pound and Eliot to Heaney and Walcott* (2009), and *Reading Postwar British and Irish Poetry* (with Nigel Alderman) (2014).

ALAN WALD is the H. Chandler Davis Professor of English Literature and American Culture at the University of Michigan. He is the author of a trilogy from the University of North Carolina Press on the U.S. literary left in the mid-twentieth century: *Exiles from a Future Time* (2002), *Trinity of Passion* (2007), and *American Night* (2012).

BARRETT WATTEN is Professor of English at Wayne State University and the author of *Frame: 1971–1990* (1997), *Bad History* (1998), and *Progress/Under Erasure* (2004). He edited the avant-garde journal *This* (1971–82) and co-edited *Poetics Journal* with Lyn Hejinian. His critical writing includes *Total Syntax* (1984); *The Constructivist Moment: From Material Text to Cultural Poetics* (2003), winner of the René Wellek Prize in 2004; and, forthcoming, *Questions of Poetics: Language Writing and Material Practice*.

CHRONOLOGY

1909	Ezra Pound, *Personae*
1912	*Poetry* magazine founded
1913	The International Exhibition of Modern Art (The Armory Show)
1914	Ezra Pound, ed., *Des Imagistes* Gertrude Stein, *Tender Buttons* *The Little Review* founded Outbreak of First World War
1915	Amy Lowell, ed. *Some Imagist Poets* *Others: A Magazine of the New Verse* founded Mina Loy, "Love Songs"
1916	H. D., *Sea Garden*
1917	T. S. Eliot, *Prufrock and Other Observations* Mina Loy, "Songs to Joannes" United States enters the First World War Revolutions in Russia Pulitzer Prize established
1918	Tristan Tzara, *Dada Manifesto* End of First World War
1919	T. S. Eliot, "Tradition and the Individual Talent" Treaty of Versailles League of Nations founded Prohibition Act passed by the U.S. Congress
1920	T. S. Eliot, *The Sacred Wood* Ezra Pound, *Hugh Selwyn Mauberley*

William Carlos Williams, *Kora in Hell: Improvisations*
The Dial reestablished as a literary magazine
Nineteenth Amendment establishes women's suffrage in the United States

1921   *New York Dada* magazine founded

1922   T. S. Eliot's *The Waste Land* published in *The Criterion,* founded that year
Claude McKay, *Harlem Shadows*
James Weldon Johnson, ed., *The Book of American Negro Poetry*

1923   Mina Loy, *Lunar Baedecker*
Wallace Stevens, *Harmonium*
Jean Toomer, *Cane*
William Carlos Williams, *Spring and All*

1924   Marianne Moore, *Observations*
André Breton, *Manifesto of Surrealism*

1925   Alain Locke, ed., *The New Negro*
Ezra Pound, *A Draft of XVI Cantos*
Scopes trial

1926   Langston Hughes, *The Weary Blues*
Fire!! magazine founded

1928   Experimental television broadcasts begin in the United States

1929   Collapse of the New York stock market
The Museum of Modern Art opens in New York City

1930   Hart Crane, *The Bridge*
T. S. Eliot, *Ash Wednesday*
William Empson, *Seven Types of Ambiguity*
Ezra Pound, *A Draft of XXX Cantos*

1931   E. E. Cummings, *Viva*
Poetry magazine publishes issue on "Objectivist" verse, edited by Louis Zukofsky

1932   Sterling A. Brown, *Southern Road*
T. S. Eliot, *Selected Essays*
Louis Zukofsky, ed., *An "Objectivist's" Anthology*

1933	Adolf Hitler elected Chancellor of Germany Prohibition repealed in the United States
1934	George Oppen, *Of Being Numerous*
1935	Marianne Moore, *Selected Poems* Wallace Stevens, *Ideas of Order*
1936	The Spanish Civil War begins
1937	Wallace Stevens, *The Man with the Blue Guitar*
1938	Cleanth Brooks and Robert Penn Warren, *Understanding Poetry* Ezra Pound, *Guide to Kulchur* Muriel Rukeyser, *The Book of the Dead*
1939	Second World War begins
1940	*View* magazine founded by Charles Henri Ford in New York City
1941	John Crowe Ranson, *The New Criticism* The United States enters the Second World War after the Japanese bombing of Pearl Harbor First commercial television broadcast in the United States
1942	Wallace Stevens, *Notes Toward a Supreme Fiction*
1944	H. D., *The Walls Do Not Fall* T. S. Eliot, *Four Quartets*
1945	Gwendolyn Brooks, *A Street in Bronzeville* H. D., *Tribute to the Angels* Bombing of Hiroshima and Nagasaki; end of Second World War Formation of United Nations The House Un-American Activities Committee (HUAC) becomes a permanent standing committee of the U.S. House of Representatives.
1946	Elizabeth Bishop, *North & South* H. D., *Flowering of the Rod* Lorine Niedecker, *New Goose* William Carlos Williams, *Paterson*, Book I (Books II–V published 1948, 1949, 1951, 1958)

W. H. Auden becomes a naturalized citizen of the United States

Ezra Pound declared insane and committed to St. Elizabeth's Hospital in Washington, DC

1947　Robert Lowell, *Lord Weary's Castle*
HUAC holds special hearings into alleged communist influence in Hollywood and the entertainment industry, leading to the blacklisting of hundreds of artists by the Hollywood studios

1948　W. H. Auden, *The Age of Anxiety*
Ezra Pound, *The Pisan Cantos*

1949　Gwendolyn Brooks, *Annie Allen*
Charles Olson, "The Kingfishers"

1950　E. E. Cummings, *XAIPE: 71 Poems*
Charles Olson, "Projective Verse"
Wallace Stevens, *The Auroras of Autumn*
Korean War begins
In a speech in Wheeling, West Virginia, Senator Joseph McCarthy gains national prominence by claiming to have a list of the names of known communists working in the State Department

1951　Langston Hughes, *Montage of a Dream Deferred*
Marianne Moore, *Collected Poems*
Origin magazine founded
Charles Olson appointed rector of Black Mountain College

1952　Robert Creeley, *Le Fou*
Archibald MacLeish, *Collected Poems, 1917–1952*
W. S. Merwin, *A Mask for Janus*

1953　John Ashbery, *Turandot and Other Poems*
Kenneth Koch, *Poems*
Charles Olson, *In Cold Hell, In Thicket*
Theodore Roethke, *The Waking*
Melvin Tolson, *Libretto for the Republic of Liberia*
City Lights Bookstore founded in San Francisco
Korean War ends

1954　Anthony Hecht, *A Summoning of Stones*
Black Mountain Review founded

The U.S. Supreme Court ruling in *Brown v. Board of Education* declares unconstitutional the racial segregation of public schools

1955   W. H. Auden, *The Shield of Achilles*
Lawrence Ferlinghetti, *Pictures of the Gone World*
Adrienne Rich, *The Diamond Cutters*
The Six Gallery reading in San Francisco

1956   John Ashbery, *Some Trees*
John Berryman, *Homage to Miss Bradstreet*
Allen Ginsberg, *Howl and Other Poems*
Denise Levertov, *Here and Now*
Richard Wilbur, *Things of This World*
Black Mountain College closes its doors

1957   Donald Hall, Robert Pack, and Louis Simpson, eds., *New Poets of England and America*
Frank O'Hara, *Meditations in an Emergency*
Wallace Stevens, *Opus Posthumous*

1958   Gregory Corso, *Bomb* and *Gasoline*
Lawrence Ferlinghetti, *A Coney Island of the Mind*
Yugen magazine founded

1959   Ted Joans, *Funky Jazz Poems*
Robert Lowell, *Life Studies*
W. D. Snodgrass, *Heart's Needle*
Gary Snyder, *Riptrap and Cold Mountain Poems*
Louis Zukofsky, "*A*," 1–12

1960   Donald Allen, ed., *The New American Poetry 1945–1965*
Robert Duncan, *The Opening of the Field*
Charles Olson, *The Maximus Poems*
Anne Sexton, *To Bedlam and Part Way Back*
Gwendolyn Brooks, *The Bean Eaters*

1961   LeRoi Jones, *Preface to a Twenty Volume Suicide Note*
The Floating Bear newsletter founded

1962   John Ashbery, *The Tennis Court Oath*
Cid Corman, *Sun Rock Man*
Robert Creeley, *For Love: Poems 1950–1960*
Barbara Guest, *Poems: The Locations of Things, Archaics, The Open Skies*

Denise Levertov, *The Jacob's Ladder*
William Carlos Williams, *Pictures from Brueghel and Other Poems*
Second Vatican Council

1963   James Wright, *The Branch Will Not Break*
The March on Washington; Martin Luther King, Jr., delivers his "I Have a Dream Speech" on the steps of the Lincoln Memorial
President John F. Kennedy assassinated in Dallas, Texas

1964   Ted Berrigan, *The Sonnets*
John Berryman, *77 Dream Songs*
Robert Lowell, *For the Union Dead*
Frank O'Hara, *Lunch Poems*
Jack Spicer, *Language*

1965   A. R. Ammons, *Corson's Inlet* and *Tape for the Turn of the New Year*
Charles Olson, *Proprioception*
Sylvia Plath, *Ariel*
Melvin Tolson, *Harlem Gallery*
First U.S. combat troops arrive in Vietnam

1966   Amiri Baraka, *Black Art*
James Merrill, *Nights and Days*
Diane di Prima, *Poems for Freddie*
Anne Sexton, *Live or Die*

1967   Robert Bly, *The Light Around the Body*
Robert Creeley, *Words*
Nikki Giovanni, *Black Feeling, Black Talk*
Anthony Hecht, *The Hard Hours*
Lenore Kandel, *Word Alchemy*
W. S. Merwin, *The Lice*
James Wright, *Shall We Gather at the River*

1968   Amiri Baraka and Larry Neal, eds., *Black Fire*
Ed Dorn, *Gunslinger*
Robert Duncan, *Bending the Bow*
Audre Lorde, *The First Cities*
Lorine Niedecker, *North Central*
George Oppen, *Of Being Numerous*
Mark Strand, *Reasons for Moving*

	Martin Luther King, Jr., assassinated in Memphis, Tennessee

Martin Luther King, Jr., assassinated in Memphis, Tennessee
Senator Robert F. Kennedy assassinated in Los Angeles, California

1969   John Berryman, *The Dream Songs*
James Schuyler, *Freely Espousing*
The Stone Wall Riots take place in New York City, launching the gay liberation movement in the United States
NASA lands the first manned spacecraft on the moon

1970   Amiri Baraka, *It's Nation Time*
Clark Coolidge, *Space*
Audre Lorde, *Cables to Rage*
Sonia Sanchez, *We a BaddDDD People*
Tottel's newsletter founded

1971   Hugh Kenner, *The Pound Era*
Galway Kinnell, *The Book of Nightmares*
W. S. Merwin, *The Carrier of Ladders*
This journal founded

1972   H. D., *Hermetic Definition*
Allen Ginsberg, *The Fall of America: Poems of These States, 1965–1971*

1973   Frank Bidart, *Golden State*
Robert Lowell, *The Dolphin*
Muriel Rukeyser, *Breaking Open*
Last U.S. combat troops withdraw from Vietnam

1974   A. R. Ammons, *Sphere: The Form of a Motion*
Leslie Marmon Silko, *Laguna Woman*
Gary Snyder, *Turtle Island*
President Richard Nixon resigns following the Watergate scandal

1975   John Ashbery, *Self-Portrait in a Convex Mirror*
Denise Levertov, *Freeing the Dust*
Kenneth Koch, *The Art of Love*
Anne Waldman, *Fast Speaking Woman*

1976   James Merrill, *Divine Comedies*

1977   John Ashbery, *Houseboat Days*
Jayne Cortez, *Mouth on Paper*

Apple Computers launches the Apple II, one of the first generation of mass-market personal computers

1978 Rae Armantrout, *Extremities*
Robert Grenier, *Sentences*
Lyn Hejinian, *Writing Is an Aid to Memory*
Audre Lorde, *The Black Unicorn*
Adrienne Rich, *The Dream of a Common Language*
L=A=N=G=U=A=G=E magazine founded

1979 Robert Hass, *Praise*
Steve McCafferey and bpNichol, *Sound Poetry: A Catalogue*

1980 James Schuyler, *The Morning of the Poem*
Louise Glück, *Descending Figure*
Lyn Hejinian, *My Life*
Sharon Olds, *Satan Says*

1981 Charles Bernstein, *Disfrutes*
Carolyn Forché, *The Country Between Us*
Sylvia Plath, *The Collected Poems*
Ron Silliman, *Tjanting*

1982 Jayne Cortez, *Firespitter*
Larry Eigner, *Water/Places/a Time*
Bernadette Mayer, *Midwinter Day*
James Merrill, *The Changing Light at Sandover*
Charles Wright, *The Southern Cross*

1983 Charles Bernstein, *Islets/Irritations*
Frank Bidart, *The Sacrifice*
Elizabeth Bishop, *Collected Poems 1927–1979*
Joy Harjo, *She Had Some Horses*
Mary Oliver, *American Primitive*
Gary Snyder, *Axe Handles*

1984 Bruce Andrews and Charles Bernstein, eds., *The L=A=N=G=U=A=G=E Book*
John Ashbery, *A Wave*
Mei-Mei Berssenbrugge, *The Heat Bird*
Robert Duncan, *Ground Work: Before the War*
Yusef Komunyakaa, *Copacetic*

1985 Amy Clampitt, *What the Light Was Like*
Susan Howe, *My Emily Dickinson*

Sonia Sanchez, *Home Girls and Handgrenades*
Gjertrud Schnackenberg, *The Lamplit Answer*

1986   Philip Dacey and David Jauss, eds., *Strong Measures: Contemporary American Poetry in Traditional Forms*
Rita Dove, *Thomas and Beulah*

1987   Gloria Anzaldúa, *Borderlands/La Frontera: The New Mestiza*
Rachel Blau DuPlessis, *Tabula Rosa*
Robert Duncan, *Ground Work II: In the Dark*
Jorie Graham, *The End of Beauty*
Ron Silliman, *The New Sentence*

1988   Ted Berrigan, *A Certain Slant of Sunlight*
Michael Palmer, *Sun*
Leslie Scalapino, *way*

1989   Ed Dorn, *Abhorrences*
Robert Hass, *Human Wishes*
Bernadette Mayer, *Sonnets*
Fall of the Berlin Wall

1990   Frank Bidart, *In the Western Night: Collected Poems*
Joy Harjo, *In Mad Love and War*
Derek Walcott, *Omeros*

1991   John Ashbery, *Flow Chart*
Billy Collins, *Questions About Angels*
Adrienne Rich, *An Atlas of the Difficult World*
Collapse of the USSR
The Persian Gulf War
The World Wide Web becomes publicly accessible

1992   Sherman Alexie, *The Business of Fancydancing*
Charles Bernstein, *A Poetics*
Louise Glück, *The Wild Iris*
Thom Gunn, *The Man with the Night Sweats*
Lyn Hejinian, *The Cell*

1994   Charles Bernstein, *Content's Dream*

1996   Mark Jarman and David Mason, eds., *Rebel Angels: 25 Poets of the New Formalism*
Susan Howe, *Frame Structures*

WALTER KALAIDJIAN

Introduction

Increasingly, contemporary critical accounts of what William Carlos Williams called "the local conditions" (1948, 146) of modern American poetry have engaged more worldly expanses of time and space, reading American verse written over the past century in the contexts of United States history and culture that participate in a decidedly global community. This collection in particular stretches the more narrow period term of literary modernism – works published between, say, 1890 and 1945 – favoring a more capacious and usable account of poetry's "modern" evolution over the entire twentieth century up to the present. Supplementing the protocols of literary "close reading" advanced by the so-called American New Critics, studies of modern American poetry have moved beyond attention to the isolated work of literature, the focus on a single author, and the domestic containments of national narration. Not unlike Ezra Pound's 1934 description of the American epic as a "poem containing history," contemporary criticism of American verse has sought to contextualize canonical and emerging poems against wider political, social, and cultural fields and forces. These and other advances in the reception of modern American poetry reflect broader and concerted efforts to question, revise, and expand the received canon of American literature.

Such revisionary initiatives date back to the latter decades of the twentieth century with Paul Lauter's "Reconstructing American Literature" project. It began as a series of conferences sponsored by the Rockefeller Foundation and Lilly Endowment, later published in the critical volume *Reconstructing American Literature* (1983) followed by Sacvan Bercovitch's scholarly collection *Reconstructing American Literary History* (1986). Changes in critical practice were further popularized that same year in the widely adopted *Heath Anthology of American Literature* (1986) and subsequently in literary histories, such as *The Columbia Literary History of the United States* (1988), and scholarly journals, such as *American Literary History* (1989), edited by Gordon Hutner. In studies of modern American poetry, several "recovery" projects, most notably Cary Nelson's *Repression and Recovery* (1989), questioned the "cultural memory" of the received canon of modern American poetry. Since then, important studies of twentieth-century American verse have unearthed a trove of new schools and movements, new authors, new manuscripts, and new cultural objects that were variously "lost," "forgotten," or politically suppressed in the reception of the modern American verse tradition. A thumbnail sketch of these titles would include Rita Barnard, *The Great Depression and the Culture of Abundance* (1995), Timothy Yu, *Race and the Avant-Garde* (1995), Michael Davidson, *Ghostlier Demarcations* (1997), Alan Golding, *From Outlaw to Classic* (1997), James Smethurst, *The New Red Negro* (1999), Rachel Blau DuPlessis, *Genders, Races and Religious Cultures in Modern American Poetry* (2001), Alan Wald, *Exiles from a Future Time* (2002), John Timberman Newcomb, *Would Poetry Disappear?* (2004), Walter Kalaidjian, *The Edge of Modernism* (2006), Adalaide Morris, *How to Live / What to Do* (2008), Jahan Ramazani, *A Transnational Poetics* (2008), Al Filreis, *Counter-revolution of the Word* (2008), Lynn Keller, *Re-making It New* (2009), Evie Shockley, *Renegade Poetics* (2011), and Maria Damon, *Postliterary America* (2011), to name a few. Thus, how modern American poetry is read and taught now differs significantly in the wake of the theoretical revolution of the past thirty years. The canon of prize-winning authors and valorized texts that have sustained modern American poetry's literary reputation – Ezra Pound, T. S. Eliot, Wallace Stevens, Robert Frost, Langston Hughes, William Carlos Williams, Marianne Moore, and Mina Loy, among others – has opened onto a democratic conversation that recovers a hitherto forgotten diversity of poetic voices. Equally important, how we read American modernist poets – whether canonical or noncanonical – differs markedly owing to the ways in which modern American verse is mediated by newer and more sophisticated understandings of nationalism, regionalism, periodization, race, sexuality and gender, ethnicity, class, and culture. Thus, the *Cambridge Companion to Modern American Poetry* eschews earlier traditions of modern American verse organized under the canonical aegis of individual talents. Instead, it accounts for modern American poetry as a discursive community, a locus not so much governed by common identities dominated by canonical traditions but rather one enlivened and enriched by what Roberto Esposito defines in terms of "plurality, difference, and alterity" (2012, 5). Toward that end, the *Cambridge Companion to Modern American Poetry* gathers together major critical voices that represent the best practices of contemporary critical approach and method.

This collection provides a sophisticated introduction to the rich archive of modern verse produced over the past century, beginning with John

Timberman Newcomb's account of what modern poets such as Alfred Kreymborg, Harriet Monroe, Louis Untermeyer, and Marguerite Wilkinson characterized as "the New Poetry" following the *fin de siècle*. In "The Emergence of 'The New Poetry'" Newcomb reaches back to the genteel canon of the Fireside Poets, who were underwritten by an insular and nostalgic resistance to the energies of modernity. In addition, he attends to the emergence of a properly modern sensibility in figures such as Stephen Crane, Edwin Arlington Robinson, and Edna St. Vincent Millay up through Robert Frost and Wallace Stevens. Intervening in the twentieth-century reception of the early modernist period, Newcomb challenges the received narrative divide between avant-garde and popular poetries promulgated by the American "New Critics" at mid-century. Instead of placing experimental modernists against popular voices of the period, Newcomb argues forcefully for recovering "a spectrum punctuated with surprising alliances and admirations between poets later assumed to be inherently opposed: Vachel Lindsay and W. B. Yeats, Allen Tate and Edna St. Vincent Millay, Ezra Pound and Carl Sandburg."

In "Modern American Archives and Scrapbook Modernism," Bartholomew Brinkman considers theories of archival preservation, provenance, and curation in the institutional formation of the modern American poetry canon, focusing on archival sites, such as the Library of Congress, the University of Chicago, and the University of Buffalo. Such centers of archival consignation, he argues, preserve a more wide-ranging modernism than is represented in volumes of selected or collected poems. Libraries of little magazines and first edition books offer – through their alternative drafts of poems, multiple versions, and early iterations – critical roads not taken. Similarly, archives of letters, drafts, and ephemeral clippings often reveal authorial intention or ambivalence inscribed in withheld or unpublished versions of poems that differ from the seemingly final drafts of canonical works. Offering close readings of Amy Lowell's and Edna St. Vincent Millay's scrapbooks, Brinkman demonstrates how modernist scrapbooking practices present a unique mode of poetry's archival preservation, one that models the most characteristic of modern literary forms: the collage poem.

Alan Golding's chapter on "Experimental Modernisms" attends to the language experiments initiated by Ezra Pound, Hilda Doolittle, T. S. Eliot, and Gertrude Stein in the early twentieth century. Beginning in the 1910s with the Imagist and Vorticist movements and the "direct treatment of the thing," this chapter's discussion of experimental modernism offers readings of Pound's early modern lyricism on view in volumes such as *Personae* (1909) and *Cathay* (1915) and in such early critiques of late Victorian culture as "Homage to Sextus Propertius" (1919) and *Hugh Selwyn Mauberley*

(1921). In addition, Pound's influence is also examined in Hilda Doolittle's early, Sapphic modernism in the compressed pastoral verse of *Sea Garden* (1916). Golding further accounts for what Pound dubbed as *logopoeia* in Mina Loy's early modern verse. The chapter also takes up the contemporaneous work of T. S. Eliot in *Prufrock and Other Observations* (1917), the prose poems that Stein published as *Tender Buttons* (1914), and Williams's inventive language experiments in *Kora in Hell* (1920) and *Spring and All* (1923). In addition to discussing representative poems from these early volumes, Golding also investigates the cultural and aesthetic contexts of the emergence of experimental modern verse in salons, such as those hosted by Alfred Stieglitz, Walter and Louise Arensberg, and Mabel Dodge in New York and those of Natalie Barney and Gertrude Stein in Paris.

In "The Legacy of New York," Cary Nelson broadens the focus on experimental modernism by considering its emergence in the American avant-garde scene associated with New York City, beginning with the 1913 Armory Show, the initial publication of *Others* magazine in 1915, and the introduction of Dadaist-influenced journals from 1915–1919, such as *291*, *391*, *The Blind Man*, *Rongwrong*, and *New York Dada*. Nelson focuses on readings of William Carlos Williams, Mina Loy, and Baroness Elsa von Freytag-Loringhoven, who published in such journals as *The Little Review*, *Liberation, Broom*, and *transition*. Moreover, Nelson underscores poetry's representation of progressive, anti-imperialist, and anti-racist political stances in, for example, The New England Anti-Imperialist League's collection *Liberty Poems* (1900), lodged against the U.S. war in the Philippines, and Claude McKay's New York-based critiques of American racism. Finally, this chapter considers poets loosely affiliated through the Greenwich Village scene including Lola Ridge, Edna St. Vincent Millay, and E. E. Cummings.

In "The Modern American Long Poem" Anne Day Dewey next offers an overview of the modern American long poem as an expanded verse form distinct from the classical epic. Unlike the epic's totalizing narratives of nation formation and heroic masculinity, the modern long poem in the United States offers, as she details, a more eclectic, encyclopedic, and differentiated account of the fragmented, nonlinear, and often transnational sprawl of modern experience. In addition to providing an account of the genre theory on, and critical reception of, the American long poem, Dewey reviews formal similarities and nuanced distinctions among major works in this subgenre by Ezra Pound, Hilda Doolittle, T. S. Eliot, Hart Crane, Wallace Stevens, and Melvin Tolson, among others.

James Smethurst, in "American Modernism and the Harlem Renaissance," offers a cultural reading of Harlem as a site of literary production during the 1920s and pays close attention to both canonical and emergent figures in the critical reception of the Harlem Renaissance as a literary movement. In addition, in accounting for the social history of race and class differences in early twentieth-century America, Smethurst explores the emergence of the "new negro" aesthetic in the work of Fenton Johnson, Jean Toomer, Langston Hughes, Claude McKay, Nella Larsen, and Jessie Fauset, among others.

Beginning with Louis Zukofsky's February 1931 *Poetry Magazine* issue on "objectivist" verse by Charles Reznikoff, Carl Rakosi, George Oppen, Basil Bunting, William Carlos Williams, and Kenneth Rexroth, Rachel Blau DuPlessis reviews, in "Objectivist Poetry and Poetics," the aesthetic tenets that initially defined objectivist poetics in manifestos such as "Program: 'Objectivists,' 1931" and collections like *An Objectivist Anthology* (1932). In addition, this chapter considers the nuanced differences among the actual poets who wrote under that rubric, including Zukofsky's original grouping and later figures associated with objectivist poetry, such as Lorine Niedecker. Finally, this chapter ends by considering the objectivist legacy as it is inscribed in the poetics of the Black Mountain School, the Beats, and Language writers.

In "American Poetry and the Popular Front," Alan Wald offers a reading in the vein of recent recovery projects focusing on American poetry that emerged from the progressive public sphere of the Great Depression. Wald offers a cultural study of how poetry came to reflect the social vicissitudes of the 1930s: widespread unemployment, economic collapse, and global conflicts, such as the Spanish Civil War. But equally important, this chapter explores the relationship between proletarianism and modernism, examining how poetry as a social discourse offered compelling literary representations that agitated on behalf of such social justice issues as workers' rights to a living wage and full employment, women's conditions of labor in the workplace as well as the domestic sphere, anti-discrimination policies for racial and ethnic minorities in employment, housing, and education, and so on. Wald devotes sustained attention to the communist presence in American poetry promoted from grass-roots organizations such as the John Reed Clubs, to groups such as The Dynamo Poets, to little magazines such as *New Masses* and JRC journals such as Detroit's *The New Force*, Grand Rapids' *The Cauldron*, Indianapolis' *Midland Left*, Hollywood's *The Partisan*, Chicago's *Left Front*, Philadelphia's *Red Pen*, and New York's *Partisan Review* as well as to workers' anthologies such as *We Gather Strength* (1933). In addition, this chapter provides overviews of representative figures who made up poetry's "popular front" during this decade: Genevieve Taggard, Herman Spector, John Wheelwright, Lucia Trent, Kenneth Fearing, Joseph Kalar, Edwin Rolfe, Sol Funaroff, Langston Hughes, and Muriel Rukeyser, among others.

Counterbalancing such popular front careers, Kieran Quinlan in "Tracking the Fugitive Poets" traces the evolution of key figures affiliated with the Fugitive Poets at Vanderbilt University during the 1920s and later Kenyon College and the American New Criticism: John Crowe Ransom, Allen Tate, and Robert Penn Warren. In addition to reviewing their representative poems, Quinlan also explores their influential theories, as Fugitives, of agrarian and distributive economics, and their critical poetics as major theorists of modern poetry in essays such as Ransom's "Criticism, Inc." and Allen Tate's "Miss Emily and the Bibliographers." The chapter concludes with a consideration of the influence of the Fugitive/New Critical legacy on mid-century modernist poets.

Next, Stephen Burt's chapter on "Mid-Century Modernism" considers a spectrum of mid-century modernist poetics defined by the mastery of fixed forms such as the sonnet, villanelle, and sestina and by common themes such as mapmaking, travel, childhood, and ekphrastic musings in the careers of canonical American poets such as Theodore Roethke, Elizabeth Bishop, Randall Jarrell, Anthony Hecht, and James Merrill. While contextualizing the immediate postwar moment out of which these poets emerge as significant figures, Burt pays close attention to the aesthetic and thematic likenesses among them, as well as to the distinctive concerns and poetic styles that distinguish each of these major figures as an individual talent.

In "Psychotherapy and Confessional Poetry," Michael Thurston discusses a group of poets led by such figures as Robert Lowell, W. D. Snodgrass, and John Berryman who turn to the analytic truths of psychoanalysis and personal explorations of self, writing what M. L. Rosenthal characterized in a 1959 review as "confessional poetry." The confessional poem, or what Helen Vendler has more recently renamed as the "Freudian lyric," increasingly engaged the psychic foreclosures, political repressions, and social containments of what Lowell dubbed as the "tranquilized fifties" defining American postwar containment culture. In attending to the "confessional" dimension of mid-century modern poetry, this chapter focuses on the particular, institutional contexts of mental illness and its treatment regimens at mid-century as formative influences in the writing of Allen Ginsberg, Robert Lowell, Anne Sexton, and Sylvia Plath.

Kaplan Harris opens "Black Mountain Poetry" with an account of the American avant-garde aesthetic scene of artists, musicians, and intellectuals located at Black Mountain College that included such luminaries as Josef Albers, Willem de Kooning, Robert Motherwell, John Cage, Merce Cunningham, and a group of poets influenced by Charles Olson, the college's rector from 1951 to 1956, and his theory of "projective verse": Robert

Creeley, Robert Duncan, Ed Dorn, Larry Eigner, and Denise Levertov, among others. In addition to reviewing the particular poetics of these figures, Harris ends with a brief discussion of Black Mountain's influence on the poetry of the San Francisco Renaissance through the works of Duncan and Creeley, editor of the *Black Mountain Review*.

Supplementing Harris's review of the mid-century avant-garde in poetry, Maria Damon's account of the Beat counterculture and the San Francisco Renaissance in "Beat Poetry: HeavenHell USA, 1946–1965" reviews the emergence of the Beat movement in poetry first in New York City, initiated through the mutually influencing associations of Allen Ginsberg, Jack Kerouac, William Burroughs, and, later, Frank O'Hara and Gregory Corso, as well as Amiri Baraka (LeRoi Jones) and Diane di Prima's collaborations for the little magazines *Yugen* and *The Floating Bear*. In addition, this chapter also accounts for the emergence of the Beat aesthetic on the West Coast through Lawrence Ferlinghetti's San Francisco-based City Lights bookstore and press and through such inaugural events as the "Six Poets at the Six Gallery" reading, presided over by Kenneth Rexroth and featuring Ginsberg, Kerouac, Gary Snyder, Philip Whalen, Michael McClure, and Philip Lamantia. In addition, to discussing these major Beat talents, the chapter also considers the contribution of writers such as Jack Spicer, John Wieners, the African-American beat poet Bob Kaufman, and female writers associated with the Beat movement, such as Helen Adam, Diane di Prima, Hettie Jones, Brenda Frazer, Joanne Kyger, and Anne Waldman.

Evie Shockley begins her study of "The Black Arts Movement and Black Aesthetics" by framing the emergence in the 1960s of the Black Arts Movement (BAM) in the context of the Black Power movement of the pre-Civil Rights era in the United States. Inaugurated in the mid-1960s by such African-American poets as Amiri Baraka and Larry Neal, who figured prominently in such venues as Harlem's Black Arts Repertory Theatre and the Umbra workshop, BAM was popularized in Baraka and Neal's landmark manifesto and anthology *Black Fire* (1968). This chapter provides an overview of poets such as Gwendolyn Brooks, who adopted a distinctively black vernacular style in the mid-sixties with her move to Dudley Randall's Broadside Press and Haki Madhubuti's Third World Press that published other Black Aesthetic poets, such as Baraka, Nikki Giovanni, Sonia Sanchez, and Etheridge Knight. In addition to presenting the BAM poetics of these central figures of that period, Shockley surveys the diverse cultural geography of Black Aesthetics as a remarkably plural community of voices, examining more contemporary poets who foreground representations of race in writing out of a distinctively African-American poetic heritage: Lucille Clifton,

Yusef Komunyakaa, and Rita Dove, as well as the Darkroom Collective poet Kevin Young and Pulitzer Prize winner Natasha Trethewey.

Ed Brunner's "New York School and American Surrealism" considers how the urban milieu of mid-century New York City fostered a community of poets and painters that included notably John Ashbery, Frank O'Hara, Jackson Pollock, Larry Rivers, Jasper Johns, and Robert Rauschenberg but also Barbara Guest, Kenneth Koch, James Schuyler, Ted Berrigan, Diane Wakoski, Ron Padgett, and Alice Notley, among others. In addition, Brunner surveys what Jerome Rothenberg and Robert Kelly, writing in a 1961 issue of *Trobar*, called "the Deep Image" in reference to the work of Diane Wakoski and Clayton Eshelman and later appropriated and popularized by Robert Bly to characterize his work with Jungian archetypes in verse. The often-surrealist style of "Deep Image" poetics also influences the aesthetic trajectories of such major figures as James Wright and Galway Kinnell. In addition to offering close readings of these poets, Brunner also considers broader examples of an American surrealist poetics variously on view in the experimental linguistic character of such important American poets as W. S. Merwin, A. R. Ammons, and John Ashbery.

Writing against the narratives of individual identity that dominated the so-called "Native Renaissance" of the late twentieth century, Janet McAdams in "Land, Place, and Nation: Toward an Indigenous American Poetics" foregrounds the importance of space and place in imagining an indigenous American poetics, a body of verse considered within what Robert Warrior characterizes as tribal frameworks of native nationalism rather than through the careers of notable single authors. Focusing on the diverse writings of figures such as Simon Ortiz (Acoma Pueblo), Diane Glancy (Cherokee), Linda Hogan (Chickasaw), Deborah Miranda (Esselen-Chumash), Gladys Cardiff (Eastern Band Cherokee), and Layli Long Soldier (Oglala Lakota), McAdams examines indigenous representations of corporeality and embodiment shaped by America's traumatic legacies of tribal removal and land theft in contemporary Native American verse.

Yunte Huang begins "Transpacific and Asian American Counterpoetics" by reviewing the Orientalist legacy in modern American poetry, examining the "blossoms of the East" shaping the American literary imaginary from Pound and the Imagists through the Beat poets. In contrast to such American Orientalism, Huang presents the diasporic poetics of Chinese immigrants who, while detained at the Angel Island Immigration Station, carved verse on the walls. In addition, Huang offers readings of Japanese internees imprisoned in American camps, such as Tule Lake, during World War II. Huang also considers the politically charged verse of Carlos Bulosan and José García Villa, examining their legacies in the work of contemporary poets, such as

Theresa Cha, Frances Chung, Jessica Hagedorn, Mei-mei Berssenbrugge, Kimiko Hahn, Lois-Ann Yamanaka, Walter Lew, and Myung Mi Kim.

Barret Watten's survey of "Language Writing" begins with the inception of the Language poetry movement in newsletters and journals such as *Tottle's* (1970), edited by Ron Silliman, *This* (1971), edited by Robert Grenier and Barrett Watten, and *L=A=N=G=U=A=G=E* (1978), edited by Bruce Andrews and Charles Bernstein, among other venues and small presses. In addition to surveying the major manifestoes and theoretical statements, such as Ron Silliman's *The New Sentence* (1987), Barrett Watten considers Language poetry's experimental precursors in such figures as Gertrude Stein as well as such movements and tendencies as literary Dadaism, Russian Futurism, Black Mountain poetry, and Oulipo. He offers accounts of the poetic careers of figures such as Charles Bernstein, Ron Silliman, Harryette Mullen, Susan Howe, Lyn Hejinian, Bob Perelman, Hannah Weiner, and Rae Armantrout, among others. This chapter ends with a consideration of the ongoing collective autobiography *The Grand Piano* and the exfoliation of Language verse into new media poetics.

Finally, Evan Kindley's study "Poet-Critics and Bureaucratic Administration" offers a reading of the figure of the "poet-critic" by focusing on the hybrid careers of key American modernists who were not only recognized for their achievement in verse composition but who actively had a hand in the formation and reception of modern American poetry not only through their shaping roles as critics and theorists but, in certain cases, as postwar administrators funded by federal programs and private foundations. The chapter begins with a working characterization of the poet-critic and then moves to a consideration of major examples of poets who were also practicing critics, such as T. S. Eliot, Marianne Moore, Archibald MacLeish, and Sterling Brown. In addition, it reviews the administrative projects of modern American verse at mid-century through a consideration of John Crowe Ransom's leadership of the American "New Critics" and R. P. Blackmur's philanthropic campaign to promote little magazines, underwritten by the Rockefeller Foundation.

"It is difficult / to get the news from poems," William Carlos Williams famously observed, "yet men die miserably every day / for lack / of what is found there" (1938, 19). Traveling now at the speed of light, digital communication and social media from anywhere on the planet reach us instantaneously and are constantly at our finger tips. Nevertheless, Williams's observation remains, arguably, more pertinent than ever. Thus, committed to poetry's singular powers to, in Pound's dictum, "make it new," the contributors to the *Cambridge Companion to Modern American Poetry* offer us an invaluable resource that is otherwise hard to come by. Together, they provide today's authors, students, and general readers doorways into American verse as it continues to evolve across formal, avant-garde, and populist traditions: a body of work that goes to the heart of the American experience in the United States and beyond.

WORKS CITED

Esposito, Roberto. 2012. *Terms of the Political.* New York: Fordham University Press.

Pound, Ezra. *Make It New.* 1934. Faber & Faber: London.

Williams, William Carlos. 1938. *Asphodel, That Greeny Flower and Other Love Poems: That Greeny Flower.* New York: New Directions.

    1948. *The Autobiography of William Carlos Williams.* New York: New Directions.

I

JOHN TIMBERMAN NEWCOMB

The Emergence of "The New Poetry"

At the turn of the twentieth century, poetry in the United States underwent a serious crisis. Many feared that the genre was coming to an end because of an accelerated modern condition of sensational amusements, telegraphic forms of communication, and ruthless market conditions that left little room for contemplation or nuance. This decline in prestige was precipitous. In 1850, poetry was central to the emergence of the first national networks of publication, dissemination, and marketing for literary works by American authors. The century's third quarter was a period of canonical consolidation around six male writers called variously the New England poets, the Schoolroom Poets, and most descriptively the Fireside Poets, a sobriquet reflecting their nostalgic embrace of preindustrial imagery and values. By 1875, this "Fireside canon" (Henry Wadsworth Longfellow, John Greenleaf Whittier, Oliver Wendell Holmes, William Cullen Bryant, Ralph Waldo Emerson, and James Russell Lowell) loomed large not just among American poets but in the nation's entire cultural identity. Their visages gazed from millions of middle-American mantels, their milestone birthdays were celebrated across the land, and most young Americans exposed to literature in schools found themselves memorizing lines penned by one or more of the great men. Not surprisingly, these six were among the first literary writers elected to the Hall of Fame for Great Americans, begun in 1900.

By 1890, however, the canonical dominance of the Fireside Poets had begun to feel oppressive to many poets, commentators, and readers. The tendency of these aging figures to generate reassuring analogical demonstrations of Christian benevolence from nearly every subject they addressed was not suited to the increasingly secular and skeptical temper of late-century life. Equally problematic was their almost total unwillingness to speak to the social, demographic, and technological forces that were transforming the United States: mass immigration, the growth of the industrial metropolis, the consolidation of huge personal fortunes and corporate infrastructures, and the acceleration of experience brought about by new media of communication and modes of transportation. In this climate of social and technological upheaval, the defining qualities of Fireside verse – didacticism, sentimentality, rhapsodic tonalities, and studied timelessness – crossed some tipping point between nostalgia and irrelevance. Yet since poetry in America had been so long and exclusively identified with this Fireside group, their perceived decline, and the consensus view that no viable successor was poised to replace them, produced a widespread sense that the entire genre was obsolete and that all the great poets had already lived and died, all the great poems were written and filed away.

The sense of crisis was exacerbated by the unwillingness of those entrenched in positions of institutional power to concede that true poetry could have anything to do with the modernizing forces that were reshaping nearly all other areas of intellectual and professional endeavor in the United States. Although many of poetry's genteel custodians perceived that the old ways were becoming moribund and meaningless, they could only respond to innovations in poetic form or subject matter with corrosive skepticism. Even those tolerant of innovation in other literary forms were unwilling to accept it in verse, as a review of Stephen Crane's volume *War Is Kind* in *The Bookman* made clear: "There is room for [Crane's] individuality in fiction ... but in the strait domain of true poesy he can only win to greatness by a closer regard for the conventionalities of rhyme and reason that the centuries have taught us are the best" (Underwood 1899, 237). The terms of this evaluation and many others of the period reveal not only the shadows of tradition looming large but also a rigid and reductive ("strait") understanding of what "true" poetry could be. In this climate, verse not conforming to conventional forms and themes was likely to be summarily dismissed as not poetry at all.

As the irresistible forces of change collided with this immovable status quo, the result was an impasse that many people interpreted as the final throes of poetry in American culture. The two decades between 1890 and 1910 featured innumerable articles in the nation's magazines pondering poetry's current straits and doubtful future with titles such as "The Poet in an Age of Science," "Has Poetry Lost Its Hold on Us?", "The Lack of Poets," "Current Neglect of Poetry," "Is Poetry Unpopular?", "The Rejection of Poetry," "Have We Still Need of Poetry?", "The Passing of Poetry," and, the most comprehensive denial of poetry's modern utility, H. E. Warner's "Will Poetry Disappear?" which answered condescendingly in the affirmative: "The result has been good indeed in former ages, but there is enough of it. Have we not all the treasures of the poet?" (Warner 1899, 288). The continued genteel insistence on treating poetry as an activity of enlightened amateurism inhibited the emergence of a modern institutional infrastructure of the sort that most other art forms, including painting, music, and architecture, had begun to enjoy. In contrast, poets in 1900 would find not one American periodical devoted to publishing verse by living writers, not one national prize or other competition designed to reward superior works, and (despite the copious publication of verses in periodicals) no systematic effort to preserve the existence of such poems past the immediate moment of their appearance.

Not surprisingly, the young Americans who aspired to become poets in this climate produced work dominated by self-doubt, skepticism, and futility. These anxieties were revealed through two interdependent motifs found everywhere in their work: the portrayal of traditions as desiccated and ghostly forces that refuse to release their hold on the living; and the troping of the contemporary poet as a vagabond wandering through desolate landscapes lacking any markers of stability or community. William Vaughn Moody's "Road-Hymn for the Start" enacts this pattern with particular clarity, beginning with a gesture repudiating the domestic traditions of American genteel poetry: "Leave the early bells at chime, / Leave the kindled hearth to blaze." But however acutely Moody's poetic vagabonds know they must depart from these phantoms, a later couplet ("We have heard a voice cry 'Wander!' / That was all we heard it say") emphasizes that they have no idea where departure will take them or what, if anything, their journey might mean (Moody 1899, 840).

The young vagabonds who came of age in the 1890s seemed to internalize the futility of their poetic aspirations even into their own health and lives. In striking contrast to the six Fireside Poets, all of whom lived into comfortable old age, a great many of these younger writers were dead by the age of forty, including Richard Hovey, Francis Brooks, William Vaughn Moody, Stephen Crane, Paul Laurence Dunbar, Guy Wetmore Carryl, George Cabot Lodge, Trumbull Stickney, and Arthur Upson. Other talented aspirants such as Ellen Glasgow, Alice Dunbar-Nelson, Carolyn Wells, and Edgar Lee Masters avoided early demise but felt compelled to give up writing poetry for other literary pursuits, many never to return.

Yet the turn of the twentieth century is not the dead zone of American poetry that most literary histories written in the high-modernist tradition assumed it to be. The crisis of confidence endured by these young writers eventually helped transform American poetry by eroding previous assumptions about its nature and practice, and by asserting key modernist qualities such as irony, skepticism, and rebelliousness as foundational to poetry in the twentieth century rather than as merely impious and inhibiting, as genteel culture had taken them to be. At times, the ubiquitous persona of the vagabond could lead not only to repudiation of traditions but also to self-renewal, as in Paul Laurence Dunbar's "Morning": "With staff in hand and careless-free, / The wanderer fares right jauntily, / For towns and houses are, thinks he, / For scorning, for scorning" (Dunbar 1905, 51). To be sure, the ebullience of these lines was not the primary note struck by fin-de-siècle poets, who found scorn easier to sustain than jauntiness, but their rejection of towns and houses for the open road, however angst-ridden and aimless it felt at the time, was a crucial step toward the potent "New Poetry" movement that emerged after 1912.

The most insightful chroniclers of the turn-of-the-century crisis were Edwin Arlington Robinson and Stephen Crane. Robinson, a melancholy character who grew up in a northern New England landscape of snow, claustrophobia, and industrial decline, chronicled this milieu with mordant wit in his "Tilbury Town" poems. "The House on the Hill" (1897) is characteristic of Robinson's inventive repurposing of traditional poetic forms in its use of the elaborate old form of the villanelle to comment on the dilemma of fin-de-siècle poets, of whom he asks, "Why is it then we stray / Around that sunken sill? / They are all gone away, / And our poor fancy-play / For them is wasted skill" (Robinson 1905, 34). All too aware that the former inhabitants of the canonical house on the hill are gone and their tradition in "ruin and decay," aspirants encounter only silence and indifference as rewards for their own "poor" efforts. The futility and obsessiveness of their struggle is troped by the rigid a-b-a rhymes required by the villanelle form. A second defining feature of the villanelle, the two-line rhyming refrain, is used ingeniously as well, as the twinned phrases evoke the contemporary poet's dilemma with stark force; the decrepitude of the canon is obvious ("They are all gone away"), but this insight allows for no new directions ("There is nothing more to say") (34).

In contrast to the diffident Robinson, Stephen Crane, the last of fourteen children born to a New Jersey minister and his pious wife, embodied the most rebellious and avant-garde impulses of fin-de-siècle American culture. Reporting for newspapers in both urban and wartime locations throughout his short adult life, Crane sought out and reproduced sensational material as intensely as any muckraking journalist, resulting in his justly famous fictional works *Maggie: A Girl of the Streets* (1893) and *The Red Badge of Courage* (1895). His verse combines the ferocious intensity of those works with searching insight into the untenable position of the modern poet, whom he figures as an avant-garde seeker bucking the common path: "There were many who went in huddled procession: / They knew not whither; / But, at any rate, success or calamity / Would attend all in equality. / There was one who sought a new road. / He went into direful thickets, / And ultimately he died thus, alone; / But they said he had courage" (Crane 1896, 18). Near the end of his life, deeply affected by the incidents of combat and colonial oppression he witnessed, Crane made a striking shift from this gnomic existential mode toward a more directly politicized poetics of critique on America's ascendancy into global imperial power:

> When a people reach the top of a hill
> Then does God lean toward them,
> Shortens tongues, lengthens arms.
> A vision of their dead comes to the weak.
> The moon shall not be too old
> Before the new battalions rise.
> Blue battalions.
> The moon shall not be too old
> When the children of change shall fall
> Before the new battalions,
> The blue battalions.
> ("Blue Battalions," Crane 1898, 182)

At length, the crisis in American poetry became an opportunity for renewed energy and innovation. Robinson and a few other fin-de-siècle poets who endured into the 1910s were finally joined by a slightly younger group less burdened by the dead hand of the past, who discovered a new confidence through experimenting with unusual verse forms and previously prohibited subject matter. These first two waves of modern American poets – those born between 1860 and 1875 who began publishing before 1900, and those born between 1875 and 1895 who began after 1912 – vary widely in styles and themes, but they share an attraction to irony, skepticism, and nonconformism and an accompanying horror of piety and sentimentality. Whether they work in meter or *vers libre*, familiar stanzaic structures or collage forms, they turn away from platitude, abstraction, and formal regularity toward more particularized forms of expression involving relaxed rhythms, simplified syntax, direct description, and precise, vivid diction. "The Microscope" by Jeanne D'Orge uses a mechanism of modern scientific investigation as an emblem for the modern poet's mission: "Only to look – / To take at random slide after slide of life, / Put it under the lens," and to see "The bloom on the wings of emotion, / The clear still wriggling of obscenity, / Or section by / section, the changing cells / Of one's own soul" (D'Orge 1916, 223).

A necessary step in the revival of American poetry's energies and fortunes was the reconstruction of its moribund institutional infrastructure. These efforts included the founding of the Poetry Society of America in 1909 (with affiliated state societies to follow), the endowment of poetry prizes and other forms of financial patronage (beginning with *The Lyric Year* contest in 1912), and, from 1905, the annual compilation of poems published in

American periodicals by William S. Braithwaite. By far the most important single step in this process was taken by the Chicagoan Harriet Monroe, who in late 1911 decided, after more than two decades of struggling with little success to get her own verse published and noticed, that she had heard enough pious pronouncements that the noble art of poetry must be kept segregated from the spoiling conditions of modernity. Declaring this position to benefit neither poets nor readers, she challenged it by founding a monthly periodical devoted to contemporary verse that would treat poets not as amateurs or charity cases but as full participants in the civic, artistic, and social life of the nation. She argued that as workers with specialized talents whose products benefited their fellow citizens, poets (no less than architects, composers, and painters) deserved to be paid for their work and whenever possible provided with respite from other forms of labor in order to concentrate on verse. To the complacent dismissals of publishers that there existed no market for poetry in the United States, Monroe insisted that the market was there if only someone would make an effort to activate and serve it. Her magazine, *Poetry: A Magazine of Verse*, proved her right by garnering passionate attention – both positive and negative – from its first issue in October 1912.

Traditionalists were outraged at Monroe's persistent assertions that the art of poetry should be fully embedded in the modern scene of automobiles, skyscrapers, and big capitalism. Many even objected to Monroe's ingenious method of funding her magazine, which involved personally securing pledges for fifty dollars per year for five years from hundreds of her well-off acquaintances. But the disapproving voices of tradition were no longer the only ones being heard. *Poetry* also catalyzed the enthusiasm of a new generation of aspiring American poets as nothing had for many years. The explosive response to Monroe's venture demonstrated that poetry, far from withering away in a neglected corner, was in fact an object of passionate devotion to many younger Americans, especially to the growing number exposed to secular humanities curricula in colleges and universities beginning after 1890, who tended to emerge from college with life ambitions more expansive than simply to serve God or to make money as their ancestors might have done. *Poetry*'s editorial positions took full advantage of this generational divide, always advocating the side of youth, passion, and innovation. To describe its policy, Monroe used the metaphor of the "open door," which recast the role of editor from a gatekeeper looking for excuses to exclude everything not conforming to immutable traditions into someone continually listening for new voices and willing to sponsor them even when their experiments might lead to controversy or even ridicule.

Traditionalists (and some judgmental modernists such as Ezra Pound and Conrad Aiken) grumbled that *Poetry*'s eclectic policies led to the appearance of much mediocre verse in its pages. Monroe cheerfully rejoined by noting that the same charge could be made against any monthly periodical filled with contemporary poetry, but that no one else had even tried to create one. Under the circumstance of that moment, as she sought to sustain a conversation about poetry in the twentieth century that was not limited to any single coterie – and with no precedent whatever that such a venture could succeed – Monroe's temperamental inclination toward encouragement and inclusivity was clearly justified, not least by the extraordinary roster of poets that *Poetry* published just within its first five years. She had created what American poets and poetry-lovers had long bemoaned as impossible: a stable and vigorous venue that publicized all the significant books of American and British verse, defended experiments in both style and subject matter, and even insisted on paying poets for their work. In 1916 editorials, Monroe reflected on the transformation since 1912: "Now all is changed. It is as though some magician had waved his wand – presto, the beggar is robed in scarlet" (Monroe 1916a, 85), so that "Never before was there so much talk about poetry in this western world, or so much precious print devoted to its schools and schisms" (Monroe, 1916b, 140). This momentous renaissance was not, of course, a matter of magic but of hard work and faith, much of it her own.

Two of the most important and distinctive poets discovered by *Poetry* in its earliest years, Carl Sandburg and Wallace Stevens, can be used to measure the vast range of the New Poetry movement. A socialist journalist of working-class origins who was then miserably writing for a trade journal, Sandburg submitted a group of his verses cold to *Poetry* in early 1914, which Monroe seized upon for the March issue, where they appeared under the title "Chicago Poems." Monroe obtained maximum impact by placing his rough-edged portrait of the city, "Chicago," on the first page of the issue, where it became a manifesto not only for Sandburg but for her proudly Chicagoan magazine. Its first lines, calling the city the "Hog Butcher for the World" and the "Stormy, husky, brawling, / City of the Big Shoulders," announced Sandburg as a hard-edged new voice in American poetry and gave Chicago two nicknames that stick to this day. Condemned by genteel critics as "an impudent affront to the poetry-loving public," "Chicago" inspired the most virulent attacks yet on *Poetry* and the irresponsible modernists who ran it, for whom "the more freakish the form of expression, the more assured the triumph" ("New Lamps for Old" 231–2). Although he only resided in Chicago through 1919, Sandburg is still indelibly associated with the city as a result of his first three volumes, *Chicago Poems*,

Cornhuskers, and *Smoke and Steel*, which chronicle the effects of the industrialized city on its populace with more insight and power than any other American poet has ever achieved.

The verse and persona of Wallace Stevens are as refined and diffident as Sandburg's are rough-edged and assertive. A Harvard-educated attorney, Stevens first appeared in *Poetry* late in 1914, and his growing friendship with the editor led to the publication the next year of a poem of staggering verbal beauty and thematic ambition, "Sunday Morning," whose blank verse cadences and cosmological meditations claimed kinship with the noble lineage of *Paradise Lost* and *The Prelude*. "Sunday Morning" advances what might be termed a philosophical or even spiritual justification for setting aside Christian belief in favor of a refreshed embrace of sensuous pleasures suffused by awareness of mortality. Thus, for Stevens, "Death is the mother of beauty," strewing "the leaves / Of sure obliteration on our paths," but also bringing us "fulfilment to our dreams / And our desires" in entirely human terms (Stevens 1923, 102). In the striking final lines, however, the poem shifts away from self-absorbed celebration of humanity toward the quiet and enduring indifference of natural processes:

> Deer walk upon our mountains, and the quail
> Whistle about us their spontaneous cries;
> Sweet berries ripen in the wilderness;
> And, in the isolation of the sky,
> At evening, casual flocks of pigeons make
> Ambiguous undulations as they sink,
> Downward to darkness, on extended wings.
>
> (Stevens 1923, 104)

The uncanny sense of detachment from everyday concerns conveyed in these lines, culminated by the self-isolation and casualness with which the pigeons glide downward toward their ultimate darkness, was applied by many early readers to Stevens himself, who seemed to them bizarrely disinterested in the impact or value of his own work. Over the ensuing four decades, however, he would become an unexpectedly prolific producer of elegant, witty, philosophically challenging poems that would engage readers and critics as powerfully as any writer of the era.

The success of *Poetry* quickly led to the founding of other "little magazines" devoted to contemporary verse. The most important of these was *Others* (1915–19), curated mostly by Alfred Kreymborg, which focused intensively on avant-garde forms of unmetered verse (*vers libre*) and, considering its tiny circulation and precarious finances, sponsored a remarkable proportion of the poets later seen as central to the period, including

Pound, Stevens, Sandburg, William Carlos Williams, Marianne Moore, Amy Lowell, and others. Also important to the emergence of the New Verse was *The Masses* (1911–17), which combined utopian-socialist politics with a strong interest in the arts, publishing verse in nearly every style available at the time, as well as the more Eurocentric *Little Review* (1914–29), founded by Margaret Anderson. The *Little Review* was eventually dominated by the high modernism of its foreign editor, Pound, and those few writers whose work he admired, most notably James Joyce, whose *Ulysses* was serialized there beginning in 1918. Although individual magazines came and went, sometimes with dizzying rapidity, the little magazine as a format remained (and a century later remains) a stable and crucial venue for formally experimental and socially unorthodox literary work.

Little magazines such as *Poetry* and *Others* were crucial to the establishment of the energetic field of activity that became known as the New Verse or the New Poetry after 1912, but equally important was the transformation of attitudes among book publishers. As late as 1911, even relative innovators, such as Mitchell Kennerley, were still routinely deflating the hopes of poets by declaring that there was no market for volumes of contemporary verse. Those publishers willing to issue verse nearly always required subventions from the author, which diminished the entire field of poetry publication into a vanity project limited to those who could afford such luxuries. This untenable situation changed abruptly after 1912, as a few publishers, both established firms, such as Macmillan and Holt, and upstart youngsters, such as Kennerley and Alfred A. Knopf, began to risk their own coin on volumes of verse.

Publishers were encouraged by the results during 1913–14, with Macmillan president George P. Brett remarking – in an article perhaps hyperbolically entitled "Poets Again Best Sellers" – on the public's sudden change of attitude toward purchasing literature. In early 1915, Macmillan hit the jackpot with its publication of Edgar Lee Masters's *Spoon River Anthology*, the contents of which had been the sensation of American literature for several months previous as they were published piecemeal in the St. Louis magazine *Reedy's Mirror*. Masters's volume, still compelling reading a century later, was a series of epitaphs in colloquial *vers libre* that told interlocking life stories of the residents of an Illinois farming town. Like Sinclair Lewis's *Main Street* and many other less-remembered novels of the period, *Spoon River Anthology* spoke to the restiveness of an increasingly secular and urban populace impatient with the narrowness and hypocrisy of small-town America. That it did so in verse that was both strikingly innovative and readily accessible struck readers as all the more remarkable.

Another publishing success of 1914–15 (for Henry Holt) was *North of Boston*, the second volume by Robert Frost, a forty year old born in San Francisco but transplanted to New England, where he was unsuccessful in farming and teaching, before going to Britain in 1912, convinced that his work would never be noticed in his own country. There, he encountered Ezra Pound and Edward Thomas, who encouraged him and helped him to find a publisher in London. The resulting volume launched a lucrative public career for Frost that lasted fifty years despite his late start. Containing several of the best-known poems of the entire twentieth century including "The Death of the Hired Man," "Home Burial," "After Apple-Picking" and "Mending Wall," *North of Boston* took the New England vernacular style pioneered by Robinson to new heights of narrative fluency and psychological insight. "Mending Wall," which months after its appearance would seem a prescient allegory of the geopolitical pathologies that had led to the Great War, develops a trivial conflict between neighbors over the wall between their property into a profoundly bleak meditation on human interpersonal relations dominated by mistrust and antipathy. Describing his neighbor as "an old-stone savage armed" who "moves in darkness as it seems to me" merely because the neighbor wants to rebuild the wall, the poem's speaker betrays a contemptuous nature that is at least as disturbing as the neighbor's unquestioning obedience to "his father's" beliefs (Frost 1915, 12–13). The multiple layers of self-questioning irony that emerge over the course of the poem belie Frost's quaint public persona and give his work a depth and darkness that allows it to speak to more demanding readers while retaining an immediate appeal to nonspecialists.

Masters, Sandburg, and Frost were among several poets, also including Amy Lowell, Vachel Lindsay, and Edna St. Vincent Millay, who after 1912 garnered a sizable and passionate audience both inside the avant-garde circles of little magazines and across literate America more broadly. These poets, sometimes termed *popular modernists*, elaborated a poetics engaged with the concerns of everyday life in relatively accessible forms, imagery, and diction. Four of the six explored the possibilities of *vers libre*, while Frost and Millay followed Robinson's example in discovering how traditional formal elements such as blank verse and the sonnet could be rejuvenated by vernacular accents and modern attitudes. The charismatic Millay projected a politically and sexually outspoken persona that made her the central American icon of the "New Womanhood" for decades thereafter. The four sonnets appearing in her volume *A Few Figs from Thistles* are characteristic in upending the florid romanticism often associated with the form in favor of an insouciant embrace of casual sexual adventuring. The last of them begins "I shall forget you presently, my dear, / So make the most of this, your little day, / Your little month, your little half a year." The speaker concludes by attributing the inconstancy of intimate relations not to the moral deficiency of individuals but to the natural desires of the human animal:

> I would indeed that love were longer-lived,
> And vows were not so brittle as they are,
> But so it is, and nature has contrived
> To struggle on without a break thus far, –
> Whether or not we find what we are seeking
> Is idle, biologically speaking.
>   (Millay 1922, 39)

As these popular modernists made their dramatic ascent into celebrity and relative wealth between 1914 and 1920, other more avant-garde strains of modernism were developing among poets who would gradually supersede them in terms of critical reputation, notably Stevens, Williams, Moore, Pound and T. S. Eliot. It would be a mistake, however, to assume that the divide between popular and avant-garde modernism that eventually shaped many historical narratives of twentieth-century American poetry was a feature of the New Poetry from its inception. In fact this divide is very much a retrospective construction of postwar New Criticism, which winnowed the canon of viable modernist poets from dozens to just a very few. Close examination of the scene of American poetry during the 1910s reveals instead a boisterous but generally harmonious coexistence between those writers later lionized as high-modernist and those diminished as popular. To be sure, there were stylistic and aesthetic divergences among individuals and some substantial differences of opinion about the quality of given poets' work, but this situation is best represented not by any sort of binary opposition but by a spectrum punctuated with surprising alliances and admirations between poets later assumed to be inherently opposed: Vachel Lindsay and W. B. Yeats, Allen Tate and Edna St. Vincent Millay, Ezra Pound and Carl Sandburg. In particular, the almost universally high standing of Sandburg and Frost through 1940 demonstrates that poets at this moment could command a large nonspecialist readership while still being seen as fully and importantly modernist by their peers.

Despite the wide variety of work it generated, the New Verse did possess a defining quality that changed American poetry permanently: a dual emphasis on formal experimentation and the expansion of poetic subject matter. Shortly after 1910, a vast range of American poets (T. S. Eliot, Claude McKay, Joyce Kilmer, and Sara Teasdale, to name only four) began working with topics that fin-de-siècle convention would have condemned as hopelessly unpoetic, particularly the spaces and social dynamics of the industrial city. Hundreds of American poems of the 1910s and early 1920s explore urban spaces from skyscraper to basement. Others consider the multifarious impact of forms of modern mass culture including advertisements, sports, cinema, and vaudeville. Still others address the characteristic social relationships of modern urban life – worker and boss, prostitute and client, political speaker and auditor, suffragette and chauvinist, self and stranger – that had been ignored by genteel poetry. This expansion of subject matter can be termed a *poetics of modernity* seeking to speak meaningfully – no matter what style it spoke in – to the conditions of twentieth-century life that most Americans were experiencing. In short, the New Verse movement cannot be considered identical to the development of Imagism, *vers libre*, collage form, or any other stylistic innovation. It was a paradigm shift in the way people saw poetry, not as a pleasant evening's diversion or as something to fill out a magazine page, but as a central form of knowledge, discovery, and commentary on every aspect of their lives.

WORKS CITED

Crane, Stephen. 1896. *The Black Riders and Other Poems*. Boston: Copeland and Day.
  1898. "Blue Battalions." In *Spanish-American War Songs: A Complete Collection of Newspaper Verse During the Recent War With Spain* edited by Sidney J., Witherbee, 182. Detroit: Sidney J. Witherbee.
D'Orge, Jeanne. 1916. "The Microscope." *Others*, May–June: 223.
Dunbar, Paul Laurence. 1905. *Lyrics of Sunshine and Shadow*. New York: Dodd, Mead.
Frost, Robert. 1915. *North of Boston*. New York: Henry Holt.
Millay, Edna St. Vincent. 1922. *A Few Figs from Thistles*. New York: Harper.
Monroe, Harriet. 1916a. "Down East." *Poetry*, May: 85–9.
  1916b. "Various Views." *Poetry*, June: 140–4.
Moody, William Vaughn. 1899. "Road-Hymn for the Start." *Atlantic Monthly*, June: 840.
"New Lamps for Old." 1914. *Dial*, March 16: 231–3.
"Poets Again Best Sellers." 1914. *Literary Digest*, April 25: 987.
Robinson, Edwin Arlington. 1905. *The Children of the Night*. New York: Scribners.
Sandburg, Carl. 1914. "Chicago." *Poetry*, March: 191–2.
Stevens, Wallace. 1923. *Harmonium*. New York: Alfred A. Knopf.
Underwood, John Curtis. 1899. Review of *War Is Kind* by Stephen Crane. In *Stephen Crane: The Critical Heritage* edited by Richard M. Weatherford, 1973, 235–7. London: Routledge and Kegan Paul.
Warner, H. E. 1899. "Will Poetry Disappear?" *Lippincott's*, February: 282–8.

2

BARTHOLOMEW BRINKMAN

Modern American Archives and Scrapbook Modernism

Edna St. Vincent Millay's are rather typical scrapbook pages from the period, pasted with envelopes, calling cards, a stray button, and construction paper hearts – all neatly labeled in fading pencil (Figure 1). The saccharine display could have been constructed by any number of young women in the first couple decades of the twentieth century, who – like their mothers and grandmothers (not to mention fathers and grandfathers) before them – turned to the scrapbook as a vehicle for chronicling personal histories and negotiating identity in an increasingly pervasive mass print culture. Even the handwritten poem was a common enough occurrence, although the skillful composition and surprising imagery of such a stanza as:

> Yet wait! Upon the sullen tide
> Two soggy, blackened biscuits ride –
> We see you soon a youthful bride

hints at the unusual talent of its compiler. These pages are representative of the "Rosemary" scrapbook (Millay Papers, Box 14, 4–5) that Millay began in 1907, when she was around fifteen years old, and concluded in 1912 (a date coincident with the inauguration of the quintessential journal of modern poetry, *Poetry: A Magazine of Verse*, with which Millay would later publish). In addition to dried flowers and sundry other mementos – as well as other notable scraps of verse – the scrapbook records through cards and newspaper clippings Millay's early poetic triumphs and setbacks. Such a scrapbook certainly reinforces the common critical image of Millay as a writer of ornately wrought romantic sonnets.

This image is complicated, however, by a second scrapbook, kept in the years between Millay's birth in 1892 and her young adulthood in 1924 (Millay Papers, Box 25), which highlights other dimensions of her life and writing. This scrapbook contains material related to Millay's time at Vassar College, including two plays she wrote there, *The Wall of Dominoes* and *Musk*, as well as clippings from such periodicals as *The Literary Digest*,

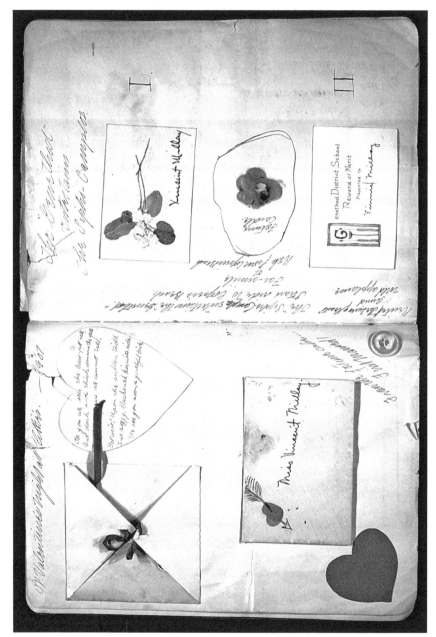

Figure 1. Edna St. Vincent Millay, "Rosemary" Scrapbook. Millay Papers Box 14, Library of Congress.

Current Opinion, and the *Boston Evening Transcript*, which publicized Millay and her work. Tellingly, the scrapbook also contains a Western Union telegram that Rebecca Horwich had sent to the young Millay on March 3, 1919 (Millay Papers, Box 25), explaining that the National Woman's Party would hold a protest demonstration during Woodrow Wilson's speech on March 20, 1919, noting that "all women must be prepared for arrest will you join us need women desperately please let us know immediately." It is unclear whether Millay attended, but the fact that she was sent such a telegram, and that she thought it a fit item to preserve in her scrapbook, highlights Millay's connection to first-wave feminism and the women's suffrage movement, which are distinct undercurrents in her verse. It also illuminates a general political dimension to Millay's life and writing evident in such poems as "Justice Denied in Massachusetts," which protested the execution of Sacco and Vanzetti, and "Say That We Saw Spain Die," which lamented the carnage of the Spanish Civil War.

These two scrapbooks, preserved at the Library of Congress, give scholars opportunities to recover and reimagine Millay's early poetic development and serve to complicate her legacy as they provide clues to biography and poetic states of mind. Millay's scrapbooks and the scrapbooks of many other celebrated modern American poets – including H. D. (Beinecke Library, Yale), Marianne Moore (Rosenbach Museum and Library, Philadelphia), E. E. Cummings (Houghton Library, Harvard), and Hart Crane (Butler Library, Columbia) – are a valuable and vastly underutilized resource for understanding modern American poetry. Likewise, the housing of these scrapbooks at some of the most prestigious libraries in the country suggests their accrued literary and monetary worth. More than mere containers of information or aids to biographical research, however, these scrapbooks are themselves complex and self-consciously organized cultural objects, often revealing processes of modern poetic production and reception. As such, they need to be studied as modern texts in their own right. Moreover, these scrapbooks are not merely one type of archival object among many. As structures for selecting, organizing, and making meaning through the juxtaposition of personal and mass print ephemera, scrapbooks are homologous to the modern poetry archive and provide interpretive models for understanding the archive's own complex form.

Modern poetry scrapbooks are a particularly important subset of the scrapbook – which generally grew out of a long commonplace book tradition and, as such critics as Ellen Gruber Garvey (2013, 20) have noted, provided some of the most salient responses to an emerging nineteenth-century mass print culture. In addition to chronicling personal and family histories (often worked on communally and handed down from generation to generation), scrapbooks served a variety of purposes in an increasingly bureaucratized world, used as reference texts for doctors and lawyers and as repositories of book reviews by newly professionalized authors from across the country (often compiled by clipping agencies charged with the task). Scrapbooks evolved symbiotically with the newspapers and magazines from which their clippings were often culled, so that by the early decades of the twentieth century they frequently exhibited a collage composition that mimicked that of mass market periodicals – predating and complicating the avant-garde collage tradition that began with the likes of Picasso and Braque.[1]

Scrapbooks are important for the history and study of modern American poetry in two key ways. First, scrapbooks kept not by poets (or at least not by poets who have garnered much critical attention) but by everyday readers suggest the varied, often previously unexamined, popular receptions and responses to modern American poetry. As a typically short, discrete, and privileged literary text, the lyric poem was, as Mike Chasar (2012, 49) has explained, "not just a general part of scrapbooking but, in some people's minds, the height of it," and it was not uncommon for people from all walks of life to keep private poetry anthologies of their favorite poets and poems. In addition to underscoring the widespread appeal of a genre that in the wake of the modernists is frequently seen as one full of high rhetoric and a bit obtuse, such scrapbook anthologies point to the popularity of poets who have fallen out of, or were never admitted to, the received canon of modern American poetry. Or they might group poems and poets together in ways that challenge common assumptions about content and form, producing constellations of meaning that for many professional critics are almost unimaginable.

Second, as I have started to suggest with Millay, scrapbooks may influence critical notions of modern poetic production for those poets who have been made central to the modern poetry canon. Such scrapbooks often acted as poetic "sandboxes" (to use a term now appropriated by the digital), allowing poets to playfully explore subjects and textual manipulations that might eventually be incorporated into their poems. This play is readily apparent in Amy Lowell's scrapbooks, kept at Harvard's Houghton Library, which present a clear case of a young poet in training. As a child, Lowell kept the *Amy Lowell Private Book* (Lowell Manuscripts, 38 (17)), a marble-covered notebook with the first pages reserved for manuscript "private" notes and later pages intended "For Pasteing" (the almost clichéd backwards "S" in the penciled heading indicating how young she was when she first started the project). Pasted pages are built from cartoon panels, taken from such periodicals as the humor magazine *Punch*, which present a knight on his steed with the caption "Campaign Equipment," and an officer presiding over a poker game reporting that "Everything Went Straight." The use of such cartoons is common in poets' scrapbooks, as they are in scrapbooks generally, although one is tempted to extrapolate from this early interest in the relationship between word and image a later embrace of Imagism, or what Ezra Pound would deride as "Amygism." At the same time, such cartoons expose the degree to which connections between word and image are largely conditioned by mass print.

While the *Amy Lowell Private Book* may suggest the first inklings of a poetic mind at work, Lowell would more self-consciously use a group of later scrapbooks as vehicles for poetic expression. *The Private Scrap-Book* (Lowell Manuscripts, 38 (24–26)), with the mock-bibliographical information "Arranged by Amy Lowell, Lowell & Co., Sevenals-Parlor, Sevenals," is given the tongue-in-cheek trappings of a published book.[2] The imitation continues with a mock preface:

> The contents of this book are made up chiefly of scraps cut out of different magazines, quotations, & one or two original pieces. The compiling of this book has taken a good deal of time, care, & property. This book will probably interest nobody but myself, so do not imagine naughty reader that you will like it because you won't. I must now skip because the dinner bell has rung.
>
> Amy Lowell.

Lowell, imagining herself as a saucier Jane Austen perhaps, addresses her potential "naughty reader" and makes the conventional offhanded gesture of meeting the dinner bell – as if the book had simply been dashed off as an afternoon diversion. The scrapbook allows Lowell to imagine an audience for her work and helps prepare her for the volumes that she would later publish, but rather than positing the "gentle reader" of Victorian convention, Lowell's reader is one who has naughtily infiltrated the scrapbook's private space where private significance is made public.

Many of the scrapbook pages are filled with constructed pictures of the many rooms at the Lowells' Sevenals ("Seven Ls") estate in Brookline, Massachusetts. These typically consist of cut-out pictures of furniture, musical instruments, bicycles, and a drawing of an owl reading a book, *Jingles and Joys*. Pages often form elaborate collages, if a bit surreal in their saturated colors (like sketches out of Monty Python), and in their attempts to reconstruct the Sevenals rooms suggest the ways in which scraps of mass print (like any texts) can only approximate the reality being represented.

As Lowell indicates in her preface, however, *The Private Scrap-Book* contains not only collaged clippings, but also "one or two original pieces." These original pieces are part of an unfinished pastoral poem sequence in the vein of Edmund Spenser's *The Shepheardes Calendar*. On the right sides of pages are full-page clippings of scenes for each month of the year, taken from the 1884 year of *St. Nicholas: An Illustrated Magazine for Young Folks*, issued when Lowell was about ten years old (though it is difficult to say if this was also the time of writing). The left sides of pages are reserved for original poems – although the sequence is cut short, only containing entries for January, March, and April. The sequence is prefaced by prose setting the scene: "In a pretty cottage at the end of the world lies Dame Nature and her twelve children. The cottage is covered with climbing roses and there is a wood, and a pond, and an orchard near it in fact it is the prettiest cottage that ever was" (Figure 2). Following this preface is a poem for January:

> There was never a leaf or bush or tree,
> The bare bows rattled shudderingly;
> The river was dumb and could not speak,
> For the weaver winter his shroud had spun;
> And a single crow on the tree-tops bleak
> From his shining feathers shook off the cold sun;
> Again it was morning, but shrunk and cold,
> As if her veins were sapless and old,
> And she rose up decrepitly
> For a last dim look at earth and sea.

The poem's competent meter and strained Romanticism contrasts starkly with the folksy image on the opposing page and accompanying text: "'Well!' said January, walking in one bright winter morning, with the snow clinging to his hair and beard, 'here I am once more, Mother; how have you got along without me all these eleven months?'"

The relationship between this printed and manuscript material can be taken at least three ways. First, if the poem is understood to be the primary text, the illustrations and printed prose passages can be read as paratextual, mimicking a device commonly used in such epic poems as *The Rime of the Ancient Mariner* and *Paradise Lost*. Second, the poetic and non-poetic texts can be read together, where they (perhaps unintentionally) make a dialogic poem, straddling high/low stylistic registers, that is more than the sum of its parts, anticipating the wide stylistic and affective terrain of such modernist poems as *The Waste Land*. Third, the printed pages can be seen as source material and inspiration for the fledgling verse. This last reading is one as concerned with the process of making as with the textual object itself and draws attention to Lowell's poetic self-fashioning. Tracing the printed scraps back to the *St. Nicholas* magazine (1884, 257), one encounters a periodical context replete with poems, stories, and other literary texts that likely would have served as early models for Lowell's writing. Following the

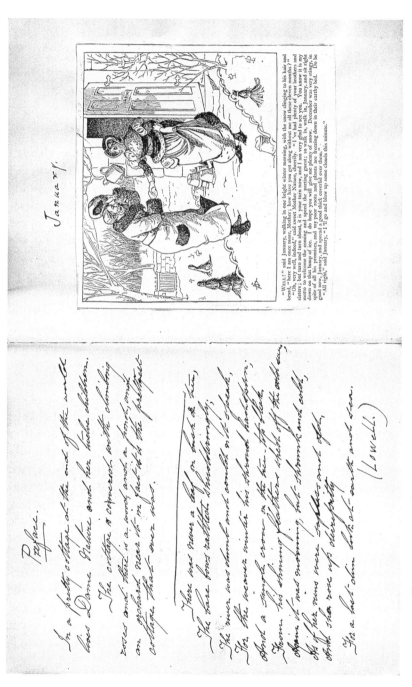

Figure 2. Amy Lowell, *The Private Scrap-Book*. MS Lowell 38 (26), Houghton Library, Harvard University.

29

"January" illustration, for example, is a poem, "The Snow-Storm," with the opening stanza:

> The old Earth lying bare and cold,
> Beneath the winter sky,
> Beheld the storm-king marshal forth
> His battle force on high.
> "Ah! soon," she said, "beneath the snow
> Full warmly I shall lie."

The poem lacks Lowell's striking imagery and personification, but the diction and tone are close to that of Lowell's own poem and may have served for her as an example of proper and successful verse (as it would have for many budding modernists). In addition to suggesting some of Lowell's unacknowledged poetic influences, serious attention to the print-cultural context into which Lowell read and from which she clipped directs attention to the popular nineteenth-century predecessors of modern American poetry who many modernist poets (and critics who have followed their lead) went to great pains to deny. Such inquiry is only possible, of course, because Lowell's scrapbooks and the source materials they incorporated are preserved in the archive.

The Rise of the Modern Poetry Archive

The poets' scrapbooks that I have been discussing are held at some of the country's most important research collections: Amy Lowell's scrapbooks at Harvard's Houghton Library and Edna St. Vincent Millay's scrapbooks at the Library of Congress. Unlike scrapbook anthologies kept by relatively unknown compilers – which are quite easily attained in antique stores, used bookstores, or through online auctions – scrapbooks kept by the most recognized and celebrated modern American poets are, not surprisingly, typically housed in institutionalized modern poetry archives. They reside alongside correspondences, drafts, and other personal papers, although they may be variously referred to as "journal," "commonplace book," or "oversized volume," sometimes making them difficult to locate. These archives are themselves a relatively recent phenomenon. They can be traced to the middle decades of the twentieth century as structures for selecting, preserving, and exhibiting the source materials and contexts surrounding modern poetry, governed by a collecting logic and attention to the ephemeral that recalls that of the modern private scrapbook.[3]

Libraries have, of course, long been collecting poetry. Until the middle decades of the twentieth century, however, the objects of this collecting typically were published books, with an emphasis on first editions and selected or collected volumes. Many academic libraries restricted their collecting to those poets who were former students or otherwise affiliated with their institutions. Both Dartmouth and Amherst, for example, were collecting books by Robert Frost.

In contrast to these libraries of published books, one of the earliest public modern poetry archives worthy of the name derived from the publishing archives of *Poetry: A Magazine of Verse*, itself a key institution for the making of modern American poetry. The *Poetry* archive was bequeathed to the University of Chicago following founding editor Harriet Monroe's death in 1936, but by 1921 (before modern poetry had reached what many would consider its 1922 high-water mark and before *Poetry* itself was scarcely a decade old), Monroe (1931, 31–6) had already willed away the archive and declared in the pages of her magazine her intentions to house a "library of modern poetry" as a permanent Chicago institution and gift to the city. Now held at the University of Chicago's Regenstein Library, the collection comprises drafts of poems by such poets as Vachel Lindsay, Rupert Brooke, Edna St. Vincent Millay, Rabindranath Tagore, and James Joyce. However, George Dillon, who succeeded Monroe as editor of *Poetry* from 1937 to 1949, exclaimed in "The Harriet Monroe Library of Modern Poetry," published in *The Courier* (May 1938, Friends of the Library, Box 1), that "by far the most valuable part of the collection, from the standpoint of research students and literary historians, is the complete file of poets' letters accumulated during the first twenty-four years of the magazine." Indeed, it is such letters as the ones exchanged between Pound and Monroe at the start of the venture that have allowed scholars to retrace many of modern poetry's first uncertain steps.

But the drafts themselves were also important. The availability of earlier, unpublished versions made genetic criticism possible as a corrective to the New Criticism's emphasis on the poem as a static, organic whole. The materials that had belonged to Monroe and *Poetry* were made publicly available in one grand gesture, providing insight into the making of a literary movement. As Jeremy Braddock (2012) has noted, the first significant attempt to approach poets individually for their materials, however, came from Charles Abbott, who created the Modern Poetry Collection at the University of Buffalo. Abbott's (1942) goal, as he would later put it, was to attain "the genuine work-sheets which the poet has used in the making of his poem – preliminary notes, the first rough draft, the various transitional stages, everything up to and including the final version, with proof sheets if textual changes are there recorded: a complete *dossier* on the composition of that particular poem" (11). Abbott wrote to poets in both the United

States and Britain and met with many of them face-to-face in the hopes of coaxing them into relinquishing their materials.

With papers by modern poets now routinely fetching thousands of dollars at auction and with some contemporary poets having standing orders for the drafts of poems that may bring in more money than the published book that comes from them, it is difficult to imagine how monetarily and culturally undervalued these materials once were. But it is clear from Abbott's responses that most poets did not grasp what he was after. Of the first fifty letters sent out, Abbott (1948, 13) received three complete silences, twenty-five fair copies, seventeen documentary histories, four promises, and a predictable response from Pound that "I don't give a damn about storing mss / in a safe." In a letter to Anna Russell dated June 22, 1958 (Modern Poetry Collection), Marianne Moore, who was constantly tinkering with her versions, and the bulk of whose papers would eventually make their way to the Rosenbach Museum and Library in Philadelphia, reacted somewhat surprisingly: "I have inexhaustible curiosity; but except as an exception – Shakespeare or Dante – an author worth reading I feel, gives enough of his mentality in what he is willing that others should see. (Also, I hear that many libraries are suffering from far too optimistic gifts of manuscript, too much script to curate.)" The most important early supporter of the Buffalo Modern Poetry Collection was William Carlos Williams, who saw the archive as an opportunity to safeguard his manuscripts during World War II. He would continue to send manuscripts and correspondences throughout his life (gradually recognizing their value) and would become instrumental in persuading other poets to donate to the collection.

Abbott's success and the increased value of the manuscripts and correspondences he collected is evident in the 1957 Library of Congress leaflet, "Literary Papers and Manuscripts" (Poetry Central File, 22 "1943–64"), pathetically subtitled "A Plea for their Preservation in the National Archives," issued when Randall Jarrell was Consultant in Poetry. Arriving rather late to the manuscript collecting game, and hoping to compete with the country's great academic and private libraries, the Library of Congress offered state-of-the-art preservation, a generous 20 percent tax break, and the opportunity to be immortalized as a literary patriot, alongside presidents, statesmen, and other great writers the library had gathered together. Many poets had already committed their works to other institutions, though the Library of Congress would score some significant victories, such as acquiring the papers of Edna St. Vincent Millay discussed earlier. There was a growing national consensus that poets' papers were worth preserving as sources of biographical information and clues as to how some of the great modern American poems had been written. Though they were often included among other archival materials, scrapbooks were not typically singled out in modern poetry collections – much of the attention going instead to correspondences, journals, and drafts of poems. Beyond simply being one item among many in the modern poetry archive, however, the scrapbook suggests an ideal form of the modern poetry archive in its negotiation of modernism and mass print culture, in its selection and preservation of poems, and in its productive possibilities, not all of which have yet been realized.

Reconstructing the Modern Poetry Archive

Unlike a collection of an author's printed works, which (even accounting for variations and diverse publication outlets) is ultimately finite, the scrapbook is an open-ended accumulation, into which another item can always be added. The scrap of verse, the hastily scrawled letter, the photograph or playbill that may have planted the seed of an idea that would eventually bear fruit as a stanza or sequence – all are potentially significant. Once selected and inserted into the scrapbook, these items resonate with others and the collection as a whole takes on new meaning.

So too with the archive. Abbot (1948, 5–7) recognized the archive's open-ended nature in his declaration that, in the Modern Poetry Collection, "there is no end to what remains still to do, since the ideal of completeness will always beckon. That impossible ideal cannot be achieved but it can be stoically sought.... We would keep constantly in front of us the goal of completeness, that desert mirage, forever vanishing to reappear in the distance." While Abbott admits to the ultimate impossibility of his task, he nonetheless aims for completeness. To even entertain the notion of completion, however, necessarily means restricting one's field of consideration. For Abbott, this restriction seems to be based largely on poetic reputation. Although he helped to open up vast new stores of poetic material worth collecting, Abbott's activities were nevertheless restricted by the unchecked assumption that he should be collecting papers from those poets who had already made a name for themselves through publication. He can hardly be blamed for this. Individual reputation still largely informs critical understandings of modern American poetry as a limited, albeit talented, tradition. Abbott's investment in a relatively few authors (and using individual authorship itself as a primary basis for collecting) does, however, have the problem of perpetuating in the archive a particular formation of modern American poetry already presented in books. Likewise, the *Poetry* archives at the University of Chicago were restricted to those poets who were published in (or at least aspired to be published in) a little magazine that may not have appealed to poets regularly appearing in *Life* or *The Daily Worker* (although there was certainly overlap among these periodicals), so that it, too, gives a particular picture of modern American poetry. The archives and manuscript collections at the Library of Congress, which counted among its most influential poetry consultants such New Critics and New Critical fellow travelers as Allen Tate and Randall Jarrell, similarly relied on ideological assumptions – such as a privileging of meaning as an organic and dynamic whole – that drove its formation.

This is not to discount the important work of the modern poetry archive, including those archives that gathered much of their material in the middle decades of the twentieth century and which may have relied on aesthetic and cultural priorities that differ from our own. These archives are invaluable for fleshing out a poet's biography or for complicating and questioning interpretations of poems often encountered only in their final published form. Rather, it is a reminder that the archive, too, is a historical construct that helps determine the history it narrates. As Jacques Derrida (1995, 16–17) puts it, the archive:

> is not only the place for stocking and for conserving an archivable content *of the past* which would exist in any case, such as, without the archive, one still believes it was or will have been. No, the technical structure of the *archiving* archive also determines the structure of the *archivable* content even in its very coming into existence and in its relationship to the future. The archivization produces as much as it records the event (emphasis in original).

The modern American poetry archive – however we choose to construct it – does not merely provide preservation of, and access to, the history of modern American poetry. Rather, in very real material ways, it *makes* the history that complements and complicates what is reproduced through print.

It is imperative, therefore, for modern poetry scholars, along with librarians and other cultural stewards charged with the task, to reflect deeply on the form and function of the modern American poetry archive and to act on that reflection. Scholars must continually reimagine the archive along with, and as a means of prompting, reconsiderations of modern poets who have been previously marginalized along racial, gender, and political lines. A prime example of such reconsideration is the Raymond Danowski Poetry Library at Emory University, a collection consisting of 75,000 volumes, along with an extensive range of broadsides, manuscripts, audiovisual materials, and other objects related to modern and contemporary poetry. The collection was thought to be the largest poetry library ever privately assembled and boasts that it "is a living entity, constantly expanding and connecting with modern-day work" as it seeks to fulfill Danowski's desire to "gather every book of poetry published in English."[4]

As laudable and important as such an archive is for the study of modern poetry, it must be recognized that the drive for constant expansion (suggesting an open-ended accumulation akin to the scrapbook) and the hope to collect every book of poetry (even when limited by such terms as "published" and "English") are inherently contradictory impulses underscoring an ultimately impossible task. To continually expand and connect with contemporary work (or old work made newly interesting) means that an archive is in a perpetually unfinished state; to complete this connection means to freeze the archive in time. In practice, the Danowski archive is even more capacious than its public declaration would suggest, including a considerable run of twentieth-century little magazines, broadsides, and other ephemera, and texts that challenge a simple pigeonholing of language and genre, making completion that more elusive.

As assumptions about what constitutes "poetry" expand to encompass previously marginalized figures, including countless popular versifiers who wrote for critically neglected mass-circulation magazines and other outlets, the problem of the archive becomes more pronounced. It is unlikely that every modern poet will find a place in the institutionalized archive, but as numerous libraries begin to publish digital surrogates of their materials online, and as these are aggregated into centralized resources, such as the Digital Public Library of America, it is reasonable to suppose that many materials could find a place online even if they were never housed in a traditional archive (though this would constitute preservation of content rather than conservation of material form).[5] Such materials would include not only digitized printed works, such as those that have been made available through Google Books and the HathiTrust, but also privately collected ephemera and other unique items as well, such as the many privately compiled scrapbook anthologies that promise valuable insight into the reception of modern poetry. But even these expansive archives are haunted by the specter of incompleteness because there will always be something more to add.

This should not be a source of anxiety. Rather, it should be a comforting thought. Although it is impossible for the archive to have the clear and final word, it can remain in the conversation, preserving, organizing, and presenting artifacts that speak to the cultural priorities of both modernism and the present day. As scholars study a richer and more complex portrait of modern American poetry than has previously been available, it is important that we retain an understanding of the modern poetry scrapbook and the rise of the modern poetry archive not only as sources of research, but also as aesthetic and cultural artifacts in themselves and as continuing examples of our responsibilities to our poetic past even as we press into the future.

NOTES

1 For more on scrapbooks as collage, see Jessica Helfand's (2008) *Scrapbooks: An American History*.
2 This volume is labeled "26," but it appears to be the first one produced.
3 The term "archive" will strike many readers as reductive. There are distinct and differing agendas governing the institutional archives of business and government agencies that may eventually be transferred to a public repository such as the National Archives and historical manuscript collections of which literary papers are often seen as a particular type. The former is typically thought to have an internal organizational logic expressed in the record that can contain several individual items, as opposed to the synthetic collections of manuscripts and other materials that take the item itself as its indivisible unit. The historical distinctions between the archive and the collection, though, are not so clear cut. Moreover, theories of the archive tended to be applied to literary collections during the period I am investigating. I have therefore chosen to use the term "archive" as general shorthand while remaining attentive to real and important distinctions between the archive and the collection.
4 This description of the Raymond Danowski Poetry Library can be found on Emory University's Manuscript and Rare Books Library webpage (marbl.library. emory.edu/collection-overview/raymond-danowski-poetry-library).
5 The Digital Public Library of America can be found at dp.la.

WORKS CITED

Abbott, Charles D. Introduction to *Poets at Work: Essays Based on the Modern Poetry Collection at the Lockwood Memorial Library, University of Buffalo*, 1–36. Edited by Charles D. Abbott. New York: Harcourt, Brace, 1948.
"Poet's Workshop." *Saturday Review of Literature*, April 25, 1942, 11.
Braddock, Jeremy. *Collecting as Modernist Practice*. Baltimore: Johns Hopkins University Press, 2012.
Chasar, Mike. *Everyday Reading: Poetry and Popular Culture in Modern America*. New York: Columbia University Press, 2012.
Derrida, Jacques. *Archive Fever: A Freudian Impression*. Translated by Eric Prenowitz. Chicago: University of Chicago Press, 1995.
Dodge, Mary Mapes, ed. *St. Nicholas: An Illustrated Magazine for Young Folks*. Vol. XI, Part I. New York: The Century Company, November 1883–April 1884. books.google.com/books?id=JhgbAAAAYAAJ.
Friends of the Library Collection. Regenstein Library, University of Chicago.
Garvey, Ellen Gruber. *Writing with Scissors: American Scrapbooks from the Civil War to the Harlem Renaissance*. Oxford: Oxford University Press, 2013.
Helfand, Jessica. *Scrapbooks: An American History*. New Haven, CT: Yale University Press, 2008.
Lowell, Amy. *Amy Lowell Private Book*, MS Lowell 38 (26). Houghton Library, Harvard University.
Millay, Edna St. Vincent. Papers. Library of Congress.
Modern Poetry Collection. University of Buffalo.
Monroe, Harriet. "Birthday Reflections." *Poetry: A Magazine of Verse* 39, no. 1 (October 1931): 31–6.
Poetry Central File. Library of Congress.

3

ALAN GOLDING

Experimental Modernisms

Make it new. – Ezra Pound
No good poetry is ever written in a manner twenty years old. – Ezra Pound
Nothing is good save the new. – William Carlos Williams
It is the new form ... that molds consciousness to the necessary amplitude for
    holding it. – Mina Loy[1]

Taken together, these statements constitute a familiar mantra for experimental American modernism, for the "experimental" is intimately connected to
this foundational category of modernist poetics, the "new." I am operating
here with a formalist definition of the new or experimental, which means
that I will not treat what one might call the social new (the New Woman,
the New Negro), addressed elsewhere in this volume, nor the "new" of the
marketplace (fashion, novelty, technological progress and the advertising
thereof). Indeed, experimental modernist craft set itself against the alienated
labor and mass production of urban-technological modernity, of emergent
Taylorism. At the risk of reinscribing an author and text-centered critical
method in a field that has come – increasingly and importantly – to empha-
size context, I focus here on significant, historically influential experimental
texts by six key figures: Ezra Pound, T. S. Eliot, William Carlos Williams,
H. D., Mina Loy, and Gertrude Stein. Certainly, I could have picked others, or more. Experimental modernist poetries are of such a scope that any
essay-length treatment will involve egregious exclusions. I have bypassed
such significant developments as Wallace Stevens's aural experiments with
playfully asemic language and his use of collage organization and almost
Oulipian repetition-with-variation to explore epistemology in *Harmonium*
(1923); Marianne Moore's genre-testing experiments in extreme citational-
ity ("what I write ... could only be called poetry because there is no other
category in which to put it"[2]); visual and typographical experimentation by E. E. Cummings, Bob Brown, or the Baroness Elsa von Freytag-
Loringhoven; Jean Toomer's mixing of period styles; and Langston Hughes's
work with blues and jazz forms and rhythms and black vernacular. But I

do assume that whatever we might mean by "modernist experiment" we recognize in the concrete form of particular texts (as well as in experimental social formations, gender positionings, and so forth). My chronological markers for the most intensive period of modernist experiment are, at the beginning, the Imagist movement and the early work of Pound, Eliot, and Stein. By the time of Louis Zukofsky's "Poem Beginning 'The'" (1928), Hart Crane's "The Bridge" (1930), and the Objectivists issue of *Poetry* (1931), we find poems already responding to earlier experimental work ("The Waste Land") and movements (Imagism), and modernist experiment is moving into a later phase.

The most widely circulated version of experimental modernism's beginnings turns on Imagism, a movement named by Pound with influence out of all proportion to its size and duration but one that, in its self-promoting collective thrust, its ambition to transform contemporary poetic practice and its use of manifestos, can lay some claim to being the first American poetic avant-garde.[3] At the same time, the original ambitions of Poundian Imagism are modest and quite narrowly literary in scope: to promote the work of Hilda Doolittle. He first used the term "Imagiste" in an August 18, 1912 letter to Harriet Monroe, editor of Chicago's *Poetry* magazine and an influential, if often ambivalent, apologist for the new poetry. A few months previous to this letter, from their base in London, Pound himself, H. D., and the English poet Richard Aldington were discussing the principles that became the foundation of Imagism:

1. Direct treatment of the 'thing' whether subjective or objective.
2. To use absolutely no word that does not contribute to the presentation.
3. As regarding rhythm: to compose in the sequence of the musical phrase, not in sequence of a metronome. (Pound 1968, 3)

In turn, Monroe published three Aldington poems, along with a mention of the new "school," in the November 1912 issue of *Poetry*, following up over the next few months with H. D., more Aldington, and what became perhaps Pound's single best-known essay, "A Few Don'ts by an Imagiste." Demonstrating the importance of sometimes ephemeral magazine publications to the circulation of experimental modernist texts, such periodicals as *The Glebe*, *The Little Review*, *The New Freewoman*, and *The Egoist* all acted as further outlets for Imagist texts and statements of poetics.

The typical Imagist poem is emotionally understated and marked by a short unrhymed (though aurally patterned) free verse line, concrete (especially visual) imagery, commonplace diction, paratactic organization, and, generally, a focus on a single scene, moment, or object. One well-known example is Pound's 1913 "In a Station of the Metro" (2003, 287), while "The Jewel Stairs' Grievance" (252), from the 1915 *Cathay*, turns Imagist method into a pedagogy with an explanatory note as long as the four-line poem. Meanwhile, in a period when T. E. Hulme associated women's poetry with imitativeness, sentimentality, and "roses, roses all the way," H. D. used Imagist techniques to invite a rethinking of women's status in both the literary and wider culture with the carefully and ironically chosen adjectives and passive verbs of poems like "Sea Rose" and "Mid-Day."[4] "Sea Rose" is written against the traditional iconography of the rose and its simultaneous association with the female and the poetic. H. D.'s 1916 poem combines vulnerability and toughness: The sea rose is "marred," "meagre," "thin," "stunted," buffeted by its environment but also "harsh," with an "acrid fragrance / hardened in a leaf" (H. D. 1983, 5). As such, it is "more precious" than the "wet rose / single on a stem" (5) of popular romance and of the predominantly male poetic tradition. While the speaker of "Mid-day" is "startled," "anguished – defeated," "scattered" in the oppressive noon heat of patriarchal culture (in which a phallic poplar thrives, "great / among the hill-stones"), the invitation comes in the closely related poem "Garden" to "rend open" or "cut apart the heat, / rend it to tatters" using the tools of verse: in an etymological pun, the wind must "plough through it, / turning it on either side / of your path" (H. D. 1983, 10, 25).[5]

Pound's contributions to a range of experimental modernisms are crucial and various, involving multiple stages and roles – as anthology editor, as inspiring irritant and resource for numerous magazine editors, as networker, as reviewer, as energetic promoter, fundraiser and even occasional patron, as critic / theorist and writer of manifestos, as creator of movements (however short-lived), as collaborator (on "The Waste Land"). Although they can seem dated today, the early poems of his *Personae* (1909) anticipate his major work by splicing elements of Robert Browning with multiple voices rendered from the Provençal of the troubadours to engage simultaneously in the revival of an obscured literary history, in prosodic experiment and in the technical challenge of using complex forms, such as the sestina. As this work with troubadour poetry evolves into poems such as "Near Perigord" (1915), one can see what became certain threads of Pound's lifelong epic, *The Cantos*, taking shape: the interest in an oblique and difficult poetry designed for initiated reader-listeners, encoding an idea of specialized learning that Pound also sees, paradoxically, as a pedagogical project in which he invites readers to join; the ideal of a poet actively engaged with contemporary politics; the use of an individual figure to get at the mind of a period. A few years later, Pound's major experiment in serial organization, "Hugh Selwyn Mauberley" (1920) – an often self-ironic meditation on his career so far – sets selective moments, figures, and texts from the history of Western high culture against a philistine present of mass-produced "tawdry cheapness" (Pound 2003, 550) and mourns the human and cultural devastation of a world war fought "for a botched civilization" (552). It does so using techniques that form much of the methodological basis of the *Cantos*: allusion, often cryptic citation, concrete imagery used concisely and metonymically to render character and situation, discontinuous organization, shifts into and out of colloquial diction and syntax.

While the *Cantos* as a long poem is treated elsewhere in this volume, these formal innovations make it central to any discussion of experimental modernisms. It was begun in 1915, with the first batch of finished Cantos (1–16) published in 1925, and continued into the final *Drafts and Fragments* (for Cantos 110–17) of 1968–9. While Pound's casual definition of the epic as "a poem including history" (1968, 86) hardly encompasses the *Cantos*, his methods for "including history" involved finding ways to juxtapose the widest possible range of voices, periods, place settings, cultures, texts, references, languages, styles, and modes of writing (much of it cited or appropriated) – narrative, historical documentary, lyric, myth, pastoral, philosophical dialogue, political satire, economic analysis, song, anecdote, gossip, memoir – all while preserving some version of the immediacy and compression associated with Imagism. This compression is accomplished in the *Cantos* via allusion, quotation, textual and imagistic fragment.

The beginning of Canto IV can give something of the flavor and purpose of Pound's palimpsestic layering:

> Palace in smoky light,
> Troy but a heap of smouldering boundary stones,
> ANAXIFORMINGES! Aurunculeia!
> Hear me. Cadmus of Golden Prows!
> The silver mirrors catch the bright stones and flare,
> Dawn, to our waking, drifts in the green cool light;
> Dew-haze blurs, in the grass, pale ankles moving.
> (Pound 1975, 13)

We begin with two lines drawing on Euripides and Virgil, followed soon after by the address to Cadmus, founder of Thebes. This juxtaposition calls up one of the *Cantos'* central themes, the destruction (here, of Troy) and building of cities – a crucial preoccupation for a poet beginning his epic project in World War I London, hoping to help initiate a renaissance that would mirror that of the fifteenth-century Italy to which he frequently returns. In the further interests of this modernist renaissance, "ANAXIFORMINGES! Aurunculeia!" summons the powers of poetry, sex, and love via invocations to Pindar's "lords of the lyre" and Catullus's epithalamium for Aurunculeia before we move into a lyric passage projecting a mythically animated semi-divine nature as another locus of value. Shifts among three languages, at least four different writers quoted or alluded to, sentence fragments, a narrative of war and a pastoral idyll, all within seven lines, this is the revolutionary method of the *Cantos* in miniature. It makes for a forbidding surface, and the extent to which that surface invites reader-learners to join its creator on a pedagogical journey or intimidates with its craggily resistant unfamiliarity is an ongoing tension within Pound's reception.[6]

There are good reasons why T. S. Eliot has been perceived, along with Pound, as embodying the most conservative aspects of modernist cultural politics: the circulation of such critical concepts as "the historical sense," "tradition," "the mind of Europe," the "objective correlative," "impersonality" (which constituted one dominant critical vocabulary in the literary academy for decades); his poetry's saturation in a relatively narrow range of western European literary canons; his essays' tone of patrician authority; the cultural positions taken in his middle-period and later prose, which seemed to become increasingly reactionary even as his cultural prestige increased. But the writer who described himself in 1928 as "classicist in literature, royalist in politics, and anglo-catholic in religion" showed up in London in 1914 as an unknown with one of the major productions of experimental modernism, "The Love Song of J. Alfred Prufrock," already under his belt.[7] In fact, Eliot had completed the poem by 1911, before any of his partners in the U. S. modernist experiment had produced anything remotely as radical. If we follow Marjorie Perloff's lead and read Eliot "not as the cultural representative he has been all too long, but with regard to his actual *practice*" (2002, 14), then, it is quite reasonable to see him as "the American avant-gardist of 1910–11" (10).

"Prufrock" brought a number of new notes into American poetry. Eliot emerged as the second major Anglophone poet of the modern city after Whitman, although with a very different tone from Whitman's celebration. In this interior monologue, Eliot's eponymous urban protagonist – alienated, isolated, ennui-ridden, crippled by social and sexual self-consciousness in ways that anticipate the population of the 1922 "Waste Land" – moves through an industrial cityscape of "half-deserted streets," "one-night cheap hotels," "yellow smoke," "lonely men in shirt-sleeves," soot, and stagnant rainwater in clogged drains to a sequence of humanly vacuous *soirées* that only exacerbate his sense of himself as "a patient etherized upon a table," a bug "pinned and wriggling on the wall" (Eliot 1963, 3–5). The poem suggested the ways in which modern subjective experience might be rendered formally: via disjunctive shifts between inner thought and short, dramatic scenes, or between levels of diction from the mundanely concrete to the pompously abstract ("a tedious argument / Of insidious intent" [3]), via rhythmic repetitions that can barely progress beyond themselves, indirectly via imagery, and via ironic use of allusion and reversal of convention ("Prufrock" both invokes and inverts the *carpe diem* tradition).

Many of these elements continue into "The Waste Land," the high point of Eliot's particular version of the collage poetics that characterize experimental modernism. Widely lauded as a powerful statement of post–World War I generational disillusionment (an intention coyly denied by Eliot himself), "The Waste Land" achieves that effect through a disconcertingly (and brilliantly) unanchored patchwork of disembodied voices, character vignettes, embedded traditional forms, shifting prosodies, allusions and citations, and shards of multiple languages. Both nostalgic for and despairing of cultural and spiritual authority, the poem's splintered polyvocality undermines any possibility of a rhetorical center and thus the very connection to canonical literary traditions to which the text aspires in its persistent allusiveness. Given Pound's editorial role in the creation of Eliot's poem, and its surface similarities to *The Cantos*, it is worth stressing some differences between their versions of modernist collage. Pound's didactic and epic ambition results in a greater range of subject matter, discourses, and sources. In particular, his documentary method – which Eliot does not use – enables him to present large chunks of non-literary material in the service of his project, while Eliot stays more strictly with literary, philosophical, and theological sources. Relatedly, Pound tends to organize around historical as well as mythological figures, while Eliot's characters are largely (though not exclusively) fictional and symbolic. And Pound tends more toward ellipsis, the half-word or tiny fragment of language, the phrase rather than the sentence. Meanwhile, as with "Prufrock," if we read it through the received lens of Eliot's cultural (self)-positionings, "The Waste Land" appears the quintessential document of modernist high cultural learnedness. It *is* that but not only that. Read for the deep strangeness of its manic shifts, its moments, even passages, of intense linguistic materiality ("Twit twit twit / Jug jug jug jug jug jug / So rudely forc'd. / Tereu" [Eliot 1963, 61]), the poem looks rather closer to the work of Eliot's most experimental contemporaries.

Only slightly later than "Prufrock," contemporaneously with Imagism, in advance of all Pound's major work and most of Eliot's, and from the radically different social and subject position of a lesbian Jew, Gertrude Stein started the experimental prose poems of *Tender Buttons* in Paris in 1912. *Tender Buttons* is often described as a kind of literary Cubism, influenced by Stein's close acquaintance with Picasso's work. In contrast, however, to the collage poetics of Eliot and Pound, who aspired to cultural syntheses through the invocation of myth, *Tender Buttons* is a counterhistorical collage. That is, if Pound and Eliot used collage to add layers of historical resonance, Stein used it to strip away layers of received meaning, clean words of their received associations, and see them afresh. Stein treats skeptically all received conventions around "representation." She uses collage to create a centerless text, one with no narrative, no governing point-of-view, no identifiable speaker, collapsing the authority of the author in a way that Pound and Eliot do not. "Act so that there is no use in a centre" (1990, 63), Stein writes. In *Tender Buttons*, the totality of the image or scene is broken into apparently disconnected parts that the reader must then reassemble. Stein's self-reflexiveness about her medium foregrounds attention to the materials (words) over attention to meaning: art as investigation of representation, then, rather than as a *form* of representation, even while individual words retain and even multiply their power to signify.

It is part of Stein's feminist project and her politically charged enactment of lesbian domesticity to question patriarchal structures at the level of language, in ways influential for numerous later writers; Stein's question "Supposing a sentence is clear whose is it?" (1975, 148) directly anticipates Susan Howe's "Whose order is shut inside the structure of a sentence?" (2007, 11–12) As with most literary collage, so with Stein parataxis is the basic structural principle: words and images juxtaposed without explicit transition or connection. *Tender Buttons* operates through alternative forms of connection – various forms of sound play and aural association, repetition and variation, pun – to proliferate open-ended possibilities of meaning without ever resolving into an interpretation (an influential feature of Stein's work for later poets from Robert Duncan to the Language writers). Here is Stein's own engagement with "Red Roses": "A cool red rose and a pink cut pink, a collapse and a sold hole, a little less hot" (Stein 1990, 24). Taking pleasure in its rhythmical balance, its alliteration, consonance, and off rhyme, this piece incorporates the flora of Stein and her partner Alice B. Toklas's domestic arrangements (a "red rose and a pink") while seeming both to suggest the violence and exploitation ("a pink cut," "a sold hole") underlying a patriarchal culture's feminization of the rose and to play with ideas of erotic heat (the literal red rose might be "cool" but in relation to the red rose as encoded eroticism, the pink is "a little less hot").

Everyday images in radically unfamiliar form, Stein operates on the premise that experiment or newness resides in particular unfamiliar forms of making. As she argues in her influential 1926 essay "Composition as Explanation," the new "thing made" is what defines an artistic generation, a coterie of makers ("the few" [Stein 1972, 514]) who realize, in the face of popular incomprehension, that "beauty is beauty even when it is irritating and stimulating not only when it is accepted and classic" (515). Stein reiterates here a widely shared assumption of experimental modernist poetics as to the effect and reception of that which is not yet seen as "beautiful." Similarly, in Mina Loy's essay-manifesto "Aphorisms on Futurism," "the new form" reshapes perception and thus creates the terms for its own eventual reception, while, like Stein's new "thing made," it also irritates: "CONSCIOUSNESS cannot spontaneously accept or reject new forms, as offered by creative genius; it is the new form, for however great a period of time it may remain a mere irritant – that molds consciousness to the necessary amplitude for holding it" (Loy 1996, 151).

More fiercely (rather than wearily) ironic than Eliot's almost contemporaneous "Prufrock," Loy's own "love song," the fractured thirty-four-part serial poem "Songs to Joannes," brought her instant notoriety just a few years later: new form as irritant indeed. The poem's tonal complexity – encompassing despair, yearning, regret at missed opportunity, a poignant sense of loss, vulnerability – is easily overlooked in the critical focus on its acerbically ironic feminist treatment of "love" as a cultural narrative and of the love poem as a genre. At the same time, it is in these latter features that the experimental force of "Songs to Joannes" resides: in the brutally sardonic anti-sentimentalism that demythologizes Cupid into a "pig ... his rosy snout / Rooting erotic garbage" and reduces "the shape of a man" to his "skin-sack" while still claiming the pleasures of "seismic orgasm" for its female speaker (Loy 1996, 53, 66); in its multifaceted parody of the love poem tradition (Song XXX is a battered, buried sonnet); in the discontinuity created by its short lines, short sections, and tonal and verbal shifts; in the performative linguistic mongrelism that mixes the bluntly colloquial, the biological ("spermatozoa" [56]), and the religious or spiritual (communion, Nirvana, crucifixion), that combines learned classical roots with bodily fluids ("cymophanous sweat" [64]). Love is sex and text here in ways shocking to many of Loy's contemporaries, both unromantic "wild oats sown in mucous-membrane" (53) and the manipulative author of those in its thrall: "Love–the preeminent litterateur," reads the four-word final section (68).

Forcefully anti-sentimental like Loy's work, William Carlos Williams's *Spring and All* – for many later readers, a germinal text of experimental modernism – was essentially lost between its 1923 publication and its 1970 reprinting. (The twenty-four untitled poems of *Spring and All* came to be well-known after the 1923 edition's loss, as Williams titled them and reprinted them in various editions of his selected and collected poems, but the whole text was unavailable for decades.)[8] In Williams's version of modernist collage, *Spring and All* blends polemical prose and poetry, theory and practice, in a hybrid mix that reads simultaneously as an extended manifesto, a statement and enactment of Williams's commitment to experiment, and a theory of the imagination (a term central to Williams that occurs rarely in the other poets discussed here). While Pound provided experimental modernism some of its most memorable slogans, few writers were more preoccupied with the "new" than Williams. The ideal of "newness" takes radically different conceptual and stylistic form in Williams, however, from what it takes in Pound and Eliot. These poets' feeling of living through a period of unprecedented and profound historical rupture involves a certain level of cultural nostalgia, and their experiments are constructed out of that conversation between literary past and present that Eliot termed the historical sense. Williams, however, considered Eliot and Pound as "men content with the connotations of their masters," their work a form of high cultural plagiarism, "rehash, repetition" (Williams 1970, 24). Close but contentious friends, Williams and Pound's differences are captured nicely in Williams's metonymic summary of one conversation: "I contended for bread, he for caviar" (26).

In persistently reflexive fashion, newness itself is often thematically the focus of modernist experiment, and "invention" is a central subject in *Spring and All*, with its dedication to "the invention of new forms" (Williams 2011, 36). *Spring and All* announces a new American poetry grounded in the social and environmental "local." In its first poem, the babies Williams delivered in his medical practice, the green shoots of spring, and new poems all "enter the new world naked, / cold, uncertain," but "rooted they / grip down and begin to awaken" (12–13). In Williams's new modernist world, "the rose" – which "carried weight of love" through centuries of literary history – "is obsolete" (30, 31) as a symbol encrusted with outmoded meanings, while "the sky is recognized as an association / is recognized in its function of accessory to vague words whose meaning it is impossible to rediscover" (19).

"Layers of demoded words and shapes" (Williams 2011, 19) required the remaking not just of poetry but of perception, and "brokenness of ... composition," "instability" (Williams 1970, 16) was the appropriate formal tool "to loosen the attention" (14) and produce "a break with banality, the continual hardening which habit enforces" (28). Beyond the shifts between his jaggedly hyperactive prose and poetry, and in ways typical of experimental modernism more generally, in *Spring and All*, Williams shifts levels of diction constantly, from the idiomatic concreteness of "twiggy / stuff of bushes" to the colloquial voicing of "Our orchestra / is the cat's nuts" to the analytic abstractness of "the decay of cathedrals / is efflorescent" to the found language of billboards and commuter train ads (Williams 2011, 12, 63, 59, 88). Despite a certain avant-garde aggressiveness in his relationship to readers and despite his skepticism toward all received forms of literariness, we find in Williams the modernist assumption of the redemptive power of art. "There is work to be done in the creation of new forms, new names

for experience" (44). The apposition in that sentence is crucial and revealing. Immediacy of attention to objects, such as a red wheelbarrow, must be
matched by immediacy of attention to the structures of language: "nothing
/ I have done // is made up of / nothing // and the dipthong // ae // together
with / the first person / singular / indicative // of the auxiliary / verb / to
have" (25). For Williams, mimesis ("plagiarism after nature" [35]) cannot be
the goal of modernist experiment. Rather, something like Viktor Shklovsky's
defamiliarization is necessary for the "invention of new forms," and the construction of those forms disrupts conventional searches for poetic meaning.[9]
Williams treats with consistent sarcasm the reader "finding there nothing
related to his immediate understanding" (1970, 21), the friends who ask of
the poet's construction (Williams's term) "but what does it mean?" (19).

   With even Williams's nativism inflected by his acquaintance with the latest
in European visual art, modernist American poetic experiment was a trans-
atlantic, cosmopolitan affair. Wherever it took place, however – in London,
in Paris, in Greenwich Village, in Grantwood or Rutherford, New Jersey – it
was also not just an individual but a socially embedded collective practice, a
cultural formation. It thrived and was discussed and generated in collective
sites for which the term "salon" can stand as partial – but only partial – syn-
ecdoche, from Pound's coopting of Yeats's and Ford Madox Hueffer's "after-
noons" in London to free-floating dinner groups to the actual salons hosted
by Alfred Stieglitz, Walter and Louise Arensberg, and Mabel Dodge in New
York, and by Natalie Barney and Stein in Paris. Janet Lyon stresses the connection between salon culture and literary and social experiment when she
theorizes the modernist salon as taking "the cultivation of cosmopolitanism
in the direction of the aesthetics of 'the shocking new,' promulgating – in
the case of Stein's salon, for example – a collective visual aesthetic rooted
in the act of scrutinizing Stein's large collection of controversially anti-rep-
resentational post-Impressionist paintings" (Lyon 2001, 35). The salon, in
Lyon's account, shaped both reception and production, and one of the most
significant for the production of an experimental poetry was one of the less
widely discussed and long-lived ones, the Arensbergs'.

   The Arensberg salon brought together Walter Arensberg – an affluent,
knowledgeable, well-connected art collector and poet with an interest in
Pound and Imagism – a young Alfred Kreymborg, Stevens, Loy, Williams,
Man Ray, and Marcel Duchamp, among others. That said, the boundaries
of the "salon" are porous conceptually and socially, and in its radiating,
multidirectional influence it is as much a term for a network, nexus, or set
of associations as it is for a physical site or social gathering. To sketch a
representative narrative: poet and editor Alfred Kreymborg first met Man
Ray through Stieglitz's 291 circle, whence Ray and Samuel Halpert invited

Kreymborg to join them in the modest property in New Jersey that became known as Grantwood Village (its own site of communal gathering and conversation) and from which Kreymborg launched his first little magazine venture, *The Glebe*. Through the publication of Pound's anthology *Des Imagistes* as the February 1914 issue of *The Glebe*, Kreymborg – himself committed to a specifically United States-based experimentalism – discovered Williams. Kreymborg subsequently met Arensberg at a party given by Allen and Louise Norton, editors of the magazine *Rogue* (which ran March–September 1915, and included Arensberg, Kreymborg, Stevens, and Loy), and part of an Arensberg circle that included Duchamp, Carl Van Vechten, and Donald Evans, publisher of *Tender Buttons*. Out of that meeting came Arensberg's sponsorship of Kreymborg's short-lived but influential magazine dedicated to the poetic "new," *Others*.[10]

"I sometimes think the Leaves is only a language experiment – that it is an attempt to give the spirit, the body, the man, new words" (Whitman 1970, [vii]): to recall Whitman's late remark about his life's work is to recall that much American poetry since Emerson, Whitman and Dickinson has its roots in the idea of a "language experiment."[11] Joan Retallack begins her 2007 essay "What Is Experimental Poetry & Why Do We Need It?" with some "linked propositions with several implications:

a) There is the shock of alterity. Or should be.
b) There is the pleasure of alterity. Or should be.
c) We humans with all our conversational structures have yet to invite enough alterity in.
d) Experiment is conversation with an interrogative dynamic. Its consequential structures turn on paying attention to what happens when well-designed questions are directed to things we sense but don't really know. These things cannot be known by merely examining our own minds."

The shock and pleasure of alterity, a certain ethical idealism (what "should be"), paying attention, "an interrogative dynamic" embodied in "structures" designed to explore "things we sense but don't really know" and to push us beyond mere introspection: these are some of the central values of what Marjorie Perloff calls the "twenty-first-century modernism" of such very different writers as Stein and Eliot as it continues to speak to the present.

NOTES

1 In order, the epigraphs come from Ezra Pound's 1935 book of the same title; Pound's 1917 essay "A Retrospect" (Pound 1968, 11); Williams's prologue to *Kora in Hell* (1970, 23); and Loy, "Aphorisms on Futurism" (1996, 151).
2 Moore 1965, 258.

3 For an important counter-argument, see Rainey 1998. Rainey sets Imagism in contrast to Italian Futurism as "the first anti-avant-garde," "a movement to end movements: informal, antitheoretical, absorbed in matters of writerly technique" and apolitical (p. 30).

4 Hulme 1955, 69.

5 Next to her Imagist work, H. D. was also writing the very different poems – usually longer and more narrative – to which Alicia Ostriker applies the useful term "revisionist mythmaking," poems like "Eurydice" that retell ancient Greek myths in the voice and from the point of view of a female figure typically overlooked in the original. See Ostriker 1986, 210–38.

6 A related ongoing issue in Pound's reception that I can only touch on here is that the claims to poetic authority implicit in his difficulty can phase chillingly into the *authoritarianism* of his increasingly virulent anti-Semitism.

7 Eliot 1928, ix.

8 *Spring and All* was published in a limited run of 300 by Robert McAlmon's Paris-based Contact Editions, and "most of the copies that were sent to America were simply confiscated by American customs officials as foreign stuff and therefore probably salacious and destructive of American morals" (Mariani 1982, 209).

9 For defamiliarization as a concept central to theories of the avant-garde and experimental modernism, see Shklovsky 1965, 3–24.

10 The sources for this narrative are Crunden 1993 and Churchill 2006.

11 The remark is reported by Horace Traubel in his foreword to Whitman 1970. In the full Whitman quotation from which I have selected, he uses the term "new" six times in the space of two sentences.

WORKS CITED

Churchill, Suzanne W. 2006. *The Little Magazine Others and the Renovation of Modern American Poetry*. Aldershot: Ashgate.

Crunden, Robert M. 1993. *American Salons: Encounters with European Modernism, 1885–1917*. New York: Oxford University Press.

Eliot, T. S. *Collected Poems 1909–1962*. 1963. New York: Harcourt, Brace & World.

    1928. *For Lancelot Andrewes: Essays on Style and Order*. London: Faber and Gwyer.

H. D. *Collected Poems 1912–1944*. 1983. Ed. Louis L. Martz. New York: New Directions.

Howe, Susan. 2007. *My Emily Dickinson*. New York: New Directions.

Hulme, T. E. 1955. *Further Speculations*. Ed. Samuel Hynes. Minneapolis: University of Minnesota Press.

Loy, Mina. 1996. *The Lost Lunar Baedeker: Poems*. Ed. Roger L. Conover. New York: Farrar, Straus, Giroux.

Lyon, Janet. 2001. "Josephine Baker's Hothouse." *Modernism, Inc.: Body, Memory, Capital*. Eds. Jani Scandura and Michael Thurston. New York: New York University Press. 29–47.

Mariani, Paul. 1982. *William Carlos Williams: A New World Naked*. New York: McGraw-Hill.

Moore, Marianne. 1965. *A Marianne Moore Reader*. New York: Viking.

Ostriker, Alicia. 1986. *Stealing the Language: The Emergence of Women's Poetry in America*. Boston: Beacon Press.

Perloff, Marjorie. 2002. *21st-Century Modernism: The "New" Poetics*. Malden, MA: Blackwell Publishers.

Pound, Ezra. 1975. *The Cantos*. London: Faber & Faber.

1950. *The Letters of Ezra Pound 1907–1941*. Ed. D. D. Paige. New York: Harcourt, Brace & World.

1968. *Literary Essays of Ezra Pound*. New York: New Directions.

2003. *Poems & Translations*. New York: Library of America.

Rainey, Lawrence. 1998. *Institutions of Modernism: Literary Elites and Public Culture*. New Haven, CT: Yale University Press.

Retallack, Joan. 2007. "What Is Experimental Poetry & Why Do We Need It?" *Jacket* 32. jacketmagazine.com/32/p-retallack.shtml.

Shklovsky, Viktor. 1965. "Art as Technique." *Russian Formalist Criticism: Four Essays*. Translated and with an introduction by Lee T. Lemon and Marion J. Reis. Lincoln: University of Nebraska Press. 3–24.

Stein, Gertrude. 1975. *How to Write*. Mineola, NY: Dover.

1972. *Selected Writings of Gertrude Stein*. Ed. Carl Van Vechten. New York: Vintage Books.

1990. *Tender Buttons: Objects, Food, Rooms*. Los Angeles: Sun and Moon Classics.

Whitman, Walt. 1970. *An American Primer*. San Francisco: City Lights.

Williams, William Carlos. 1970. *Imaginations*. Ed. Webster Schott. New York: New Directions.

1969. *Selected Essays*. New York: New Directions.

2011. *Spring and All*. New York: New Directions.

4

CARY NELSON

The Legacy of New York

Where to begin? That is the obvious opening question for any narrative account of the emergence of modern American poetry. It is also in many respects a question whose answer can powerfully determine everything else you say about the topic. Any single given answer marks not only a signal moment of origin for modernism but also eliminates or marginalizes other traditions that begin at other moments and in other contexts. Even an account that credits several instructive origin stories may identify some as major or stigmatize others as minor. Both a number of canonical poets and a still larger number of critics have preferred modern origin stories grounded in a fundamental break with the past, while some poets have valued a sense of continuity with predecessors more highly.

Alternative modern poetry narratives also inevitably jettison particular audiences for poetry. It is not therefore just the diversity of our poetic heritage that is at stake in these decisions. We also risk losing the aesthetic, religious, aspirational, social, and political investments that particular audiences made in American poetry at any given time. We risk losing knowledge of the cultural work different kinds of poetry were able to do, the social functions poetry served in people's lives, and fundamentally the range of meanings poems and poetry had in American history. To write one story that does justice to all these imperatives for our acknowledgement is probably impossible, but it is possible to register alternatives and to write history that reflects on its own problematics. Some of the key poetry collections we need to understand early twentieth-century literary history, as we will see, were not published until the past twenty years.

In the modern poetry narratives that have dominated criticism for decades, several dates stand out – the appearance of *Poetry* magazine in Chicago in 1910, the opening of the Armory show (officially titled the International Exhibition of Modern Art) in Manhattan in 1913, and the first publication of *Others* magazine in New York in 1915. These events, two of them set in New York, typically help facilitate narratives about telling literary innovation and a dramatic break with the literary past. In retrospect, at least, Ezra Pound's rallying injunction to "make it new" has come to seem the implicit intent driving the whole history of modernist invention. Yet we also know that some of what was new took its inspiration from Walt Whitman and, even if unknowingly, took up a tradition lying in wait to be inaugurated by Emily Dickinson decades after her death.

In their shared deployment of syntactical elision and disjunction, their associational leaps, their demands on the reader, their reflections on gender, and their assaults on convention, the poems of Dickinson and Mina Loy can now be said to be in conversation with one another. Dickinson wrote "Tell all the Truth but tell it slant" in the late 1860s. Loy's "Songs to Joannes" began to appear in *Others* in 1915. Although *Poetry* and *Others* had some poets in common, including Pound, poems like Loy's helped give *Others* a more consistently experimentalist image. Below, Dickinson is on the left, Loy on the right, one using the dash, the other the caesura:

Title divine – is mine!	Spawn of Fantasies
The Wife – without the Sign!	Silting the appraisable
Acute Degree – conferred on me –	Pig Cupid his rosy snout
Empress of Calvary!	Rooting erotic garbage
Royal – all but the crown!	"Once upon a time"
God sends us Women –	Pulls a weed white star-topped

(53)

Loy moved to New York in 1916. Her "Songs" display only elliptical and minimalist vestiges of narrative. As it begins, the speaker has already failed at conventional romance – steeped in all the drama of stereotyped emotions – yet opts instead not for unreflective animal sexuality but for something like a verbally inventive biological union. The sequence relentlessly offers up the illusory dramas of gender ("I am the jealous storehouse of the candle-ends / That lit your adolescent learning") only to reject them; repeatedly, in their place, Loy offers us versions of intercourse that invent figures for bodily fluids and anatomy: "laughing honey," "spermatozoa ... in the milk of the Moon," "Shuttle-cock and battle-door." Some critics have concluded that these are images of degraded lust; they seem instead to be antiromantic but celebratory. Moreover, their variety and surprising capacity to recode the rhetoric of romance ("honey," "the milk of the Moon," "pink-love," and "feathers" above all reposition romance tropes) demonstrate that a degendered human sexuality – one freed of cultural clichés about men and women – need not be impoverished. The rediscovery and reevaluation of Loy's work was finally made possible by the publication of a reliable collected poems in 1996.

Other writers associated with the New York circle around Alfred Kreymborg's magazine *Others* (1915–1919) included William Carlos Williams and Marianne Moore. The group was co-founded by Kreymborg and photographer Man Ray and would include multimedia artist Marcel Duchamp. Moore's first poems had conventional stanzaic forms, but she soon returned to them, introducing prototypically modernist indentation and dislocation. "The Fish" was first published in fixed four-line stanzas in *The Egoist* in 1918, the same year she moved to New York, but when she published the poem in *Others* the following year its lines ebbed and flowed in a more radical use of the page. Still more fundamental to her poetics, however, was her distinctive use of quotation and popular textual resources. Notably, her use of quotation in her poems is as elaborate as that of T. S. Eliot, but to quite different purposes. If Eliot performed magisterial allusiveness, Moore aimed for something more complex and subversive – recreating the broad cultural constitution of knowledge and understanding. At their most ambitious, her poems braid multiple sources of social and philosophical investigation, all the while reaching out to popular texts more readily than major aesthetic achievements.

"Marriage" (1923) and "An Octopus" (1924) are her intertextual triumphs. On one level, "Marriage" is a strikingly even-handed demolition of the illusion that either party to a marriage can so divest himself or herself of self-absorption and self-interest as to make a union possible. "He loves himself so much," she writes, "he can permit himself / no rival in that love" (68). But the poem is much more than an analysis of the pitfalls in gender relations. It actually moves centripetally and centrifugally at the same time, treating marriage not only as a site on which individuals and the culture as a whole act out their contradictory investments in independence and community but also as a figural resource that informs all compromised institutions in the culture. Thus the poem is at once about the marriage two people make and about the marriage the states made to form one country – "Liberty and union / now and forever" (70). Both require "public promises / of one's intention / to fulfill a private obligation" (62) and both "can never be more / than an interesting impossibility" (63). Marriage is an institution constructed by contractual idealization and a model for comparably problematic institutions of other sorts. Marriage in the poem is effectively thus both victim and purveyor of illusions within the culture.

Unlike Moore, Williams's incorporation of the popular was not primarily textual but experiential. Though Williams was born near Paterson, New Jersey, and established a medical practice there that he maintained through much of his adult life, his literary life was mostly centered in New York

City. From 1916 to 1923, Williams successfully established a new poetics grounded in colloquial American speech. His medical practice helped balance his life by keeping him in touch with lower middle class families, their lives and language. His lyrics, including "The Red Wheelbarrow" and others often separated from *Spring and All* (1923), as a result seem transparent and accessible, yet they are actually both unstable and infinitely interpretable. Nearly a hundred years later, critics still cannot decide where his investments lie in "The Young Housewife" (1916):

> At ten A.M. the young housewife
> moves about in negligee behind
> the wooden walls of her husband's house.
> I pass solitary in my car.
>
> Then again she comes to the curb
> to call the ice-man, fish-man, and stands
> shy, uncorseted, tucking in
> stray ends of hair, and I compare her
> to a fallen leaf.
>
> The noiseless wheels of my car
> rush with a crackling sound over
> dried leaves as I bow and pass smiling.
>   (*Collected Poems*, 57)

The poem masquerades at once as a piece of literal reportage and a fantasy surveillance, a celebration and critique of voyeurism. We cannot be certain whose innocence wanes most notably in the poem's autumnal season, the speaker's, the young housewife's, or even the reader's, for we too are implicated in the poem's final recognition. Indeed, no fixed reading of Williams's short poems will survive sustained reflection, for – despite their straightforward narrativity – they remain so ambiguous and unresolved that one interpretation continually displaces or reverses another.

When *The Waste Land* appeared, Williams realized he was in firm opposition to its elitist cultural ambitions. Meanwhile, he maintained fellow traveler status with the radical Left, publishing in Communist Party-affiliated magazines and supporting the cause of the Spanish Republic from 1937–9. And he was moved to create complex mixed genres that combined political reflection with Dadaist uses of his signature transparent speech.

Other vibrant early to mid-twentieth-century movements, some centered in New York, were devoted not to breaking with earlier traditions but rather to updating or transforming them. I take the moment of 1898–9 as one key modern origin, although not all the poets participating in that moment of consolidating political and social critique were in the least aware of one another's work. But within given literary and ethnic communities, there was a very strong sense of common cause and mission.

The historical impetus was dual but somewhat comparably motivated – the final push to eliminate the last vestiges of Native American independence and the U.S. war in the Philippines. Both events occasioned powerful anti-imperialist poetry of a sort the United States had not seen before. Among the Five Nations, we saw (or we could have seen had we known to look) Native American poetry written in criticism of American empire, poetry that linked racism in the Philippines to racism in the American West. And in Boston, New York, and elsewhere in the East, we saw anti-war poetry that was also anti-imperialist and anti-racist. It is a tradition that sustained itself through the rest of the twentieth century and beyond, taking us through the Harlem Renaissance, the Black Power Movement, the Vietnam War, and the war in Iraq. To insist that modern American poetry "begins" in 1910 or 1913 is to make a studied effort to marginalize, disempower, or wholly erase the very notion of an anti-racist and anti-imperialist tradition that synthesizes the resistance to empire in the United States and links it to comparable struggles in Latin America, the Caribbean, and elsewhere.

All scholars have assumed that it was not until the 1960s that individual Native American poets decided to write poems in English as opposed to traditional chants and songs, which were often not only anonymous but also transcribed and adapted for English-speaking audiences by missionaries and anthropologists. Only recently has the rich nineteenth- and twentieth-century tradition of Native American poems in traditional forms been rediscovered; a selection was not reprinted until the 2011 collection *Changing is Not Vanishing*. Most of these poems were written for Native American newspapers and magazines that never reached a larger American audience. The poems at stake dealt not only with nature and with Indian culture and history but also with national and international events. Parodying Edwin Markham's instantly famous 1899 poem "The Man With the Hoe," Creek poet Alexander Posey in "The Fall of the Redskin" (1901) wrote of an Indian leaning "against a witness tree … The emptiness of treaties in his face" (188). He references the Boer War, then describes a comparable gaze from a "Filipino … humanity betrayed, / Plundered, profaned, and disinherited." The Filipino "Cries protest to the judges of the courts, / A protest that is also made in vain" (189). Posey thus compares American imperialist aggression against peoples of color at home and abroad and links the various broken agreements that litter U.S. history. In "The White Man's Burden" (1899) Too-qua-stee (DeWitt Clinton Duncan), a Cherokee, parodies Rudyard Kipling's infamous poem of the same title and takes up God's voice: "Go tell those white men, I, the Lord of hosts, / Have marked their high presumption, heard their boasts ... Should just minorities be made to yield / That wrong majorities may be upheld?" (200). Again, the injustices against peoples of color are linked, and the principles that would bring them both justice invoked: "The red man, and the black, whom fate debars / From whited temples, see me in the stars" (199).

At the same moment that Too-qua-stee and other Native American poets were writing, The New England Anti-Imperialist League issued *Liberty Poems* (1900), "inspired by the crisis of 1898–1900." Among the other books of poems focused on the genocidal war in the Philippines published that year was Morrison I. Swift's *Advent of Empire.*[1] Like Posey and Too-qua-stee, Swift and the contributors to *Liberty Poems* understood that race was at the center of the crisis, a crisis provoked by imperialism that not only produced a murderous assault on the island's inhabitants but also jeopardized American democracy and the ideals supposedly underwriting the nation's social contract. Edmund Vance Cook's "Shoot Him Down" opens "Ay, beat the Filipino back! / 'All men are equal born and free,' / Was only meant for you and me" (4). David Greene Haskins Jr.'s "What is the White Man's Burden?" characterizes Kipling's poem as "The Christian Pirate's Plea" (73). And Henry Labouchere's "Retort to Kipling," reprinted from *London Truth*, opens with this stanza:

> Pile on the brown man's burden,
> To gratify your greed;
> Go, clear away the "niggers"
> Who progress would impede.
> Be very stern; for truly
> 'Tis useless to be mild
> With new-caught, sullen peoples
> Half devil and half child.
>
> (90)

Kipling's poem was published in New York's *McClure's Magazine* in February 1899 with the subtitle "The United States and the Philippine Islands," and it exhorted Americans to take full responsibility for their recent conquest. How much if any sarcasm Kipling intended in his characterization of the Filipinos as "Half devil and half child," a phrase Labouchere quotes directly, is unclear, although Kipling does warn that, as a colonial power, Americans will reap "the blame of those yet better / the blame of those ye guard" (216). In any case the poem treats colonialism as an historical inevitability and thus has been repeatedly parodied and attacked, both in *Liberty Poems* and elsewhere. *Liberty Poems* reprints a poem from the New York literary periodical *Ainslee's Magazine* (1897–1926) and draws other poems not only from Boston but also from writers in Ashville (North Carolina), Chicago,

New York, San Francisco, Washington, and various towns and cities in New York State. Five poems are by New York City poet Ernest Crosby, who would later include a Kipling parody "The Real White Man's Burden" in his 1902 collection *Swords and Plowshares*.

It is unlikely that the East Coast members of the Anti-Imperialist League were reading *Indian Journal* or *Daily Chieftan*, the venues in which "The Fall of the Redskin" and "The White Man's Burden," respectively, first appeared. Too-qua-stee's 125-line poem was reprinted the same year in *Indian Chieftan*, but that gave it wider distribution only within the Native American community, although both groups of writers were familiar with abolitionist discourse. Posey did not have a true collected poems until 2008, which was the first time "The Fall of the Redskin" was reprinted in over a hundred years. As a result, critical comments on his poetry are painfully misinformed. What we do know now is that American Indians were, unsurprisingly, following the news, reading widely, and writing rhymed and unrhymed metered political poems of considerable ambition. The constellation of these two turn-of-the-century groups of anti-racist, anti-imperialist poetry – now placed in dialogue with one another – unearth the multi-faceted tradition that had a major resurgence with Claude McKay and Langston Hughes in New York in the 1910s and 1920s and that gathered further strength with the poets of the Left in the Red Decade of the 1930s.

Born in Jamaica, McKay came to the United States in 1912. Several of his most influential early sonnets were published in *The Liberator* while he lived in New York and served as co-executive editor of the magazine from 1919 to 1922. His towering sonnets remain some of the fiercest indictments of American racism ever written. "Outcast" (1922) invokes the slave trade to depict what it means, as a racial "other," to live as though an alien in one's own country:

> For the dim regions whence my fathers came
> My spirit, bondaged by the body, longs.
> Words felt, but never heard, my lips would frame;
> My soul would sing forgotten jungle songs.
> I would go back to darkness and to peace,
> But the great western world holds me in fee,
> And I may never hope for full release
> While to its alien gods I bend my knee.
> Something in me is lost, forever lost,
> Some vital thing has gone out of my heart,
> And I must walk the way of life a ghost
> Among the sons of earth, a thing apart.
> For I was born, far from my native clime,
> Under the white man's menace, out of time.
>
> (*Complete Poems*, 173–4)

McKay's speaker harbors a spiritual and historical relation to Africa, but it is forever lost to him as a reality. Nonetheless, he carries it as a lack, a wound, that haunts him while he wanders a white world which still holds him in bondage, discriminated against, confined to poverty, and racially barred from white centers of power.

McKay's poems are as much a part of the New York legacy as the experimental verses inspired by modernist painting. Moreover, McKay adopted the sonnet not in reaction against experimental modernism but rather in an effort to install his revolutionary agenda within the heart of literary tradition. His collected poems, finally published in 2004, presents nearly a third of his poems for the first time. To credit his and other eloquent politically committed voices as formative ones in modern American poetry is also to reposition American poetry partly within a transnational project of anti-racist and anti-imperialist critique. That also helps us not only understand but also give full attention to the transformative history of Whitman's heritage. Perhaps our most unapologetically American of major poets, Whitman's embrace of his nation's belief in its manifest destiny is transformed among his international followers into the reverse, a revolutionary impulse toward popular resistance to state power. Beginning early in the twentieth century and continuing to the present day, Whitman's catalogues, his democratizing outreach, and his long lines have empowered a political aesthetic that Whitman himself could not have foreseen. Part of that re-articulation of Whitman's voice and style was centered in New York, but it spread across the globe. That transformative work also helped progressive poets disarticulate Whitman's gay advocacy from his nationalist ideology. Later in the century, that impulse would bear fruit in the work of Robert Duncan, Allen Ginsberg, and many other poets.

The dramatic reversal of fortune that accompanied Whitman's evolving influence also played out in the influence the emerging experimental tradition would have in the United States. T. S. Eliot's *The Waste Land* (1922) and, by the 1930s and 1940s, the solidifying politics of Pound's *Cantos*, gave experimental modernism not only a culturally elitist cast but also strong links to conservative or fascist politics. Progressive poets from William Carlos Williams to Edwin Rolfe – among them a number either working in the New York area or publishing in New York venues like *New Masses* – struggled with that apparent legacy, railed against it at times, and then began to re-articulate experimental techniques to very different social agendas. The effort to link experimentalism with leftist political projects would also sustain itself throughout the century. Among its towering achievements are Melvin Tolson's *Libretto for the Republic of Liberia* (1953), which replaces Eliot's Eurocentric range of reference with an extraordinarily rich set of quotations, allusions, and explicit references that create a composite history at once European, African, and American.

The literary inspirations for the widening field of experimental poetry were matched by developments in the visual arts. While the most notable stimulus was the Armory Show – with Marcel Duchamp's "Nude Descending a Staircase" its signature painting – the movement that came to be known as New York Dada, partly linked with the Armory show, was equally influential. Francis Picabia was also in the Armory Show and given still more space in gallery 291. Officially inaugurated in Zurich in 1916, the movement established itself in the United States in such 1915–19 New York magazines as *291, 391, The Blind Man, Rongwrong,* and *New York Dada.* Walter Conrad Arensberg was both a Dada patron and a poet. His "Axiom" appeared in *The Blind Man* in 1917:

From a determinable horizon
                              absent
                   spectacularly from a midnight
                   which has yet to make public
                                     a midnight
                   in the first place incomparably copied
     the other
              in observance of the necessary end
                                     guarantees
     the simultaneous insularity
                     of a structure
                     self-contained
     a little longer
              than the general direction
                                     of goods opposed
                                     tangentially.

"Axiom" is a rather early example of a poem that uses linguistic associations to take a poem across multiple domains, from cultural understanding to nature to economics, in this case in service of an anti-capitalist subtext.

The New York Dadaists were largely all anti-war, anti-colonialist, and anti-bourgeois, but none had quite so anarchist and unconventional a literary style or personal presence as Baroness Elsa von Freytag-Loringhoven. Freytag-Loringhoven arrived in New York from Berlin in 1910 and remained in the United States until 1923. She established herself as a figure in the New York avant-garde as she began writing poetry furiously a few years later. She published scattered poems in *The Little Review, The Liberator, Broom,* and *transition,* the first two edited in New York and the third arriving in Manhattan near the end of its run. Freytag-Loringhoven was working on a book of her poems at the time of her death in 1927. It was never completed. A full evaluation of Freytag-Loringhoven would have to wait until the remarkable collection of her work *Body Sweats* was published in 2011.

In poems such as "Affectionate," "Kindly," and "A Dozen Cocktails – Please," she features portmanteau words rich with instructive meaning ("Phalluspistol," "Kissambushed," "Icefanged," "wombcrucible," "bloodsuckled," "spirittesticle"), surrealist set pieces ("Wheels are growing on rosebushes"), compressed sacrilege ("And God spoke kindly to mine heart – ... He said: 'Thou art allowed to fart!'"), and ribald sexual celebration ("No spinsterlollypop for me – yes – we have / No bananas – I got lusting palate – I / Always eat them") (*Body Sweats*, 200, 86, 48). These are mixed with associational reverie, sound experiments, and rants variously celebratory and denunciatory, as in this representative passage from "MINESELF – MINESOUL – AND – MINE – CAST-IRON LOVER" (*Body Sweats*, 285):

> Costly he looketh a toad – creature that is – demands bloodright
> And balance – – – has it – finds it – SQUATS on it!
> Costly he looketh in grandeur – magnitude – eyes stony –
> darkcentered – – – gazing undisturbed at good and evil
> for him – – – thinking ceaselessly – – – unwinkingly
> – – – dreams – TOADDREAMS!
> SQUATING IN SHADOW DARKNESS UPON CENTER OF CRIMSON
> THRONE

One of her more infamous pieces was the long 1921 "THEE I CALL 'HAMLET OF WEDDING-RING' CRITICISM OF WILLIAM CARLOS WILLIAMS'S 'KORA IN HELL' AND WHY" (*Body Sweats*, 291–313), but Williams himself would have a failed relationship with her, end up being somewhat inspired by her, and in "Descent of Winter" (1928) create a Dadaist mixed poem and prose sequence:

> Someone should summarize these things
> in the interest of local
> government or how
> a spotted dog goes up a gutter –
>
> and in chalk crudely
> upon the railroad bridge support
> a woman rampant
> brandishing two rolling pins
> (*Collected Poems*, 310)

Dada would continue to have an impact on American poets in New York and elsewhere but not primarily through overt movement affiliation. Much the same story can be told about surrealism and American poetry, a movement in which poetry and the visual arts were also intertwined. Indeed Dada and surrealism themselves were interrelated, sharing interests in Left politics and practices like automatic writing. Surrealism, however, added an explicit commitment to unconscious motivation and to dreams as a resource. It also developed its American strain slightly later, beginning in the 1920s and 1930s and achieving a high point with Charles Henri Ford's New York magazine *View* (1940–7). Some would argue that Dada, in effect, was transformed into surrealism, but it is worth distinguishing the two sets of literary and artistic commitments. Surrealism first achieved wide visibility in the United States in the 1930s at the very moment when so many writers were becoming affiliated or aligned with the Communist Party. The question of whether surrealism could be a vehicle for radical political advocacy, despite the Party's general preference for realism, would then be widely debated in New York and other east coast magazines. Dada, on the other hand, was credited with a committed political edge throughout its history.

The first decades of the century did not include the formation of even anything like the loosely affiliated group of poets and painters that came to be called the "New York School" of the 1950s and 1960s. What New York documented from 1900 to 1930 instead was diversity; it was a ferment, a cauldron of intersecting and diverging poetries, one that no linear narrative can encompass. There is a telling 1922 photograph early on in *Body Sweats* that images part of what New York offered. Claude McKay and Baroness Elsa are posing together richly costumed. McKay wears a dress, carries a scepter, and has a string of pearls dangling from his royal hat (Figure 3).[2] Freytag-Loringhoven exhibits herself in one of her self-made costumes with a swirling hat that exceeds any effort at description I can muster. She leans on McKay as if jauntily flirting with him, but in a posture embodying her own aggressive sexuality. The photo reminds us that McKay was doubly othered, as both black and gay. Yet the photograph is striking in a different way for literary scholars. In the way that we conventionally divide and conquer our literary history, these two writers inhabit separate worlds and separate narratives. Claude and Elsa could meet in the flesh in New York, indeed McKay recalls her visits to *The Liberator* (where he published one of her poems) in his 1937 autobiography *A Long Way from Home* (104–5), but they do not meet in our histories of modern poetry. And yet they did meet, the founding poet of the Harlem Renaissance, who wrote in fixed forms, and the single most radical Dadaist experimentalist poet of the period. As they were working, Dorothy Parker was beginning to become famous for the savagely witty poems she would publish in *Vanity Fair*, *The New Yorker* and other magazines, and Charles Reznikoff was writing his early imagist poems in Brooklyn, sometimes based on New York settings and with a political edge. Here are two of his untitled poems from 1918:

Figure 3. George Grantham Bain. Claude McKay and Baroness Von Freytag-Loringhoven. Photograph. George Grantham Bain Collection, Library of Congress, Washington D.C. Prints & Photographs Division, LC-DIG-ggbain-33941.

On Brooklyn Bridge I saw a man drop dead.
It meant no more than if he were a sparrow.

Above us rose Manhattan;
below, the river spread to meet sea and sky.

(4)

The shopgirls leave their work
quietly.

Machines are still, tables and chairs
darken.
The silent rounds of mice and roaches begin.

(5)

We might remember that New York's Greenwich Village became Lola Ridge's home when she moved there in 1908. She published in Emma Goldman's radical magazine *Mother Earth* and issued *The Ghetto and Other Poems* in 1918, meanwhile surviving by writing advertising copy, publishing stories, and being employed as a factory worker, artist's model, and illustrator. She began to publish in both well-known and experimental magazines, becoming associate editor of *Others* and American editor of *Broom*. *New Masses* made her a contributing editor in 1926, and the following year she was arrested protesting the execution of Sacco and Vanzetti, events which later inspired her *Dance of Fire* (1935). Here are a few of the opening stanzas from "The Ghetto":

> The heat...
> Nosing in the body's overflow,
> Like a beast pressing its great steaming belly close,
> Covering all avenues of air...
>
> The heat in Hester street,
> Heaped like a dray
> With the garbage of the world.
>
> Bodies dangle from the fire escapes
> Or sprawl over the stoops...
> Upturned faces glimmer pallidly -
> Herring-yellow faces, spotted as with a mold,
> And moist faces of girls
> Like dank white lilies,
> And infants' faces with open parched mouths that suck at the air
> as at empty teats.   (3)

Edna St. Vincent Millay moved to Greenwich Village in 1917. If McKay turned the sonnet into a vehicle for revolutionary anger, Millay made it more deeply anti-romantic than anyone had before. Here are the opening lines from "Sonnets from an Ungrafted Tree" (1922):

> So she came back into his house again
> And watched beside his bed until he died,
> Loving him not at all.   (606)

McKay and Millay together, writing in Manhattan, transformed the character of one of our most fundamental literary forms, yet they tend not to meet in literary history either. E. E. Cummings moved to Greenwich Village in 1924, already well on the way to establishing his own brand of experimental modernism. Here is "Buffalo Bill's" (1920):

Buffalo Bill's
defunct
    who used to
    ride a watersmooth-silver
              stallion
and break onetwothreefourfive pigeonsjustlike that
                                  Jesus
    he was a handsome man
                      and what I want to know is
    how do you like your blueeyed boy
Mister Death

New York was throughout the century a vibrant center for the arts as well as itself a repeated visual and poetic topic. From Whitman's "Mannahatta" and "Crossing Brooklyn Ferry" through Lola Ridge's "Broadway" and "Wall Street at Night," Marianne Moore's "New York," Claude McKay's "The Tropics in New York" to Hart Crane's "The Bridge," then eventually on to Frank O'Hara's "The Day Lady Died," James Merrill's "An Urban Convalescence," and finally the poetry of 9/11 and Occupy Wall Street, no other American city has been so rich a site of literary variety or so thoroughly imaged and offered as a symbol at once of American potential and disaster.

NOTES

1 For comments on Swift's *Advent of Empire*, see Cary Nelson, *Revolutionary Memory: Recovering the Poetry of the American Left*.
2 George Grantham Bain, "Claude McKay and Baroness v. Freytag," photograph, in *Body Sweats*, 15. The photograph is reproduced from the George Grantham Bain Collection in the Library of Congress.

WORKS CITED

Arensberg, Walter Conrad. 1917. "Axiom." *The Blind Man* No. 2 (May): 8.
Crosby, Ernest. 1902. *Swords and Plowshares*. New York: Funk & Wagnalls.
Cummings, E. E. 1920. "Buffalo Bill's." *The Dial* 67: 1: 23.
Dickinson, Emily. 1955. "Title divine – is mine!" In *The Poems of Emily Dickinson*, Vol. 2. Ed. Johnson, Thomas J. Cambridge, MA: Harvard University Press, 758.
Freytag-Loringhoven, Elsa von. 2011. *Body Sweats: The Uncensored Writings of Elsa von Freytag-Loringhoven*. Eds. Gammel, Irene and Suzanne Zelazo. Cambridge, MA: MIT Press.
Kipling, Rudyard. 1910. "The White Man's Burden." *Collected Verse of Rudyard Kipling*. Toronto: The Copp Clark Co., 215–17.
Loy, Mina. 1996. *The Lost Lunar Baedeker*. Ed. Roger Conover. New York: Farrar, Straus and Giroux.

Liberty Poems. 1900. Boston: Published for the New England Anti-Imperialist League by The James H. West Co.

McKay, Claude. 1970. *A Long Way from Home*. New York: Harcourt Brace.

2004. *Complete Poems*. Ed. William J. Maxwell. Urbana: University of Illinois Press.

Millay, Edna St. Vincent. 1956. *Collected Poems*. New York: Harper & Brothers.

Moore, Marianne. 1967. "Marriage." *Complete Poems*. New York: The Macmillan Company: 62–70.

Nelson, Cary. 2001. *Revolutionary Memory: Recovering the Poetry of the American Left*. New York: Routledge.

Posey, Alexander. 2008. *Song of the Oktahutche: Collected Poems*. Ed. Matthew Wynn Sivils. Lincoln: University of Nebraska Press.

Reznikoff, Charles. 2005. *The Poems of Charles Reznikoff: 1918–1975*. Ed. Seamus Cooney. Jaffrey, NH: David R. Godine.

Ridge, Lola. 1935. *Dance of Fire*. New York: Harrison Smith and Robert Haas.

1918. *The Ghetto and Other Poems*. New York: B. W. Huebsch.

Swift, Morrison I. 1900. *Advent of Empire*. Los Angeles: The Ronbroke Press.

Tolson, Melvin. 1970. *Libretto for the Republic of Liberia*. New York: Collier-Macmillan.

Too-qua Stee (De Witt Clinton Duncan). 2011. "The White Man's Burden." In *Changing is not Vanishing: A Collection of American Indian Poetry to 1930*. Ed. Robert Dale Parker. Philadelphia: University of Pennsylvania Press, 199–202.

Williams, William Carlos. 1986. *The Collected Poems of William Carlos Williams, Vol. I: 1909–1939*. Ed. A. Walton Litz & Christopher MacGowan. New York: New Directions.

1923. *Spring and All*. Dijon, France: Contact Publishing Co.

5

ANNE DAY DEWEY

The Modern American Long Poem

Although the long poem genre includes a range of forms – sonnet sequence, verse novel, serial poem, prose poem – epic is central to Modernist experimentation. Whereas epic poems traditionally represent a culture's values, heroic ideals, and social-cosmological world view, often through narration of the culture's origins in war, both national identity and epic form grow increasingly unstable in the twentieth century. Nations' geographical and cultural integrity become more permeable to imperial and trade relations, transnational flows of steam and air travel, and immigration, while cataclysmic world war reveals nationalism's destructive power, challenging Eurocentric views of civilization and progress. Modernism's rupture with traditional forms of representation challenges epic fusion of social order, hero, and the poet's public voice, extending late Victorian fascination with personae and masks in dramatic monologue, Imagism's focus on the concrete image, and Cubist decomposition of the object into constituent structures of perception and medium. Breakdown of epic unity prompts what Smaro Kamboureli terms the "openness" of the long poem, its novelization of epic (and lyric) forms through "incorporation of various genres and its simultaneous resistance to generic labels" that sets genres in dynamic dialogue (1991, 26, xii, 46), ultimately establishing the long poem as an intensely dynamic genre in its own right. Thus, whether we view genre as an attempt to produce transcendent unity absent from the artist's historical conditions (Lukács 1988, 38–9), "an interpretive abstraction" that constitutes the object it claims to know (Jackson 2005, 10), or a "set of expectations" or "literary norms to which texts may be related and by virtue of which they become meaningful and coherent" (Culler 1975, 145), the modern long poem is a genre in crisis and transformation.

Even before the twentieth century, epic poetry had not come easily to American poets. Not only was the United States forged in the era of democratic revolutions that challenged traditional epic's aristocratic heroes and supernatural machinery, but U.S. self-fashioning as a revolutionary culture springing from the American wilderness rendered epic conventions inappropriate. John McWilliams identifies obstacles to these conventions, such as that the War for Independence is too recent and painful to have acquired legendary status; moreover, ideals of an agrarian and pastoral rather than military republic – coupled with the idealization of the farmer rather than warrior hero – compounded the problem of defining the religious or cosmic dimension of the American universe (1989, 16–35). Not until the nineteenth century did Walt Whitman's "Song of Myself" (1855) fuse these elements into an inclusive democratic voice evolving with a future-oriented nation, animated by the divine spirit of nature.

> I celebrate myself, and sing myself,
> And what I assume you shall assume,
> For every atom belonging to me as good belongs to you,
> ....
> My tongue, every atom of my blood, form'd from this soil, this air,
> Born here of parents born from parents the same, and their parents the same,
> ....
> I permit to speak at every hazard,
> Nature without check with original energy.   (Whitman 1973, 28–9)

The poem's opening sings not military heroism but individual self, vital to nation because of its physical origin in nature's "energy," which connects Whitman to others as part of revolutionary growth. Nature is also the source of the eroticism that binds Whitman as "caresser of life" "mad ... to be in contact" with others and renders the body politic cohesive (1973, 29).

Pre-World War I Cubist experiments in prose poetry disrupt this hard-won unity, foregrounding everyday domestic and feminine content against masculine, public epic while dismantling the continuities of space and time that constitute national tradition. Gertrude Stein's 1914 *Tender Buttons* critiques realism's transparency by reclassifying things into modes of interacting with them – objects (seeing), food (ingesting), rooms (inhabiting) – to expose their role in constructing sex-gender binaries. Her "Patriarchal Poetry" (1927) extends critique to narration, recording not men's heroic nation-founding but women's ongoing struggle to achieve identity within the nation through the repetition of "Let her be let her let her let her be let her be let her be let her be shy let her be let her be let her try. / Let her try. / Let her be" (Stein 1980, 120). This vivid representation of history thwarting women's ambition shifts to construction of alternative contexts for women's poetic activity in Stein's intensely abstract "Stanzas in Meditation" (1932), where radical recontextualization of self in space and time rejects public conventions of identity and fictions of nationhood. Similarly, William Carlos Williams's *Kora in Hell* (1920) uses diary jotting to generate new patterns by "seeing the thing itself without forethought or afterthought but with great intensity of perception," a rupture Williams associates with femininity (his mother's disorienting "dark mood") as well as the Cubist decontextualization of freeing objects from conventionally ordered structures so as to "improvise novelty." "A stained-glass window that had fallen out and lay more or less together on the ground was of far greater interest than the thing conventionally composed *in situ*" (Williams 1970, 8).

Poets apply these techniques to representing nation in order to express cultural disorientation after World War I. Marjorie Perloff interprets T. S. Eliot's *The Waste Land* (1922) as the "culmination" of the cosmopolitan prewar avant-garde's collage, "attenuated hypotaxis," and Cubist experimentation (2002, 33, 20–2). Both emblematic and influential in transforming epic to seek shared transnational roots that can heal a shattered postwar West, *The Waste Land* portrays the crisis of a culture that has lost Whitman's vital organic and erotic unity. Eliot's metropolis is no pinnacle of civilization but an "Unreal City" (1971, 39), a chaotic mass of strangers. Lacking common institutions and traditions to ground mutual understanding, polyglot voices from past and present become a Babel of fragments coordinated only by impersonal workday clocktime. Unlike Whitman's "caressing" narrator, Eliot's Tiresias – a prophet whose knowledge derives in part from experience of both masculine and feminine sexuality – is a jaded voyeur "foresuffering" the mechanical affair of clerk and typist, the potential embrace of his "throbbing between two lives" reduced to "the human engine... / Like a taxi throbbing" (Eliot 1971, 43–4).

Eliot's search for solutions produces elements Jahan Ramazani views as common to "modernist bricolage": "translocalism, mythical syncretism, heteroglossia, and apocalypticism" (2009, 101). Failure of community marginalizes the poet, leaving him to adopt a prophetic voice or mine the rubble of tradition for saving belief. While the poem's final exploration of sacred truths in common Indo-European roots (the Sanskrit *Upanishads*) addresses a "friend," intimacy never materializes, leaving "each in his prison" witnessing apocalyptic destruction (Eliot 1971, 49). Metropolis, persona, and language disintegrate in the poem's closing: "London Bridge is falling down falling down falling down / ... Why then Ile fit you. Hieronymo's mad againe. / Datta. Dayadhvam. Damyata. / Shantih shantih shantih" (Eliot 1971, 50). Without community, poetry becomes "mad" babble, the sacred Sanskrit evoking peace mere fragments, powerless to work ritual transformation.

A number of Modernist long poems trace a poet-prophet's search through history for mythic forms to revive culture. Seeing poets as "steam-gauges of that nation's intellectual life," Ezra Pound defines epic as "a poem including history" and seeks to make the poetic image active in history (1968,

58, 86). His lifelong project *The Cantos* (1917–69) experiments with the power of the image as "vortex" or "radiant node or cluster" of ideas (Pound 1960b, 88) and the ideogram or constellation of images signifying an idea to "extend the borders of knowledge" (Pound 1960a, 26). *The Cantos* seek exempla of ideal forms emerging in and shaping history: Renaissance noble-man Sigismundo Malatesta's temple, Confucian philosophy, the language of American law. History resists Pound's transformative efforts, however. He comes to perceive the ideal as undermined by the formless energy of the material, demonized in his principle of "usury." Whether economic currency or formless "mud," this independent agency of the material destroys beauty, for "with usury has no man a good house / made of stone, no paradise on his church wall" (Pound 1969, 250). Embracing the dream of an enlight-ened ruler's ability to impose harmonious forms on society, Pound supports Mussolini's fascism during World War II and is arrested for treason. Written from the extreme conditions of a detention camp, Pound's "Pisan Cantos" (1948) question his "vanity," as "lone ant from a broken anthill from the wreckage of Europe" who "tried to make a paradiso / terrestre" (1969, 521, 458, 802). *The Cantos* remain incomplete, Pound's inability to end them per-haps tacit recognition that paradise exists "only in fragments" (1969, 438).

Other Modernist long poems of epic scope seek alternate principles of cultural unity. William Carlos Williams's *Paterson* (1926–58) asserts the local as universal, its exploration of his city Paterson's history attempting to unite culture and nature through the controlling metaphor of "a man like a city and a woman like a flower / – who are in love" (7). Nature's forms pro-vide no unity for culture but refract into multiple, indeterminate images. The Passaic River and falls represent alternately a metaphor of the poet's life, the "noise" of an unknown source "animat[ing]" city dwellers unconscious of their natural origins, thought "jostled as are the waters approaching / the brink," sexual attraction as "the stream / that has no language," and fluid materiality "encasing [words] / in a sort of thick lacquer," rendering nature the sheen on a primarily verbal reality (Williams 1992, 6–7, 23, 81). Nor does Williams's collaged historical material cohere to represent place but creates an unending counterpoint of voices challenging the poet – Allen Ginsberg revealing a seedy side of Paterson unknown to Williams himself or the disgruntled lovers and women poets who feel he has slighted them – and among which he is less a crafter of forms than a dog pursuing smells (Williams 1992, 3). *Paterson*'s images of poetic process shift from organic growth to violent rearrangement whose energy releases new, generative combinations: the burning library, radioactivity, the atomic bomb.

Like *The Cantos* and *Paterson*, Melvin Tolson's *Harlem Gallery* remains unfinished. Tolson plans an epic journey from slavery to the Promised Land

but completes only *Book I, The Curator* (1965). Tolson's dizzyingly centrif-
ugal attempt to place Harlem's culture in the fractured temporal and spatial
terrain of African American, African, and European traditions develops a
"diasporic," "liminal," "dialogic" representation of nation that Kathy Lou
Schultz identifies as "Afro-Modernist epic" (2013, 43, 69, 81). Poems that
achieve closure tend to abandon documentary collage. Although Muriel
Rukeyser's *U.S. 1* (1938) uses journalistic and legal testimony to record
Kentucky miners' struggle to obtain justice for the silicosis contracted in
unethical working conditions, the poem traces the trial's drama to resolution. H. D.'s *Trilogy* (1944-6) foregrounds poetic transformation of sound
and image to reimagine ruined World War II London as a peaceful Atlantis
governed by a new matriarchal deity, "the Lady." Her *Helen in Egypt*
(1961) attributes war to gender antagonism between the masculine "iron-
ring" army defending the walled city of Troy and women as "writing," mere
ciphers or token prizes (H. D. 1961, 51, 22), and imagines the reconciliation
and mutual transformation of Helen and Achilles outside history.

Hart Crane's *The Bridge* (1930) and Muriel Rukeyser's *Theory of Flight*
(1935) render the new technological forms of suspension bridge and airplane governing metaphors for culture, recognizing both violence and
beauty in their sublimity. Crane's New York rises from the subway tunnel as
mechanical maw consuming the body to the Brooklyn Bridge's new music
of the spheres, "Our Meistersinger, thou set breath in steel," its "cordage,
threading with its call / One arc synoptic of all tides below – / Their labyrinthine mouths of history" harmonized in a new Atlantis's "arching strands
of song" (Crane 1986, 99, 83, 105). While Rukeyser's airplane inspires
both sublime panoramic vision and the terror of aerial warfare, "reflecting
/ all history in a bifurcated Engine" (23), the propeller's engine-igniting
"contact" models the transformative "dynamics of desire" in erotic attraction, technological power, and the crowd galvanized to unity if the people
will only "say yes" (1978, 24, 46). Significant of post-Modernist strategies,
Zukofsky's *"A"* (1927–75) adopts a strict formal plan. In the crucial transition between the first and second halves of *"A"* – 9, composed in 1938 and
1948, respectively, Zukofsky abandons integration of medieval, Marxist,
and scientific world views to cross formal elements of source texts (the
rhyme scheme of a Cavalcanti poem, the vocabulary of Marx's *Capital*, and
a sound pattern replicating the mathematical formula of the conic section)
to generate new patterns. Such formal techniques radically undermine traditional continuities of narrative, voice, and poetic agency, a shift Burton
Hatlen interprets as "movement beyond a Modernist poetics of nostalgia
for a lost Absolute into a Postmodernist poetics of finitude – and, thus, of
possibility" (1992, 23).

In the 1930s and 1940s, various cultural forces challenged epic voice: skepticism as to whether poets could speak for a whole culture (Bernstein 1980, 271–2), fascist rhetoric of heroism and nation, New Critical preference for short epiphanic lyrics, and Cold War retraction of poetry to the private sphere (Brunner 2001, 158–9). In this vein, Jeffery Donaldson traces the anxiety of W. H. Auden's generation about how to reach a "real or constructed" audience in its fragmented culture, showing how Auden's mock-epic "Letter to Lord Byron" (1937) (1995, 36–7) betrays concern that its subject is trivial. Fascism intensifies challenges to writing politically engaged poetry. Auden's 1944 Christmas Oratorio "For the Time Being" expresses helplessness that public language is inadequate to comprehend "this Horror starting already to scratch Its way in? / Just how, just when It succeeded we shall never know." Auden's ironic report that "on account of the political situation, / There are quite a number of homes without roofs, and men / Lying about in the countryside neither drunk nor asleep" shows fear anesthetizing public rhetoric against dire reality or expressions of heroism (1968, 135–6).

For Edward Brunner, this "restless search for a viable public space" renders "the long poem … invaluable for the invitations it offers to enter new linguistic and semantic territory" (2001, 123, 131). A number of poets experiment with extended lyric and sonnet sequences that enable private meditation against an epic horizon. M. L. Rosenthal and Sally Gall propose the "modern poetic sequence" as "the result of sheer, psychically powerful need … to mobilize and give direction to otherwise scattered energies" (1986, 9). Varied lyric sequences by Wallace Stevens, Gwendolyn Brooks, and John Berryman address loss of the public unity that sustained epic aspirations. Stevens's "Examination of the Hero in a Time of War" (1942), in Rachel Galvin's interpretation, adapts the traditional sonnet sequence's tracing of a love relationship to the citizen's affective relationship to the hero, showing how patriotic rhetoric prevents empathy (2013, 24). "The hero is not a person" but a monumental "emblem" and "a feeling / In a feeling mass, a blank emotion, / An anti-pathos" (1981, 276–7). "The Man with the Blue Guitar" (1936) replaces the hero's inhumanity with poetry's power to tune perception to a more beautiful, humane key "of things as they are and only the place / As you play them, on the blue guitar, / Placed, so, beyond the compass of change, / Perceived in a final atmosphere" (Stevens 1981, 167–8). The blue guitar, blending medium (Picasso's blue paintings) and mood (African American blues), recombines mere sound to transport the listener, "atmosphere" as the feeling that pervades place transforming or re-"composing" the senses. Music, "like the reason in a storm; / And yet it brings the storm to bear" (1981, 169), projects an ideal counterpoint to the turbulence of "things as they are." The "final" atmosphere, like Stevens's "Supreme Fiction," asserts the imaginative world as telos and the most significant element of reality. Rachel Cole's argument that Stevens makes aesthetic pleasure ethical by constructing forms of intimacy, tenderness, and erotic attentiveness "not to interpellate but to satisfy the reader" (2011, 388) renders poetry vital to a humane body politic.

In contrast to Stevens's lyrical reconstruction of social relationships, Brooks's *Annie Allen* (1949) combines short lyrics, mock epic, diary, and loose sonnet form (including sonnet-ballad) to represent her marginalized protagonist's maturation in the romance between "chocolate" Annie and a "tan man." Brooks's mock epic "Anniad," its rhyming couplets reminiscent of Pope's *Dunciad*, traces both characters' quests for belonging in white culture by embracing its ideals – the tan man through patriotic combat in World War II and Annie through emulation of the New Criticism's ornamental, time-transcending beauty, "pretty tatters blue and red, / Buxom berries beyond rot" (1987, 103, 99). When failure to achieve these ideals leaves Annie disillusioned, the sonnet sequence of "The Womanhood" re-anchors voice in neighborhood community and in Annie's more meaningful love as mother of "the Children of the Poor." Brooks recognizes the inadequacy of traditional forms to sing this community, and the poem's closing urges self-discovery through local solidarity by urging people to "rise. / Let us combine. There are no magics or elves / Or timely godmothers to guide us. We are lost, must / Wizard a track through our own screaming weed" (1987, 140).

Although Berryman's lyric sequence "Homage to Mistress Bradstreet" (1953) creates intimate community in conversation with a literary predecessor, *The Dream Songs* (1959–69) recount white Henry's failed romance with a remote, abstract "world" to a black friend, Mr. Bones. Against the potential for mutual caring in this cross-racial friendship, impersonal institutions construct the public sphere and the individual's relationship to it. While the sonnet-like, eighteen-line poems are rife with epic allusions, Berryman's confessional lyric renders the citizen victim and celebrity, forms of selfhood forged by a seductive public sphere, in which "all the world like a woolen lover / once did seem on Henry's side. / Then came a departure. / Thereafter nothing fell out as it might or ought. / I don't see how Henry, pried / open for all the world to see, survived" (1986, 3). Unlike Brooks's local community modeled on family, Berryman's world is a "woolen lover," disconcertingly inanimate, warm but possibly scratchy, with overtones of "wooden" insensitivity. Impersonal agents thwart hope and the desire for justice, leaving the poet's persona "pried open" to an unbearable public gaze. Henry's Whitmanic catalogues identify not with fellow citizens but with damaging impersonal forces in the body politic, "the enemy of the mind," "a teenage cancer," "two eyes screwed to my [television] set" (Berryman 1986, 24). Poetry serves official institution as Henry gains fame, serving the literary-political establishment by writing essays on "The Care & Feeding of Long Poems" or toadying to the president "during his 10 seconds in the receiving line / on the problems of long poems" (Berryman 1986, 376).

The cross-racial aesthetics these mid-century poems exemplify begin to fracture with the growing gap between local community and the massified public arena, a gap intensified by ethnic literatures emerging in the 1950s and 1960s that express group identities often rooted in local community and poetic practice. In *Epic and Empire*, David Quint argues that the "legitimat-ing function" of epic forms to "naturalize or universalize an official ideol-ogy" makes epic a significant genre for establishing new communal identities through the interaction between "topical allusion and literary allusion" (1993, 15). In Langston Hughes's *Montage of a Dream Deferred* (1951), for example, the geographical limits of Harlem structure the imaginary limits of African American culture bounded by the demographics of racial and class oppression, Harlem's streets occasioning the contact through which this cul-ture emerges. The opening "Parade" asserts the powerful experience of race consciousness in a black crowd for a speaker who *"never knew / that many Negroes / were on earth, / did you? / ... / A chance to let / PARADE! / the whole world see / PARADE! / old black me!"* (Hughes 1994, 389). Mixing bebop and other African American musical forms, Hughes juxtaposes brief lyrics and scraps of conversation to sketch both the unity and the fissures in a community-in-becoming that spans urban northerners and those recently arrived from the rural South, divergent ghetto and bourgeois ideologies, and old and young, as well as family, religion, and love increasingly shaped by despair. Haunting silences of unresolved mourning for slavery, racial trauma, and archival voids due to African Americans' omission from written record make Hughes's long poems of the 1950s, as Kathy Lou Schultz observes, epics of absence as well as presence, challenging contemporary myths of U.S. national unity (2013, 93–117).

Hughes's integration of private lyric voices into epic represents one sig-nificant innovation (among others) generated by the emerging poetics of minority cultures. Susan Stanford Friedman observes similar strategies in women epic poets' incorporation of novelistic or lyric conventions that rec-ognize multiple, intimate, and personal experiences as forceful elements of their culture's world view. Although some poets adopt a more public voice (for example, Allen Ginsberg's "Howl" (1956) with its Whitmanic cata-logues describing Beat generation gay subculture), the blending of epic and lyric voices is a productive strategy in Sharon Doubiago's feminist epic *Hard*

Country (1982) or Rodolfo Gonzales's documentation of Chicano identity in *I Am Joaquín / Yo Soy Joaquín* (1967), poems that combine multiple voices and elements of collective culture to map communal experience. Conversely, lyric and sonnet sequences become powerful vehicles to politicize the personal in lesbian love lyrics like Marilyn Hacker's sonnet cycle *Love, Death, and the Changing of the Seasons* (1986). Lynn Keller shows how Hacker's "performative revelation of the arbitrariness and conventionality of inherited forms" that structure seemingly "natural" relationships between lover and beloved highlight gender as artificial and malleable (1997, 185). Theresa Hak Kyung Cha's *Dictee* (1982) extends generic hybridity to radical recontextualization of genre as one of multiple official discourses and local practices (pedagogical, patriotic, medical, astronomical, religious, cinematic) imposed on the body to produce citizen and nation.

If return to the local (including translocal) provides one basis for form in the long poem, particularly for distinct ethnic or subcultural traditions, some postwar poets revisit Modernist long poems and find not fragments of uncompletable wholes but a bricolage generative of new experimental possibilities. For Ron Silliman, "the problem ... of the whole's relation to its parts and ultimately to irreducible elements" disrupts representational and linguistic subordination, generating "surface" patterns of parataxis and contiguity (1992, 19). The New American poets' open form aesthetic seeks freedom from metaphysical or lyric/subjective enclosure in a processual poetics that records the poet's dynamic interaction with the environment. Similarly, Joseph Conte interprets serial and procedural forms as responses to scientific theories of a chaotic or unbounded universe. Whereas serial forms are fluctuating and provisional, procedural forms become attractive models of poetic creativity for their "radically exploratory" nature (Conte 1991, 24–5, 40). Robert Creeley's *Pieces* (1969) and Robert Duncan's *Structure of Rhyme* and *Passages* – which emerge sporadically throughout his work from 1960 onward – each develop serialism differently. Creeley combines words in abstract constellations whose meaning the reader discovers to be local and provisional as their context shifts. Duncan extends Stevens's conception of language as cosmic architecture to exploit rhetorical, etymological, and musical correspondences that wrench words out of conventional contexts and generate new harmonies and meanings, thereby altering the "grand collage" of culture. Such mutable, unstable order is reinforced by the formal characteristics that Brian McHale identifies as emerging when material elements of culture are granted creative agency: pluralization of fictional worlds, heterotopias, scrambling of the literal and figurative, and deconstructive or self-erasing orders in which meaning, truth, and reality are shifting and discontinuous.

Such techniques also reflect the power of mass culture, media, and language to alter our world. John Ashbery resumes Stevens's meditation on cultural rhetoric but dissolves Stevens's intimacy between poet and reader into an indistinguishable "I" and "you" whose collective mentality is constructed by the colloquial idiom that utterly mediates our relation to reality. In Ashbery's long poem *Flow Chart* (1991), colloquial language is a flow chart, whose ambiguous agency, as Nick Lolordo observes, both creates and predicts its subject even as it maps and invents its process (2001, 757). Self-awareness is fleeting, emerging in epiphanic recognition of "what a city this is! In what rich though tepid layers you can / almost detect the outline of your head and then / you know it's time to read on" (Ashbery 1991, 216), scenes in which the individual appears as mere outline or deformation in a more substantial collective reality. Ed Dorn's pop epic *Gunslinger* (1968–75) satirizes the similar power of mass culture to displace the local, the media of its cartoon landscape mutating beyond control. The poem stages the battle between mythic cowboy Slinger and elusive capitalist magnate Howard Hughes – who adopts the guise of the latest mass consumer trends, from fast to ethnic food – with as sidekicks a third person construct "I," structuralist philosophers, and figures like "Kool Everything." Influenced by Marxist and poststructuralist thought, Language poets return to prose poetry to critique the ideological power of linguistic structures to control thought. Ron Silliman's "new sentence" composition juxtaposes sentences unconnected by common scene or event to force new paratactic correspondences. Rosmarie Waldrop's dialogues between masculine and feminine interlocutors in *Curves to the Apple* (2006) show how the language of self hews to the gendered body and attempts to reconfigure identity, while Lyn Hejinian's autobiography *My Life* (1980) recombines sentences remembered since childhood in new contexts to reveal self as the life of language in memory emerging from collective language.

If contrasting the poetics of ethnic and subcultural writers seeking cultural representation in epic and lyric traditions with those of poets who work in experimental forms provides a useful though oversimplified way to approach poetic culture from the 1950s to the 1970s, creative interplay between these aesthetics takes off in the 1980s. Three examples suggest the potential of such interplay. James Merrill's *The Changing Light at Sandover* (1982) exploits the parody and pastiche of a mock occult epic to construct its own universe, in which, as Aidan Wasley argues, Merrill becomes a puppet of tradition, but a selective tradition of his invention (2011, 90–2), empowering subsequent poets to manipulate poetic tradition as material for their own constructed reality. Adrienne Rich's "An Atlas of the Difficult World" (1991) maps local communities as elements of fractured national or global spaces created by class, race, and gender differences. Although using radically different techniques to represent institutions and agents shaping history, both Susan Howe and Rita Dove are haunted by and attempt to recover voices lost to history. The long poem's mixing and recontextualizing of historical materials, perspectives, and forms establishes the genre not only as distinct and self-transforming but as a significant source of insight into the interactions, rifts, and lines of force traversing its poetic landscape.

WORKS CITED

Ashbery, John. 1991. *Flow Chart*. New York: Alfred A. Knopf.
Auden, W. H. 1968. *Collected Longer Poems*. London: Faber and Faber.
Bernstein, Michael André. 1980. *The Tale of the Tribe: Ezra Pound and the Modern Verse Epic*. Princeton, NJ: Princeton University Press.
Berryman, John. 1986. *The Dream Songs*. New York: Farrar, Straus and Giroux.
Brooks, Gwendolyn. 1987. *Blacks*. Chicago: Third World Press.
Brunner, Edward. 2001. *Cold War Poetry: The Social Text in the Fifties Poem*. Urbana: University of Illinois Press.
Cole, Rachel. 2011. "Rethinking the Value of Lyric Closure: Giorgio Agamben, Wallace Stevens, and the Ethics of Satisfaction." *PMLA* 126.2: 383–97.
Conte, Joseph M. 1991. *Unending Design: The Forms of Postmodern Poetry*. Ithaca, NY: Cornell University Press.
Crane, Hart. 1986. *The Complete Poems: The Centennial Edition*. Ed. Marc Simon. New York: Liveright.
Culler, Jonathan. 1975. *Structuralist Poetics: Structuralism, Linguistics, and the Study of Literature*. Ithaca, NY: Cornell University Press.
Donaldson, Jeffery. 1995. "The Company Poets Keep: Allusion, Echo, and the Question of Who Is Listening in W. H. Auden and James Merrill." *Contemporary Literature* 36.1: 35–57.
Eliot, T. S. 1971. *The Complete Poems and Plays 1909–1950*. New York: Harcourt, Brace & World, Inc.
Friedman, Susan Stanford. 2005. "Gender and Genre Anxiety: Elizabeth Barrett Browning and H. D. as Epic Poets." *Tulsa Studies in Women's Literature* 5.2: 203–28.
Galvin, Rachel. 2013. "'Less Neatly Measured Common-Places': Stevens' Wartime Poetics." *Wallace Stevens Journal* 37.1: 24–48.
H. D. *Helen in Egypt*. 1961. New York: New Directions.
Hatlen, Burton. 1992. "From Modernism to Postmodernism: Zukofsky's 'A'-12." *Sagetrieb* 11.1 & 2: 21–34.
Hughes, Langston. 1994. *The Collected Poems*. Ed. Arnold Rampersad, New York: Vintage Books.
Jackson, Virginia. 2005. *Dickinson's Misery: A Theory of Lyric Reading*. Princeton, NJ: Princeton University Press.
Kamboureli, Smaro. 1991. *On the Edge of Genre: The Contemporary Canadian Long Poem*. Toronto: University of Toronto Press.
Keller, Lynn. 1997. *Forms of Expansion: Recent Long Poems by Women*. Chicago: University of Chicago Press.

Lolordo, Nick. 2001. "Charting the Flow: Positioning John Ashbery." *Contemporary Literature* 42.4: 750–74.

Lukács, Georg. 1988. *The Theory of the Novel: A Historico-Philosophical Essay on the Forms of Great Epic Literature*. Trans. Anna Bostock. London: The Merlin Press.

McHale, Brian. 2004. *The Obligation toward the Difficult Whole: Postmodernist Long Poems*. Tuscaloosa: University of Alabama Press.

McWilliams, John P., Jr. 1989. *The American Epic: Transforming a Genre, 1770–1860*. Cambridge: Cambridge University Press.

Perloff, Marjorie. 2002. *21st Century Modernism: The "New" Poetics*. Oxford: Wiley-Blackwell.

Pound, Ezra. 1960a. *ABC of Reading*. New York: New Directions.

    1969. *The Cantos*. New York: New Directions.

    1960b. *Gaudier-Brzeska: A Memoir*. New York: New Directions.

    1935. *Literary Essays*. Ed. T. S. Eliot. New York: New Directions.

Quint, David. 1993. *Epic and Empire: Politics and Generic Form from Virgil to Milton*. Princeton, NJ: Princeton University Press.

Ramazani, Jahan. 2009. *A Transnational Poetics*. Chicago: University of Chicago Press.

Rosenthal, M. L. and Sally M. Gall. 1983. *The Modern Poetic Sequence: The Genius of Modern Poetry*. New York: Oxford University Press.

Rukeyser, Muriel. 1978. *The Collected Poems*. New York: McGraw-Hill Book Company.

Schultz, Kathy Lou. 2013. *The Afro-Modernist Epic and Literary History: Tolson, Hughes, Baraka*. Hampshire: Palgrave Macmillan.

Silliman, Ron. 1992. "I Wanted to Write Sentences: Decision Making in the American Longpoem." *Sagetrieb* 11.1 & 2: 11–20.

Stein, Gertrude. 1980. *The Yale Gertrude Stein*. New Haven, CT: Yale University Press.

Stevens, Wallace. 1981. *The Collected Poems*. New York: Alfred A. Knopf.

Wasley, Aidan. 2011. *The Age of Auden: Postwar Poetry and the American Scene*. Princeton, NJ: Princeton University Press.

Whitman, Walt. 1973. *Leaves of Grass*. Ed. Sculley Bradley and Harold W. Blodgett. New York: W. W. Norton & Company.

Williams, William Carlos. *Imaginations*. New York: New Directions, 1970.

    Paterson. 1992. Revised edition. Ed. Christopher MacGowan. New York: New Directions.

6

JAMES SMETHURST

American Modernism and the Harlem Renaissance

The subject of Modernism and the Harlem or New Negro Renaissance has motivated intense and often heated discussion since, at least, the appearance of Houston Baker's *Modernism and the Harlem Renaissance* twenty-five years ago. Actually, the subject antedated Houston Baker's work in that many earlier discussions of the Harlem Renaissance took the movement to task for being insufficiently modern (or at least not up to date with the cutting edge of "high" modernism). Nathan Huggins's groundbreaking *Harlem Renaissance* is no doubt the most important example of this sort of criticism in early Harlem Renaissance scholarship – though, indeed, Harlem Renaissance artists themselves made much the same point, notably Wallace Thurman in his 1932 roman à clef *Infants of the Spring*. It should be added that another critical take on the Renaissance was put forward by critics of the Black Arts Movement, notably Larry Neal, who did much to promote the reissuing of long out of print works of the movement but also criticized it for being overly invested in modernist notions of aesthetics, alienation, and primitivism at the expense of the actual culture and realities of black people – a position that had also been articulated back in the late 1920s by various black radicals, notably the Communist William L. Patterson and socialist Hubert Harrison. In both cases, the basic premise, though from very different ideological stances, was that the Harlem Renaissance, despite its significant energies and some artistic accomplishments, was ultimately a failure.

Baker took this question head on and asked other simple questions. Who says the Harlem Renaissance was a failure? Was it a failure? Baker, still emerging from what one might think of as his high nationalist mode answered the first question by pointing out that those who judged the movement insufficiently modern (or ineptly modern) were judging it by a reductive notion of white "Anglo-Irish" modernism that had been enshrined in U.S. literary scholarship by the New Critics and the New York Intellectuals, a yardstick that was simply inadequate for judging the project(s) of the artists of the Harlem Renaissance (and indeed the generation of writers and artists that preceded them). Instead, Baker proposed that there were at least two major strands of artistic modernism in the United States, a white one and a black one, which emerged from different antecedents and proceeded down different paths, for the most part. As he might have said then, their codes (in all the senses of code) were fundamentally different.

Since then, scholars of many stripes have taken at least partial exception to Baker's work at that point in his career, arguing that the Harlem Renaissance was a central locus of U.S. modernism, with much impact on both black and white (and, Latina/o and Asian American) artists. Another way of putting it, in New York terms anyway, is that there was a tremendous interaction between uptown and downtown, between Harlem and the Village, social, sexual, artistic, and political, that left a profound mark on U.S. modernism. One of the earlier and perhaps the most publically prominent of these studies is Ann Douglas's 1996 *Terrible Honesty: Mongrel Manhattan in the 1920s*, which was published by a major commercial press rather than an academic one. (It might be added, though, that many accounts of U.S. bohemia from 1900 to 1920, notably Christine Stansell's *American Moderns: Bohemian New York and the Creation of a New Century* (2000), either implicitly or explicitly see "white" bohemia and "black" bohemia as almost completely disjunct.

However, the argument of this essay is that the relationship between white modernists (and primarily white cultural institutions and sites) and black modernists (and primarily black cultural institutions and sites) was basically dialectical. The presence of the work of African American artists and intellectuals (and, generally, their physical selves) in an otherwise very segregated society was a defining characteristic of primarily "white" bohemia in the United States (and the presence of the work and selves of white artists and intellectuals of "black" bohemia) from the very beginning. Even in places, such as New Orleans and the bohemian circle anchored by *The Double-Dealer* magazine, where official segregation made the regular physical association of African American artists and white artists on some level of equality difficult before the radical challenges to Jim Crow in the South during the 1930s, there was a pronounced, if often problematic, interest in African American literature and culture. (*The Double-Dealer*, for example, was the first journal to publish the work of Jean Toomer and published an early positive review of *Cane*.) In large part, this was because the peculiar location of African Americans in the social, legal, political, popular, and "high" cultures of the United States with the onset of the "Nadir" of Jim Crow forced black authors (and other artists) to explore what one might think of as typically modernist themes of alienation, dislocation, fragmentation, and commodification very early on, providing a certain sort of artistic roadmap – even if some early (and later) white modernists, such as Sherwood Anderson, also saw African Americans as the antithesis of such "civilized" discontents. Because of a longstanding African American concern with sexual freedom (especially in the sense of the free choice of sexual partners) as well as with the racist attribution of an immoral sexual abandon to black men and women – an attribution that had its roots in the slave era but took on new life and new meanings during Jim Crow – black authors took up the subject of sexuality and pushed the boundaries of sexual representation in ways that influenced early white modernists, such as Gertrude Stein in the "Melanctha" section of the 1909 *Three Lives* that so many white (and some black) modernists claimed as a breakthrough of U.S. fiction.

Among many black artists and intellectuals, there was both a pride that a number of them and their peers (and elements of African and African American expressive cultures) were a part of the forefront of modernist experimentation and a sense that African American "high" art, especially literature, theater, and visual art, lagged behind the basically white (and often European) avant-garde and needed to catch up. (It needs to be noted here that this African American artistic self-consciousness was not unique and was closely related to a general U.S. cultural self-consciousness that saw U.S. literature and art as underdeveloped as compared with Europe.) Two major responses generated by the notion of needing to catch up with Europe (and, perhaps to a lesser degree, with white U.S. modernists) were a sense of the need to participate more fully in an international (and possibly, but not necessarily, a U.S. national) modernist cultural movement, which would include integration of black subjects (in both the literary and philosophical senses) into that movement and the creation or further development of distinctly African American literature both formally and thematically. Of course, since white writers from at least the time of Mark Twain were notably concerned and drew on what they saw as demonstrably "authentic" African American language, literature, art, and culture, the general circulation of ideas and works of modern "Negro" art and literature entered into U.S. (and world) modernism as a whole so that one might see the dialectic of African American literature and modernism as resembling the Marxist idea of a dialectical spiral development upward.

One can see this dialectic at work in the very notion of a "New Negro Renaissance" in the 1920s (the term "Harlem Renaissance" was a product of a much later revival of critical interest in that cultural moment). After all, if one is speaking about the early part of the movement before 1925, when Jean Toomer, Claude McKay, Jessie Fauset, and Georgia Douglas Johnson were virtually the only major poets or fiction writers normally associated with the Harlem Renaissance to publish a book (and McKay and Fauset were basically at the beginning and Toomer and Johnson near the end of their book publishing careers), it is hard to argue that it was a more obviously productive period for black writers than, say, the 1890s and early 1900s, when the leading white literary critic William Dean Howells praised both Charles Chesnutt and Paul Laurence Dunbar (arguably the most successful poet of the period, black or white) in the pages of *Atlantic Monthly* and Pauline Hopkins, Alice Dunbar-Nelson, and Frances E. W. Harper were at the height of the "Women's Era" of African Americans writing published novels and collections of short stories and poems that, at least in the case of Harper's poetry, sold as much or more than any book of poetry in the Harlem Renaissance. As has often been noted, the term "New Negro" itself considerably antedated the Harlem Renaissance.

So what made the New Negro Renaissance "new"? What made the idea of a "Renaissance" in the more modern artistic and political sense of a "birth" rather than a "rebirth" plausible and even convincing? It was the connection of African American literature and art to a matrix of intersecting national and international avant-garde or vanguard movements, including modernism in the arts. One set of related movements was the new or newly invigorated nationalist movements of the internal colonies of the great European empires, such as those of the Irish, the Czechs, the Finns, and so on, in the late nineteenth and early twentieth centuries as well as the exponential growth of freedom movements in the external colonies and among African-descended people, such as the Indian National Congress, the South African Native National Congress, the Pan-African Movement, and the Garvey Movement and the beginning of the Négritude Movement in France in the early twentieth century.

Another movement was the post-Bolshevik Revolution international Left. While responses to the October Revolution were mixed among black leftists, with some, notably A. Phillip Randolph and Frank Crosswaith, becoming adamantly anti-Communist, there was a decidedly changed environment of revolutionary political possibility that nurtured the New Negro Renaissance. While the Communist Left did not have the influence in Harlem and other black communities that it would gain in the 1930s – as such scholars as Bill Maxwell, Jeffrey Perry, and Mark Solomon have shown – Communists, left Socialists, and socialist-minded nationalists (or nationalist-minded socialists), such as Cyril Briggs, Otto Huiswoud, Claude McKay, Richard Moore, and Hubert Harrison, and organizations and institutions such as the African Blood Brotherhood and its journal *The Crusader* and the Communist-led journal *The Liberator*, coedited for a time by Claude McKay and Mike Gold, exerted important influences on the scope and tone of the Harlem

Renaissance. One might see this influence even in A. Phillip Randolph's and Owen Chandler's *The Messenger*, one of the major journals of the Harlem Renaissance, which, at least in its early days, displayed a militant socialist and race-conscious stance, extolling for example African American armed resistance to racist violence as a hallmark of the "New Negro," and thereby distinguishing itself from both W. E. B. Du Bois as well as Booker T. Washington in terms that anticipate similar Communist "Third Period" criticisms of Du Bois later in the 1920s.

Finally, "New" and "Renaissance" connoted literary and artistic modernism in the United States, as in the "New Poetry" and the "Chicago Renaissance" of the early twentieth century (that is, of *Poetry* magazine, *The Little Review*, *Others*, and the radical North Side bohemia of Towertown and Bughouse [Washington] Square, not the later black movement of the 1930s and 1940s). That is to say, "the Negro" was fully participating in the "new spirit" of the arts internationally. Again, there was some tension between the idea that African American artists were helping to constitute this new spirit and the notion that they, especially writers, dramatists, and visual artists, needed to catch up, to catch this spirit – though one also sees the longstanding belief dating back to the rise of U.S. modernism and continuing to our own time that black writers, visual artists, theater workers, and "art" music composers were lagging behind African American popular and folk musicians and needed to follow their aesthetics, their models of the artist's relationship to audience, their self-pride, and so on. To a considerable extent, some – particularly Alain Locke in *The New Negro* – used the revolutionary aesthetics of modernism to displace and mute the revolutionary and revolutionary-nationalist political aspects of the Harlem Renaissance. Nevertheless, Locke could sound pretty Bolshevik when addressing a Left-leaning audience, as when he spoke before the early Négritude crowd in the Paris-based salon of the Nardal sisters (Paulette and Jane). There was also, however, a decidedly Left modernist tendency in the Harlem Renaissance, as seen in the African American contributions to such journals as *The Liberator* and the early *New Masses* and the activities of Claude McKay (a Communist for much of the Renaissance who attended the fourth Communist International congress in Moscow), Langston Hughes (who published poetry in Communist journals through the second half of the 1920s and the early 1930s), Eric Walrond (an early contributing editor to *New Masses*), Jean Toomer (another early *New Masses* contributing editor), and Fenton Johnson.

Fenton Johnson is a fascinating case of how the different strands of the Harlem Renaissance came together both in his work and its reception by other black artists and critics who projected Johnson as a sort of ur-black modernist even if Johnson basically had ceased to publish by the mid-1920s.

Although basically the same age as Claude McKay and Nella Larsen (and actually younger than Jessie Fauset), Johnson had a literary career that antedated most of the writers closely identified with the Renaissance (with the exceptions of Georgia Douglas Johnson and James Weldon Johnson, if one considers them to be primarily associated with the New Negro Renaissance). Johnson was never really a resident of Harlem or anywhere else in New York, although he did spend a year at the Columbia School of Journalism. He was a product and pretty much a lifelong resident of the South Side of Chicago with brief sojourns at Columbia and in Louisville, Kentucky.

Johnson was a fairly regular visitor to New York and published in 1916 what appears to be the first work (the poem "Harlem: The Black City") using the new ghetto in central Harlem as a literary landscape, antedating (or revising) what many consider to be the start of the Harlem Renaissance by a few years. He was extraordinarily connected in the also new South Side ghetto as his family was an integral part of the network of political operatives, entrepreneurs, and – not to put too fine a point on it – gangsters, gamblers, and numbers moguls, forming the power elite of Bronzeville linked to the very similar white networks that basically ran the city. This included his uncle John Johnson (a numbers and gambling mogul), his father Elijah Johnson (a partner in his brother's gambling operations and nightclub owner), Jesse Binga (the realtor and leading black banker in Chicago before the Depression and frequent underwriter of Fenton Johnson's literary projects, who was married to Johnson's aunt), and Robert Abbott (a banking partner of Binga and founder of the *Chicago Defender*, which became arguably the leading black newspaper in the United States). This patronage network gave Johnson, paradoxically enough, tremendous access to the social and cultural institutions of black Chicago (and beyond), including the *Defender*, which promoted Johnson as the up and coming leader of literary Bronzeville, favorably reviewing or covering Johnson's books, journals (substantially funded by Binga), readings in black literary circles both in Chicago and elsewhere (particularly New York) in the 1910s. He was also an integral part of the interracial bohemian modernist scene centered in the Near North Side of Chicago, publishing in Harriet Monroe's *Poetry* magazine and Alfred Kreymborg's journal *Others*. As Lorenzo Thomas notes, Kreymborg in particular saw his relationship to Johnson as an essential part of his modernist-bohemian (and Left) challenge to the cultural and social order of the United States (Thomas 2000, 35).

Johnson also positioned himself as part of a black artistic and political vanguard, particularly in the years immediately before and after the end of World War I in 1918. He spoke (or read poetry) before a black socialist club in Harlem. His journal *Champion Magazine*, while not precisely

Left, nationalist, or modernist in its aesthetics or politics, was open to all three overlapping (in black art and letters) tendencies, beginning to feel its way toward what a radical black modernism that interacted with the larger world of international modernism might be. In his own poetry, Johnson began to experiment with using the forms, tropes, diction, and rhythms of black vernacular music, particularly the spirituals and, to some degree, ragtime and the blues as the basis of a new black poetry. Johnson's last published poetry (at least in his lifetime), in such venues as Kreymborg's *Others* and James Weldon Johnson's landmark anthology *Book of American Negro Poetry*, was a colloquial, almost prosy free verse that was (and is) frequently described as resembling that of white Chicago poet Carl Sandburg. However, as this poetry evolved, it took on a more objective, more stripped-down tone and diction than that of Sandburg. While never appearing in book form, it seems that Johnson was attempting to create in these poems, including what are now his most frequently anthologized poems "Tired" and "The Scarlet Woman," a collective portrait of the new black ghetto, particularly Chicago's Bronzeville, anticipating similar efforts later by such poets as Langston Hughes, Gwendolyn Brooks, and Melvin Tolson.

Even though Johnson's publishing career for all intents and purposes ceased as the Harlem Renaissance began to take off, even as late as the preface to the 1931 edition of the *Book of American Negro Poetry*, James Weldon Johnson positioned the work of Fenton Johnson as an integral part of U.S. literary modernism:

> It is also a fact that Johnson belongs in that group of American poets who in the middle of the second decade of the century threw over the traditions of American poetry and became the makers of the "new" poetry. He was among those writers whose work appeared in *Others* and in *Poetry: A Magazine of Verse*.   (Johnson 1931, 141)

James Weldon Johnson, then, early on used the work of Fenton Johnson to propose a history of the "New Poetry" and literary modernism in which African Americans were an integral part as well as to present one model of how literature by a black author and how a black literature could be truly modern.

The other early Harlem Renaissance model for African American participation in U.S. modernism and U.S. bohemia and for the creation of a distinctly black modernism was Jean Toomer. Toomer has long been understood, really from the period of the Harlem Renaissance itself, as the epitome of the black modernist, again, both in terms of his writing, notably the genre-defying *Cane* (1923), and his prominent participation in predominantly, though not entirely, white bohemian circles. Paul Rosenfeld, one of the first critics to attempt to survey U.S. artistic modernism at length, included an entire chapter on Toomer and *Cane* in his 1925 *Men Seen: Twenty-Four Modern Authors*, somewhat to the bemusement of the book's anonymous reviewer at the *New York Times*. Toomer was famously reluctant to identify himself as a "Negro," but both his friend the white bohemian Waldo Frank and favorable reviewers identified Toomer as black and his work as an authentic, perhaps *the* authentic, expression of the black folk spirit or what John McClure, in *The Double-Dealer* called "the Negro's South" (McClure 1924, 26) in modernist U.S. literature, recalling the similar terms in which William Dean Howells praised the "dialect" poetry of Paul Laurence Dunbar. Despite the similarity to Howells' praise of Dunbar, some reviewers, such as McClure, seemed to present Toomer as doing something that had never been attempted before:

> The Negro has given to America its only beautiful folk poetry. "Cane" may be a landmark in American literary history because it represents the injection into our polite letters of the emotional ecstasy of the black man.
>
> (McClure 1924, 26)

Toomer was unhappy with his identification as a Negro by Frank and others because of his projection of himself as a potential member of a new "American race" that is neither white nor black, but cast rather as part of his larger modernist project of individual and social reintegration. That is to say, like other modernists of various stripes and identities, he takes up what he sees as the problem of modern isolation, fragmentation, and warring selves (racial, gendered, sexual, economic, intellectual, natural, and, spiritual) rendered in terms of a stylistically and generically fragmented version of the black migration narrative of the Jim Crow era. This narrative, in such works as Paul Laurence Dunbar's *The Sport of the Gods* and James Weldon Johnson's *Autobiography of an Ex-Colored Man*, features a black protagonist (or group of protagonists) who yo-yo between North and South, finding both intolerable: the urban North being a place of rootlessness, isolation, and materialism (while still racist in the extreme) and the South remaining a place of the black folk, of a fading, but still present rootedness (while unbearable because of intense and often violent racial oppression). One aspect of *Cane* – seen earlier also in Du Bois's *The Souls of Black Folk*, which much influenced Toomer – is a sense that not only do black subjects travel the North-South axis, but so do ideas and even economic influences so that the South itself is undergoing a sea change, transformed by the materialism and alienation of the industrial capitalism associated with the urban North. In the "Karintha" and "Esther" stories/prose poems of *Cane*, one does not have to leave the South to go so to speak up North.

Whatever Toomer's desire personally and artistically to transcend what he saw as the prison of the Negro/white binary, many black artists and intellectuals (and white artists and intellectuals) held him up as an even more achieved model of a genuinely black modernism than Fenton Johnson. After all, Fenton Johnson's project of portraying the black South Side never came to full fruition while *Cane* was a realized work. And, as with Fenton Johnson, when Toomer basically stopped publishing (or was unable to publish) what might be considered belletristic literature after 1929, it was black artists, critics, and scholars who really kept his reputation alive for decades, not white scholars of modernism, at least until the revival of interest in the Harlem Renaissance during the 1960s and 1970s, again largely initiated by African American scholars, critics, and cultural activists.

Both Toomer and Johnson, then, not only demonstrated the cutting edge participation of African Americans in the various artistic insurgencies taking place more generally in the United States, but also inspired other black writers to create a distinctly black and distinctly modern art and literature. Langston Hughes, for example, who was fascinated by the sonnet and the other song-based forms of Western European lyric poetry that formed the backbone of the English lyric verse tradition, created a genre or sub-genre of African American lyric poetry based on popular and folk song forms identified with African Americans, most notably the blues. Others, including Dunbar, Fenton Johnson, Toomer, and James Weldon Johnson had undertaken similar projects, though generally drawing on the spirituals. It is worth noting, however, Hughes chose the blues not only because of its amenability to such lyric poetry, but also because it was a product of the modern urban industrial era; his early blues poems, such as "The Weary Blues," are generally set in urban landscapes. Again, it is worth emphasizing that Hughes drew on the sounds, tropes, rhythms, rhyme schemes, and other formal and thematic resources of the blues to represent what Amiri Baraka would later characterize as the "changing same": a tradition that constantly revolutionizes and renews itself. Thus, the blues (like jazz) represented a significantly verbal black expressive modernity.

Other poets of the Harlem Renaissance, including Countee Cullen, Gwendolyn Bennett, Helene Johnson, Claude McKay, and Sterling Brown (who was also associated with poetry rooted in black folk forms, including the blues, the work song, and the badman song), took older European/North American forms, notably the sonnet and the ballad and used the associations of these forms to their own particular ends. For example, the association of the sonnet with love, particularly in the enormously popular and comparatively recent sonnets of Elizabeth Barrett Browning, made McKay's bitter and angry sonnets that indicted U.S. racism, racist violence, and class oppression (and, indeed, "America" itself) all the more shocking and powerful, harkening back to the political sonnets of Milton, Wordsworth, and Shelley, but with a violent tone missing from those earlier sonnets. One possible date for the beginning of the Harlem Renaissance was the appearance of McKay's protest-sonnet "If We Must Die" in *The Liberator*, which was understood by readers, particularly black readers as calling for armed resistance against the violent race riots (pogroms, in fact) that swept the nation in 1919, employing a tone of determined pride and anger seldom heard in black poetry to this point, a sonic equivalent, perhaps, of the Left national African Blood Brotherhood (to which McKay belonged for a time). Helene Johnson in "Sonnet to a Negro in Harlem" similarly used the popular association of the verse form with a studiedly high culture to give a conflicting (one might say dualistic) complexity to a praise poem to a young black man loitering on a Harlem street. Like Edna St. Vincent Millay, Cullen and Bennett used the sonnet's association with love to engage contemporary politics of sexuality and gender in a moment in which received gender identity and roles as well as racial identity and roles were being challenged. In the case of Cullen, his position as a black gay man in the 1920s – complicated by being a believing Christian at a time when homosexuality was considered a sin by virtually every (if not every) Christian denomination – infused his poetry with a considerable anguish and tension.

In fact, if one takes a new openness about and engagement with sexual expression to be a hallmark of modernist literature, as was, in fact, how the artistic avant-garde was widely understood in the U.S. during the 1910s and 1920s (and, after all, Joyce's *Ulysses* was denounced and prized at least as much for the freedom of its sexual depictions as for its radical form), then the literature of the Harlem Renaissance was perhaps the most radical beachhead of literary modernism in the United States. There is no other large body of work by U.S.-published, mostly "mainstream" presses during that era in which openly gay and lesbian characters appear so frequently. In addition to Cullen's erotic poetry, such novels as Langston Hughes's *Not Without Laughter*, Claude McKay's *Home to Harlem* and *Banjo*, and Wallace Thurman's *The Blacker the Berry* and *Infants of the Spring*, and James Weldon Johnson's *Autobiography of an Ex-Colored Man* (published anonymously in 1912, but reissued in 1927 under Johnson's name) all contain openly gay or lesbian characters, which in turn raises the possibility within the frame of the novels that their homosocial relationships are in fact homosexual or homoerotic relationships. One might push this further and suggest that the more recent readings of homosocial relationships in such novels as Nella Larsen's *Passing* and Jean Toomer's *Cane* as gay or queer are also strengthened by the body of works in which clearly gay and lesbian characters appear, often in some sort of bohemian or socially subterranean milieu. In that context, if one is generally familiar with the fiction of the New Negro Renaissance, it would be surprising if such a possibility did not occur.

Consequently, the way that homosexuality inflected the Harlem Renaissance and its relationship to modernism generally did not simply reside in the fact that the circuits that connected modernism and bohemianism uptown in Harlem to modernism downtown (and to the publishing industry) were to a large extent gay or queer circuits, as significant as these connections were for the circulation of black literature and art beyond the ghetto. But also non-normative sexuality, whether in a basically heterosexual modality as in Jessie Fauset's novel *Plum Bun*, featuring various bohemian social and sexual relationships outside of marriage, or in a largely gay or queer modality, was a prominent feature of many Harlem Renaissance works, pushing the boundaries of U.S. literature in ways understood as avant-garde. Of course, questions of sexual freedom and sexual choice (and, by extension, sexual repression and sexual coercion) had been major features of African American literature, particularly by women, since the first half of the nineteenth century, in large part a legacy of chattel slavery. In that sense, the impetus for pushing the boundaries of the representation of sex and sexuality in the Harlem Renaissance issued not simply from modernist or bohemian sources, but out of African American literature, culture, and politics over the previous century and more, in turn, influencing modernism generally.

Returning to the questions explicitly and implicitly posed by Houston Baker's book – whether the Harlem Renaissance was sufficiently modern and achieved (and, hence, "successful"); whether it was a part of a larger phenomenon that we call "modernism" generally or a part of an African American modernism distinct from "white" modernism; and whether, if a part of a larger modernism, it lagged behind or was in the vanguard – one is tempted to say "all of the above." A significant premise of both the Harlem Renaissance and the broader networks of the "new poetry" and other concepts of a new U.S. literature and art, was the African American participating in and even, sometimes, leading the cutting edge of that literature and art in the "Jazz Age," when even T. S. Eliot's "The Waste Land" was regarded as a jazz poem by some white critics. At the same time, many black writers and critics in belletristic and more theoretical works spoke of the need for African American artists to participate in what they saw as an international (not white), multifaceted and multivalent modernism. While some of these writers saw their work as that of modernist internationalist citizens of letters, others viewed their work as part of a modern African American literature that was under construction, but based on principles and cultural resources derived from the African American people (who were in fact a people or something like a "nation," as Third International Marxists increasingly understood the term, as a group with a common history, culture, historically-based psychology, language, and so on). And, it was this group development of a black modernist art that then helped ensure African American participation in international modernism (and modern politics) on the basis of equality and respect, even as black people maintained the right and even the obligation to pursue artistic (and political) self-determination.

WORKS CITED

"Advance Guard of the New Movement in Literature." 1925. *New York Times*, April 26: Book Review, 2.

Baker, Houston. 1987. *Modernism and the Harlem Renaissance*. Chicago: University of Chicago Press.

Douglas, Ann. 1995. *Terrible Honesty: Mongrel Manhattan in the 1920s*. New York: Farrar, Straus, and Giroux.

Johnson, James Weldon, ed. 1931. *Book of American Negro Poetry*. New York: Harcourt, Brace.

McClure, John. 1924. "*Cane* by Jean Toomer" *The Double-Dealer*, January: 26

Smethurst, James. 2011. *The Afro-American Roots of Modernism: From Reconstruction to the Harlem Renaissance*. Chapel Hill: University of North Carolina Press.

Stansell, Christine. 2000. *American Moderns: Bohemian New York and the Creation of a New Century*. New York: Metropolitan Books.

Thomas, Lorenzo. 2000. *Extraordinary Measures: Afrocentric Modernism and Twentieth-Century American Poetry*. Tuscaloosa: University of Alabama Press.

7

RACHEL BLAU DUPLESSIS

Objectivist Poetry and Poetics

Any discussion of objectivist poets and poetics in U.S. poetry must address that key term. Each definition will have virtues except the most obvious – capital O Objectiv*ism*. There was no such movement then, no "-ism" – no manifesto, no like-minded mutually supportive grouping, no headline magazine, no performances, no excommunications – all characteristics of literary movements.[1] An objectivist ethos is fundamentally a poetics without a movement. The roles of Ezra Pound as an instigator and William Carlos Williams as a bridge figure from the modernist teens were vital. And various poets underwrote this poetics: Charles Reznikoff beginning in the late teens, Louis Zukofsky beginning in the late 1920s–mid-1930s, Basil Bunting and Williams working throughout their careers within objectivist projects and their Poundean trace, and George Oppen, Lorine Niedecker, and Carl Rakosi in the thirties and then, after particular career interruptions, again in the late 1950s through the 1970s (in Rakosi's case – decades beyond).[2] How may we understand something both genealogically diffuse and historically influential? This essay defines "objectivist" as a set of claims in poetics and as a multi-generational nexus of writers propelling a late modernist poetics into contemporary writing.

The term "objectivist," some say, originated in an opportunistic publicizing move that accrued long-term credibility. Special editor Louis Zukofsky was compelled to name his February 1931 issue of *Poetry* magazine – he thereupon called it "'Objectivists' 1931." Note the specificity of the date as a localized sounding, and the ironic forceps of quotation marks around the key word. Two crucial terms, "sincerity" and "objectification," centered his introductory essays. In that issue and in the 1932 *An "Objectivists" Anthology*, Zukofsky published both contemporaries and older modernists, illustrating his interests in poetic craft, "NOT" in any new movement (Zukofsky 2000a, 214).[3] Despite Pound's hovering presence urging a movement indebted to Imagism/Vorticism (and thus to himself), Zukofsky refused to spearhead a specific group differentiated from the modernism in

89

which he claimed a serious place. Between 1927 and 1932, Zukofsky wrote seven incisive critical assessments of modernist/objectivist poetry, defining "objectivist" as concerning foundational poetic practices: an optically exact critical-poetical "lens" to bring "particulars" into exacting focus via sight, sound and analytic thought (Zukofsky 2000a, 12; Zukofsky 2000b, xi). In 1958, Zukofsky redacted several of these essays from the late 1920s to excise any hint of an -ism, insisting forcefully on his universalizing commitments to excellent writing.[4]

A second view, also historically accurate, shows that the objectivist formation did briefly possess at least one characteristic of a movement – a network for mutual publication. With An "Objectivists" Anthology and texts by Williams, Reznikoff and Oppen from 1931–5, one sees like-minded poets involved in TO, Publishers (financed by Oppen, edited by Zukofsky) and then in The Objectivist Press collective, with a short life but a distinguished list. The poets involved volunteered enough money to participate in the latter imprint. That pared-down demand excluded the financially marginal (but theoretically central) Zukofsky from publishing a book. However, despite the scant meetings of this distribution network, and further, despite long-term engagements among and between these poets – specific relationships of friendship, affection, acquaintanceship, respect, deep bonds or coolness over decades and whole careers – the objectivists are still less a "group" than loosely affiliated realist writers in a Pound/Williams tradition with a radical modernist attitude in poetics.

The term "radical" points simultaneously toward an experimental poetics and a progressive politics. A third view sees Objectivists as poets propelling a politically progressive or Marxist (radical) modernism in an aesthetically experimental (radical) mode. This overview statement demands precise ideological, biographical, and historical qualification for each poet, but it is generally accurate. However, the occlusion of Popular Front ideals, "historical amnesia" about Communism and Socialism, and the political repression of the American left in the 1950s – as well as the principled resistance to explicit political poetry among these poets – make this a complex point (Lowney 2006, 7).

Charles Reznikoff's influential work (from the twenties on) features reticent diction, understated perception, the humble and sorrowful framed by compassionate implacability. His work is psalmic (inflected with Hebraic modes), notational, similar to "Chicago School" vignettes, but ethically committed to negativity and resignation, not to upbeat populist affirmation. He is the poet of extreme condensation, apparently beyond poetic artifice, with an inexorable vision of the human condition *in extremis*. Reznikoff (born 1897), though influenced by Pound's "imagism," seemed, to the younger Zukofsky, to offer an alternative modernism: exact articulation of what is seen and heard, rigorous economy of presentation, the discipline of social witness reflecting immigrant, working class, and *shetl* life. Reznikoff's *Testimony* (two volumes, 1965, 1968) and *Holocaust* (1975) are key examples of a documentary poetics, constructing searing accounts of U.S. industrial accidents and Nazi-fascist genocide redacted from public records and court cases. This work frames the horrors and crimes to which Europe's Jews were subjected along with the economically and politically powerless. Reznikoff's works are devastating in their simultaneous sincerity (these things really happened; these things are true) and objectification – a list-like account without moralizing or any sense of meaning through transcendence.

All the poets in the objectivist formation were acutely aware of the struggles of the common person within the crises of capitalism: poverty, labor struggles, an increasingly polarized economic landscape in the late 1920s and beyond, and the stock market crash precipitating worldwide economic Depression in 1929. Indeed, Oppen's *Discrete Series* (1934); Zukofsky's contrast in *"A"*-1 between a fashionable concert (with a redemptive text – Bach's St. Matthew Passion) and militant organizing; Reznikoff's poignant, restrained depictions of urban poverty; Williams's dynamic snapshots of quotidian life and of the jaunty defiance of ordinary people; and Niedecker's "conversational – metaphysical" works on real life in rural poverty all manifest an investigative, progressive sensibility tuned to social and historic reality (Niedecker 1986, 46). All tried variously to reconcile their versions of radicalism or Marxism with their writing careers.

Though objectivists were a late modernist set of leftists and realists, objectivist work is not Popular Front poetry, but rather a transposition of a Poundean sensibility to a leftist vision. Zukofsky claimed that objectivist poetry would necessarily point toward progressive values and economic justice but without instrumentalizing goals to convert, to arouse, or to polemicize. The poets as worker-artisans of the real were to see, to record, to register contradictions and ambiguities, to think and meditate in a condensed, humane, realist poetry beyond any powerful political-cultural "line," but always with a sense of social inequality and the intricacies of injustice. The objectivists' materialist sense of literary realism about the human condition and their comprehension of the language as a material medium led to a poetry of thought, of economic and social observation, and of textual experimentalism. The complex materialist *world* as represented by the complex materialist *word* formed the rigorous dialectic of objectivist practice.

The materiality of the signifier as a precise and penetrating element is an essential objectivist claim, yet this "word" might not be spoken only sparely;

it had its own historical layers and obscure twists. Zukofsky's sestina and essay-poem, "Mantis" and "'Mantis,' An Interpretation" (1934) illustrate "objectification": the invention of a structure adequate to the self-debating complexity of thoughts. Zukofsky's sestina is an intense, notably oblique and idiosyncratic poem concerning his radical politics yet his squeamishness about "the people." He meditates allegorically on a deracinated, frightened praying mantis in a subway station, blown against the poet, who flinches at the gawky, out-sized insect. For Zukofsky, the sestina is the only form that captures the wavering back-and-forth of his thoughts on economic injustice, his political, social, personal observations, his mix of desire, fear, repulsion – plus his need to resist surrealism, the poetics with which his colleague-in-poetry, Lorine Niedecker, was then involved. The model sestina (Dante's "Al poco giorno") captures "thought's torsion" – "la battaglia delli diversi pensieri," a phrase from *Vita Nuova*, Chapter 14. Zukofsky then extended this work to express this dialectics of word and world – if his sestina has a totalizing modernist (Joycean) intensity of form through objectification, his "interpretation" created a postmodernist essay in impatient, notational sincerity. With this double poem, Zukofsky reinvented both the elaborations of closure and the openness of gloss; he straddled pre-modern (Dantean), modern, and contemporary modes of practice. The work acknowledges how political feelings suffuse subjective, personal experience.

A fourth way to see the objectivist formation notes the fact that most (though hardly all) of the poets were raised in versions of Judaism, itself having various differential manifestations.[5] Here a religious culture and not a religious affiliation is at issue – not affirmations of cultic particularism but an amalgam of attitudes: skepticism and critical negativity rather than redemptive fulfillment (for Judaism, no Messiah has yet come); utopian hope combined with a "quarrel with God" particularly about social justice; a use of such motifs as exile, exodus, diaspora, nomadism, along with historical debates over assimilation; frankness about anti-Semitism (in certain poems of Oppen, Rakosi, and Reznikoff); a metaphorically "Talmudic" textual intricacy (Zukofsky); and a resistance to the saturated Christianizing of literary culture propelled by T. S. Eliot in this period. Zukofsky's *80 Flowers* (1978) "answered" Eliot's *Four Quartets* (1935–42) by an alternative secular and naturalistic evocation of words' material, etymological force combined with arguably Eliotic motifs of time/thyme, the rose, the dance, the light, the scientific (not Christian transcendent) patterns of "liveforever," made into a dry-mortared wall of complex words in an intense procedural pattern. Reznikoff's "Hanukkah" gives a critical-aesthetic torque to Judaism: "the rebellious Jews / light not one light but eight – / not to see by but to look at" (Reznikoff 2005, 242). In his later poetry of philosophical starkness,

Oppen proposed the incessant, quarrelling and vectoring position-testing and "whirl wind" ontological and syntactic vastness as the objectification of a secular (but not un-spiritual) Hebraic-critical attitude – comparable to Edmond Jabès.

A fifth way to understand the term "objectivist" proposes that an "objectivist nexus" was conjoined and set in motion by these poets' individuated readings of Zukofsky's original terms "sincerity" and "objectification." Sincerity is aligned with clarity, with unadorned statement, with a generally anti-rhetorical stance, and with situational enactments of complex thinking within a text. Objectification is aligned with honesty about the material world of objects, with language and (sometimes intricate) poetic textuality as material facts, and with the goal of a poised poem as a fully wrought object. The poets' rich and particularized debates with these rubrics are beyond the scope of this essay to elaborate, but the terms – veridical, historically and socially investigative, resistant to social and poetic pieties and rhetorical blandishments, and leading in general to austere, intransigent works – set a standard for the poetic act. The "objectivist" position within late modernism has thus come to signify "a non-symbolist, post-imagist poetics, characterized by a historical, realist, anti-mythological worldview" (DuPlessis and Quartermain 1999, 3). Objectivist poetics values concision and exactness and makes an ethical claim of sincerity in thought; such a poetics is resistant to grand theory, overgeneralization, mythic thinking, and poeticized sublimity with its vatic claims.[6]

"Sincerity" and "objectification" do not emerge in a literary or historical vacuum. While Eliot and Pound remained inspirations and irritants to these younger poets, the practices and poetics of objectivists occur explicitly to resist the political and spiritual-institutional shifts of these modernist mentors. As left-realist poets, they reject the fascist and anti-Semitic turn in Pound (beginning by the mid-twenties), and they reject the politically conservative and Christianizing claims of Eliot (beginning by 1927). In later Pound and Eliot, abstract system, authoritarian institutions, and nonsecular claims seemed to trump local specificity. Therefore, Pound, with his mytho-informational model in *The Cantos,* and Eliot, with his adhesion to "universalizing" redemptive Anglicanism, became reduced (because reductive) models for these younger poets. Objectivists resisted fixed, un-situational ideas, the privileging of mythic transcendence, and claims of universal values and permanence in favor of local and situational investigation.

These criteria of clarity of vision, intensity of form, accuracy of diction, and social relevance have many analogues in modern/contemporary art and music. Spareness, attention to the materials, a Bauhaus-like sensibility of unadorned clarity contribute to an aesthetics of "objectification." This allies the objectivist ethos with such movements as *Neue Sachlichkeit*, with interests in the everyday, the social-critical, the unsentimental, or with modernist minimalist atonality, critical of prior musical rhetorics. Such spareness enhances and highlights intellectual and formal complexity and enacts intense in-dwelling luminosity. This does not mean that objectivists all were similar stylistically nor the same across their careers. Far from it; they ranged from an economic, factual-journalistic plain diction (Reznikoff with his poetry of witness, or the rakish, conversational Rakosi) to an intense condensation of ontological insight in notational, "folkish" observations with a proverbial flair (Niedecker). Their range includes a Poundean lyric sense fusing Old English prosody, the English song tradition, and an outrider "northern" attitude combined with a satiric Horatian elegance (Bunting), to a quasi-philosophic declaration of intransigent propositions and vertiginous aphorisms (Oppen), to a hermetic, conceptually finessing and impacted verbal surface (Zukofsky). These individual stylistic outcomes can, however, be attributed to specific poets' interpretations of sincerity and objectification within whole poetic careers.

Any diagrammatic or binarist contrast of a symbolist/incarnational and objectivist/realist poetics could become reductive, but, despite qualms, here are some pedagogic observations. "Symbolist" prosodies tend to be strophic, saturated metrically (the pentameter is not heaved away); they employ diction relatively uniform in social origins, a hypotactic/subordinating syntax, and metaphor, based on vertical relations of images. Objectivist prosodies tend to be line-based, often jagged with oblique syntactic probing, with a free verse orientation; they rely on a wide social range of speech-based discourses, parataxis and page-space (including interior white space), and metonymy (side-by-side image-materials). Symbolist poetics tend to be forensic and closural in structure, based in step-by-step argument (as in W. B. Yeats), building to a carefully managed epiphanic climax, a still or heightened moment. Poetry is often equated with the word "lyric" or "lyric narrative" and seeks transcendence. In objectivist poetics, organization is collage-like, without explicit teleological relations of the parts, but with thematic crossing points. Poetry, not only "lyric" or "ode," can be "essay-poem," long poem, life-poem. The poem is a visual and epistemological "projective field," in Charles Olson's poetics, with modes of "disjunction, ellipsis, [and] constellation" organizing "fragment" (Olson 1997, 239–49; Bernstein 2013, 7). Poesis is the imitation of the situated act of thinking, with insight dispersed across the terrain of the poem, not structurally gathered, but continuous and open-ended.

In objectivist poetics, Imagism becomes cognitive. The objectivist ethos is not just a way of purifying diction or of isolating one describable "moment" or "thing" but of exploring thinking via the poem. This thought can be abstract and conceptual as well as concrete. Reading one of William Carlos Williams's infamous hyper-short poems within the lively splay of *Spring and All* (1923), readers sometimes focus only on the "red wheelbarrow" and the "white chickens" as the shiny materials of a realist if neo-pastoral content; what they might better consider from an objectivist viewpoint is the verb "depends," the visual text, and Williams's intensely informative line breaks as means to "objectification" (Williams 1986, 224). Some of the crucial innovations in poetry that derive from this realist poetics are seriality and modular construction, anti-transcendent parataxis and montage, field poetics and collage, documentary poetries including citation strategies, and a strong commitment to the material, visual, and sonic text.

Perhaps the most distinctive contribution of objectivist poetics is the mid-length to very long serial poem. Seriality is a way of joining small units or fragments into one larger poem by sequencing these insights in meaningful ways. Serial poems are characterized by leaps of self-debating thought, multi-directional vectors of argument, coordination by juxtaposition, and emotional and epistemological gaps. The pulses of argument are present; the progression of argument occurs inferentially and disjunctively. A serial poem produces structures of thought and places things in meaningful sequence (a trajectory of emotion, a pressure of thought) without necessarily creating one narrative line; in this it is distinguished from a poem sequence. Such a work may not seek wholeness or totality, but rests on insoluble dialogic relations among the sections. In a serial work, meanings are built by the ordering or sequencing of the parts, by the nature and cut-splice of the parts (image, phrases, lines, words), by the white spaces or structural caesurae among the parts, and by the varied intellectual and emotional relations of leap or suture among these elements. The sequencing tactics of seriality make individual units gain in implication, but appear, paradoxically enough, perpetually suggestive and incomplete.

From the moment of the serial critical haibun *Spring and All* (1923), and with full awareness of the intellectual and structural challenges of Pound's *Cantos* (written from 1913–72), of Eliot's long poems in 1922 and in the 1940s, and of *Paterson* (1946–58) by Williams, objectivist poetics often took shape in mid-length serial poems. These include *Briggflatts* by Bunting (1965), *Discrete Series* (1934), "Of Being Numerous" (1968) and "Some San Francisco Poems" (1972) by Oppen, book-length documentary works such as *Holocaust* (1975) by Reznikoff and "Wintergreen Ridge" (1968) and "Paean to Place" (1966–8) by Niedecker, and – a long poem in twenty-four sections paralleling the great modernist examples –"*A*" (1978; "*A*" 1–12 in 1959) as a consummate, career-staking achievement by Louis Zukofsky. As a mode of practice, seriality is one way of extending a lyric into a long poem but without monumentality, without any necessary continuous narrative or any systematizing philosophical position, and even without conclusion/ resolution. Formally, the sections and the clashes of position among sections dramatize the dilemmas to which they testify.

In objectivist terms, poetry "serve[s] as a test of truth," as Oppen said – meaning situated truth, true to what you saw and felt at a particular juncture (Oppen 2007, 32). This may be philosophically problematic (it is not a Platonic or absolutist definition of truth) but it may also be ethically inspiring. In Oppen's own existential *dérive*:

> It is possible to find a metaphor for anything, an analogue: but the image is encountered, not found; it is an account of the poet's perception, the act of perception; it is a test of sincerity, a test of conviction, the rare poetic quality of truthfulness. (Oppen 2007, 31–2).

This "encounter" provokes ontological shock within a historical moment. From this moment comes faceted or vectored thoughts, some self-debating and contradictory, as sections of a poem. Argument or development are not pre-formulated by normative ideas or normal structures of poetic texts but leap from each other by association, extended elastic logic, and self-debate. Thus, seriality is a critique of totality (as in Frankfurt School thinking) in favor of the veridical nature of the fragmentary insight. As a formal mode, seriality becomes the "objectification" of sincerity.

This is clearly a realist ethos – but not necessarily a representational one. One sees this poetics in Lorine Niedecker's early poems of hyper-associative consciousness – as when she pasted lively, personalized aphorisms over the anodyne mottoes in a calendar in "Next Year or I Fly My Rounds, Tempestuous" (1934). In her "Paean to Place" (1966–8), she writes a pensive autobiography and credo in allusive, richly sounded short sections, all streaming together like the swampy Wisconsin lake-with-river on which she lived most of her life. The credo involves a validation of marginality, a humanist /Darwinian anti-transcendence with an eye to renewal, a lyrical anti-sublimity, and an evocative sense of psychic adjustment to the real.

One sees this poetics when Oppen uses the serial form to articulate a radical political and ontological skepticism. In Oppen's serial Vietnam War poem "Of Being Numerous" (1968), there are epic topics but no epic means – it is a grand work resisting grandeur. It concerns neither nation-building nor hero – yet there is a soldier, at least one war, and a nation, and a speaker who examines hopefully, painfully, skeptically, the nation being built and rebuilt. The poem emerges from the sixties' political crisis around legitimacy and war. And this revolutionary moment provokes Oppen's political questions – on war atrocities and responsibility; on whether and how democracy is possible; whether people can live in communities effectively; whether there can be a civic covenant; how one assesses the most intimate bonds during devastating historical times. Oppen's is a writing that begins as if from the beginning – devoid of certainty and absolutes, evaluating the adequacy of insight, statement and word. Oppen's oeuvre in general is centered by serial poems presenting social and personal dilemmas registered with unembellished clarity and unresolvable ambiguity.

So too Zukofsky's "*A*" – a poem with the scale of *The Cantos* of Pound or *The Maximus Poems* of Olson; this long poem (composed in spurts over forty years) employs the self-different sections characteristic of seriality. Its twenty-four long sections offer a panoply of genres – from shortest section ever in a long poem (four words as one full section) to a full length play, to oblique redactions of world history, to a sonnet sequence, also including a family narrative, a career-summarizing cantata (assembled by Celia Zukofsky) citing prior work by Zukofsky himself, epistles, philosophic debate, chronicle. This dazzling and often hermetic array of many genres in a serial sampler of high hermeneutic challenge is a secular modernist version of Hebrew Scriptures (in the mandated twenty-four books) with Zukofsky as both editor and writer.

A poetics claiming realist values will, by definition, cut against the grain of some assumptions and claims of poetry as a genre – the terms used would be transcendent, heightening, seeking beauty, attending to uplift, interested in poetic craft (such as rhyme) as a symbol of the special cultural status of poetry and the poetic. The importance of objectivist "sincerity" is its allowance for historically situational thinking without institutional-spiritual claims. The evocative term "objectification" also brought with it the clarity of vision, the precision, the sense of commonplace objects, a thingy-ness, a willingness to treat "objects" (including emotions) as worthy of scrutiny and to employ words and dictions from whatever discourse realms, including vernacular "a-poetic" language. If one defines an objectivist poetics as the realist intertwining of word and world and a generally secular (not mythic) orientation, then an expanded field of objectivist writing would include William Bronk, Cid Corman, Robert Creeley, Langston Hughes, David Ignatow, Denise Levertov, Marianne Moore, Naomi Replansky, and Harvey Shapiro constellated into this "nexus" by distinctive affiliations in poetics.[7]

The issue of delayed impact differs from the question of direct influence: the realist ethos and the critical, investigative and resistant poetics of objectivist writing can be said, retrospectively, to have had a relationship with other almost contemporaneous movements in U.S. poetry. Yet each group had a different and differential relationship to what are technically "forbearers" but in fact are contemporaneous peers, particularly in the 1960s–1970s. This strange temporality occurs because objectivist writers all had periods of silence, interrupted writing careers, painfully intermittent access to publishing, and low reception, often in the late 1940s through the mid-1960s. Objectivist poets – individually rediscovered and appreciated after about 1960–5 – become, in critical and poetic retrospect, the center of a constellation of contemporary U.S. poetry. During their actual careers, however, none felt at the center of anything, especially given their marginalizing, intransigent commitment to radical poetics – socially progressive and linguistically experimental. So objectivist poetics may only now be said to exist in a constellation with various poetic movements from the 1960s and 1970s, although objectivist poets were generally older than these apparent peers.[8]

Aspects of objectivist poetics may be found in at least three named or identifiable poetic groups in the contemporary period. The notion that thought, insight, and perception are not simply represented or written up afterward into a poem but are the structure of the poem on the ground of its making emerges in New American poetics (sometimes also called Black Mountain Poetries or Projectivist poetry, and attuned to Olson's "Projective Verse" manifesto [1950]). The emphasis on poetic sincerity within the act of thought – a projectivist claim – and on notable documentary and historical materials inside the poem occur in Olson, as well as Paul Blackburn, Robin Blaser, Ed Dorn, Robert Duncan, LeRoi Jones (now Amiri Baraka), Joanne Kyger, bpNichol, John Wieners. Within this formation, only Robert Creeley's intense condensation, syntactic energy, and secular (non-mythic) attitudes are fully parallel to objectivist sensibility.

Where a Beat sensibility is concerned (the work of Gregory Corso, Diane di Prima, Lawrence Ferlinghetti, Allen Ginsberg, Bob Kaufman, Michael McClure, Ed Sanders, Gary Snyder, Anne Waldman), one may note Oppen's un-seduced review (in *Poetry*, 1962) where he suggests that beyond Ginsberg's passionate "declamatory" poetry, he might want to begin "the task of rigorous thought" (Oppen 2007, 24). Objectification means the poem as an exact object – its structure is not validated or backed up by personal charm, charisma, manner, or adhesion to modes of dramatic performance. The Beats are notably vatic and grandiosely, eclectically spiritual; in contrast, objectivists are not, yet the Beat concern for marginal people, daily life, outcasts, and political dystopia are parallel. The ethos that animated Beat poetry – identifying with downtrodden people in society, naming political hypocrisy, and raising these up to ecstatic claims and judgment is one heritage of "realist" poetics.

Objectivist poetics is not only about the material world as such. Their materialist orientation has another important and complicating aspect – attention to the materiality of the medium (rhythms, diction, syntax, visual/sonic text the substance of the language, historical discourses, conventions of representation and their ideologies). Thus the materialism of the word itself is expressed as a realist poetics. Ruptures of language and syntax and ruptures of conventional discourses have homologies with ruptures of consciousness based on critique of ideology. In this way, Language Poetry claimed allegiance to the difficult, procedurally elegant and learned Zukofsky (as well as to Gertrude Stein). In Zukofsky, the vagaries of textuality itself, and the histories of discourses, lettristic and semantic play with language, witty proceduralism, and intense syntactic condensation are characteristic practices. This has analogues with Kabbalistic textuality in Judaism – a religious adhesion that Zukofsky rejected, but a cultural-linguistic stance of some conceptual influence on him. A materialist poetics in Zukofsky develops a full-scale, material hermeticism combined with a procedural experimentalism, all with a trace of the Marxism he once professed. This complex of concerns advances into the work of such Language-oriented poets as Bruce Andrews, Charles Bernstein, Michael Davidson, Carla Harryman, Lyn Hejinian, Bob Perelman, Ron Silliman, and Barrett Watten; Rae Armantrout has analogues rather with Niedecker. Zukofsky was also one of the modernist poet-critics (as, of course, were Eliot, Pound, Stein, Moore, and Williams), an influential subject position in today's radical poetics overall, with Language Poetries, among others, contributing to the analytic claim that poetics and poetry are inseparable activities.

Beyond "named" poetic formations, there is no doubt that the objectivist ethos has affected U.S. poets whom one could even call "neo-objectivist," formed in some interchange both with objectivists and with a generalized post-Holocaust, European-influenced sensibility. These include Norma Cole, Beverly Dahlen, Rachel Blau DuPlessis, Michael Heller, Susan Howe, Hank Lazer, Michael Palmer, Jerome Rothenberg, John Taggart, and Rosmarie Waldrop.

In general, because of their delayed critical reception, spotty anthology presentation, quite uneven in-print availability, and odd non-status as a "group," objectivist poets have just in the past decades begun to be read, critically assimilated, and finally understood as fundamental in every way to Anglo-American late modernism.

NOTES

1 Some poets in this formation did not ever meet or met only at the ends of their careers. Even the key anthology was only designated "An" not "The" and retained the quotation marks (Zukofsky, ed. [1932], 1975). Various literary critics do, however, use "Objectivism" as a notational shorthand.

2 Zukofsky, Oppen, and Williams all wrote essays and reviews. Reznikoff, Rakosi, and Niedecker's discussions of poetics took place mainly in letters. With the exception of Niedecker, interviews with these poets provide sources for discussions of their poetics. Basil Bunting, a British Poundean, is often included on this objectivist roster.

3 There are also "extra" poets in both the issue and the anthology; Kenneth Rexroth is the best known now. As for exclusions – Niedecker is absent; she was influenced precisely *by* that issue of *Poetry*.

4 *Prepositions+* importantly includes both original and redacted essays.

5 The exceptions are Bunting, Williams (considered an objectivist), and Niedecker – the only woman and also the sole non-urban poet among these.

6 If Zukofsky was the founding theoretician in poetics, George Oppen, back from Mexican political exile (in 1958) and returning to poetry, was the instigator of the objectivist resurgence.

7 This and subsequent alphabetical poet-lists are constructions to be taken with a grain of salt.

8 Objectivist poetics is normatively anti-surrealist, and thus all the blandishments of the New York School generations and the neo-surrealism of Clayton Eshleman and Robert Kelley were of no interest to them. The exception: Niedecker made serious surrealist work in the 1930s.

FURTHER BIBLIOGRAPHY INCLUDING WORKS CITED

Bernstein, Charles. 2013. *Recalculating*. Chicago: University of Chicago Press.

Bunting, Basil. *The Complete Poems*. 1994. Richard Caddel, Associate Editor. Oxford: Oxford University Press.

DuPlessis, Rachel Blau and Peter Quartermain, eds. 1999. *The Objectivist Nexus: Essays in Cultural Poetics*. Tuscaloosa: University of Alabama Press.

Lowney, John. 2006. *History, Memory, and the Literary Left: Modern American Poetry, 1935–1968*. Iowa City: University of Iowa Press.

Nicholls, Peter. 2007. *George Oppen and the Fate of Modernism*. Oxford: Oxford University Press.

Niedecker, Lorine. 2002. *Collected Works*. Ed. Jenny Penberthy. Berkeley: University of California Press.

    1986. *"Between Your House and Mine": The Letters of Lorine Niedecker to Cid Corman, 1960–1970*. Ed. Lisa Pater Faranda. Durham, N.C.: Duke University Press.

Olson, Charles. 1997. *Collected Prose*. Eds. Donald Allen and Benjamin Friedlander. "Projective Verse" (1950): 239–49. Berkeley: University of California Press.

Oppen, George. 2002. *New Collected Poems*. Ed. Michael Davidson. New York: New Directions.

    1990. *The Selected Letters of George Oppen*. Ed. Rachel Blau DuPlessis. Durham, NC: Duke University Press.

    2007. *Selected Prose, Daybooks, and Papers*. Ed. Stephen Cope. "The Mind's Own Place" (1962): 29–37. Berkeley: University of California Press.

Quartermain, Peter. 1992. *Disjunctive Poetics: From Gertrude Stein and Louis Zukofsky to Susan Howe*. Cambridge: Cambridge University Press.

Rakosi, Carl. 1995. *Poems 1923–1941*. Ed. Andrew Crozier. Los Angeles: Sun and Moon Press.

Reznikoff, Charles. 2007. *Holocaust* (1975). Boston: A Black Sparrow Book, David Godine, Publisher.

2005. *The Poems of Charles Reznikoff, 1918–1975*. Ed. Seamus Cooney. Boston: A Black Sparrow Book, David Godine, Publisher.

Williams, William Carlos. 1986. *The Collected Poems Volume I, 1909–1939*. Eds. A. Walton Litz and Christopher MacGowan. New York: New Directions.

Zukofsky, Louis. 1978. "*A.*" Berkeley: University of California Press.

1991. *Complete Short Poetry*. Baltimore, MD: Johns Hopkins University Press.

Zukofsky, Louis. 2000a. *Prepositions+: The Collected Critical Essays* (1967, 1981). Mark Scroggins, ed. Hanover: Wesleyan University Press

Zukofsky, Louis. 2000b. *A Test of Poetry* (1948). Hanover: Wesleyan University Press.

Zukofsky, ed. 1975. *An "Objectivists" Anthology*. (TO, Publishers, 1932). Folcroft, PA: Folcroft Library Editions.

8

ALAN WALD

American Poetry and the Popular Front

The Landscape of the 1930s

At the dawn of the politically turbulent 1930s, eminent as well as apprentice U.S. poets discovered that one did not need a clear day to see the class struggle. For the more passionate youngsters, a trip to the offices of the Communist Party's *New Masses* magazine at 31 East 27th Street in New York City or a meeting of the John Reed Club at 1427 Michigan Avenue in Chicago seemed as fated and fateful as Ernest Hemingway's direct path to Gertrude Stein's apartment at 27 Rue de Fleurus in Paris in March 1922. Imaginations were swiftly dazzled by Marxist images of social justice and the search for suitable rhythms was not far behind. Even the more wary, established writers were under pressure from the environment and shifting public consciousness to think in altered ways about their craft and speak of the world more directly.[1] When new problems are posed, new ideas about speech, expressions, and vistas are required.

Soon the landscape of the early Great Depression itself became a text to be read by poets from all regions and age groups. According to one literary textbook from the decade, "By 1931, there was a poet on every soap box" (Anderson and Walton, 581); in 1932, the leading Marxist critic V. F. Calverton (1900–40) declared literary radicalism "a mainstream affair" (Calverton, 26). With the help of appropriate language and forms, writers were giving narrative shape to the desperate facts of sudden impoverishment and growing anxiety. As can be seen in the 1934 poem "American Jeremiad" by Alfred Kreymborg (1883–1966), the new poetry assumed a prophetic and sometimes ominous voice, using the times as raw material but searching for an agent of change to articulate humanity's destiny: "What shall a lover sing when half the land / Is driven cold and lives on dank despair? / As long as inhumanity's in the hand / That runs the race and whips the poor apart, / Lovers must all embrace a bloody air / And strangle men who starve the human heart."[2] The March 1935 poem "I, Jim Rogers" by Stanley Burnshaw

(1906–2005), uses visionary speech to describe a process of psychic transformation: "you're never alone any more: / All of your brother-millions /
(Now marking time) will stand by you / Once they have learned your tale!"[3]
Increasingly, poets would depict workers as politically embryonic beings
acquiring a class consciousness. Their belief was that a fuller knowledge of
one's social role would generate a new type of proletarian who would act
on new principles.

Certain images began to turn up with unusual frequency in verse organized around social observances and historical witnessing: darkened facto-
ries, silent machines, agitated crowds, raised fists, and hungry faces. Urban
immigrant structures of feeling emerged in narratives expressing contempt
for the false front of a corrupt society, including the illusions of romantic love, class-biased indoctrination through formal education, and ways in
which economic inequality contravenes political freedom. In the sardonic
verse of Kenneth Fearing (1902–61), the older line between high art and
mass art is broken down as the reader is jolted into a reapprehension of
the human condition. In the soliloquies of Alfred Hayes (1911–85), pun-
gent, aching phrases are used to communicate an acute awareness of dashed
hopes. In the writings of many others, childhood experiences are linked to
adult fears of social catastrophe and the protest picket line becomes established as a significant symbol of depression culture.

After Hitler came to power in Germany in 1933, a militant yet humanistic
social and artistic vision also began to cohere, incorporating and transfigur-
ing many of these elements into a more optimistic resurrection of national
traditions. A range of liberals and Leftists promoted "the people," plebeian
and often multi-ethnic. Carl Sandburg (1878–1967), Stephen Vincent Benét
(1898–1943), Norman Rosten (1913–95), and Margaret Walker (1915–98)
worked toward heroic narratives with a beginning, middle, and end, creating epics of an emerging new society. The worker themes of the early 1930s
remained active elements, but now poets pushed harder toward the discern-
ment of certain truths rising above the circumstances of daily life under
the rubric of "People's Art." The center of this emerging mental picture of
the world was the possibility of working people taking hold of levers of
the economy while a longed-for tidal wave of justice and human solidarity
overwhelmed fascist barbarisms at home and abroad. Such a "vision of the
1930s" found a rough political correlative in 1935, when the Communist
International proclaimed the Popular Front policy.

What all this meant for modern poetry cannot be pigeonholed. Radical
poems of the 1930s and after are not a separate phenomenon from the
broader literary culture, even when their authors are political outsiders
to the national consensus. Verse of the Depression era grew out of earlier

and contemporaneous literary traditions while adding new elements and subtracting or transforming others. From 1929 to 1939, abrupt political changes reconfigured the geography of poetic thinking, aesthetic coordinates of unique conjunctures become gradually fixed, and what amounted to a new historic period stamped poetic strategies with some enduring characteristics. For subsequent decades, an afterlife of idealized memories of Popular Front culture, as a Camelot moment of radical innocence when history and hope seemed to rhyme, would episodically emerge in various shapes. Yet the succession of poetic forms and sensibilities did not keep identical time with the sequence of even world-shaking events. If one takes a closer look, many of the leitmotifs and methods of Depression-era poetry had been adumbrated by the rebel writers of previous years.

Proletarianism and Modernism

Early twentieth century verse in *The Comrade* (1901–5), *The Masses* (1911–17), and *The Liberator* (1918–22) showcased gritty realism, denounced war, promoted early feminism ("the new woman"), reveled in savage cultural satire, and produced haunting portraits of social victims that sometimes addressed racism and the oppression of immigrants. Carl Sandburg, a socialist before World War I, wrote of ordinary people and the ugliness of capitalism. Influential collections of radical poetry appeared during the 1920s, many inspired by the worker-bards of the Industrial Workers of the World (IWW) and the rhythms, meters, and romantic-democratic sensibility of Walt Whitman (1819–92). Such premonitory volumes include the *Proletarian Song Book* (1923), *Poems for Workers* (1927), *Poems of Justice* (1929), and *An Anthology of Revolutionary Poetry* (1929).

Then there was the growing presence of modernism. Since the publication in 1922 of *The Waste Land* by T. S. Eliot (1888–1965), conscious allusion and deliberate quotation became venerable means of heightening or congealing one's effects and deepening one's meaning of reference. But modernism was always a highly contested terrain, disposed to a range of political and philosophical appropriations. Poets less desolate, willfully difficult, and anti-romantic than Eliot used modern language to yoke analogous innovative practices to promoting their personal preoccupations: the impact of new types of technology on the arts, the fragmentation of contemporary life, experimentation in sex, an attraction to European aesthetics and African American music, stoic seriousness about a godless universe, and the creation of a new avant-garde in culture. Hart Crane (1899–1932), in particular, diverged from Eliot by responding positively to the aesthetic beauty of the industrial city, inventively incorporating the machine as object and symbol into his verse.

The political commitment that came with the 1930s announced the need for a social poetry that was a public art accentuating the impact of society on humanity. Yet such collectivist and purposeful primary goals were never exclusive ones. To be a social poet did not require one to be always angry and never reflective, thinking of one's art as little more than a propaganda delivery machine. After all, the most widely-read poet among writers of that era after Eliot was William Butler Yeats (1865–1939), an ardent political nationalist whose poetry was inflected by symbolism and mysticism. Soon the radicalizing W. H. Auden (1907–73) moved to third or even second place in popularity, and his work was simultaneously animated by themes of the fragility of personal love and the unseen psychological effects of preceding generations.[4] No study of what are plausibly the outstanding younger talents of that decade – Muriel Rukeyser (1913–80), Kenneth Fearing, Langston Hughes (1902–67), and John Wheelwright (1897–1940) – can be comprehensive without remembering that one function of poetry is to convert traumatic pain, personal and social, into order. A leading pro-Communist poet, Horace Gregory (1898–1982), was aptly described as having "one foot in the Waste Land and the other rather uncertainly in some communist future" (Anderson and Walton, 580). Kenneth Patchen (1911–72), habitually to the Left of Communism, is best remembered for haunting lyrics of intimate feeling.

A few radical outliers, such as regional-agrarian Georgia-born Don West (1906–92), sought authenticity in what modernity was leaving in the dust in *Crab-Grass* (1931) and *Between the Plow-Handles* (1932). Self-proclaimed practitioners of proletarian poetry such as George Henry Weiss (1898–1946), H. H. Lewis (1901–85), W. S. Stacy (dates unknown), and Jim Waters (dates unknown), and ardent promoters of the genre, such as the bohemian couple Ralph Cheyney (1896–1941) and Lucia Trent (1897–1977), also favored a vernacular culture untainted by the fancy taste of high society or the predilection for kitsch of the masses. Characteristically, Weiss employed conventionally rhymed English verse forms while Stacey wrote in free, irregular, unrhymed verse. Yet such writings were hardly walled off from modernist temptations.

One celebrated "worker-writer," a classification of the time for which considerable proletarian job experience was a requirement, was Joseph Kalar (1906–72). A mill employee on the northern Minnesota Iron Range, Kalar was as close to his subject as lips are to teeth. In a few outstanding poems, such as the 1931 "Warm Day in Paper Mill Town," he provided "a political inflection to modern imagist poetics" (Kalaidjian, 156–7). Truly a worker in words, he used harsh language in his recreations of the daily realities of proletarian life even as one finds in his work haunting portraits suggestive of the precision and sharp language of Ezra Pound (1885–1972) and linguistic experiments that recall the inventive compound words of E. E. Cummings (1894–1962). Championed in the official Communist press for his class status, Kalar was privately something of a dissident. What galled him especially were an unwanted pressure to introduce explicit revolutionary and abstract internationalist ideas into poetry and a negative assessment among super-Leftists in the urban East that poems of the "local reality" of his mid-West small-town culture were "defeatist" and "passive" (Kalar, 19).[5]

Labyrinthine bodies of work should not be distorted to fit a simple thesis, and the boundaries between various groups in the 1930s are obviously not a watertight fit, but the poetry that prevailed was that of neither the regional and small town proletarians nor Kalar's sectarian antagonists in New York. Rather, it was a sophisticated version of social modernism, a literary culture in which collage, reportage, free verse, Marxist perspectives, and proletarian language all meet in the common use of modernist formal strategies to heighten and interrogate a recognition of the economic, political, and cultural crisis. Poems that imbricate modernist montage and socialist reportage shine through like pebbles in a clear stream in the pages of the collection *We Gather Strength* (1933) and *Dynamo* magazine (1934–6), as well as other little magazines and small press publications. Outstanding practitioners include not only Fearing, Rukeyser, Hayes, and Hughes, but also Edwin Rolfe (born Solomon Fishman, 1909–54), Sol Funaroff (1911–42), Herman Spector (1905–59), and Ben Maddow (who often wrote as "David Wolfe," 1909–92). This was a trend continuous with (not opposed to) modernism, but tells a different narrative about modernist poetics than the ones predominant among literary historians before the 1989 publication of Cary Nelson's *Poetry and Repression: Modern American Poetry and the Politics of Cultural Memory, 1910–1945*.

Nelson famously wrote, with special reference to the radical poetry of the 1930s, "we no longer know the history of the poetry of the first half of this century; most of us, moreover, do not know that the knowledge is gone" (Nelson, 4). A glance at leading academic studies of U.S. poetry of that moment, such as David Perkins' *A History of Modern Poetry: Modernism and After* (1987), and Jay Parini, editor, *The Columbia History of American Poetry* (1993), confirms the proclamation. But Nelson's eloquence and original research, his blend of contemporary theory about literariness and canonicity, and his use of striking magazine illustrations, precipitated a climate change in scholarship. Only a few years earlier, efforts by Jack Salzman, Charlotte Nekola, and others had sought to promote a fresh look at the

1930s radical poetry legacy that elicited but a modest response in scholarship.[6] Nevertheless, a short time after Nelson's book, U.S. poetry studies was transfigured by a steady onslaught of new scholarship rethinking and introducing neglected texts to academe and beyond.

The most conceptually daring of the post-Nelson narratives of modern poetry is Walter Kalaidjian's *American Culture Between the Wars: Revisionary Modernism and Postmodern Critique* (1993), which exponentially expanded the field of modernism through the "politicized coupling of image and text, art and journalism, poetry and visual agitation" (3). James Edward Smethurst's *The New Red Negro: The Literary Left and Afro-American Poetry* (1999) is a transformative study of how the cultural institutions of the Literary Left significantly shaped a new relationship of African American poetry to vernacular African American culture. Nancy Berke's *Women Poets on the Left: Lola Ridge, Genevieve Taggard, Margaret Walker* (2001) presents three case studies of the socially conscious verse of radical women poets. Michael Thurston's *Making Something Happen: American Political Poetry Between the Wars* (2001) provides sustained close readings of poets of both the Left and Right in historical context to ask, "How does political poetry make something happen?" (16). These and additional studies in the new millennium established the sundry ways in which poetry of the 1930s articulated a fresh patterning of concerns that gave widespread priority to social questions and social commitment, even as complementary and contradictory impulses stemming from an author's unconscious were hardly erased.

The Communist Presence

Beyond a need for inquiry into intimate life, there is the issue of treating political commitment in a candid and precise manner. After the McCarthy era, "Communist" became more of a boo-word than a label for an adherent of any coherent doctrine. How does one demythologize the Communist presence to reveal a diverse collection of individuals who may have looked to Moscow as their religious capital but lived lives in different environments and of varying political valences? It is certainly dismaying to see scholars trying to rescue or damn individuals by denying or declaiming that they held "real" Communist Party membership. Few well-known poets were "organized" party members in the relatively conventional manner of an Edwin Rolfe, Isidor Schneider (1896–1975), Margaret Walker, James Neugass (1905–49), George Oppen (1908–84), Carl Rakosi (1903–2004), or Joy Davidman (1915–60). Many were so devoted to the cause of the USSR that they did not need formal membership to be regarded as trustworthy by the Party's political and cultural hierarchy, as was the case with Stanley Burnshaw, Genevieve Taggard, Langston Hughes, Alfred Kreymborg, Horace Gregory, and Muriel Rukeyser. Both types of writers, as well as others, saw themselves as individuals submerged in the same ideological cause, and in all cases their eccentricities determined a variety of unique appropriations of Marxist perspectives and responses (or non-responses) to changing Communist policy. Students of this poetry do not need bombshell revelations about who paid Party dues or signed a pro-Soviet petition, but when Communist affiliations are treated vaguely and evasively as part of a rushed, patchy biopic, the element of political commitment feels artificial and inert as a category of analysis because it makes so little narrative or psychological sense.

As the early 1930s radicalization ripened into the Popular Front, the role of the Communist presence in cultural activity remained similar but not identical. Meeting in groups and participating in literary discussions, Communists and their literary allies were a vanguard with a palpable impact on broader layers of writers. Yet those at arm's length from the Party were by no means duped or indoctrinated when drawn toward the Popular Front. In many ways, they already shared, or were driven by, Depression conditions to embrace, a goal of putting their special skills to use on behalf of the vision of the 1930s. And they did not need hectoring *New Masses* critics to make the mistake of sometimes overvaluing literary expression that was more urgent than subtle.

The challenge of the Depression era to all poets was an excruciating tangle of anti-capitalist and anti-fascist necessities along with a utopia that never was, or that lasted for only a brief spurt after October 1917. A version of political correctness was in the air; only a few radicalizing poets and critics seemed to remember that critical and subversive energies could coexist with racist, authoritarian, and fascist ideologies in literary works. These broader-minded poets were likely to be drawn to the quasi-Trotskyism and pro-modernism of the post-1936 *Partisan Review*, or to Trotskyism itself. This stratum included Delmore Schwartz (1913–66), John Wheelwright, Harvey Breit (1909–68), Florence Becker (1895–1984), Harry Roskolenko (1907–80), Robert Duncan (1919–88), and Sherry Mangan (1904–61). In contrast, the *New Masses* seemed to think that reading the poetry of T. S. Eliot mostly exposed one to an aesthetics of death, or that a book like Edmund Wilson's *Memoirs of Hecate County* (1946), a novel facing obscenity charges, was threatening the nation's moral health.[7]

By making radical art a citadel to be defended from attack by outsiders, the more doctrinaire Communist writers increasingly militarized their own aesthetic judgments when it came to the tricky question of how to yoke an aesthetics of responsibility to an ethics of witness and testimony. Such instrumentalizing of poetry brings risks – the subsumption of complexities of political conflict to empty and vain slogans, an intellectual foundation in pious, dogmatic sentiments, and an over-reliance on the rhetoric of indignation. On the occasions when one's verbal palette was reduced to a two-dimensional demotic voice, hardly a Left poet was free of at least some episodes of such banality, often accompanied by vitriol and finger-pointing dependent on a language of power and domination. At the same time, just as there could be subtlety and sophistication in critical rejections of high modernists such as Eliot, what appeared to be sloganeering tropes in verse might be turned, Brechtian-fashion, toward a subversive humor.

In the early 1930s Michael Gold (born Itztok Isaac Granich, 1894–1967) was much in demand as a public speaker, debater, and performer; a divo of flamboyant proletarianism with a repertoire of street-wise arias. His finest 1930s poems, such as "Ode to Walt Whitman" and "Tom Mooney Walks at Midnight," seem formulated in the heat of the moment, mostly from the gut and the heart.[8] But Gold, the bad boy of Left poetry, was something of a manners challenge to everyone in his devout, emotionalistic Stalinism and occasional pink-baiting of gay men. What should not be missed is that there was more than a little nose-thumbing in Gold's verse, columns, and reviews; more than a guardian of Communist rectitude, he thought of himself as a gleeful rebel against cherished beliefs and sacred taboos of the ruling elite, shocking cultural snobs and flabbergasting Rotarians.

In the long-run, though, it was the craft-conscious Kenneth Fearing who made a bigger hit as a studied ironist, exemplified by his cool, sardonic tone in "Dear Beatrice Fairfax," and louche characters and deadpan dialogue in "St. Agnes' Eve." His strategy of attacking bourgeois society ingeniously in terms of its own slogans and typical jargon was widely imitated, but one still finds an infinite variety of contrasting techniques within a common vision as one traverses the chapbooks and little magazines of the Literary Left.

Muriel Rukeyser, in poems like "Fifth Elegy: A Turning Wind," uses a scientific terminology alternating with subjective lyricism to address personal intricacies and struggles shaped by the disorder of the present.[9] Tillie Lerner, in "I Want You Women up North to Know," displays a fierce commitment to an interracial proletarian community of women. Alfred Hayes, like Robert Frost (1874–1973), held that a poem is drama or nothing; in his narratives "In a Coffee Pot," "Singleman," and "In a Home Relief Bureau," he relies on a crisp, clear, and direct voice. In the quest for formal structures to channel the intensity of feeling, Langston Hughes also became a dramatic poet, but he spoke of African American life through multiplicity of voices, making greater use of his extraordinary gifts of ear and eye, timing and phrasing.

Like Hughes, the work of Sterling Brown (1901–89) was especially admired for its treatment of race in terms of class differences.

The Popular Front saw a new step in the process through which a version of radical feminism reinvented Marxism as a gender-alert form of cultural practice. Sometimes the topics of verse by Genevieve Taggard, Ruth Lechlitner (1901–89), and Joy Davidman (1915–60) were specifically female issues, such as motherhood, abortion, or women taking collective action as part of a larger struggle. The everyday existence of women could be scrutinized for its own significance, or there might be a steady, unromantic attentiveness to the immediate lived experience of women as prisoners of family and the larger world. More often, women participated in poetry that addressed power and money, the dangers of self-absorption, and material oppression. This change that came in the 1930s was striking and enduring; formerly, women poets were associated with the tradition of private and domestic verse, but under the blows of the Depression, and in tandem with the rise of social movements, they felt motivated to assume a voice of authority to speak directly of the experiences of hunger and exploitation and of the threat of Nazism. Although the politics of women's separatism was avoided and same-sex desire masked or repressed, the writing of the Left-wing women provided significant antecedents of feminist poetry and fiction of the 1960s and after.

Marxism and Communist-initiated activism were mostly beneficial to energizing new dimensions in poetry. Yet in pre-and-post Popular Front days, there was always a distinctly negative aspect to the official Communist presence. Behind the scenes operated the Party's Cultural Commission, with V. J. Jerome (born Jerome Isaac Romain, 1896–1965), a Teutonic taskmaster, at the helm. Jerome's own articles and pamphlets today read like a ghastly monument to sectarianism. But there were other *Daily Worker* and *New Masses* critics who could occasionally be seen as "going thug," throwing every knife in the sectarian arsenal and conducting miniature treason trials replete with denunciations. In the middle of the decade, H. T. Tsiang (1899–1971), a relatively prolific Chinese-born Communist author living in New York City, was publically smacked around by the editors of the *New Masses* in an all-too-familiar manner: "Mr. Tsiang is not much of a writer and his career as a revolutionist is such as to hinder rather than help.... His opportunism is combined with arrant individualism. Tsiang's chief literary influence is the decadent Gertrude Stein.... Organizations of Chinese workers have repudiated him and his self-seeking tactics."[10] Such public degradation ceremonies cannot be blamed on Communist doctrine alone; competitive masculinities are often at the core of literary assaults, and even in the non-Left press, one finds a macho, alpha male tone of rivalry for dominance.

Legacy of the Popular Front

When urgent causes and ideologies enter the picture, the question will always be whether poetry is to be assessed as art or treated as a diagram of political attitudes. The movement of the 1930s Left was never as rigidly hierarchical or stage-managed as its harshest critics suggest. Rank-and-file writers could exercise reciprocal influence, and one can find many maverick poems and book reviews by poets in Party-led publications. Indeed, without Party-initiated organizations and its diverse publishing projects, U.S. culture of the era would be much-diminished while some outstanding writers would never have launched their careers. But any author who came under suspicion of disloyalty to the Soviet regime, or who strayed too far into obscure or difficult stanzas, might be subject to the firing squad of the Cultural Commission or those who instinctively carried out its work.

For the Left political movement of the 1930s, the Communist International was the most important institution and ultimately determined broad strategies. Collective organizational forms led to common projects, but there was a contrast between the first and second half of the decades. Prior to 1935, the Communist forces foolishly focused on "Red" unions, heroically propagandized for "Self-Determination in the Black Belt" (southern regions with a majority African American population), senselessly excoriated social democrats and the New Deal as "social fascist," unwisely promoted the Communist Party as an electoral alternative under the slogan "Toward a Soviet America," and admirably built cultural organizations and publications that promoted little-known and working-class artists. After 1935, the central focus became the Democratic Party and the New Deal, CIO unions, mobilizing on behalf of the Spanish Republic, and promoting the broad-based League of American Writers that featured prominent and commercially successful writers.

Ideally, Popular Front poetry would mean singularities that act in common, usually grouped under categories such as "the people" and "anti-fascist." But there is a longer history to those individuals providing guidance for the League of American Writers and selecting material for anthologies. In 1934, the Soviet Writers Congress tried to impose cultural policy on a world Communist movement via conventions of "Socialist Realism," a style of realism that judged art by its relation to the political objectives of the USSR. English translations of these speeches were read, but the resulting deliberations for the United States did not simply parrot the Soviets. U.S. poets and critics expanded on theoretical and critical insights by augmenting them and drawing on the national tradition of cultural criticism in creative ways, including an openness to new forms and sensibilities. One finds

examples of the highlighting of the examinations of appropriate poetic strategy in the April-May 1934 "American Writers Congress Discussion Issue"
of *Partisan Review* and in the record of the first Congress, *American Writers
Congress* (1935). Much of the innovative poetry, and social modernist literary strategies, for which the 1930s is best remembered, has its roots in this
pre-Popular Front era of "class against class." The outstanding scholarly
books, cited earlier, engage both periods.

After the Popular Front, it was the new pro-liberal democracy and anti-
fascist political line that was the main subject of discussion for writers.
One emblematic moment was the publication of the celebratory review of
Sandburg's *The People, Yes* (1936) by Archibald MacLeish (1892–1982) in
the September 1936 *New Masses*: "What [Sandburg] says to those who have
attempted to spell the name of their own cause out of the cracked letters of
the Liberty Bell is this: Why turn back? Why say the people were right *then*?
Why not say the people are right still? ... He points out the one great tradition in American life strong enough and live enough to carry the revolution
of the oppressed. That tradition is the belief in the people" (25–6). Here,
there is no discussion of the art of the poetry to accompany such sentimental
(and non-Marxist) political abstractions. A year later, nothing substantial
appeared about poetic form and function in the proceedings of the Second
Congress of the League of American Writers, *The Writer in a Changing
World* (1937). Many poems were read, mostly from other countries, but the
featured talks were political ones on "The Democratic Tradition in American
Letters," "Spain and American Writers," "Writers Fighting in Spain," and
"The Dialectics of Culture Under Nazism."

What is most likely the primary retrospective collection of verse on the era,
that contained in the League of American Writers' *War Poems of the United
Nations* (1943), is empty of literary criteria and has received no consideration among scholars. While collections of poetry on the Spanish Civil War
are essential documents of the 1930s, and there are wonderful writings on
the subject from later decades by unexpected authors, very few by Leftists
from the late 1930s have invited much scholarly work beyond several by
Edwin Rolfe, Langston Hughes, and Muriel Rukeyser.[11] The U.S. Marxist
critical legacy of the late 1930s does not help much, either. For the Left,
it was an era during which salesmanship, not judicious reviewing, was too
often the norm, and not much has been reprinted. The goal of Marxist criticism should have been to establish organic links between the private and the
social, always remembering the observation of Walter Benjamin that "the
tendency of a literary work can only be politically correct when it is literarily
correct" (221).

The vaunted ideals of the Popular Front are so inspiring that a scholar can be tempted to regress to the perspective of its advocates of sixty years ago. This muddles the grave significance of the political contradictions known today – the Moscow Trials, the attack on the Spanish Far Left, the catastrophe of the Hitler-Stalin Pact – as well as evidence that the poetry expressive of the sensibility of the late 1930s may be less aesthetically and intellectually compelling when detached from roots in the preceding "class against class" era. Like a mine that silently explodes, the really existing Popular Front in culture collapsed, leaving no viable foundations after World War II. It was replaced mostly by sentimental myths serviceable to later political agendas.

The first of these came through the exertions of the remnants of the Communist movement and its allies during the 1950s. Superhuman efforts were made to oppose colonialism, wage war against domestic racism, and preserve Left-wing unions, but the cultural movement was also built on dubious claims about the innocence of Julius and Ethel Rosenberg in the face of espionage charges and an insistence that fascism had already seized the decisive levers of power in the United States. The interest in the Popular Front was next revived among the social movements generated during the 1960s, which inspired the university scholarship in later decades, still hard at work today in recovering and interpreting the legacy of the 1930s.

By the time of the New Left radicalization, however, the organized working class and the centrality of a revolutionary political party were replaced in political strategy by other actors and organizational forms as more plausible vectors of social transformation. The unavoidability of "presentism" made it possible for those in search of ancestors and a usable past to revisit the history of the Left selectively. At the outset, they tended to reclaim cultural activity that could be understood more like contemporary political causes such as feminism, Black Arts, and multiculturalism; later, the more academically-inclined reimagined the era through interpretative tools inflected by at least the vocabulary and some of the ideas of contemporary deconstruction and postmodernism. Always present in the background was the demonizing inheritance of McCarthyism, which was never effectively killed off and could be revived as needed by anti-radicals (journalists, politicos, academics) as the radicalization ebbed. Neo-McCarthyism's attendance has understandably produced a counter-tendency to circle the wagons, too often resulting in a muting in literary scholarship about the late 1930s of any thorough or candid assessment of its shaping political enigmas. A new story of the Popular Front as more precisely enacted in poetry is required, one based on what we have learned from the totality of events and a more rigorous contextualization of the art.

NOTES

1 See the compelling study by Milton A. Cohen, *Beleaguered Poets and Leftist Critics: Stevens, Cummings, Frost, and Williams in the 1930s.*
2 The poem first appeared in *New Republic* 78, 1011 (18 April 1934): 203.
3 The poem originally appeared in the *New Masses* and was reprinted in Stanley Burnshaw, *The Iron Land.*
4 The claim that these three poets were the "most sedulously read" around 1930 is made by Joseph Warren Beach, *Obsessive Images: Symbolism in the Poetry of the 1930s and 1940s, 4.*
5 See the well-introduced collection of Joseph Kalar's writings by Ted Genoways, *Papermill: Poems, 1927–35.*
6 See *Social Poetry of the 1930s, Writing Red: An Anthology of American Women Writers, 1930–40* and *The Revolutionary Imagination: The Poetry and Politics of John Wheelwright and Sherry Mangan.*
7 See D. S. Mirsky, "The End of Bourgeois Poetry," and Charles Humboldt, "A Trotskyite in Love."
8 Both were published in the *New Masses.*
9 Published in Muriel Rukeyser, *A Turning Wind,* 34.
10 "Between Ourselves," New Masses, 27 August 1935, 30.
11 See the excellent collection edited by Cary Nelson, *The Wound and the Dream: Sixty Years of American Poems about the Spanish Civil War.*

WORKS CITED

Anderson, George K. and Eda Lou Walton. 1939. *This Generation: A Selection of British and American Literature from 1914 to the Present with Historical and Critical Essays.* Chicago: Scott, Foresman and Company.
Beach, Warren. 1960. *Obsessive Images: Symbolism in the Poetry of the 1930s and 1940s.* Minneapolis: University of Minnesota Press.
Benjamin, Walter. 1934. "The Author as Producer." In *Reflections: Essays, Aphorisms, Autobiographical Writings.* Ed. Peter Demetz. Trans. Edmund Jephcott. 1978. New York: Harcourt Brace Jovanovich: 220–38.
Berke, Nancy. 2001. *Women Poets on the Left: Lola Ridge, Genevieve Taggard, Margaret Walker.* Gainesville: University of Florida Press.
Burnshaw, Stanley. 1936. "I, Jim Rogers." In *The Iron Land,* 99–102. Philadelphia, PA: Centaur Press.
Calverton, V. F. 1932. "Leftward Ho." *Modern Quarterly* 6, Summer: 26–32.
Cohen, Milton A. 2010. *Beleaguered Poets and Leftist Critics: Stevens, Cummings, Frost, and Williams in the 1930s.* Tuscaloosa: University of Alabama Press.
Fearing, Kenneth. 1934. "Dear Beatrice Fairfax." *New Masses,* 6 March: 33.
1927. "St. Agnes' Eve." *New Masses,* April: 31.
Gold, Michael. 1935. "Ode to Walt Whitman." *New Masses,* 5 November: 21.
1934. "Tom Mooney Walks at Midnight." *New Masses,* 2 January: 19.
Hayes, Alfred. 1934. "In a Coffee Pot." *Partisan Review* February: 12–15.
1936. "Singleman." *Poetry* May: 34–5.
1938. "In a Home Relief Bureau." *New Masses,* 10: 115.
Humboldt, Charles. 1946. "A Trotskyite in Love." *New Masses,* 7 May: 22–3.

Kalaidjian, Walter. 1993. *American Culture Between the Wars: Revisionary Modernism and Postmodern Critique*. New York: Columbia University Press.

Kalar, Joseph. 2006. *Papermill: Poems, 1927–35*. Edited by Ted Genoways. Champaign: University of Illinois Press.

Kreymborg, Alfred. 1934. "*American Jeremiad.*" *New Republic* 78, 1011 18 April: 203.

MacLeish, Archibald. 1936. "The Tradition of the People." *New Masses*, 1 September: 25–6.

Mirsky, D. S. 1934. "The End of Bourgeois Poetry." *New Masses*, 13 November: 17–18.

Nekola, Charlotte and Paula Rabinowitz. 1987. *Writing Red: An Anthology of American Women Writers, 1930–40*. New York: Feminist Press.

Nelson, Cary. 1989. *Repression and Recovery: Modern American Poetry and the Politics of Cultural Memory*. Madison: University of Wisconsin Press.

2002. *The Wound and the Dream: Sixty Years of American Poems about the Spanish Civil War*. Champaign: University of Illinois Press.

Olsen, Tillie. 1934. "I Want You Women Up North to Know." *Partisan* 4, March.

Rukeyser, Muriel. 1939. *A Turning Wind*. New York: Viking.

Salzman, Jack and Leo Zanderer, eds. 1978. *Social Poetry of the 1930s*. New York: Burt Franklin & Co.

Smethurst, James Edward. 1999. *The New Red Negro: The Literary Left and Afro-American Poetry*. New York: Oxford University Press.

Thurston, Michael. 2001. *Making Something Happen: American Political Poetry Between the Wars*. Chapel Hill: University of North Carolina Press.

Wald, Alan. 2002. *Exiles From a Future Time: The Forging of the U.S. Literary Left*. Chapel Hill: University of North Carolina Press.

1983. *The Revolutionary Imagination: The Poetry and Politics of John Wheelwright and Sherry Mangan*. Chapel Hill: University of North Carolina Press.

9

KIERAN QUINLAN

Tracking the Fugitive Poets

The Fugitive Poets – John Crowe Ransom, Donald Davidson, Allen Tate, and Robert Penn Warren – are part of the modern literary movement of the twentieth century that includes T. S. Eliot, Ezra Pound, Robert Frost, William Carlos Williams, and a host of other writers, and yet, as Southerners originally living in the provincial Tennessee capital of Nashville, slightly apart from that mainstream generally associated with the more cosmopolitan modernisms of London, Paris, and New York. Moreover, they all went on to become Agrarians in the 1930s – hardly the most urbane of choices – and shaped what until recently was the received narrative of the Southern Literary Renascence. However, this regional perception is a little misleading for a group some of whose members lived for extended periods in New York, Paris, and Rome, two of whom (Ransom and Warren) were Rhodes Scholars, and all of whom directly influenced many of the leading American poets of the mid-century and later. Collectively, the Fugitive poets propagated the most effective literary critical movement of the century and so shaped the teaching of college English for several decades. Again, Ransom's second book, *Grace After Meat*, was published in 1924 by Leonard and Virginia Woolf at the Hogarth Press in London on the recommendation of Robert Graves and Eliot; Tate became a close friend of the latter, and the English novelist and editor Ford Madox Ford was to spend a good deal of time among them in Tennessee in the 1930s. In other words, from the very beginning, the Fugitives had diverse national and international connections that partly belied their provincial roots. And even at the local level, there were creative tensions among them from the start, Ransom being the professor, Tate and Warren his imitative but also gifted and rebellious students. Finally, while they significantly altered their social and artistic views as they negotiated the contingencies of the passing decades, their legacies, both collective and individual, remain a matter of lively contention in the twenty-first century.

The original group began in 1915 with members of Vanderbilt University's English Department and other Nashville luminaries gathering informally to discuss issues in contemporary philosophy and literature at a time when great change was in the air. It got its second wind – partly inspired by H. L. Mencken's superbly hyperbolic attack on the South in 1917 as being "almost as sterile, artistically, intellectually, culturally, as the Sahara Desert" – following World War I when the group was expanded to include the precocious Tate and Warren and shifted its interests to sharing and critiquing their own poems, in many ways the prototype of the now-familiar writers' workshop (Mencken 2010, 229). Then, in 1922, they began publishing *The Fugitive*, a literary journal aimed at "flee[ing] from nothing faster than from the high-caste Brahmins of the Old South," which was to have a lifespan of just three years (Ransom 1922, 1). What they had in mind was an alternative to the prevailing celebrations of the Southern Lost Cause written in what Tate later referred to as "Confederate prose" (Tate 1968, 579). Southern gentility would be displaced by Southern realism, or at least by an ironic stance all the more powerful because veiled in a gentlemanliness of diction. But 1922 was also the year of *Ulysses* and *The Waste Land*, the twin pillars of modernism in English, and the Fugitives were divided on that movement, Ransom skeptical about it while the younger Tate and Warren were attracted to its purposely discordant melodies. In the background, meanwhile, lay a disturbing awareness of the Harlem Renaissance that was challenging received notions of blackness as it sought, like the white Southerners, to find a place in the sun of cultural respect long denied to its particular group.

Most of Ransom's best poems appeared in *The Fugitive*; most of the poems for which Tate and Warren are remembered, as we shall see here, came afterward. Ransom's are short, intricate, playful, and characterized by occasionally quaint usage, a kind of jolt for the reader that immediately draws attention to what the poet called the "texture" of the work. A striking number of them are about death, which Ransom approaches from a variety of angles but always with a seriousness noticeably undercut by humor and irony. In "Bells for John Whiteside's Daughter," for example, while the little girl's "brown study" is our first encounter with her, there is a playfulness in the descriptions of her directing the geese homeward as the "Lady with rod that made them rise / From their noon apple-dreams and scuttle / Goose-fashion under the skies!" (Ransom 1978, 7). Yet, according to Ransom, the poem is not a memorial for a child's actual death but a philosophical exploration of "the disintegration or nullification" of values that death itself inevitably presents (Ransom 1985, 169).

In "Captain Carpenter," Ransom deals with the same topic even more humorously (the scene is reminiscent of the comical dismemberment of the Black Knight in *Monty Python and the Holy Grail*), so that the protagonist has all his limbs cut off in a series of foolhardy, quixotic encounters with male and female adversaries:

> And Captain Carpenter parted with his ears
> To a black devil that used him in this wise
> O Jesus ere his threescore and ten years
> Another had plucked out his sweet blue eyes.
>
> (Ransom 1978, 44–5)

"Necrological," which gave the Fugitives their first sense of their potential as poets, has a friar visit a battlefield to meditate on the bodies of those slain, "some gory and fabulous / Whom the sword had pierced and then the grey wolf eaten." He reasons initially that "heroes' flesh was thus." But the more he sees, the more shaken the friar becomes until "he sat upon a hill and bowed his head / As under a riddle," and feels his own cosmic vulnerability with no divine shield to protect him, a recurrent trope with Ransom (Ransom 1978, 42–3). It is in his most playful poem, "Janet Waking," about the demise of a young girl's "dainty-feathered" hen that Ransom is most rueful; in the end, Janet "would not be instructed in how deep / Was the forgetful kingdom of death" (Ransom 1978, 12).

By the time that Tate began to make his name, Ransom had almost ceased writing poetry apparently because he felt he had little more to say in the medium. From the outset, Tate was drawn to Eliot's modernism. When a classically trained Ransom famously criticized *The Waste Land* in 1923 in the *New York Literary Post Evening Review* as "the apotheosis of modernity" that "seems to bring to a head all the specific modern errors, and to cry for critic's ink of a volume quite disproportionate to its merits as a poem," Tate publicly attacked his mentor in defense of the "distracting complexity" of the new age (Ransom 2001, 167). In many ways, the poem for which Tate is best known – "Ode to the Confederate Dead" – is a 1928 version of Eliot's masterpiece set in a Southern context. Far from being a celebration of those who fought for the Lost Cause – such as was Henry Timrod's popular "Ode" of 1866 – it is an account of a present day Southerner: one who fails to find meaning in the Confederates' sacrifice because he is plagued by the same self-absorbed modernity and spiritual infertility blighting the lives of Eliot's protagonists. In the "desolation" of the Confederate graveyard, any expectation of finding inspiration in the "inexhaustible bodies" buried there is quickly checked:

> The brute curiosity of an angel's stare
> Turns you, like them, to stone,
> Transforms the heaving air
> Till plunged to a heavier world below

> You shift your sea-space blindly
> Heaving, turning like the blind crab.
> (Tate 2007, 20)

This crab image is also reminiscent of Eliot's "The Love Song of J. Alfred Prufrock" with its dysfunctional protagonist unable to cope with ordinary reality. Tate's subsequent essay on his ode, "Narcissus as Narcissus," is a brilliant combination of self-deprecation, philosophical explanation, and technical analysis that also, of course, suggests that Tate too suffers from being a modern man with a "locked-in ego" (Tate 1968, 598).

By the late 1920s, however, the South-fleeing Fugitives had moved on to their next phase, or rather retreated to their original regional fortress. After all, they were white men with minds like Faulkner's Quentin Compson's that was full of "back-looking ghosts" and with a keen awareness of what they – and mainline historians at Columbia and Chicago – perceived as the political abuses of the Reconstruction era (Faulkner 1990, 7). Tate was writing exploratory biographies of Stonewall Jackson and Jefferson Davis as he puzzled over the South's defeat. If Mencken's first attack on the South had caused the Fugitives imaginatively to flee its nostrums, his newspaper reporting of the shenanigans of the Monkey Trial in Dayton, Tennessee, in 1925 – a comedy of ignorant fundamentalists and superstitious witch-hunting that many outsiders felt was all too reflective of this benighted region – led them to become defensive of the South and hence to champion it without regard to the truth or otherwise of Darwin's theory. They were also acting in opposition to the New South movement, dedicated to economic growth and now called into question by the pending Great Depression. They likely felt attacked too by the writers of the Harlem Renaissance, who looked none-too-sympathetically to their region and its notorious lynchings, which had dramatically increased since the end of World War I.

In their 1930 manifesto, *I'll Take My Stand: The South and the Agrarian Tradition* (the first part of the title a line from the southern anthem "Dixie," although Tate and Warren had wanted a title that would reflect its anti-Communist stance), they set "a Southern way of life against what may be called the American or prevailing way," representing the struggle succinctly as "Agrarian *versus* Industrial" (Twelve Southerners 2005, xli). While they claimed to have no truck with the Old Confederacy, Ransom's essay had the defiant title of "Reconstructed but Unregenerate." The Agrarians vigorously attacked industrialism as leading to "overproduction, unemployment, and a growing inequality in the distribution of wealth" and even went so far as to proclaim that "the true Sovietists or Communists ... are the Industrialists themselves" (xlv). Factory labor was a drudge that destroyed the soul of the laborer. More importantly, the industrialization of society led to an illusion of human capability and the loss of a sense of a Divine, thunderous, and mysterious ruler. They also railed against the modern advertising and consumer culture that came in industrialism's wake. Against all this, "the culture of the soil is the best and most sensitive of vocations, and ... should have the economic preference and enlist the maximum number of workers" (li).

Racial matters intruded, however, in this presentation of an idealized rural South. Ransom misstepped when he claimed in an aside that "slavery was a feature monstrous enough in theory, but, more often than not, humane in practice" (14); Warren, then pursuing his Rhodes at Oxford, reluctantly submitted an essay on the subject in which he argued for justice for blacks but followed Booker T. Washington's acceptance of a separate but equal segregationist policy. Overall, as Michael Kreyling observes, "the more the Agrarians struggled to deny that race was any part of southern identity, the more race ensnared them" (Kreyling 2005, 62). Meanwhile, Tate's recommendation of a feudal religion as necessary for the sustenance of Southern traditions was hardly likely to win over either die-hard fundamentalists or sober members of the mainline Protestant denominations already virulently hostile to Catholicism in any form. Tate's subsequent involvement in 1936 with the European Distributist movement, inspired by papal encyclicals, which was making similar efforts under the aegis of such writers as Hilaire Belloc and G. K. Chesterton in England, and through which Eliot was also drawing attention to the threat of ecological disasters caused by the rapid expansion of an industrial economy, probably led to even deeper suspicions (Agar and Tate 1936; Conkin 2001).

In its day, the Agrarian project was an impractical fantasy for the New South, threatening to the so-called New Negro (many African Americans had recently fled the region in the Great Migration to the industrialized North for work and acceptance), and offensive to the political and social aspirations of the "New Woman." But it was commented on widely then and later, and even long after the originators had themselves abandoned the cause. When Louis D. Rubin wrote an introduction for a new edition of *I'll Take My Stand* in 1961, he noted its dated racial rhetoric but commended its defense of a humanistic ideal; when Rubin added an even newer introduction in 1977, he explained that he had chosen not to deal with the racial issue earlier because most of the Agrarians had changed their views by then and should not be judged by the standards of a later period; he also stressed their relevance to the growing interest in ecological matters (Rubin 1977, xi-xxii, xxiii-xxxv). By 2005, Susan Donaldson, in the most recent introduction to the book, treats the Agrarians more critically as the defenders of an eroding male white hegemony that was ultimately defeated by the triumvirate of forces it had opposed, disparaged, or ignored (Donaldson

2005, ix-xl). Nevertheless, Southern Agrarianism remains a subject of interest, reinforced by a new awareness of its more practical articulations of the 1930s, Mark Jancovich offering a rather surprising quotation from Tate to prove the point: "The end in view is the destruction of the middle class capitalist hegemony" (Jancovich 1993, 26).

Following their Agrarian interlude, Tate and Warren returned to poetry and literary criticism. In fact, although Warren's earliest poems had appeared in the later issues of *The Fugitive*, it was not until the 1930s that he emerged as a poet in his own right with *Eleven Poems on the Same Theme* (1935). Here he shows the influence of Ransom, Eliot, and Tate and also his freedom from them. Warren's essential concern is with an original sin – though not in a strictly religious sense – that has rendered all our enterprises subject to derailment (which is also the theme of his enormously successful novel of 1947, *All the King's Men*). In his poem titled "Original Sin: A Short Story," the persistent intimacy of this condition is vividly portrayed:

> You have moved often and rarely left an address,
> And hear of the deaths of friends with a sly pleasure,
> A sense of cleansing and hope, which blooms from distress;
> But it has not died, it comes, its hand childish, unsure,
> Clutching the bribe of chocolate or a toy you used to treasure.
> (Warren 2001, 32)

"The Ballad of Billie Potts," the first of Warren's long narrative poems can be seen as an illustration of his thesis: A nineteenth-century innkeeper father who has initiated his son into his routine of killing passing strangers on the Kentucky trail ends up mistakenly murdering the young man years later when he reappears as an unidentified traveler. In what will become a typical strategy of his, Warren interrupts energetic, colloquial exposition with reflective commentary, sometimes masterfully, sometimes, as Ransom noted, to jarring effect (41–51). In the years that followed, Warren would go back and forth between fiction and poetry, easily becoming the most prolific of the Fugitives.

In 1937, John Crowe Ransom left Vanderbilt to take up a position at Kenyon College in Ohio where he would shortly afterward found the *Kenyon Review*, one of the three or four most significant literary periodicals in America that would publish many of the major poets, fiction writers, and literary critics of the next several decades. A couple of years earlier, Warren and a fellow Rhodes Scholar who had also been at Vanderbilt, Cleanth Brooks, founded the *Southern Review* at Louisiana State University, an equally influential journal. Ransom's growing influence is also shown in the fact that when he departed Vanderbilt, three of his most promising students followed him: Robert Lowell, Randall Jarrell, and Peter Taylor. It was in the same year also that Ransom published "Criticism, Inc.," one of the founding documents of the literary movement that was to receive its popular name from the author's 1941 *The New Criticism* (Ransom 1941).

The term New Criticism, sometimes seen as the ongoing pursuit of the political goals of agrarianism under another name, gave a formal American identity to a critical approach that had been gathering momentum since its early advocacy in England by T. S. Eliot and I. A. Richards in the 1920s, and its usage by the Fugitives themselves in their practical criticism of one another's poems. Back in his Fugitive days, Ransom had already defined irony, a key New Critical term, as "the rarest of the states of mind, because … the whole mind has been involved in arriving at it, both creation and criticism" (Ransom 1967, 64). Now, with its focus on the literary text as a self-contained organic unit held together by irony and paradox, New Criticism provided a useful way of approaching literature at a time when how to teach the subject at university level was still uncertain and when professors in the humanities felt threatened by the growing importance of the hard and soft sciences with their emphasis on repeatable techniques and measurable results. In fighting for academic acceptance, the New Criticism's first adversary was the historical approach then prevalent in English departments. Thus, Ransom declares in his essay that "Criticism must become more scientific, or precise and systematic" in the way that disciplines such as psychology and economics may be regarded, that is as inexact but self-justifying enterprises (Ransom 1968, 239). He does not deny the value of historical scholarship as preparatory to understanding older authors, such as Chaucer, whose mindset is somewhat alien to ours, but he does deny its sufficiency since the student needs tools with which to analyze the text. Ransom wants "technical studies of poetry" that treat "its metric; its inversions, solecisms, lapses from the prose norm of language, and from close prose logic; its tropes; its fictions, or inventions, by which it secures 'aesthetic distance' and removes itself from history." The proper criticism of a poem should ask "what it is trying to represent that cannot be represented by prose." For Ransom, the poem is "nothing short of a desperate ontological or metaphysical manoeuvre" that the critic must analyze (347). Thus we have "the prose core to which he can violently reduce the total object, and the differentia, residue, or tissue, which keeps the object poetical or entire." The "good critic" focuses on this "residuary quality" (349).

Although the Fugitive-New Critics frequently differ among themselves in nuance and terminology, Tate's 1940 essay "Miss Emily and the Bibliographers" is also a complaint that the historians fail to make aesthetic judgments about the texts they so lovingly seek to preserve: what is needed is "a relevant judgment" of a text based on its "form, coherence of image and metaphor, control of tone and of rhythm, the union of these features" (Tate 1968, 149). He objects to those who no longer believe "that the arts give us a sort of cognition at least equally valid with that of scientific method" (150). Unless we develop the capacity and the tools to make literary judgments (and basically judgments about artistic form), we are left with the ridiculous notion that "History" makes the decisions. For Tate, on the contrary, and following Eliot, "the literature of the past lives in the literature of the present and nowhere else ... it is all present literature" (153–4).

In subsequent years, critics would expand and refine Ransom's (and Tate's) principles, and they would be disseminated most of all by Warren and Brooks in *Understanding Poetry*, first published in 1938, a widely used textbook for at least three decades. More bells and whistles were added to the original effort to focus on the text itself with the creation of a unique terminology – injunctions to avoid fallacies of authorial intention, reader responsiveness, paraphrase as a substitute for the original poetic text, and to detect communication heresies and fallacies that substituted propaganda for art. In this way, a kind of clerisy was formed in the teaching of literature throughout the United States, although the New Critics themselves rarely conformed to New Critical orthodoxy. In its purest form, New Criticism – which always favored poetry over fiction and the Metaphysicals and Moderns over the Romantics and the Victorians – may have aimed at the one true interpretation of a text; in reality, it led to a plethora of often forced interpretations with no end in sight. Still, it is widely acknowledged that their methods helped generations of students to acquire an appreciation of the literary arts, not least those first-generation college students who had entered the academy through the post–World War II GI Bill.

The New Criticism would reign almost supreme until the mid-1960s when history, linguistics, psychology, feminism, and politics reasserted their rightful and needed place in the interpretation of literature. And, just as the New Critics had overthrown the previous generation of plodding historicists, Deconstructionists (in a way propounding a form of New Criticism in their hyper-intense focus on the text to disassemble its parts), New Historicists, Feminist and Psychoanalytic critics among many others would replace them in turn even as core New Critical practices remained stubbornly – and probably usefully – in place. Often accused of being elitist because of their labyrinthine terminology, the New Critics had generally written in a more accessible prose than that which followed, and, at the same time, they had prepared the way for what came afterward; Ransom, for example, was described in the 1990s as a "proto-deconstructionist" (Jancovich 1993, 92).

Opponents of the New Criticism also liked to point out that it was very convenient for the children of the Old South to focus exclusively on the text and thus ignore the region's lamentable racial history. Moreover, the narrative of the Southern Literary Renascence that the Fugitive-Agrarians and their followers established tended to be exclusionary; the literary break-through had come in the early twentieth century when male writers – and, substantially, the Fugitives themselves – began to take a more critical view of their inheritance, rather than in the work of George Washington Cable, Kate Chopin, and other writers a generation earlier. Of course, it was this very exclusion, both at the social and literary levels, that led, unintentionally, to flowerings elsewhere. As Thadious Davis remarks, "It was precisely because of the South that Harlem could become the center of black America and of a major literary and cultural movement, the New Negro Renaissance" (Davis 1985, 291).

By the 1950s, Tate and Warren had altered their views on racial matters both in their poetry and their prose, distancing themselves from Donald Davidson, who maintained an ever stronger segregationist stance in the face of the growing Civil Rights movement. Ransom criticized both the white South's intransigence against change and the North's insistence on it. Coming out, and perhaps in an effort to redeem his earlier racial positions (he had refused to meet Langston Hughes in Nashville in the 1920s), Tate wrote about a childhood visit with an elderly African American member of his own ancestral family. In "The Swimmers," he depicts the quintes-sential scene of a racist South, the lynching of a black man. In the poem, set in Kentucky in 1911 and composed in terza rima, Tate and four child-hood friends discover the victim, his neck still in a noose, at their swimming hole. Later, finding the body that was dragged into the nearby town, Tate reflects:

> Alone in the public clearing
> This private thing was owned by all the town,
> Though never claimed by us within my hearing.
> (Tate 2007, 135)

The complicity of the "respectable" white community is acknowledged in the revelation of their hypocrisy. Tate explained later that the lynching was not the result of a presumed rape but rather because a black tenant farmer had shot his white landlord, who had been cheating him.

One might see Warren's long narrative poem on a crime committed by one of Thomas Jefferson's nephews in Kentucky as a similar mark of repen-tance, although Warren had already written extensively on African American issues in *Who Speaks for the Negro?* (1965) and elsewhere. In *Brother to*

Dragons, Jefferson's innocence about the evil side of our nature is presented, his earlier hope:

> Of a time to come
> If we might take man's hand, strike shackle, lead him forth
> From his own monstrous nightmare – then his natural innocence
> Would dance like sunlight over the delighted landscape.

(Warren 1979, 29)

His nephew's actions in horrifically killing a young slave for merely breaking a jug, however, gives the lie to this hope, ending with a wiser acceptance of our human lot in a "confirmation of late light" (132). In its dialogue between a past Jefferson and a present "RPW" – a persona not too distinct from the author – the poem is perhaps also predictive of the current controversies about Jefferson's miscegenated legacy.

In their separate ways, the three main Fugitive poets ended up in places different from where they had started out: Tate as a religionist in the tradition of Eliot; Warren a wise meditator on a tangled Southern past; Ransom converted to secular ideas he had once vehemently opposed. But perhaps the most important achievement of the Fugitives has been their direct influence on the poets and writers who immediately came after them – Lowell, Jarrell, Taylor, James Dickey, E. L. Doctorow – and on the poets and critics who became resident fellows at the Kenyon School of Letters: Delmore Schwartz, Irving Howe, and many others. These followers too often showed opposition as well as influence, as in 1960 when Tate's mentee Lowell would write "For the Union Dead," a celebration of a black Massachusetts regiment that fought in the Civil War and a poem inspired by and responsive to "Ode to the Confederate Dead." The writers who appeared in the pages of the *Kenyon Review* and the *Southern Review* – John Berryman, Katherine Anne Porter, Eudora Welty, and Flannery O'Connor among them – also gave witness to the Fugitive-Agrarian-New Critical influence, though Beat poet Robert Duncan would publicly criticize Ransom as editor for first accepting then rejecting his homosexual poems in 1944, a *cause célèbre* in American gay literary history (Janssen 1990, 139–40). An important and often unnoticed contribution of the Fugitives is that they inspired a writerly culture in and beyond their region at the many campuses at which they taught.

The legacy, or perhaps legacies, of the Fugitives, then, remains contentious in the way that those of Jefferson, Twain, Eliot, and Faulkner do: Their heritage represents the "original sin" of political stances that are no longer acceptable; nevertheless, the Fugitives also leave behind creative explorations that still inspire the imaginations of their readers. Defenders of such writers would like to see the politics left out and only the art left in, although today that is no longer an option. But the value of saying "that which could not be said otherwise" remains. Ransom's poems on death – commended of late by Seamus Heaney and Ted Hughes – will continue to touch readers who know little about the author; Tate's poetry is difficult by most judgments and is less frequently anthologized; Warren's fiction – especially *All the King's Men* – and his narrative poems will also attract dedicated readers. The ideology of New Criticism and some of its mechanics have passed into history, but its practical effects endure. Even the Agrarian inheritance will be remembered, perhaps ahistorically, by environmentalists and others, if only because, as critic Scott Romine has noted, "their localized culture war predicted the broader forms that cultural warfare would assume over the course of their century and into the next" (Romine 2008, 4).

WORKS CITED

Agar, Herbert, and Allen Tate, eds. 1936. *Who Owns America? A New Declaration of Independence*. Boston: Houghton Mifflin.

Conkin, Paul. 2001. *The Southern Agrarians*. Nashville, TN: Vanderbilt University Press.

Davis, Thadious M. 1985. "Southern Standard-Bearers in the New Negro Renaissance." In *The History of Southern Literature*. Eds. Louis D. Rubin, Jr., Blyden Jackson, Rayburn S. Moore, Lewis P. Simpson, and Thomas Daniel Young. 291–313. Baton Rouge: Louisiana State University Press.

Donaldson, Susan. 2005. Introduction to *I'll Take My Stand: The South and the Agrarian Tradition*. Baton Rouge: Louisiana State University Press.

Faulkner, William. 1990. *Absalom, Absalom!* New York: Vintage.

Jancovich, Mark. 1993. *The Cultural Politics of the New Criticism*. New York: Cambridge University Press.

Janssen, Marian. 1990. *The Kenyon Review 1939–1970: A Critical History*. Baton Rouge: Louisiana State University Press.

Kreyling, Michael. 2005. "Teaching Southern Lit in Black and White." *Southern Cultures* 11.4: 47–75.

Mencken, H. L. 2010. *Prejudices: First, Second, and Third Series*. New York: Library of America.

Ransom, John Crowe. 1922. "Foreword." *The Fugitive* I:1.
　1941. *The New Criticism*. New York: New Directions.
　1985. *Selected Letters*. Baton Rouge: Louisiana State University Press.
　1978. *Selected Poems*. New York: Ecco Press.
　1925. "Thoughts on the Poetic Discontent." *The Fugitive* IV: 63–4.
　2001. "Waste Lands." In T. S. Eliot, *The Waste Land*. Ed. Michael North. New York: W. W. Norton. 167–70.
　1968. *The World's Body*. Baton Rouge: Louisiana State University Press.

Romine, Scott. 2008. *The Real South: Southern Narrative in the Age of Cultural Reproduction*. Baton Rouge: Louisiana State University Press.

Rubin, Louis D. 1977. Introduction to *I'll Take My Stand: The South and the Agrarian Tradition*. Baton Rouge: Louisiana State University Press. xi–xxii, xxiii–xxxv.

Tate, Allen. 2007. *Collected Poems 1919–1976*. New York: Farrar, Straus, and Giroux.

1968. *Essays of Four Decades*. Chicago: Swallow Press.

Twelve Southerners. *I'll Take My Stand: The South and the Agrarian Tradition*. 2005. Baton Rouge: Louisiana State University Press.

Warren, Robert Penn. 1979. *Brother to Dragons: A Tale in Verse and Voices*. Baton Rouge: Louisiana State University Press.

2001. *Selected Poems of Robert Penn Warren*. Baton Rouge: Louisiana State University Press.

10

STEPHEN BURT

Mid-Century Modernism

This chapter introduces, by examining one moment in their writing lives, a set of poets who found recognition, by about 1950, at national magazines, trade presses, and universities and who remain admired, studied, and imitated (if indirectly) today. These poets are sometimes called mid-century modernists, or "the middle generation," because they came after the High Moderns – for them, T. S. Eliot, Ezra Pound, Wallace Stevens, Marianne Moore, Hart Crane, W. C. Williams – they had grown up reading; they became the first generation for whom, as F. O. Matthiessen put it, "much of 'the new poetry' is no longer new" (Matthiessen 1950, xxi). They stand out not least for how much their poems learn to do, how subtle their language can be, without challenging the definitions of "poetry" that they received and that they passed down in turn. If modernists sought to make it new, these poets believed they had something to preserve; literary history has viewed them (sometimes quite misleadingly) as "conservative." Yet inseparable from their efforts at conservation, their attempts to renew older modes and forms (from seventeenth-century stanza shapes to Romantic notions of voice), these poets put forward a skepticism, or a pessimism, about the postwar world; about when (if ever) to trust representation, and about when, and whether – outside the redoubt of poetry – social life could be a source of value at all.

The older members of this set of poets could have been called, forty years ago, the generation of Robert Lowell; they might be called, today, the Elizabeth Bishop circle. Lowell wrote poems about Bishop, poems adapted from her prose, and poems that imitated her poems. Randall Jarrell lived with Lowell at Kenyon College in 1937–9 (both young men had moved there to study with John Crowe Ransom), introduced Bishop to Lowell in 1947, wrote the first major critical essays on both, and learned from Bishop in his own late poems. "Jarrell emerged as the ideal contemporary reader of Bishop and Lowell," writes Thomas Travisano, although no one emerged as the ideal reader for Jarrell (Travisano 2003, 59). All three poets became "established," winning such prizes as the Pulitzer and the National Book Award, and serving at the Library of Congress in the position then called Consultant in Poetry, now Poet Laureate. When Jarrell died, Lowell commemorated him in verse; when Lowell died, Bishop did as much for him. Their coevals during the 1940s and 1950s included John Berryman, Theodore Roethke, Delmore Schwartz, Karl Shapiro, and May Swenson. The African-American writers Melvin Tolson, Robert Hayden, and Gwendolyn Brooks also adapted and consolidated modernism after midcentury; their discoveries, like Berryman's and the later Lowell's, appear elsewhere in this book.

These poets provided immediate models – and, sometimes, classroom instruction – for the "mainstream" poets who began publishing after the Second World War, among them Richard Wilbur, Howard Nemerov, Katherine Hoskins, James Merrill, Louis Simpson, and Anthony Hecht; many (like Jarrell and Shapiro) had served in that war. Critics quickly singled out that younger generation for its reliance on models of order and civility, for its deft use of pre-modern forms, and for its symbiosis with institutions; Jarrell joked that each one could receive "a Guggenheim fellowship, a *Kenyon Review* fellowship, and the Prix de Rome" (Jarrell, *Third* 1969, 299). *The Beautiful Changes* (1947) and *Ceremony* (1950) made Wilbur the most imitated, the most celebrated, the most ostensibly representative. Jarrell complained in "Fifty Years of American Poetry" (1962) that many poets of the 1950s had "so to speak, come out of Wilbur's overcoat," with "academic, tea-party, creative-writing-class" verse that "tamely satisfied the rules or standards of technique." Wilbur himself, on the other hand, made "true works of art," "little, differentiated, complete-in-themselves universes" showing "the bright underside of every dark thing" (Jarrell, *Third* 1969, 331–2).

Much of Wilbur's cohort appeared in *New Poets of England and America* (1957), edited by Donald Hall, Robert Pack, and Louis Simpson, with a preface by Robert Frost. Along with most of those named earlier, the volume's fifty-three poets included John Hollander, William Meredith, W. S. Merwin, Adrienne Rich and James Wright, all of whom won the Yale Younger Poets prize when it was judged by W. H. Auden; the onetime leader of younger British poets had settled in New York City and become "his adopted nation's chief arbiter of poetic fashion and form" (Wasley 2011, xiv). Hecht wrote, and Jarrell tried to write, a whole book about him.

Many of these poets would alter their styles radically during the 1960s. Some who did not would do their best work much later. Anthony Hecht helped to liberate the Flossenburg concentration camp; the Holocaust and the problem of evil reverberate through his highly wrought verse. Drawing on Jewish lore, and on the ideas of his colleagues at Yale, Hollander would explore theories of language, aesthetics, and form in intricately playful book-length works such as *Powers of Thirteen* (1983). Merrill would bloom, with *Water Street* (1962), into a great poet of social comedy, of Proustian autobiographical reflection, and of same-sex love, while exercising cosmic ambitions in his own three-book poem *The Changing Light at Sandover* (1976–82).

All these poets responded, directly and indirectly, to the end of the Great Depression and to the war, when Jarrell instructed navigators for bombers, and Lowell, "a fire-breathing Catholic C. O.," was jailed for refusing to serve. All took account, in the tones and the forms of their poems, of at least some large-scale changes in American culture after the war – intellectual turns from Marx toward Freud, the Cold War and the Red Scare, the influx of U.S. tourists and U.S. money into Western and Central Europe, the expansion of higher education, the civil rights movement, and the growth of youth culture.

And yet to read their most original poems – those of the 1940s, and those from long afterward – is to see how much these poets worked to stand apart, to imagine some distance from public history; they could not help being "post-modernist" (a term first applied by Ransom to Jarrell), but they worked to be postwar (Longenbach 1997, 77). They wrote poems imbued with self-doubt, whose careful discoveries, rueful ironies, and dialogues with the past reacted to recent violence and to their own distrust of national mission, historical progress, religious salvation, or radical artistic novelty. They wrote Atlantic poems, in which Americans (and American language) reconsider Europe (and European artistic forms); they wrote ekphrastic poems, looking at architecture or at art. They wrote about apparently powerless people – enlisted soldiers and airmen, students, children. And they wrote poems about making, and rebuilding, carefully, for a postwar world: in an ambience of self-control and reconstruction, they were also poets of doubt.

John Ciardi's *Mid-Century American Poets* (1950) was "the first anthology to propound a concise aesthetic for postwar poetry" (Brunner 2000, 43). Its seventeen poets, all born in the 1910s or 1920s, included Lowell, Jarrell, Bishop, Shapiro, Schwartz, Wilbur, and Muriel Rukeyser, poets then "impossible to ignore" (Brunner 2000, 51). Ciardi's further choices included himself, John Holmes (now remembered as Anne Sexton's teacher), E. L. Mayo, and the self-described "New Conservative" polemicist Peter Viereck (Filreis 2008, 44–5, 274–83). Because he asked poets to pick their own poems, his anthology (as Brunner emphasizes) shows us how these writers saw themselves.

Ciardi's own view emphasized a chastened, democratic approachability. He described his choices as latecomers, able to learn from high modernists – and able to eschew the (often left-wing) excesses of both the 1910s and the 1930s: "The poets writing today are in a better position to write good poetry, in part because some of their ancestors showed them the perils of loud poetry" (Ciardi 1950 [hereafter *MCP*], xi). Today's poems could not "exist to confirm moral, political, or religious judgments" (*MCP*, xxii). And yet they were no hermetic aesthetes: "These poets *want* to be understood" (*MCP*, xxix). Modernism and modernity together gave resources – toolboxes, palettes, libraries – with which to rebuild, although the verbal structures that resulted might look fire-damaged, incomplete, stormy, or rickety indeed. "If Donne could use a compass," wrote Mayo, "so can we use ... a pressure-gauge or an instrument board; thanks in some measure to the poets of the thirties, there are no longer any taboos on what we may use as raw material for our metaphors" (*MCP*, 143).

Mayo's choice of images – drawn from wartime aviation – is no accident. If the prose in Ciardi's volume addresses the present, the poems overwhelmingly look back to, and come out of, the Second World War. Jarrell led off his selection with a bleaker than bleak poem entitled "The State." In its harsh anapests, all human beings become helpless victims, destroyed by force and ideology: "When they killed my mother it made me nervous, / I thought to myself, it was *right*" (*MCP*, 185). When they take the man's "cat for the Army Corps / Of Conservation and Supply," however, "there's nothing. I'm dead and I want to die" (*MCP*, 185). Jarrell followed "The State" with one of the first American poems about the mass murder of Jews in Europe, "A Camp in the Prussian Forest." Jarrell would write for the rest of his career about helpless victims, in war zones and out of them, people who had their individuality, their ability to represent themselves *as* selves, taken away, victims of what Hannah Arendt (a close friend of Jarrell's) would teach her peers to call totalitarianism; his poems could try to give them back that selfhood or give up on it, as in "The Death of the Ball Turret Gunner," a five-line anthology favorite, with its acrid finale: "When I died they washed me out of the turret with a hose." (*MCP*, 198)

When Jarrell's lines could slow down and admit more acoustic variety – when they became more like conversation, less like epitaphs – they would admit exactly the vulnerable individuality, the childish curiosity, the play, that impersonal systems were out to destroy. The arrangements in Jarrell's poems – of lines, of images, of speakers – seem most optimistic at their most tentative, because the personhood of the people in them is new, or fragile, or hard to preserve. "A Game at Salzburg" recalls Jarrell's teaching at the Salzburg Seminar in American Civilization in 1948 (Pritchard 1990, 171).

Because its speech rhythms take time to establish themselves, the lines must be quoted at length:

> A little ragged girl, our ball-boy;
> A partner, ex-Afrika Korps –
> In khaki shorts, P. W. illegible.
> (He said: "To have been a prisoner of war
> In Colorado is a *privilege*.")
> The evergreens, concessions, carrousels,
> And D. P. camp of Franz Joseph Park;
> A grey-green river, evergreen-dark hills.
> Last, a long way off in the sky,
> Snow-mountains.
>
> Over this clouds come, a darkness falls,
> Rain falls.
> On the veranda Romana,
> A girl of three
> Sits licking sherbet from a wooden spoon;
> I am already through.
> She says to me, softly: *Hier bin i'*.
> I answer: *Da bist du*.
>
> (MCP, 191)

"A Game" may look now like the poems of high-culture sightseeing, of "self-conscious tourists, with a mission," that Wilbur and his peers would write by the valise-ful (von Hallberg 1985, 72). Bishop, too, would respond to the vogue for travel poems: "Should we have stayed at home and thought of here?" she wrote in "Questions of Travel" (Bishop 1983, 93). But "A Game" is in fact an immediately postwar poem, a poem of international recovery, with very little "tourism." Rather than seeing the sights, the poet plays tennis and learns a child's German (as in Jarrell's later poem "Deutsch Durch Freud"), displaying less skill than the former P. W. does in English. Seeing how much reconstruction work remains to be done ("displaced persons" live in a public park), the quietly bilingual rhymes (Korps-war, through-*du*) also acknowledge prior literary moments of consolidation, of international force majeure kept at bay: its green-on-green, its layers, its girl interlocutor, point gently to William Wordsworth's "Lines Composed a Few Miles above Tintern Abbey."

Ciardi reprinted Jarrell's review of Lowell's *Lord Weary's Castle* (1947) in lieu of new prose from Lowell himself. Lowell's early poetry, Jarrell explained, reflects his heterodox faith: "In his poems the Son is pure liberation from the incestuous, complacent, inveterate evil of established society, of which the Law is a part" (MCP, 162). (He made Lowell sound, in retrospect, like

Allen Ginsberg.) Lowell's most elaborate, and most admired, early work, "The Quaker Graveyard in Nantucket," commemorates his cousin "Warren Winslow, dead at sea." Winslow's death alters nature: "Wherever winds are moving and their breath / Heaves at the roped-in bulwarks of this pier, / The terns and sea-gulls tremble at your death" (*MCP*, 171) (Winslow's destroyer sank – though the poem nowhere says so – because of its officers' own navigational error [Fender 1973]). The elegy imitates John Milton's "Lycidas" in cadence, in cosmic ambition, in its overtone of self-announcement. It is also a war poem: "The guns of the steeled fleet / Recoil and then repeat / The hoarse salute." Lowell, Jarrell remarked, "seems to be condemned both to read history and to repeat it" (*MCP*, 162–3). The violence of Lowell's language might shock, then as now: "Atlantic, you are fouled with the blue sailors, / Sea-monsters, upward angel, downward fish" (that last phrase quotes *Paradise Lost*) (*MCP*, 173). What seems to have stood out, what these wrenching rhythms emphasized, for Lowell's first readers was less the carnage (they could have found that in the headlines) than the heady, allusive plunge into a tradition. The poem offers its centuries of oceanic terror as a kind of alternative – the only plausible alternative – to a narrow focus on the here and now.

Lowell, whose bipolar disorder resulted in periodic breakdowns and hospital stays, soon came to see his periods of greatest confidence (religious, literary or erotic) as manifestations of a disease. "After the Surprising Conversions" recalls a Puritan who "dreamed / That he was called to trumpet Judgment Day / To Concord. In the latter part of May / He cut his throat" (*NPEA*, 184). "Thanksgiving's Over," from *The Mills of the Kavanaghs* (1951), portrays a German-American Catholic afflicted with suicidal religious mania. Her dreamt words are Lowell's early, forceful style writ frighteningly, parodically large:

> "I heard
> The birds inside me, and I knew the Third
> Person possessed me, for I was the bird
> Of Paradise, the parrot whose absurd
> Garblings are glory."
>
> (Lowell 2006, 47)

Soon after, Lowell wrote *in propria persona* about leaving the Church and leaving Rome on a train. "Beyond the Alps" (1952) became simultaneously an early example of the 1950s tourist poem and a farewell to his early mode: "Life changed to landscape. Much against my will / I left the City of God where it belongs" (Lowell 2006, 53).

Lord Weary's Castle, Jarrell declared, "was as much of an event as Auden's first book" (*MCP*, 158). Auden by then had become an authority figure for

many Americans besides Jarrell; the styles that Auden developed in America –
Horatian, learned, playful, ambassadorial – provided models for a postwar
mode. Wilbur's own poetry would compare (following Auden and Frost)
his poetic goals to "feigning" and flirting, asserting in "Ceremony," "What's
lightly hid is deepest understood" (*MCP*, 8). (Compare Auden's "'The Truest
Poetry Is the Most Feigning.'") The aspect of play, of taking serious truths
unseriously, even of camp, was something that Auden and Bishop bequeathed
to Merrill, whose later work paid homage to both poets by name. Merrill's
(1989) memorial poem to Bishop lauded her caution, her only apparently
impersonal style, which "refused to tip the scale of being human / By adding unearned weight"; the "W. H. Auden" whose spirit becomes a character
in *Sandover* warns (along with other characters) against technology-driven
overconfidence: "WE HERE TREMBLE ON A CRUST SO FRAGILE / IT
NEEDS GOD'S CONSTANT VIGIL TO KEEP US AFLOAT" (Merrill 2001,
666; Merrill 2006, 391). Not only Auden's verbal power but his versatility
made him a model; so did his cultured insistence, in his American phases, that
while religion might have to take itself seriously, poetry could be approached
as technique, as a game – it had no serious purpose save, perhaps, "to disin-
toxicate and disenchant" (Auden 1962, 27).

1950s poets, if they were playing a game, tried to show they had mas-
tered its tough rules. "Collections seemed incomplete without a sestina,"
quips Brunner, though *Mid-Century Poets* and *New Poets of England and
America* held just one apiece, respectively Bishop's "A Miracle for Breakfast"
and Hall's sestina about sestinas, "Sestina," whose end words include "dull"
and "sestina" (Brunner 2000, 161; *NPEA*, 96). Such forms could be seen
as signs of professionalization, badges for craftsmen in a new white-collar
trade, or ways to contain otherwise unmasterable experience. Bishop and
Hecht wrote multiple sestinas, some of them – "The Book of Yolek," "Sestina
(September rain falls on the house)" – among their strongest, saddest, best-
known poems.

The earliest model for these sestinas seems to have been Auden's sestina
beginning "'We have brought you,' they said, 'a map of the country,'" where
an unreliable map enables a sexual "consummation" (Auden 1991, 68).
Maps, ubiquitous in wartime, became representative figures for poems: representations of our world that could not be mistaken for it, involved with
but distinct from public history. Elizabeth Bishop finished "The Map" in
1935, but it made perfect sense as the leadoff poem in her first book, *North
and South* (1946):

> Land lies in water; it is shadowed green.
> Shadows, or are they shallows, at its edges
> showing the line of long sea-weeded ledges

where weeds hang to the simple blue from green.
Or does the land lean down to lift the sea from under,
drawing it unperturbed around itself?
(Bishop 1983, 3)

Names that cross boundaries, political designations that do not match physical ones, suggest, in the free verse that makes up the poem's middle stanza, "the printer here experiencing the same excitement / as when emotion too far exceeds its cause." The map – like the language in the poem, like Bishop's point of view – held off the violence that its manmade boundaries could suggest: "More delicate than the historians' are the map-makers' colors." Holmes's "Map of My Country" (1943) reads like an homage to Bishop: "A map of my native country is all edges, / The shore touching sea, the easy impartial rivers / Splitting the local boundary lines." Yet unlike Bishop's, Holmes's long lines could scarcely be clearer: His poem will provide a map for the individual, the part of the self not determined by public events: "On my own map of my own country / I shall show where there were never wars, / And plot the changed way I hear men speak in the west" (*MCP*, 215). Shapiro's "The Geographers" (1944), included in Matthiessen's *Oxford Book of American Verse* (1950), also toggled back and forth between the map as alterable thing in itself, and as a means of representation: Geographers promise "New numbered money, bright new postage stamps ... Yet seen from Jupiter things are of old; / Wars cannot change the shape of continents" (Matthiessen 1950, 1077).

Jarrell's maps end up less sententious, and sadder; the limits in their means of representation reveal not just limits to temporal power, but also the limits, the pathos, and the impotence of the private emotional life vouchsafed to everybody, which everybody must lose. That is one loss in the title poem from Jarrell's *Losses* (1948), anthologized both by Matthiessen and by Ciardi, in which deceased airmen (like those Jarrell trained) speak as "we." Their repeated words echo Auden's sestina; they say:

We died on the wrong page of the almanac,
Scattered on mountains fifty miles away ...
We died like ants or pets or foreigners.
(When we left high school nothing else had died
For us to figure we had died like.) ...

When we died they said, "Our casualties were low."
They said, "Here are the maps"; we burned the cities.
(Matthiessen 1950, 1097–8; Fussell 1989, 62)

The bomber crews died (like Winslow) due to a mistake in representation, because the map was not the territory; they graduated (or not) from high schools that could not give them the time, or the knowledge, to speak as themselves, as "I" rather than "we."

Bishop had her own reasons to scrutinize maps. She had lived, as a child, in Nova Scotia and Massachusetts, as an adult in Paris, New York, and Key West, before settling in Brazil from 1951 to 1967 with her partner, the Brazilian political figure Lota de Macedo Soares. Her sense of the distance between the map and the territory, between a representation and the things or the people it hoped to represent – or to control, or to preserve – extends almost through every poem she wrote, along with her "unusual focus on the physical world" (Pickard 2009, 7). The Canadian harbor in "Large Bad Picture" (1942) holds

> a fleet of small black ships,
> square-rigged, sails furled, motionless,
> their spars like burnt match-sticks.
>
> And high above them, over the tall cliffs'
> semi-translucent ranks,
> are scribbled hundreds of fine black birds,
> hanging in n's, in banks.
>
> (MCP, 269)

In quatrains whose rhythmic precariousness belies their syntactic balance, Bishop envisions the large scale of the harbor, with its impressions of disaster – what the painter thought his painting showed – but she also envisions the letter-like marks on canvas, "n's," notable failures of representation. These ships, like their painter, are not going anywhere: "Apparently they have reached their destination. / It would be hard to say what brought them there, / commerce or contemplation" (MCP, 269). It would be hard to say, too – Bishop's politely skeptical style, "airy, reticulated to let in light" makes it hard to say – to what extent more skillful art could yield better ends or finer consolation (Vendler 1988, 299).

The poem addressing visual art, or ekphrasis, became as popular in the 1950s as the sestina and the tourist poem, and for some of the same reasons – it could display familiarity with European high culture, ambassadorial civility, and technical competence, and it too had a model in Auden, from whose "single influential poem" "Musée de Beaux Arts" (1938) "the modern subgenre has primarily developed" (Fowler 1982, 115). (Hollander would later write a lavish, informative book all about ekphrases, The Gazer's Spirit [1995].) And like those other subgenres, the ekphrasis at its best could say a lot, quietly, about postwar fatigue, aesthetic heritage, and existential doubt: How do we know that anything makes sense to preserve, that anything will survive? How do we know when (if ever) to trust a representation? Wilbur's mordant "Museum Piece" admires the "grace" and "strain" in Degas and his dancers. Yet the quatrains conclude:

> Edgar Degas purchased once
> A fine El Greco, which he kept
> Against the wall beside his bed
> To lay his pants on while he slept.
>
> (*MCP*, 10)

Who is to say that art must be worth more than that? Who is to say, and how could we confirm, and what (if anything) should we give up to protect a heritage of high art? So Hecht asked in the typically saturnine lines of "La Condition Botanique," in *New Poets of England and America*; Hecht's lengthy work, too, is a tourist poem, finding in Europe:

> Fancy cigar boxes, and eyes
>
> Of ceremonial masks; and all
> The places where Kilroy inscribed his name,
> For instance, the ladies' rest room in the Gare du Nord,
> The iron rump of Buddha, whose hallowed, hollowed core
> Admitted tourists once but all the same
> Housed a machine gun.
>
> (*NPEA*, 116)

("Kilroy Was Here" was a ubiquitous graffito, associated with American servicemen.)

The figures in Jarrell's poems, too, wonder whether to trust what they see. In his great long poem "The Night Before the Night Before Christmas" (1948), a well-read girl wonders whether anything or anyone, any work of art or impression or utterance, can make her inner life seem real to her:

> In her room that night she looks at herself in the mirror
> And thinks: "Do I really look like *that*?"
> She stares at her hair:
> It's really a beautiful golden – anyway, yellow …
> No, it's no use.
> She thinks: What do I *really* look like?
> I don't know.
>
> Not really.
>
> *Really.*
>
> (Jarrell 1969, *Complete*, 42)

What unites these poems – the strongest poems by the most prominent poets from these anthologies of the 1950s – is not just a careful postwar sensibility or a heightened interest in technique, not even a wish to go back beyond modernism (as they understood it) for resources, without giving modernism up. Rather these poets (Lowell, Bishop, Jarrell, Wilbur, Hecht, and their most thoughtful peers) wrote poems that asked who and what and when to trust, and whether we should ever trust words, or works of art, or societies, or adults. In this respect they echoed the meditative, melancholy late poems of Wallace Stevens, whose elaborately thoughtful "supreme fictions" had made him, by 1950, "for many younger poets one of the most encouraging examples" (Matthiessen 1950, xxix). Stevens had "blazed with artifice" in *Transport to Summer* (1947) and *The Auroras of Autumn* (1950), before turning to poems of old age and self-doubt (Stevens 1997, 443). In "The Plain Sense of Things," from *The Rock* (1955), "A fantastic effort has failed, a repetition / In a repetitiousness of men and flies." And yet even this bleak aftermath reflects the shaping presence of human consciousness: "All this / Had to be imagined as an inevitable knowledge, / Required, as a necessity requires" (Stevens 1997, 428).

Stevens had become America's greatest poet both of abstraction and of old age. His middle generation successors gravitated instead toward childhood: "You will have no trouble," Roethke told Ciardi's readers, "if you approach these poems as a child would, naively, with your whole being awake" (*MCP*, 68). Childhood for Roethke's – and Bishop's and Jarrell's – generation served broadly (as Travisano and Richard Flynn have stressed) as a problem, a refuge, a source – instinctive, creative, mysterious and vexing – against the literally incredible programs and institutions of adult life (Travisano 1999, 75). Jarrell wrote four children's books and translated fairy tales; Roethke, Ciardi and Wilbur later produced fine volumes of children's verse. If Bishop's poems of childhood are invitations to look, and Jarrell's often invitations to listen, then Roethke's became invitations to move, wrestle, dig, burrow, fly: "follow me further back / Into that minnowy world of weeds and ditches / When the herons floated high over the white houses ... And my intent stretched over the buds" (*MCP*, 81). Wilbur's poems for, or about, children, by contrast, value wit, reserve, introversion, and delicacy, along with all-ages wordplay:

> It's hard to think in crowded places where
> Loud music, squeals and clatter fill the air,
> And brainless persons holler "Yo!" and "Hey!"
> That's why *idea* is found in *hideaway*.
> (Wilbur 2005, 576)

The quatrain from Wilbur's sequence *The Pig in the Spigot* (2001) should give pleasure to preteens still discovering how to make harmless patterns with letters and words: but it is still, decades later, a postwar poem, an all-ages condensation of Auden's "The Shield of Achilles" (1952). Later in the same sequence Wilbur finds "an *arf* in *warfare*," "a *bug* in *bugle*," and in "mustn't," which holds "TNT," a warning to children: "You're not to blow things into smithereens" (Wilbur 2005, 576, 578).

Childhood seemed, to the coming generation, perhaps the last space free of institutional control: in Rich's "Versailles" (another tourist poem), "the cry of closing rings / For us and for the couples in the wood / And all good children who are all too good" (*NPEA*, 267). Wildness, for this style, lies elsewhere; diligence, with a component of anger, lives here.

The postwar poets I have been admiring would not have described themselves as politically conservative. Jarrell thought Viereck "imbecile" (Jarrell 1985, 310). Wilbur, while serving as the first U.S. Poet Laureate in 1987–8, wrote just one poem, "A Fable," denouncing Reagan's "defense-initiative" (Wilbur 2005, 107). All these poets did, however, see themselves as trying to conserve something, or to preserve it, or to defend it; that thing could be variously the private life, the gains of modernism, or the sense of a past that extended beyond it. They were also trying to avoid, as they said, grand programs: not only (as Alan Filreis has emphasized) the programs of the American left, whose unapologetic adherents could become pariahs, but also the patriotically institutionalized optimism of the Second World War, the "whole fictive world projected by wartime Public Relations," whose "plethora of show-business and fraud" continued into the Cold War, if not to the present day (Fussell 1989, 163).

The poets of midcentury could thus turn to humbly perfected forms, to games and to crafts, to "mere" tourism, to homemade, useless things, to "play" (a key word for Bishop, Jarrell, Rich, Roethke, Wilbur, and others), because they had trouble believing in anything else. Wilbur insisted that art should "declare its artificiality," its "partial and provisional attempt" (*MCP*, 7). Jarrell told the editor Margaret Marshall in September 1945 "I feel so rotten about the country's response to Hiroshima and Nagasaki that I wish I could become a naturalized dog or cat. I believe our culture's chief characteristic, to a being from outside it, would be that we are *liars*. That all except for a few never tell the truth" (Jarrell 1985, 130). Jarrell and his peers, Wilbur and his, are sometimes viewed as contributors to a consensus, to an emerging set of 1950s institutions designed to affirm academia or American life, but the truth in their best poems and prose is far otherwise: They saw one another as sometimes appalled observers, attentive to a *longue durée*, inclined to use inherited tools to cast a kind of controlled doubt over everything that schools could teach them, everything that most other adults believed.

And yet to end that way makes these poets sound more often grim, less often a pleasure, than the experience of their verse reveals. These poets' work – those who changed in the 1960s and 1970s and those who did not – remains part of a consolidation, or a rebuilding, or a making of new connections, between the past and the present, or between the recent (modernist) and the distant past, or between the United States and Europe; but it also remains a record of how literary and artistic craft and care could support notions of play and hope and individuality when larger goals were not in view. Wilbur's selection in *New Poets of England and America* concluded with the stately anisometric quatrains of "For the New Railway Station in Rome." Its arrangements respond to centuries of poems about Roman ruins and to the new ruins of the world war. "Echoing in its light/ And cantilevered swoop of reinforced concrete / The broken profile of these stones," Rome Termini station (completed in 1950) seems to ask (quote marks are Wilbur's):

> "What city is eternal
> But that which prints itself within the groping head
> Out of the blue unbroken reveries
> Of the building dead?
>
> "What is our praise or pride
> But to imagine excellence, and try to make it?
> What does it say over the door of Heaven
> But *homo fecit*?"
>
> (*NPEA*, 335–6)

Homo fecit, "human[s] made it": The new Roman Heaven in the Eternal City belongs to its practical, present-day builders. Like all Wilbur's best poems, it remains "committed to the continuity of the world despite its bent towards self-annihilation" (Gery 1996, 115), and it repurposes terms with religious or aristocratic heritage to a present (pluralistic and secular) moment. A hostile reader could attack the poem, and the station, and the whole set of poets, as a valorization of craft that cannot but serve capital; it makes more sense, and seems more generous, to see it as careful homage from Wilbur's America to a not-entirely-rebuilt trans-Atlantic civilization, a way to acknowledge life and invention – and an absence of destructive ambition – in what had been a wreck, not long ago.

WORKS CITED

Auden, W. H. 1991. *The Collected Poems*. Ed. Edward Mendelson. New York: Vintage.

Auden. W. H. 1962. *The Dyer's Hand*. New York: Random House.

Bishop, Elizabeth. 1983. *The Complete Poems 1927–1979*. New York: Farrar, Straus and Giroux.

Brunner. Edward. 2000. *Cold War Poetry*. Champaign-Urbana: University of Illinois Press.

Ciardi, John, ed. 1950. *Mid-Century American Poets*. New York: Twayne. Cited in text as *MCP*.

Fender, Stephen. 1973. "What Really Happened to Warren Winslow?" *Journal of American Studies* 7:2: 187–90.

Filreis, Alan. 2008. *Counter-Revolution of the Word: The Conservative Attack on Modern Poetry, 1945–1960*. Chapel Hill: University of North Carolina Press.

Fowler, Alastair. 1982. *Kinds of Literature*. Cambridge, MA: Harvard University Press.

Fussell, Paul. 1989. *Wartime: Understanding and Behavior in the Second World War*. New York: Oxford University Press.

Gery, John. 1996. *Nuclear Annihilation and Contemporary American Poetry* Gainesville: University Press of Florida.

Hall, Donald, Robert Pack and Louis Simpson, eds. 1957. *New Poets of England and America*. New York: Meridian. Cited in text as *NPEA*.

Jarrell, Randall. 1969. *The Complete Poems*. New York: Farrar, Straus and Giroux.

1969. *The Third Book of Criticism*. New York: Farrar, Straus and Giroux.

1985. *The Letters of Randall Jarrell*. Ed. Mary Jarrell. Boston: Houghton Mifflin.

Longenbach, James, 1997. *Modern Poetry after Modernism*. New York: Oxford University Press.

Lowell, Robert. 2006. *Selected Poems*, expanded ed. New York: Farrar, Straus and Giroux.

Matthiessen, F. O. ed. 1950. *The Oxford Book of American Verse*. New York: Oxford University Press.

Merrill, James. 2006. *The Changing Light at Sandover*. Ed. J. D. McClatchy and Stephen Yenser. New York: Knopf.

2001. *Collected Poems*. Ed. J. D. McClatchy and Stephen Yenser. New York: Knopf.

Oostdijk, Diederik. 2011. *Among the Nightmare Fighters: American Poets of World War II*. Columbia: University of South Carolina Press.

Pickard, Zachariah. 2009. *Elizabeth Bishop's Poetics of Description*. Montreal: McGill-Queen's University Press.

Pritchard, William. 1990. *Randall Jarrell: A Literary Life*. New York: Farrar, Straus and Giroux.

Stevens, Wallace. 1997. *Collected Poetry and Prose*. Ed. Frank Kermode and Joan Richardson. New York: Library of America.

Travisano, Thomas. 1999. *Mid-Century Quartet*. Charlottesville: University Press of Virginia.

2003. "Reflecting Randall Jarrell in the Bishop-Lowell Letters." In *Jarrell, Bishop, Lowell & Co*. Ed. Suzanne Ferguson. Knoxville: University of Tennessee Press. 58–72.

Vendler, Helen. 1988. *The Music of What Happens*. Cambridge, MA: Harvard University Press.

Von Hallberg, Robert. 1985. *American Poetry and Culture, 1945–1980*. Cambridge, MA: Harvard University Press.

Wasley, Aidan. 2011. *The Age of Auden: Postwar Poetry and the American Scene*. Princeton, NJ: Princeton University Press, 2011.

Wilbur, Richard. 2005. *Collected Poems 1943–2004*. New York: Harcourt.

11

MICHAEL THURSTON

Psychotherapy and Confessional Poetry

Confessional poets are crazy. Don't take my word for it; their biographers and critics are happy to provide supporting detail. Robert Lowell suffered severe manic episodes and deep depressions, was institutionalized on several occasions, and wrote with anguish of the ways his behavior harmed friends and loved ones (Mariani 1994, 341–7). Indeed, Lowell's mental illness is so defining an element of his image that Paul Mariani begins his biography of the poet with a picture from an institution (Lowell's 1954 hospitalization at the Payne Whitney Clinic in New York, his fourth serious episode of mania or depression in a five-year period). Anne Sexton and Sylvia Plath attempted suicide, spent time in institutions, endured electroconvulsive therapy, and ultimately ended their own lives (Alexander 1991, 221–5, 320–30; Middlebrook 1991, 345–93). As Dawn Skorczewski reminds readers, Sexton's first published poems were written while she was institutionalized at Westwood Lodge, in the Boston suburbs (Skorczewski 2012, xii). John Berryman's depression was exacerbated by severe alcoholism, and, after numerous hospitalizations, he finally took his own life as well (Mariani 1996, 343–6; 499–501). The illnesses, treatments, and institutionalizations of Allen Ginsberg are similarly familiar (Morgan 2006, 114–21). The very document that names and defines "confessional poetry" links this work to its authors' psychopathologies: In his 1959 review of Lowell's *Life Studies*, M. L. Rosenthal coined the term, writing that "because of the way Lowell brought his private humiliations, sufferings, and psychological problems into the poems ... the word 'confessional' seemed appropriate enough" (Rosenthal 1967, 26). And as early as 1973 – while Lowell and Sexton and Ginsberg were all still living and writing – Marjorie Perloff could deplore critical treatments that reduced the work of a poet like Lowell to a "portrait of the artist as a mental patient" (Perloff 1973, 174).

Recent scholarship has moved well beyond salacious or snooping detail about the poets' mental illnesses to examine the roles played in their work by discourses of treatment and cure, especially the Freudian psychoanalysis with which the poets were familiar (whether they entered into such analysis as patients or not). This work effectively shifts attention from the biographical facts of mental illness to the ways poetic texts are formed by the conventions of talk therapy, the dynamics of transference, the Freudian family drama of Oedipal desires and conflicts, and the "dream work" of condensation and displacement.[1] While psychoanalysis – as treatment and as powerful cultural script – is clearly at work in the poetry of Lowell, Berryman, Plath, Sexton, Ginsberg, and others, it was not the only therapeutic practice experienced by these poets, and it is not the only practice that informs their poems. Coded references (and some not-so-coded references) to newly developed tranquilizers, to electroconvulsive therapy, to lobotomy, and to the routines and regimes of institutional treatment occur in the poems as well. Attention to these (attention that effects a shift of focus from "psychoanalysis" to "psychotherapy") enables us to explore additional avenues by which the poems are in dialogue with the circumstances not only of their authors' lives but also of the tumultuous American society in which they lived. These poetic explorations of drug and convulsive therapies and of the routines of institutional life reveal the poets' understandings and performances of the construction of the subject in American society during the postwar decades.

Confessional poets were not crazy about the label "confessional." As Miranda Sherwin writes, "Without exception, the confessional poets despised and resisted the label," and all of the poets included under the rubric "argued that their work was only nominally autobiographical" (Sherwin 2011, 7). Many of these poets' smartest readers have chafed at the label as well. Dissatisfaction with "confessional" has led some to offer new, more accurate characterizations of this poetry, and these often turn to psychoanalysis as a descriptive vocabulary superior to "confessional" (with all of that word's implications). Helen Vendler, for example, writes that the "most inclusive rubric, perhaps, that can be proposed for the lyric poetry written in America immediately after World War II is 'Freudian lyric'" (Vendler 1995, 31). The term suits, she argues, both because many poets (including those labeled confessional, among others) "found in the therapeutic hour (and its textual support in Freud's writings) not only themes for their poetry but also new formal procedures shaping it." For those poets who experienced one or another version of the talking cure, the specific practice of weekly hour-long sessions in which intimate episodes were not only narrated but also analyzed offered a means for bringing previously unavailable subject matter into verse. This subject matter would not serve simply as the expression of personal emotion, but would, instead, be set as a text for analysis within the poem, a provocation for the poet's and the reader's search for significance.

Even for poets who had never set foot in a therapist's office (but also for those who had spent many hours weekly in such places), the broader cultural presence of Freudian topoi made Freud's ways of framing profound emotional difficulty available as a readily comprehensible code.[2]

More recently, Sherwin has argued that Vendler's "Freudian lyric" is too narrow a label. She offers, instead, "psychoanalytic poetics" as a term that more flexibly captures the ways psychoanalytic tropes influenced the work of the confessional poets. One way to understand the distinction is to compare Vendler's focus on Freudian analysis as formal model to Sherwin's emphasis on psychoanalysis as master narrative. For Vendler, the strict formal limits of Berryman's *Dream Songs* (eighteen lines in three six-line stanzas) mimic the strict temporal limits of the therapeutic (fifty-minute) hour, and the sequence of poems mimics the recursively anecdotal character of analysis. While Berryman deploys a division of the subject into characters that can be mapped onto the Freudian Id (the part of the psyche characterized by untrammeled desire) and Superego (the part that demands self-denial and compliance with law), and while the sequence dramatizes the slow emergence of an Ego that might enable the performance of an integrated "self," Vendler argues, the real value of the Freudian model for the poet is its structure, which allows Berryman implicitly to invoke, comment on, and revise other, older narrative and thematic structures. Sherwin emphasizes, instead, the way Berryman stages, through the conflict between the Id and the Superego and through the balance of specific biographical resonance and more general references to familial dynamics, a straightforward and recognizable Oedipal conflict (in which the child unconsciously desires his mother and wishes the death, or even symbolically kills, his father).

Both of these critics focus part of their discussion on "Dream Song #29," and we can see how "Freudian lyric" and "psychoanalytic poetics" differ by comparing their readings of this often anthologized poem. The poem announces its theme, guilt, as a palpable and almost overwhelming presence:

> There sat down, once, a thing on Henry's heart
> só heavy, if he had a hundred years
> & more, & weeping, sleepless, in all them time
> Henry could not make good.
> (Berryman 1969, 33)

Famously, it concludes with Henry's inability to find the foundation for his guilt; while he might think he has committed murder, he can find no one missing when he "reckons them up." Vendler reads this "cognitive dissonance" as a kind of traumatic repetition that is amenable not to "confession" (because Henry has "no sin to confess") but, instead, to the analysis conducted during the "therapeutic hour" (Vendler 1995, 49). Through that analysis, Berryman arrives at an emblem of the psychic material rendered unavailable to Henry's conscious mind by the process of repression. The poem, read in Vendler's Freudian terms, illustrates at once the illusory foundation of the analysand's free-floating guilt (no murder) and the actual foundation of his anxiety ("pathological scrupulosity").

Where Vendler keeps her focus on the contents of Henry's (and Berryman's) psyche, Sherwin reads the poem precisely for the way it denies readers access to individual guilt and, instead, participates in a "universalizing trend" (Sherwin 2011, 74). From the first stanza's insistent location within Henry (on his heart, in his ears), the second shifts to an image outside Henry. The "chime" in Henry's head in the first stanza becomes, in the second, actual "bells" that speak to him: "too late." It is, Sherwin argues, this newly dawning "awareness of the outer world" that enables, in the final stanza, a "psychological movement" toward "health and recovery." This movement is not the Freudian uncovering of repression; it is, instead, a broader integration of inner and outer worlds that disproves the first stanza's "thing on Henry's heart." While Sherwin does not mention it, the diction in the third stanza seems to bear her out on this integration. Where the first stanza focuses inward and the second outward, the third brings the two together. Henry "thought" and "reckons," but he also twice acknowledges the external fact that "Nobody is ever missing."

A good deal of recent scholarship on confessional poets has worked through the psychoanalytic to the ideological in ways that capitalize on the implicit invitation to read the psychoanalytic work of confessional verse in and against its historical moment. Paul Breslin's perceptive readings of Ginsberg, Lowell, and Plath in *The Psycho-Political Muse*, for example, set these poets against the horizon of psychoanalysis's cultural popularity in the 1950s and its absorption into the radical political thought of Herbert Marcuse and Norman O. Brown in the 1960s in order to delineate the cultural work of confessionalism's "representative victim." In *Pursuing Privacy in Cold War America*, Deborah Nelson juxtaposes shifting legal definitions and delineations of privacy during the postwar decades with the poetry of Lowell, Plath, and Sexton, showing how the poems' psychoanalytical explorations of inner tension register the cultural tensions around and arising from privacy concerns. Noting (along with other critics) the "preponderance of anxious and hostile poems about fathers in the confessional corpus," Nelson deftly maps the psychoanalytic onto the political: "This anxiety about the hostility to fathers then reveals the special relationship that the patriarch enjoyed with respect to privacy" (Nelson 2002, 60). Where Nelson adumbrates the discourse of psychoanalysis with the evolution of privacy through legal opinions, Adam Beardsworth reads Lowell for the present absence of the bomb. The emptiness of the severe depressive's psyche, Beardsworth argues, stands in Lowell's work as a figure for the nothingness that would follow nuclear annihilation (Beardsworth 2010, 97). Negating his culture's norms through his encounter with (and acceptance of) nothingness, Lowell emerges as the atomic poet par excellence.

For Sylvia Plath and Anne Sexton, most critics find the psychoanalytic opening onto the politics of gender and domesticity. The range of devices each of these poets brings to her lyric practice helps to link those political anxieties to vocational questions; language and poetry are perhaps more explicitly at stake in the work of Plath and Sexton than in the work of other poets labeled confessional. Jo Gill illuminates the links between gender, the domestic, and the poetic vocation in early poems by Anne Sexton by focusing on the multivalent significance of narcissism in the work (Gill 2004, 62). In her book on Sexton's confessional poetics, Gill goes further, situating Sexton's work in the specific matrix of 1950s and 1960s suburbia to show how the poet depicts "the self in the modern suburban home as dislocated and fragmented" (Gill 2007, 58).

Freud offered Sylvia Plath a key to her own emotional experience (and that of others) from early on; while a student at Smith College, she diagnosed her anxiety as arising from penis envy and an inferiority complex and she readily explained the infidelities of her boyfriend, Dick Norton, in terms of "a mother complex" (Alexander 1991, 89). Michael Davidson draws on the significance of Freud to the poet in his rereading of Plath's performance of gender. Tracing a profound gender ambivalence from Plath's early journals and letters through her late poems, Davidson argues that the mythic vocabulary she drew (at least in part) from the psychoanalytical work of Freud and Jung masks a repeated "presumption of speech ... whereby the male being addressed ... becomes identified with the female subject speaking" (Davidson 2004, 182).

In a variety of ways, then, psychoanalysis enlivens the confessional poem and reveals links between the poem and its moment. While Berryman, Ginsberg, Lowell, Plath, and Sexton all were at once interested in Freudian psychoanalysis as a cultural discourse and engaged, at one time or another, in a version of the psychoanalytic talking cure, all of these poets also endured other therapeutic interventions. As Elliot Valenstein notes, convulsive therapies were deployed in the majority of American mental institutions between the mid-1930s and mid-1950s (Valenstein 1986, 52), and, as Andrea Tone shows, new tranquilizers were widely used and celebrated in the 1950s and 1960s (Tone 2009, 27). These, too, find their ways into the work of confessional poets. Tranquilizers, electroconvulsive therapy, and the routines of institutionalization address the body as a site for the exercise of power more directly than do the rhetorical and narrative devices of psychoanalysis. In their explorations of the full range of treatments for mental illness in mid-century America, the confessional poets perform the drama, still familiar to readers, of the subject produced by disciplinary practices and their underlying discursive formations.

This is perhaps most vividly apparent in Allen Ginsberg's *Howl*. The poem is famously addressed to Carl Solomon, whom Ginsberg had met when both men were patients in the Columbia Presbyterian Psychiatric Institute in 1949, and the entirety of its third section is an apostrophe to Solomon organized around the refrain "I'm with you in Rockland," a New York mental hospital in which Solomon had been committed. Near the end of the long first section, Ginsberg finds the best minds invoked in the poem's famous opening line, the "angel-headed hipsters" (including himself) in the same "total animal soup of time" in which he locates Solomon (Ginsberg 1984, 126; 130). Having "presented themselves on the granite steps of the madhouse," they are subjected to the range of treatments available in the 1950s and are given "the concrete void of insulin Metrazol electricity hydrotherapy psychotherapy occupational therapy pingpong & amnesia" (Ginsberg 1984, 130). This catalog is worth hovering over for a moment, for its constituents illustrate the strong connection between manipulation of the body and an ideal of mental health during this historical moment. The first three items here are forms of convulsive therapies; they all derive from an understanding that unhealthy psychological cycles must be interrupted, that the brain and nervous system must be directly addressed in order to "normalize" or regulate the patient's mind (Valenstein 1986, 45–6; 50–2). All were intended to "jolt" the patient's system (usually diagnosed as abnormal, depressed, or schizophrenic) into "normal" functioning. Insulin shock therapy, introduced in the 1920s, used heavy doses of insulin to induce daily comas (Valenstein 1986, 46–8). "Metrazol" was a brand name for the stimulant, pentylenetra-trazol, which, in sufficiently high doses, induced convulsions in the patient (Valenstein 1986, 50). Electroconvulsive therapy brought about brief seizures through the application of electricity in order to alter "abnormal" functions in the brains of depressives and schizophrenics (Valenstein 1986, 50–2). All of these therapies tended to produce "successful" outcomes when success was defined as docility and compliance; power applied to the body could indeed bring the mind into a socially acceptable orderliness (or at least the appearance of it).[3]

Ginsberg marks one end of a continuum of critical attitudes toward somatic therapies, institutional regimes, and prescription drugs. The work of Lowell, Sexton, and Plath offers a range of responses to and interpretations of the production of the subject by these practices. While Lowell, for example, does not suggest revolution against it, he does sadly limn the disciplining of the subject by the routines of treatment. Taken together, the late poems of *Life Studies* survey a good deal of the landscape of mental illness and its treatment from the late 1940s to the end of the 1950s. The poems of the volume's last section shift attention from the routines and therapies of institutional life to the medications that enable a life outside in the world. Both "Memories of West Street" and "Man and Wife" prominently mention one of the chief new technologies for the maintenance of "mental health," the pharmacological tranquilizer: "These are the tranquillized *Fifties*," he writes in the first line of the second stanza of "Memories of West Street," and in the first line of "Man and Wife" he describes himself as "Tamed by *Miltown*" (Lowell 1959, 87). The italicized noun here names the Wallace Laboratories brand name for the tranquilizer, meprobamate (Tone 2009, 50). Released for prescription use in 1955, the drug quickly became enormously popular for its combination of sedative properties and fairly low toxicity. By the time it appeared by name in Lowell's poem, Miltown had developed the reputation of a wonder drug (Tone 2009, 27–8). What is clear in Lowell's poems, however, is the drug's inadequacy. In "Man and Wife," though the couple is "tamed" by the tranquilizer, they are caught in an emotional struggle so powerful that it expands to infect every aspect of the world around them. The Marlborough Street Lowell describes in "Memories of West Street" as "hardly passionate" is on fire in "Man and Wife," flamed and fueled by the mania of which the speaker has supposedly been cured and left, as "Home After Three Months Away" has it, "frizzled, stale and small."

In "Memories of West Street," the decade has been "tranquillized" and the speaker is sedately "book-worming," but the poem's structural logic seems to confirm the meekly negative judgment on "cure" delivered at the end of "Home After Three Months Away." The poem's four stanzas divide so that two internal stanzas emphasizing violence are framed by two in which the central figure is artificially calm. The framing stanzas offer the speaker himself, quietly reading in his house on "hardly passionate Marlborough Street" (and tranquilized, as we can infer from the poems that surround this one in *Life Studies*) and, at the other end of the poem, the crime boss Lepke, awaiting execution. On the surface, little seems to connect these two figures, the poet and intellectual on the one hand and the murderer and extortionist on the other. Both, though, occupy spaces set apart, the poet in his house and the prisoner in his "little segregated cell." Each of these is a space of privilege: The poet reads and studies because he teaches only one day a week and the criminal enjoys "things forbidden the common man."

Finally, each is artificially maintained in his calm. Lepke moves in "a sheep-ish calm" as a consequence of his lobotomy, and the violence with which he is at once prevented from the poet's "agonizing reappraisal" and left to focus without interruption on his execution is, in an attenuated way, gener-alized to the speaker and his society by the crucial "tranquillized" in the sec-ond stanza. Objectors to the state, whether conscientious or criminal, must be controlled, whether by institutionalization, drugs, surgery or "the electric chair" (Lowell 1959, 86).

The catalog of therapies sketched in these poems helps us to see beyond psychoanalysis to the broader range of treatments narrated or examined in the work of Lowell's fellow confessional poets. While psychoanalysis is important in both the biography and the work of Anne Sexton, for example, some of her most powerful poems focus on the mechanics of institution-alization rather than the dynamics of Freudian analysis. From such early poems as "You, Doctor Martin" (published in 1960 in Sexton's first book, *To Bedlam and Part Way Back*) to "Angel of the Love Affair" in the 1972 volume, *The Book of Folly*, the mental hospital and its regimes and accou-terments recur in her work. "The Double Image" encapsulates these with haunting economy:

> I pretended I was dead
> until the white men pumped the poison out,
> putting me armless and washed through the rigmarole
> of talking boxes and the electric bed
>   (Sexton 1988, 28).

The institution responds to the emotional and spiritual pain that drives the speaker's suicide attempt (not her first) by addressing her body, first empty-ing her of the drugs she has taken and then subjecting her to electric shock. Later in the poem, Sexton touches on the occupational therapy that figures often in her narratives of "recovery": "I made moccasins that I would never use" (Sexton 1988, 29). The body is kept busy, set to hollow labor, in order to still the mind and render the subject productive (as the term is defined by the society's dominant voices). Sexton examines the routinized surveillance and physical control with which the "mad" are "treated" in more detail in "You, Doctor Martin," and here, perhaps more than in any other confes-sional poem, the bio-political significance of mutually reinforcing regimes of psychotherapy is acutely registered. Sexton keeps an intense focus not on Doctor Martin and his talk but, instead, on the ways the patients' bodies are controlled and monitored. Standing in lines, eating on cue and in uni-son, watched even when they are alone, the patients are infantilized by their treatment. Unmade by the institution, the speaker is, like the moccasins she stitches, remade in a shape more useful than that of a "mad" queen: "Now I am myself / counting this row and that row of moccasins / waiting on the silent shelf" (Sexton 1988, 10).

Sylvia Plath endured institutionalization, electroconvulsive therapy, and insulin shock therapy, as well as rigorous psychoanalysis, after periods of depression and a suicide attempt at age twenty. I want to conclude with a discussion of Plath's work because, more than that of any of the other confessional poets, Plath's poetry shows how an awareness of the broad landscape of psychotherapies in the 1950s can illuminate the poems' figurative language. More than this, Plath's work also evinces an ambivalence toward these therapies and their effects that complicates our sense of the subject produced by them. It is tempting to read Plath's figurations of treatments for mental illness as critiques of the institutions of mental health analogous to the critiques of American gynecological and psychiatric medicine that Luke Ferretter reads in *The Bell Jar* (Ferretter 2008, 127). The complexity of Plath's poetic handling of this imagery, however, renders her critical position more ambivalent.

Anne Stevenson, among others, has written of the possible long-term effects Plath suffered from the treatment she endured first as an outpatient during the summer of 1953 and then, after her suicide attempt, at McLean Hospital. While many might not agree with Stevenson that Plath's "ECT may have substantially contributed to her cool, logically-arrived-at decision to do away with herself" (Stevenson 1989, 44), it is more difficult to dispute her claim that the "psychiatric treatment Sylvia Plath received in the 1950s now seems almost as barbaric as the rituals of eighteenth-century Bedlam" (Stevenson 1989, 47). It is clear that the interacting set of therapies Plath experienced had powerful effects that reverberate throughout her career. Among those effects is an emphasis on the subject as constructed by forces and powers beyond her control.

The array of therapies aimed at "curing" the mind by controlling the body are most obviously in play in a poem like "The Hanging Man" (a poem not among those Plath clearly intended to publish but which Ted Hughes included in the 1965 *Ariel*), whose speaker "sizzle[s] in blue volts" and awakens in a "world of bald white days" (Plath 1966, 77). Here, Plath absorbs the experience of electroconvulsive therapy into a mythic system of reference, alluding obliquely to *The Waste Land* (where Madame Sosostris does not see this card as she performs a Tarot divination) and to the figure of Christ ("pinned … in this tree").

In the later poems Plath wrote for *Ariel*, a less explicit and less tightly formal dramatization of bio-political therapies yields a more powerfully complex exploration. "Tulips" is among the earliest of the poems written for the volume; Plath composed it in March, 1961, only a month after suffering a miscarriage (and less than a year after the birth of her first child, Frieda) and shortly after a long hospital stay for appendix surgery. The hospital imagery in "Tulips" can therefore obviously be read as referring to these experiences. Against the horizon of her treatments for depression, though (which included anti-depressant drugs, electroconvulsive therapy, and insulin-shock therapy), it is difficult not to see the poem as a comment on these therapies as well. However, unlike the responses to therapy in the work of Ginsberg or Sexton, "Tulips" is ambivalent. Lying quietly in a bed surrounded by "white walls," propped up on a pillow and passively taking in all that happens around her, the speaker is at once powerless, forced to take in her surroundings like an eye held open, and "a pebble" tended by the nurses as "water / Tends to the pebbles it must run over" (Plath 2004, 18). What is striking in this poem, especially when read alongside Sexton's poems on institutionalization, is the speaker's generally positive affect regarding her treatment, even (perhaps especially) the treatments that empty her of memory, attachment, and personality. It is the reminders of her life outside the white walls – the titular tulips, which are "too excitable," and the photograph of her husband and child – that cause the trouble. On the one hand, this diction recalls Plath's youthful jealousy at the hospitalization of her college boyfriend, Dick Norton; "Sick with envy," she had written in her journal when Dick entered a sanitarium in upstate New York. While she was suffering one of her overwhelming depressions and wanted to "crawl back abjectly into the womb," Dick was "lying up there, rested, fed, taken care of, free to explore books and thoughts at any whim." On the other hand, the featureless setting, the speaker's passivity and powerlessness, and the imagery of drowning ("I watched my teaset, my bureaus of linen, my books / Sink out of sight, and the water went over my head") recalls the poet's descriptions, throughout her journals and letters, of the oblivion offered by suicide. Holding these two poems together, however, we see Plath exploring the comforts of momentary amnesia and disconnection (effects of convulsive therapies), even as she resists the "hooks" of those practices and institutions that would bring her back to the "self" she wished to escape. If the "blue volts" that shock the hanging man into prophetic vision are the currents of electroconvulsive therapy, they are at once torture and power. If the "Communion tablet" figuring the peace on which the dead close is a pill, it is at once the relinquishing of connection and the promise of reemergence from figurative death into dangerous life. In Plath's complex confessional work, the disciplinary apparatus of mid-century psychotherapy appears in all its multivalent and contradictory richness. Much madness, here as in the work

of her afflicted contemporaries, leads readers to divine a richer sense of
mid-century American subjectivity.

NOTES

1 On these well-known concepts, see Sigmund Freud (2010).
2 Regarding "code" here we might usefully recall Roman Jakobson's definition
of the term as a mode of signification commonly held by both addresser and
addressee in a communicative situation (Jakobson 1971, 570–1).
3 As Valenstein writes, although convulsive treatments were not (at least until the
late 1950s) "subjected to rigorous or effective criticism within psychiatry" (1986,
53), their "successes" were widely proclaimed and celebrated in the popular
press.

WORKS CITED

Alexander, Paul. 1991. *Rough Magic: A Biography of Sylvia Plath*. New York:
Viking.
Beardsworth, Adam. 2010. "Learning to Love the Bomb: Robert Lowell's Pathological
Poetics." *Canadian Review of American Studies* 40.1: 95–116.
Berryman, John. 1969. *The Dream Songs*. New York: Farrar Straus and Giroux.
Breslin, Paul. 1987. *The Psycho-Political Muse: American Poetry since the Fifties*.
Chicago: University of Chicago Press.
Davidson, Michael. 2003. *Guys Like Us: Citing Masculinity in Cold War Poetics*.
Chicago: University of Chicago Press.
Ferretter, Luke. 2008. "'Just Like the Sort of Drug a Man Would Invent': *The Bell Jar*
and the Feminist Critique of Women's Health Care." *Plath Profiles* 1: 136–58.
Freud, Sigmund. 2010. *The Interpretation of Dreams*. Translated by A. A. Brill. New
York: Sterling.
Gill, Jo. 2007. *Anne Sexton's Confessional Poetics*. Gainesville: University of Florida
Press.
2004. "Textual Confessions: Narcissism in Anne Sexton's Early Poetry." *Twentieth-
Century Literature* 50.1: 59–87.
Ginsberg, Allen. 1984. *Collected Poems, 1947–1980*. New York: Harper and Row.
Jakobson, Roman. 1971. "Language in Relation to Other Communication Systems."
In *Selected Writings, Volume 2: Word and Language*, 570–9. The Hague:
Mouton.
Lowell, Robert. 1959. *Life Studies*. New York: Farrar Straus and Cudahy.
Mariani, Paul. 1996. *Dream Song: The Life of John Berryman*. 2nd Edition. Amherst:
University of Massachusetts Press.
1994. *Lost Puritan: A Life of Robert Lowell*. New York: W.W. Norton and
Company.
Middlebrook, Diane Wood. 1991. *Anne Sexton: A Biography*. Boston: Houghton
Mifflin.
Morgan, Bill. 2006. *I Celebrate Myself: The Somewhat Private Life of Allen Ginsberg*.
New York: Viking.
Nelson, Deborah. 2002. *Pursuing Privacy in Cold War America*. New York: Columbia
University Press.

Perloff, Marjorie. 1973. *The Poetic Art of Robert Lowell*. Ithaca: Cornell University Press.

Plath, Sylvia. 1966. *Ariel*. New York: Harper and Row.

    1982. *The Journals of Sylvia Plath*. Ed. Frances McCullough. New York: Dial Press.

    2004. *Ariel: The Restored Edition*. New York: Harper.

Rosenthal, M. L. 1967. *The New Poets: American and British Poetry Since World War II*. New York: Oxford University Press.

Sexton, Anne. 1988. *Selected Poems of Anne Sexton*. Edited by Diane Wood Middlebrook and Diana Hume George. Boston: Houghton Mifflin.

Sherwin, Miranda. 2011. *"Confessional" Writing and the Twentieth-Century Literary Imagination*. Houndmills, Basingstoke: Palgrave Macmillan.

Skorczewski, Dawn M. 2012. *Accident of Hope: The Therapy Tapes of Anne Sexton*. New York: Routledge.

Stevenson, Anne. 1989. *Bitter Fame: A Life of Sylvia Plath*. Boston: Houghton Mifflin.

Tone, Andrea. 2009. *The Age of Anxiety: A History of America's Turbulent Affair with Tranquilizers*. New York: Basic.

Valenstein, Elliot S. 1986. *Great and Desperate Cures: The Rise and Decline of Psychosurgery and Other Radical Treatments for Mental Illness*. New York: Basic.

Vendler, Helen. 1995. *The Given and the Made: Recent American Poets*. London: Faber and Faber.

12

KAPLAN HARRIS

Black Mountain Poetry

Two views dominate the poetry associated with the Black Mountain school. The first centers on Black Mountain College (founded 1933), a small experimental arts school in North Carolina where poet Charles Olson served as final rector from 1953 to 1956 and where a number of young poets converged, among them Robert Creeley, John Wieners, Robert Duncan, Hilda Morley, Ed Dorn, Joel Oppenheimer, and Jonathan Williams. The second centers on Creeley's *Black Mountain Review* (1954–7), founded in Mallorca and featuring a contributor list of not only his close correspondents Denise Levertov, Larry Eigner, Paul Blackburn, Cid Corman, Irving Layton, and Gael Turnbull, but also an international network of writers, not least the Beats on the eve of their rise to fame. The two views are sometimes at odds. In 1968, when Martin Duberman asked whether Black Mountain poetry possessed a "quality in common of style or content," Creeley sought to set him straight: "I think there's a confusion here, implicitly, simply that 'Black Mountain' as a school of poetry refers more to the locus of the *Black Mountain Review*, the particular writers who contributed to that magazine and who really come for the most part from the previous relation to *Origin* in the early 1950s. So that to speak of a 'Black Mountain School of Poetry' as if it had reference to the students at Black Mountain or to the fact of the college is a little deceptive." Creeley defines the poetry, then, according to a network of magazines, including Corman's *Origin*, that came together around the open field poetics of Olson's "Projective Verse."

While the *Black Mountain Review* tends to be the starting point for literary scholars, and the college itself for Duberman, the continuing significance of Black Mountain poetry is probably best understood through the mutual relationship between the two. Black Mountain poetry was less a poetic revolution in its own right than a changing of hands after World War II, when the international intelligentsia among the faculty conferred its prestige on the emerging American avant-garde. The original faculty of the 1930s and 1940s counted among its members an all-star roster of European modernists whose authority was necessary for elevating the reputation of the start-up college. Without their affiliation, it is hard to imagine the poets who arrived in the 1950s earning lasting fame from the otherwise fly-by-night operation that briefly sustained their backwoods utopia. Nor is it easy to imagine the careers of major poets launched from a college literary journal. The faculty who voted to allocate resources for the *Black Mountain Review* wanted to boost recruitment more than they wanted to burn down the literary establishment. Olson convinced the faculty to support the magazine only after the usual advertisements and fliers proved ineffective and the school was becoming desperate for warm bodies in the classroom. As editor, Creeley transcended such parochial intentions by embracing the Pound-Williams tradition. His model was the little magazine of modernism. Building on the artistic renown of the college, he was wildly successful at bringing together mid-century experimentalists with his peers (or "company" as he called them). Grove Press editor Donald Allen ultimately crowned them the leading postwar generation in the bestselling anthology *The New American Poetry: 1945–1960* (published 1960), and they have been packaged as a more or less coherent group since.

§

The story of the school's founding is well known. John Andrew Rice was a fiery Southern progressive intellectual who established Black Mountain College after his dismissal from Rollins College in the spring of 1933. Although an investigation by the AAUP (then two decades in existence) eventually ruled that the college had violated Rice's intellectual freedom, by then he had already assembled a cadre of faculty, students, and donors for a new enterprise in the Blue Ridge Mountains outside of Asheville, North Carolina (Duberman 1972, Harris 1987). The facilities at the Black Mountain were less ivory tower, more "run-down summer camp" (Rumaker 2003, 16). Rice successfully persuaded his cohort that the future of higher education depended on a model of governance by faculty and students rather than overpaid administrators or regents on a corporate board (Harris 1987, 164–5). Bucking professional-school norms, Rice and his colleagues envisioned a progressive curriculum that placed the arts at the center. They evaluated students on originality instead of grades from standardized tests that measure a narrow subset of skills. As Mary Emma Harris explains, Rice thought emotions should be emphasized as much as intellect during student training: "The measure of education was to be qualitative, not quantitative; its method, an active process rather than the passive absorption of a pre-scribed body of information" (Harris 1987, 7). Rice's great antagonist was naturally University of Chicago "Great Books" proponent Robert Maynard Hutchins. Rice once chided Hutchins that "Gertrude Stein's *Lectures in America* is headier than Aristotle's *Poetics* or Horace's *Ars Poetica*" (quoted in Harris 1987, 15). This top-down overhaul and emphasis on student self-realization – in some ways anticipating Paulo Freire's *Pedagogy of the Oppressed* (1970) – made the teaching opportunities attractive to rising names from art, design, music, dance, and architecture. Robert Motherwell and Willem de Kooning joined the art faculty. Visionary mathematician Buckminster Fuller constructed geodesic domes on the serene hillsides half a century before chemists named a spherical carbon molecule buckminsterfullerene in his honor. Visiting lecture series and summer programs welcomed renowned guests such as Walter Gropius, Albert Einstein, and William Carlos Williams.

The quirky college drew the attention of the national press in large part thanks to famous faculty who came seeking refuge from Nazi Europe. The most celebrated of the arrivals were painter Josef Albers and textile artist Anni Albers, who were driven out of the Bauhaus by Berlin police in 1933. Large endowed universities in the United States attempted to lure Albers, but he accepted Rice's offer because there was "no ecclesiastical, political, or state control and no established tradition or faculty to contend with" (Harris 1987, 10). Albers found it a relief to be free from the "Picas-sobia," "Mattise-itis," and "Klee-tomania" of the reigning art curriculum (Duberman 1972, 50). Black Mountain permitted Albers – who served as rector in the 1940s – to construct his own curriculum among the Appalachian shoals and red clay forests. Although he became best known for his research on the square, the assignment that proved most influential to his students concerned matiére studies. Albers defined matiére as the surface character of a material as experienced both by hand and eye. He commanded his students to bring everyday objects or "unsung detritus" to class: wet strips of paper, apple seeds, glass shards, insect nests, eggshells, rubber tubes, or muddy tires. His students took the exercise to heart by expanding the materials of their practice. Most famously, Robert Rauschenberg became the enfant terrible of postmodernism when he developed the combine method – a clear corollary of the matiére scales. Albers's innovations ultimately spawned an anything-goes attitude across the small campus. Another teacher, Franz Kline, covered his canvases with house paint that could be procured at the hardware store in town. John Cage, a frequent visitor to the school starting in the 1940s, used ordinary objects as anarchic stage props in *Theater Piece no. 1* (1952), an event considered a forerunner to the Happenings that swept arts of the 1960s (Katz 2003, 75). Olson and M. C. Richards read poetry on stepladders, participants blew whistles, David Tudor played a piano, Edith Piaf records played at double speed, a barking dog trotted across the stage (Katz 2003, 138–9). When the poets became the center of the college life in the 1950s, they too embraced the ordinary and everyday, as exemplified in the Americana that fills out the bulk of Olson's *Maximus Poems* and reflects his fascination with the odds and ends of settlement and trade.

Although the college benefited from the prestige of its faculty, the budget was always on the brink of bankruptcy. Enrollment peaked at around a hundred students and more often hovered less than two dozen. Balancing an unconventional curriculum with fiscal limitations often meant concocting ingenious plans, such as assigning work duty for the mess hall and the campus farm. The faculty even opened a mica mining operation right on the campus grounds in an effort to raise revenue during the war. Creeley recalls, "There are few colleges whose president, bursar and professors might be found on a Sunday morning, pulling classic gunk out of a clogged up main drain so as to allow the student toilets to function" (Creeley 2002, 303). Although the Forbes family provided funds (albeit anonymous) at crucial moments, and the GI Bill brought an influx of tuition in the postwar years, the need for donors was always a pressing concern (Harris 1987, 110). Matters were complicated by the school's unpopularity with locals. Germans on the faculty stirred suspicion during the war, and the acceptance of black students full time in 1945 unsettled Jim Crow-supporting neighbors (Harris 1987, 111). A reputation for tolerating anarchists, communists, and homosexuals further diminished the likelihood of friendly relations in the Bible Belt. In one notorious altercation, a local farmer punched a professor after the writer Paul Goodman took a leak in the woods at a baseball game (Harris 1987, 169).

Into these straitened circumstances stepped Charles Olson, first as monthly lecturer in 1948, then as full-time rector in 1953. Olson carried the credentials of Harvard graduate study and was heir apparent of Pound's historical poetics. He was an archive rat whose obsession with primary sources led him to Melville's marginalia in a fragile edition of *Hamlet* (causing acclaim among Melville scholars). Olson salvaged his unfinished dissertation in *Call Me Ishmael*, an eccentric book on the nineteenth-century whaling industry that reminded readers of Pound's *Spirit of Romance* or William Carlos Williams's *In the American Grain*. His curriculum vitae, however, was not alone what landed him the top spot at Black Mountain College. Born in 1909, the son of a postman and labor organizer in Massachusetts, raised in the fishing town of Gloucester, Olson proved to be a choice hire for a college where getting dirty was part of the job. In the early 1940s, he had devoted his considerable energies to domestic politics, and unlike most poets, he knew the ins and outs of organizations and leadership. He had written pamphlets for the Office of War Information that encouraged immigrants to support the Allied Powers, and he had served a stint on Roosevelt's reelection staff with the notion that he might eventually pursue a career as a political insider. Olson was deemed too eccentric, in the end, for the Truman staff, and he soon found himself unemployed and disillusioned about change from within institutions of power (Clark 1991, Maud 2008). In the 1940s, he was also publishing poetry for the first time and visiting Ezra Pound, whose Rome radio broadcasts in support of Mussolini had led to his incarceration at St. Elizabeth's Hospital. The two met regularly, they exchanged ideas, but their eventual fallout over the older poet's anti-Semitism served as impetus for Olson to embark on a new historical epic, *The Maximus Poems*, around 1950 (Seelye 1975).

Olson wrote his most important work while at Black Mountain College. He composed "Projective Verse" (1950), the vastly influential manifesto that grew out of correspondence with Robert Creeley and Frances Bolderoff (Butterick and Blevins 1980–1996, Maud and Thesen 1999). His major accomplishment was to define verse according to the body rather than traditional poetic form. The words "breath" and "breathing" appear nineteen times in the ten-page piece. The proposed unit of composition, the syllable, appears sixteen times. Olson demands "COMPOSITION BY FIELD" or use of the entire page "as opposed to inherited line, stanza, over-all form, what is the 'old' base of the non-projective" (Olson 1950, 13). These mantras are among the most quoted principles of poetic composition in the last half century. He seized on Creeley's statement, "FORM IS NEVER MORE THAN AN EXTENSION OF CONTENT," to reflect a pragmatic strain of modernist experimentation. He composed in a bombastic style that echoed the macho posturing of avant-garde manifestos. Another mantra, drawn from Edward Dahlberg's idea that "ONE PERCEPTION MUST IMMEDIATELY AND DIRECTLY LEAD TO A FURTHER PERCEPTION," captured the imagination of readers who felt suffocated by the lockstep conformism of the era's *The Man in the Grey Flannel Suit* or *The Organization Man*. Projective verse requires "getting rid of the lyrical interference of the individual as ego, the 'subject' and his soul, that peculiar presumption by which western man has interposed himself between what he is as a creature of nature … and those other creations of nature" (Olson 1950, 20). When he insinuates that lyric poets are puppets of imperialism – a shot over the bow of the reigning Confessionalists of his day – he carves out a rival space that Black Mountain soon occupied.

§

Black Mountain College was broke by 1956. Enrollment numbers dropped, unpaid faculty packed their bags, and Olson soon oversaw the closing of doors and dismantling of day-to-day operations. While he would spend his remaining years in western New York and Gloucester, a great many of the names associated with the school migrated westward to San Francisco, among them Michael Rumaker, Edward Dorn, Fielding Dawson, John Wieners, and Robert Creeley. It was an exodus of sorts, or a re-centering of energies, and the poets' writing quickly adapted to the new locus among the San Francisco Renaissance and the Beats. Wieners, for instance, wrestled with sexual norms and Cold War bohemia in "A poem for cock suckers" and "A poem for the insane" from *The Hotel Wentley Poems* (Aurhahn Press, 1958). Inspired by Olson's archaeological interests (see *A Bibliography of America* for Ed Dorn), Dorn turned to the Western frontier in the poems of *The Shoshoneans: The People of the Basin-Plateau* (1966) and *Gunslinger* (1968). Even those poets never directly associated with the college could not help but be affected by the relocation of their cohort. Galvanized by student movements that germinated in the Bay Area, Levertov embraced the role of poet activist as the decade wore on, serving as influential poetry editor of *The Nation* and later falling out with longtime friend Duncan over the place of poetry in the political arena (Bertholf and Gelpi 2004). Larry Eigner's stripped-down variant of projective verse tied Olson's notion of "polis is this" to minute observations from his home in Massachusetts – where cerebral palsy prevented his ability to travel widely like his peers. As the network of Black Mountain poets expanded, however, he published an enormous body of work across a vast geographic footprint, reaching audiences throughout North America in such magazines as *TISH* (Vancouver), *Gay Sunshine* (San Francisco), and *El Corno Emplumado* (Mexico City).

Why were the Black Mountain poets welcomed in San Francisco rather than treated as rivals or interlopers? The answer partly has to do with the meteoric rise in fame that resulted from their association with Creeley's *Black Mountain Review*. Creeley (born 1926) was an aspiring writer with New England roots and a WWII veteran of the American Field Service on the Indian subcontinent when he entered the poetry scene. In the late 1940s, he married, dropped out of Harvard, and moved to a farm in New Hampshire where he began soliciting contributions for a little magazine that would feature his own generation side by side with established poets of modernism. Not any elder poets would do, however. Creeley fiercely rejected T. S. Eliot and the New Critics. He favored Ezra Pound and William Carlos Williams, one a national pariah and one a rabidly anti-Eliot spokesperson for homegrown modernism. At the ripe age of 23, Creeley reached out to each by introducing himself as a pigeon farmer and requesting editorial guidance. (Who could say no?) Although his first magazine never came to fruition – Corman used some of the gathered contributions when editing *Origin* – the resourceful Creeley was soon corresponding with a vast network of new or neglected poets, among them Charles Olson, Larry Eigner, Robert Duncan, Denise Levertov, Louis Zukofsky, and Jonathan Williams.

Creeley's publishing breakthrough came when he relocated his family to Mallorca and established the Divers Press in 1952 and then the *Black Mountain Review* in 1954. Divers Press was much like Black Mountain College in its aspiration to merge international modernism with a steadfast devotion to a "hand-craft" ethos. As Creeley wrote in an advertising prospectus from 1953:

> Printing is cheap in Mallorca, and for a small press like our own it means freedom from commercial pressures. It means, too, that we can design our books in a way that we want, since they are handset and made with an almost forgotten sense of craft. Above all, it is our own chance to print what we actually like and believe in. (Creeley 1953)

Readers discovered speculations on the origin of language in Olson's *Mayan Letters* (1953), Old Provençal translations in Paul Blackburn's *Proensa* (1953), and campy medievalism in Duncan's *Caesar's Gate: Poems, 1949–1950* (1955), the latter illustrated with photographic cut-ups by Duncan's partner, the American visual artist Jess Collins. Readers also found H. P. Macklin's *A Handbook of Fancy Pigeons* (1954), not a work of literature at all, but as its title indicates, a guide for the identification of birds. Creeley disavowed economic interests while embracing the artistic prestige of modernism and its successors, as when he published Lorine Niedecker, Kenneth Rexroth, William Carlos Williams, and Louis Zukofsky in the *Black Mountain Review*. Most important for legitimizing the venture was the fact that Creeley ambitiously courted associates of Pound, whose addresses he simply lifted from the distribution lists of the now-forgotten *Pound Newsletter* (Smith 2014, 130). Translators of *The Cantos* are found throughout the *Black Mountain Review*: Olson memorializes Rainer M. Gerhardt (Germany) in "The Death of Europe"; René Laubies (France) supplies paintings in the first issue; and Katue Kitasano (Japan) designs the covers of the first four issues. The Kitasano connection shows again the international network that the *Black Mountain Review* and Divers Press sought to harness. Kitasano, who edited *VOU* magazine in Tokyo, had early on featured Japanese translations of Creeley in 1951, alongside work by Rexroth and Jackson Mac Low. Creeley, in turn, issued Kitasono's full collection *Black Rain: Poems & Drawings* (1954) under the Divers imprint. The *Black Mountain Review* ultimately re-centered this network in the West, in San Francisco, when Creeley published Jorge Luis Borges alongside Allen Ginsberg and Jack Kerouac in the final issue – right as *Howl* and *On the Road* were set to become landmarks of a generation.

The larger phase of establishing Black Mountain poetry's reputation began with Grove's *New American Poetry 1945–1960*. The Black Mountain poets were a promising acquisition for Donald Allen, the editor whose role at Grove Press found him competing with James Laughlin's New Directions for a share of the counter-canonical poets in the 1950s. Allen in fact worked for New Directions for almost a year, and when first hired at Grove, his one calling card was his translation of Gabriel García Lorca: the martyred poet whose populist pedigree has been championed in poems by Amiri Baraka (then as LeRoi Jones), Robert Creeley, Robert Duncan, and Jack Spicer. Because Laughlin controlled a virtual monopoly on Pound, Williams, and H. D., it was understandable that Allen cultivated the emerging, self-published coterie of the New York School, the San Francisco Renaissance, the Beats, and Black Mountain. Because the Grove imprint carried the distinction of European avant-garde, it was strategically positioned to confer value on the counter-culture that it came to publish (Glass 2013). The first issue of Grove's magazine *Evergreen Review* headlined Jean-Paul Sartre, Samuel Beckett, Henri Micheax, Albert Camus, and Eugene Ionesco, and the second issue leveraged these marquee names to arouse interest in the largely unknown voices of the "San Francisco Scene." That second issue subsequently became a bestseller against the backdrop of the 1957 obscenity trial for *Howl*. Although the focus is San Francisco, the issue signals an affinity with Black Mountain throughout, ranging from contributors who studied or taught at the college to Philip Whalen's "Homage to Robert Creeley." Of special note is the longest selection, a forty-page short story, "The Desert," written by Olson's student Michael Rumaker, followed in distant second place by Kerouac's seventeen-page "October in the Railroad Earth." Henceforth Grove fashioned its brand as a deserving Black Mountain successor: *Evergreen Review* featured Duncan and Olson in 1957, Creeley in 1958, and Wieners and Levertov in 1959.

The seeds of the anthology began when Allen tried to formulate a business model to publish emerging poets in cheap, quickly produced trade editions that could compete with the New Directions "Poet of the Month" pamphlet series. He had two goals at the outset. The first was to market a series as "less concerned with masterpieces and more with showing what is going on" (Allen 1958). Rather than prizewinners who were crowned by juries of tenured professors, Allen wanted American bohemians who could cross racial and class lines and function as antennae for events behind the headlines. The Black Mountain poets turned out to be ideal candidates, and better yet, their interests in Mayan archaeology, Provencal troubadours, and French surrealists complemented the cosmopolitan image at Grove. Allen's second goal, one that he ultimately discarded, was to open the anthology with a selection of modernist precedents, as he wrote to Olson in 1959: "10 to 15 pages of the older generation, chosen from their work published since 1945: WCW, Pound (1 canto), M Moore, HD, EEC, Wallace Stevens – stressing those works that show the techniques that have been of influence, etc., on the new poets, but the choices would also inevitably show how different the new poets have grown to be, i.e., that way indirectly showing what the new poetry is, etc." (Maud 2005, letter 9/9/1959). Olson, who complained about the "aunties" and "grandpas" in a letter dated 9/12/1959, ultimately persuaded Allen to make a clean break and present the new generation on its own terms (Maud 2005, 59). The poets of the anthology were left to seek cultural legitimacy beyond the inherited high modernism, as they did in the influential appendix of their "Statements on Poetics." In the end, Allen situated Black Mountain alongside the Beats, the San Francisco Renaissance, and the New York School, but he implicitly conferred the highest rank on Black Mountain when he kicked off the poetry section with Olson's magisterial long poem "The Kingfishers." The poem was a strategic editorial decision because it reiterated the call for an experimentalist ethos: "What does not change / is the will to change." The first of its dense allusions, "Albers & Angkor Vat," evoked the avant-garde and Cold War internationalism in a way that perfectly aligned with the Grove Press catalog, while also reminding readers of the Albers-Olson connection at Black Mountain College.

§

The New American Poetry opened the door to wider readerships in the United States and beyond. Creeley, Dorn, Duncan, Levertov, and Olson headlined with Ginsberg at the Vancouver Poetry Conference of 1963. The Berkeley Poetry Conference of 1965 gathered an even larger roster by adding Wieners and numerous younger Bay Area poets to the schedule. In the 1960s, Dorn and Wieners facilitated a vibrant exchange with the British Poetry Revival, especially Tom Raworth and J. H. Prynne. Although Montreal poet Irving Layton had served on the editorial board of the *Black Mountain Review*, the number of collaborations with Canadians later grew by vast leaps thanks to *TISH* magazine in Vancouver and Coach House Press in Toronto. And in campus corridors? Because Black Mountain poets rigorously elaborated statements and manifestos about their practice and because they generated such a large critical body about one another (reviews, introductions, published correspondence), their reception by literary scholars was in many respects a matter of codifying an existing discourse. The 1970s witnessed special issues of the journal *boundary2* on Olson and Creeley and the first wave of monographs including Charles Altieri's *Enlarging the Temple: New Directions in American Poetry During the 1960s* (1979) and Don Byrd's *Charles Olson's Maximus* (1980). The college itself achieved mythic distinction thanks to Martin Duberman's *Black Mountain: An Exploration in Community* (1972), Mary Emma Harris's *The Arts at Black Mountain College* (1987), and more recently Vincent Katz's *Black Mountain College: Experiment in Art* (MIT, 2002). The regular editions of the poetry from independent, university, and large publishing houses were increasingly supplemented by biographies (Olson, Creeley, Dorn, Duncan, and Levertov), correspondence, and monographs, most recently Anne Day Dewey's *Beyond Maximus* (2007). The pressure to be included on syllabi was already evident in the 1970s when the Black Mountain poets assumed a crucial place in anthologies patently designed for undergraduate classrooms, such as Richard Ellmann's *Norton Anthology of Modern Poetry* (1973), in which page counts for Olson (12), Duncan (9), Levertov (10), Creeley (10), and Dorn (10) roughly competed with establishment icons Elizabeth Bishop (9), Randall Jarrell (14), Dylan Thomas (11), Adrienne Rich (12), and Sylvia Plath (11).

The poetic community sometimes viewed this academic assimilation as betrayal and grounds to reject their influence and teaching. Former Black Mountain student Fielding Dawson balked at Duberman, "They've made sleek and new that rough, old and irrational force which fought so hard to survive even itself, and they've dressed up the corpses for the marketplace" (Dawson 1973). Robert Grenier eulogized Olson in the first issue of *THIS* magazine, and he was a lifelong friend of Creeley, but he also issued a famous proclamation, "I HATE SPEECH," that was incommensurable with a projective poetics for which the unit of measurement was the breath. The Language poet Charles Bernstein faulted Olson's "excessive" historical allusions in The *Maximus Poems*: "The escalating plethora of proper names, chronologies, unsubstantiated references and quotes, shipping inventories, geographic data constantly distract: lead away from any grounding of the poem in the actual experience of words" (Bernstein 1986). Bernstein charges Olson with a nationalist agenda that is politically and ethically suspect: "The poem falls prey to the impulse to justify America by the appropriation and overlaying of privileged texts (such as the Hesiodic myths, so specifically rooted in their own geographical and historical context) that are ingeniously contorted to appear relevant but are only relevant with the wildest leap of Gnostic imagination" (Bernstein 1986).

The last decade of interest tends to address the structure of gender and cultural identity in Black Mountain poetry. Michael Davidson and Rachel Blau DuPlessis lead the way with feminist and queer interventions in the largely male ensembles, or what Davidson calls "compulsory homosociality" (Davidson 2004). DuPlessis has fundamentally intervened in the reception of Olson by demonstrating that his radicalism – even the critique of masculinity among his peers – still retains "the powers and privileges of normative manhood" (DuPlessis 2006). Turning to Creeley's *For Love*, DuPlessis discerns the pattern of "an antic, unbowed, playful, appropriative attitude to gender anxiety" where Creeley's markers of masculine vulnerability are converted into reclamations of power (DuPlessis 2012, 98 and 102). Other endeavors involve the historical recovery of neglected women artists and poets at Black Mountain, among them the poet Hilda Morley (Conniff 1993). Heriberto Yépez signals a postcolonial turn when he reads Olson's writing as "biocriticism of the geopolitical" (Yépez 2013). Finally, the field of disability studies has begun to consider the case of Larry Eigner, whose poetics operates less according to rules of representation of disabled experience or narrative, more as an ontology (Davidson 1999, Hart 2010, Luck 2012). As distance grows from the years of the college and the *Black Mountain Review*, it is less generational strife among practicing poets than such critical and historical analysis that sustains the ongoing interest in the poetry.

WORKS CITED

Allen, Donald M. 1958. Letter to Barney Rosset, 6 April 1958. Donald Allen Papers. MSS 3 Box 75 Folder 2. *Mandeville Special Collections Library.* San Diego: University of California, San Diego.

Allen, Donald M. ed. 1960. *The New American Poetry.* New York: Grove Press.

Bernstein, Charles. 1986. "Undone Business" in *Content's Dream: Essays 1975– 1984.* Los Angeles: Sun and Moon Press.

Butterick, George F. and Richard Blevins, eds. 1980–1996. *Charles Olson and Robert Creeley: The Complete Correspondence.* 10 volumes. Santa Barbara, CA: Black Sparrow Press.

Bertholf, Robert and Albert Gelpi, eds. 2004. *The Letters of Robert Duncan and Denise Levertov.* Stanford, CA: Stanford University Press.

Clark, Tom. 1991. *Charles Olson: The Allegory of a Poet's Life.* New York: Norton.

Conniff, Brian. 1993. "Reconsidering Black Mountain: The Poetry of Hilda Morley." *American Literature* 65.1: 117–30.

Corrigan, Matthew, ed. 1973–4. "Charles Olson: Essays, Reminiscences, Reviews," Special issue of *boundary 2* 2.1–2.

Creeley, Robert. 1953. *Divers Press Prospectus.* Mallorca: Divers Press.

"Response to Martin Duberman's interview questions on Black Mountain, from the late 1960's." http://writing.upenn.edu/pennsound/x/Creeley.php

2002. "Olson and Black Mountain College," in *Black Mountain College: Experiment in Art*. Ed. Vincent Katz. Cambridge, MA: MIT Press.

Davidson, Michael. 1999. "Missing Larry: The Poetics of Disability in the Work of Larry Eigner." *Sagetrieb* 18.1: 5–27.

2004. *Guys Like Use: Citing Masculinity in Cold War Poetics*. Chicago: University of Chicago Press.

Dawson, Fielding. 1973. *On Duberman's Black Mountain and B.H. Friedman's Biography of Jackson Pollock*. Toronto: Coach House Press.

Duberman, Marin. 1972. *Black Mountain: An Exploration in Community*. New York: W. W. Norton.

DuPlessis, Rachel Blau. 2006. "Manhood and its Poetic Projects: The Construction of Masculinity in the Counter-cultural Poetry of the U.S. 1950s." *Jacket* 31. Accessed August 10, 2013.

2012. *Purple Passages: Pound, Eliot, Zukofsky, Olson, Creeley, and the Ends of Patriarchal Poetry*. Iowa City: University of Iowa Press.

Ellmann, Richard and Robert O'Clair, eds. 1973. *Norton Anthology of Modern Poetry*. New York: Norton.

Glass, Loren. 2013. *Counter-Culture Colophone: Grove Press, Evergreen Review, and the Incorporation of the Avant-Garde*. Stanford, CA: Stanford University Press.

Hart, George. 2010. "'Enough Defined': Disability, Ecopoetics, and Larry Eigner." *Contemporary Literature* 51.1: 152–79.

Hallberg, Robert von. 1978. *Charles Olson: A Scholar's Art*. Cambridge, MA: Harvard University Press.

Harris, Mary Emma. 1987. *The Arts of Black Mountain College*. Cambridge, MA: MIT Press.

Katz, Vincent, ed. 2003. *Black Mountain College: An Experiment in Art*. Cambridge, MA: MIT Press.

Luck, Jessica Lewis. 2012. "Larry Eigner and the Phenomenology of Projected Verse," *Contemporary Literature* 53.3: 461–92.

Maud, Ralph and Sharon Thesen, eds. 1999. *Charles Olson and Frances Boldereff: A Modern Correspondence*. Hanover, NH: University Press of New England.

Maud, Ralph, ed. 2005. *Poet to Publisher: Charles Olson's Correspondence With Donald Allen*. Vancouver: Talonbooks.

Maud, Ralph. 2008. *Charles Olson at the Harbor*. Vancouver: Talonbooks.

Olson, Charles. 1947. *Call Me Ishmael*. New York: Reynal & Hitchcock.

1950. "Projective Verse vs. The Non-Projective." *Poetry New York* 3: 13–22.

Paul, Sherman. 1981. *The Lost America of Love: Rereading Robert Creeley, Robert Duncan, and Ed Dorn*. Baton Rouge: Louisiana State University Press.

Rumaker, Michael. 2003. *Black Mountain Days* Asheville, NC: Black Mountain Press.

Seelye, Catherine, ed. 1975. *Charles Olson and Ezra Pound: An Encounter at St. Elizabeths*. Grossmann: New York.

Smith, Rod, Peter Baker, and Kaplan Harris. 2014. *The Selected Letters of Robert Creeley*. Berkeley: University of California Press.

Spanos, William V., ed. 1978. "Robert Creeley: A Gathering," Special issue of *boundary 2* 6.3/7.1.

Yépez, Heriberto. 2013. *The Empire of Neomemory*. Translated by Jen Hofer, Christian Nagler, Brian Whitener. Oakland, CA: Chainlinks.

13

MARIA DAMON

Beat Poetry: HeavenHell USA,
1946–1965

> That silent beat makes the drumbeat, it makes the drum, it makes the
> beat. Without it there is no drum, no beat ... the silent beat is beaten by
> who is not beating the drum, his silent beat drowns out all the noise, it
> comes before and after every beat, you can hear it in the beatween, its
> sound is.
>
> Bob Kaufman (1967, "Oct. 5, 1963")

In the poem excerpted here, which doubled as a letter written to the *San
Francisco Chronicle*, African-American beat poet Bob Kaufman riffs on the
word "beat," as disillusionment with the social conditions he finds in San
Francisco after a devastating New York sojourn grinds up against his faith
in poetry, in jazz, in human emotion, and in the power of declaring himself
outside of society as a "not white" person – a condition for which he is
profoundly grateful. His otherworldly insistence on the silence of the beat
counters popular understanding (then and now) of the Beats as noisy senti-
mentalists, "holy barbarians" whose histrionic rooftop yawps were indeed
barbaric but whose sensibilities were holy only in their own misguided per-
ceptions (Podhoretz 1958, Lipton 1959). Kaufman does, however, ascribe to
himself as "Poet" the foundational role of prima causa, the underlying beat
itself. And more, he claims the silent beat behind and between the sounded
beat: the invisible hand, the maker that is the substance and ground of all
life. Kaufman points to and claims as his identity – indeed, his signature – a
central absence or, more properly, a plenitude that is not recognized as such:
the silence from which emerges and around which sound is organized; we
can usefully understand this silence as contradiction. This type of generative
oxymoron (silence/beat, abject/sacred, disillusionment/utopian strivings,
street vernacular/literary language, vulnerability/cool), in which a dialectical
synthesis is resisted in the interest of prolonging a productive tension, characterizes Beat writing. Although most of the Beat writers we have come to
recognize as "important" (Gary Snyder, Allen Ginsberg, William Burroughs,

Jack Kerouac, the latter of whom continues to appeal stubbornly and complicatedly to a primarily popular rather than scholarly readership) were white (often in qualified ways) and, indeed, seemingly rarely silent, the predicament Kaufman sets forth here can be read as paradigmatic of some crucial Beat concerns, however buried they may be beneath the accrual of myth, bombast, and hagiography/opprobrium. In a sense, Kaufman here calls the Beat literary movement out by pointing to its failings: in trying to get behind the façade of the desperately convention-bound 1950s, they simply erected another cultural bifurcation. Kaufman's poetics were more invested in *poeisis*, that is, the pre-formal "real" of an organic making-process, than in poetry per se. And that "real" was intimately connected to his subject position, that of a Black man in a still-segregated United States in which "beat" meant beatings and lynchings in addition to the backbone of bebop, the then-experimental edge of jazz, and the abjection of voluntary poverty.

By suggesting that there is something behind "the [perceptible] beat," Kaufman's poem complicates conventional understanding of beat literature's "nakedness" – the aspiration to reveal, the hope that what you see is what you get – along multiple axes. Contrary to the forthright "candor" (a key term, along with "nakedness," in Allen Ginsberg's lexicon) that Beat writing strove for, Kaufman insists on a kernel of unsayability, of silent solitudes "crowded with loneliness" (Kaufman 1965, 15) of unassimilable, underlying experience that gives rise to all the music, the pulsations of quotidian life and its resulting apprehensible art, the base and superstructure of life in the United States, circa 1946–65. Perhaps this is what post-Freudian psychoanalysts call the "real"; if so, Kaufman is claiming "realness" as his identity. Looking at the Beat generation, a Negrophiliac but primarily white art movement, from an oblique angle, as Kaufman does, brings unexpected and perhaps counter-intuitive insights that can enrich our perspective on what is still – in spite of a by now decade or two of serious scholarship on the subject – a somewhat sensationalized and stereotyped countercultural community and its artifacts.

The postwar United States was a dramatic collision, and, metonymizing the nature of domestic arrangements in the era, it was an unhappy "marriage of Heaven and Hell": a figure that, thanks to Allen Ginsberg's passion for William Blake, suggests itself as paradigmatic for the Beats' project (Blake 1793). Indeed, as Jack Spicer – one of the three most prominent members of the San Francisco Renaissance, a movement that had a relationship of adjacency to the Beats – remarked, "[Bohemia] is a Hell full of windows into Heaven" (Spicer c. 1951–2). Against the tragic/triumphant contradiction of the United States' emergence as an economic and military superpower out of the ashes of the atom bomb and the crematoria, the Beats posited their own oxymoronic yoking: drugs and spirituality, purity and abjection, voluntary poverty in a nation of dollars, the derangement of the senses as response to the strict regulation of pragmatism, the street as a viable alternative to the university.

The Cold War atmosphere dominating the United States in the 1950s and early 1960s lent itself well to stark political and ideological divisions, even as a powerfully emergent middle class softened class divisions and enhanced upward social mobility through the democratization of education and home ownership via the GI bill, which subsidized veterans' college costs as well as home and property mortgages. Economic expansion and enhanced opportunities were accompanied by a narrowing of possibilities in the world of ideas, culture, and life choices. In the wake of the war, with fascism ostensibly safely defeated, and particularly after the revelations of the true conditions of Stalin's USSR after his death in 1952, communism was cast as the ultimate evil, and loyalty oaths to the U.S. constitution were instituted as criteria for employment in many public institutions (including public universities) even though a few decades previously a range of socialist and communist parties had participated fully, albeit oppositionally, in American public life. One could say that in the wake of the Nazi genocide of Jews, Romany people, and attacks on leftists, and queers, the U.S. government – in the grip of demagogue Senator Joseph McCarthy – sought to administer a social death to Communists and their sympathizers, while formal and informal policies encouraged state-sanctioned homophobia and at least socially, if not legally, acceptable anti-Semitism: All this added to the already racially segregated nature of American life.

This retreat from tolerance of political difference accompanied an ideological expansion of the idyll of the suburbs, aided by Henry Ford's undermining of public transportation systems in favor of a national highway system that enabled, on the one hand, the development of relatively isolated middle-class communities that were neither urban nor rural, and on the other, the wild cross-country rides chronicled in, most famously, *On the Road* (Kerouac 1957). With the collapse of the political Left, the only revolutionary alternatives rested with what we now call "lifestyle," a depoliticized revolution against engagement itself; a once-proud potential labor force now saw labor, whether as management, manual worker, or the emerging corporate culture (epitomized by the "man in the gray flannel suit," the responsible paterfamilias, etc.), as an undertaking bereft of promise or fulfillment – a waste of time. The term "alienation" migrated from a Marxist lexicon for labor conditions under capitalism to become a psychological descriptor for an individual who cannot "adjust" to his or her societal circumstances. Men who were slated for middle-class status and all the constrictions that entailed could only dissent by "dropping out," a kind of passive resistance to the military-industrial complex that increasingly came to define the discourse of the public sphere, and women who had been active in the workforce during the war were now expected to aspire solely to suburban domesticity. The Beats substituted their own masculine ideal: flawed but potent (non-normative) masculinities, such as queerness or athletic powers, good looks, non-normative intelligence, non-conformist cool, off-beat verbal inventiveness.

Contemporary feminist scholars such as Barbara Ehrenreich (1986) and Elaine Tyler May (1990) have written sensitively about, respectively, the rebellious options open to upwardly mobile men (corporate shill on the one hand, playboy or beat on the other), and the trope of "containment" – a strategy to prevent the spread of communism, of the "disease" of homosexuality, and of the oozing ungovernability of unfettered female sexuality – that came to characterize both foreign and domestic policy on the one hand, and the return of restrictions placed on middle-class women and their opportunities "outside the home" on the other. A bohemian counterculture became visible as one of the few modes of expressive culture that did not conform to the stultifying options available. Not surprisingly, "loneliness" became a key trope in anthropology, sociology, philosophy, and literature, and made its way into Beat thematics and sensibility: Bob Kaufman's first book was entitled *Solitudes Crowded with Loneliness* (Kaufman 1965), and John Wieners's explorations of devastating emotional isolation continue to reverberate, to the degree that he has been called the most "destitute" English-language poet (Sutherland 2012). The ways in which language-making served as self-soothing practice as well as companionship worked in tandem and in tension with the Beats' great emphasis on community. As a desirable alternative to the fully enfranchised but "hollow [white] men" of the 1950s and 1960s, white male Beats, envious of what they saw as alternative embodiments, were drawn to deterritorialized not-quite-people: Blacks, women, migrant workers, and so on, and figured them as angels, ghosts, or shadows. However, as Kaufman makes explicit in "Bagel Shop Jazz," these "shadow people" suffered their own "secret terrible hurts" with stoic cool, moving uneasily as mascots/objects among their white confrères.

At the mainstream level, the poetic landscape reflected this inward turning, suburban isolationism and containment in its valuing of tight, highly wrought lyric verse. Academically prized poetry, or what contemporary poet Charles Bernstein has catchily termed "official verse culture," valued formal control and hermeticism, and politically conservative poet-scholars like Allen Tate, Robert Penn Warren, and John Crowe Ransom were in ascendancy (Bernstein 2001, 246). The poem as "well-wrought urn," with its intimations of (immortality as) stasis and containment (the ur-trope of the Cold War), was presented as ideal to young aspiring poets in the academy. Beat poets, as might be expected, vehemently rejected as claustrophobic and ethically untenable this kind of formalism, primarily practiced by the New Critics, Fugitive Poets, Southern Agrarians, and other movements then dominating the academic poetry scene, that – taking their cue from T. S. Eliot's concept of the "objective correlative" and disavowal of the personal in "Tradition and the Individual Talent" – emphasized the autonomy of the work of art, its compressed, intricate, and depersonalized nature, and the "dramatic irony" that arose from its internal and strictly textual contradictions (Damon 2012, 130). "I don't like dreams where a right sound / Can put a minor emotion in amber" (Spicer 1980, 84) wrote Jack Spicer, referring to the ossified (indeed "lapidary") nature of the lyric whose musical structure dignifies relatively trivial inner events.

This protest against closure and purity as glib evasions of the complexities of life, language, and the relationship between them took a range of forms and subjects. The Beats as well as members of the San Francisco Renaissance countered the sterility they experienced in academically sanctioned poetry with tropes of nakedness, madness and abjection, ecstasy, suggestions of underworldly activities coupled with otherworldly aspirations (a coupling signified by the word "beat" itself, in its reference to "beatitude" "beat it," and being "beat down to [one's] socks," in the words of Herbert Huncke, the queer hustler and petty criminal who inspired Burroughs and Ginsberg), and the driving rhythms and improvisational flair of jazz or vernacular street speech mixed with modernist references. The Beat personality was a combination of an aloof, stoic, omniscient cool and "ignu": Ginsberg's term for an impish, childlike holy fool sensibility epitomized by, for example, Charlie Chaplin, Harpo Marx, Beat actor Taylor Meade or even Peter Orlovsky, Ginsberg's own longtime partner. The naïf coupled with the laconic hipster or the logorheaic, confessionally compulsive, "angelheaded" poet best embodied by Ginsberg himself, or his amphetamine-driven compatriot the "outsider writer" Neal Cassady, countered images of the poet as polysyllabic but perfectly controlled, the tweedy professor who always knew what he was talking about and was not interested in expanding that knowledge or putting himself at risk by venturing beyond the safety of verse as formal container. Formally, the Beats and the Renaissance poets favored long lines, emulating Whitman's expansiveness (Allen Ginsberg, Robert Duncan); avoidance of traditional verse structures (with the notable exception of Helen Adam's eerie poems, modeled on the supernatural Scots ballads she grew up with but updated to include contemporary subject matter such as heroin addiction and Beatnik life); short, broken lines or even words (Wieners, Spicer,

Joanne Kyger) that fragmented language itself at the level of the phoneme in order to both open up words and defamiliarize them, drawing attention to their obdurate materiality. San Francisco Renaissance poets especially used the concept of the "open series" to resist the tight, one- or two-page poem that suggested false resolution through bon mots and rhythmically pleasing aperçus: Robert Duncan's ongoing "The Structure of Rime," "Passages," and "The H.D. Book" were composed over the course of forty years and were as yet – deliberately – incomplete at the time of his death in 1989; Boston-based poet Stephen Jonas's "Orgasms" and "Exercises for the Ear," and Spicer's belief in books over poems, in collectivities over singularities – that communities of poems need each other as much as communities of people do – form a powerful argument through example of alternatives to the tightly contained lyric, although many among the San Francisco Renaissance poets, especially Spicer and Duncan in their early work, demonstrate mastery of that form as well. Surrealistic imagery (Kaufman, Ted Joans, LeRoi Jones/ Amiri Baraka, Philip Lamantia, Lawrence Ferlinghetti, Ginsberg, Gregory Corso), jazz (Kaufman, Joans, Jones/Baraka, Kerouac, ruth weiss, Diane di Prima, Ray Bremser, David Meltzer, among others), queer love and sex (anticipating the emergence of gay liberation) (Ginsberg, James Broughton, Wieners, Duncan, Spicer, Robin Blaser), unorthodox domestic arrangements and frank eroticism (di Prima, Duncan, Ginsberg, Lenore Kandel), drug addiction or experimentation (Wieners, Ginsberg, Kaufman), and squalor all featured as preferred thematic or imagistic touchstones, while often the language worked both to ground itself in street vernacular and to disorient through experimentation – Arthur Rimbaud's mandate to "derange all the senses" in order to be "absolutely modern" was taken to heart, to varying degrees, both experientially and textually. A belief in the authenticity of the "self" (with, of course, some complexity, complication, and friction, as Kaufman's insistence on a beat behind the beat demonstrates) meant that techniques of dissociation and defamiliarization could not simply be surface tricks to achieve a novel literary effect; they had to come from putting oneself at risk of actual dissociation, "madness" and then "candor" about it. (Both these terms are Ginsberg's.) However, not surprisingly, the very attempt to make the signified mesh perfectly with the signifier led to crises in stability and sanity – loss of "self" by putting too much pressure on the concept. The Beat path is strewn with tragedy and waste, much of it due to the unacknowledged impossibility of baring all, especially for those who, like Kaufman, inherited a socio-historical legacy of pain that could not be simply addressed by personal confession and social transgression. The unspeakable – or the real, the beat behind/between the beat – was the suffering of the many American underclasses, whose existence went largely unacknowledged in the 1950s–1960s public discourse, and for all its attempts to voice some of this suffering, the Beat movement succeeded primarily in romanticizing it as a literary and lived gesture that merely exacerbated the untenability of the yoking of Heaven and Hell.

The inevitably impossible attempt to reconcile these polarities also drew on French existentialism, which, along with certain accouterments of beat attire (the beret, for example, as a symbol of bohemian dissent), made its way to the United States in the postwar return of veterans and the influx of refugees and immigrants. The same trajectory held for psychoanalysis and psychoanalytic theory via the Jewish intelligentsia fleeing Europe before, during, and immediately after the war. Both existentialism and psychoanalysis emphasized individual rather than class struggle, and the struggle was to find meaning in the anomie of a post-atomic life without conceding to a newly consumerist public sphere, rather than achieving economic and social justice. Both of these approaches to the inner life emphasized spontaneity: Psychoanalysis, for Beat purposes, depended on uncensored introspective speech – "candor" in the form of a flow of words, aimed at unmasking secrets or mutable truths concealed even from oneself – while existentialism, as well as a street version of hipster existentialism, focused on action.

A third strain of philosophical influence from abroad was that of Buddhism, particularly Zen, which entered the United States from the West Coast, initially via Chinese and Japanese immigrants in the early part of the twentieth century, but also from U.S. war veterans returning from duty in the East after WWII. Figures such as Gary Snyder, Philip Whalen (who became a Zen priest and abbot), Lew Welch, Ginsberg, and, less seriously but with more popular impact, Kerouac studied and helped to popularize the meditation practices, the philosophy of spontaneous insight (and hence spontaneous writing, epitomized by the axiom "first thought best thought"), and interdependence of phenomena of East Asian Buddhism. This turn to Eastern perspectives was a key factor in reconciling the vexed issue of the "self," as by dissolving a faith in the static" "self or identity one transcends the painful division of "inauthentic" self – the dreaded "phony" or that company man in gray – and the "real" self that cannot fit into an overly rigid society (the division between appearances and reality, signifier and signified) is obviated.

As for English and U.S. American influences, African-American culture – especially music, speech, and vernacular culture – on the one hand and the Romanticism of Thoreau, Poe, Melville, and especially Whitman, as well as that of Blake, Keats, and Shelley, on the other hand, helped to define both philosophical and literary antecedents. And clearly, the French *maudit* tradition of Francois Villon, Charles Baudelaire, Lautréamont, Antonin Artaud, and

especially the teenaged Arthur Rimbaud, whose outlaw sensibilities and dis-
solute lifestyles, combined with otherworldly sensitivity, laid the template for
much beat life, poetry, and poetics. All of these, mixed with an appreciation of
the multiple vernaculars of the "old, weird America" – new to them – inspired
Beat poetry and Beat affect. As might be imagined, the Beats preferred to
deploy a widely eclectic lexicon and linguistic sensibility that obliquely drew
from a host of sublanguages and argots that reflected their ethnic roots: French-
Canadian joual, Yiddish, paisano Italian refracted through jive talk, the language of Black hipsters and musicians, the drug subculture, Neal Cassady's
drifter-con-man hobo talk as poetic media, mixed with the emerging ad-speak
of Madison Avenue and the social clichés of the time.

While the West Coast Beats and San Francisco Renaissance enjoyed a
relationship of adjacency and rubbed elbows at some of the same bars,
cafés, and nightclubs in North Beach and found refuge in the city's history of
anarcho-socialism and ludic political activism, there were significant distinctions with regard to style, poetics, aesthetic values, and world view. While
Walt Whitman was an object of affection for both groups, he served as a
model primarily for the Beats in his expansive embrace of the nation and his
democratic range; among the San Francisco Renaissance poets, or at least
Jack Spicer, there was suspicion of his populist optimism. The 1950s homoerotic experience with the cruelties of social ostracism precluded such easy
democratic utopianism as Whitman seemed to embody. Closer to home both
temporally and spatially, Kenneth Rexroth, who predated both movements
by a generation and was regarded by them, with Oedipal ambivalence, as a
forefather both supportive and limiting, conducted experiments with reading imagistic, free verse poetry to a jazz accompaniment, held philosophical-
political salons in his home, and presided over the famous reading at the Six
Gallery at which Ginsberg debuted his most famous work, "Howl," which
became the subject of a landmark censorship trial after its publication.
Ginsberg's notoriously incendiary reading has overshadowed the other five
readers who also participated in the event: Jack Spicer, Michael McClure,
Philip Whalen, Philip Lamantia, and Gary Snyder, all of whom went on
to make serious lifelong careers of poetry. The San Francisco Renaissance
poets, who actually considered their inaugural moment to be in Berkeley,
in 1946, where Robin Blaser, Robert Duncan, and Jack Spicer were students, were, according to Richard Cándida Smith (1996), less averse than
the Beats to domesticity, although their domesticity was of a homoerotic
nature, and slightly embarrassed by Beat excesses of personal melodrama.
In the last poem he wrote, Jack Spicer famously criticized what he saw as
Ginsberg's rise to celebrity status using a glib philosophy of universal love
(epitomized by Ginsberg's having been elected to represent the Kral Majales,

King of the May, by Czech students at a major festival in Soviet-dominated Czechoslovakia in 1965):

> If the [Czech police] had attacked
> The kind of love (not sex but love), you gave the one hundred
>   thousand students I'd have been very glad. And loved the
>   policemen.

(Spicer 1975)

The title of this group of poems, "Ten Poems for Downbeat," suggests some of Spicer's exasperation with the already tired tropes of beatdom. If some of the Beats were "queer," misfit outsiders in the idiom of the day, the San Francisco Renaissance poets were "gay," seeing themselves as belonging to a community, however "half-hid," as Whitman characterized "manly love" in his "Democratic Vistas," an essay that makes the bold claim that homoerotic affection underlies and is the foundation of American democracy (Whitman 1982). The concept of a "gay community" was barely emergent; the first gay community center opened in 1966 in San Francisco, almost twenty years after the San Francisco Renaissance poets recognized themselves as a community formation. While the road was an ur-trope for the Beats, the home was sacred space for the San Francisco Renaissance poets. Companionship, friendship, community of poems and of people were common themes in their work: Jack Spicer devoted an entire book, *Admonitions,* to letters to friends, in which he spelled out his poetics and closely related philosophy of friendship. Robin Blaser's lines sum up the poetry/politics/friendship continuum thus: "The clown of dignity sits in a tree. / The clown of games hangs there too. / Which is which or where they go / the point is to make others see / That two men in a tree is clearly / the same thing as poetry" (Blaser 2009).

Although they moved in a cultural and domestic environment that included freelance intellectuals like Paul Goodman and Philip K. Dick (both were at one time roommates of Jack Spicer or Robert Duncan), the core San Francisco Renaissance poets considered their intellectual and aesthetic genealogy to be based at the University of California, Berkeley, where they had studied with the poet Josephine Miles and the medievalist intellectual historian Ernst Kantorowicz. Both of these figures made a deep impression on Blaser, Duncan, and Spicer, the former for her precise, Dickinsonian poetics, and the latter in his connection to the legendary German symbolist poet Stefan George, whose elitist, secretive, and homosocial/homoerotic circle of intellectuals and writers (known as the *Georgekreis*) inspired the young U.S. poets in spite of its eventual fascistic overtones and connections with pre-WWII national socialism. The resonance of George in the life of the principals of the San Francisco Renaissance is so strong that the term

Spicerkreis has emerged in contemporary scholarship on these poets. The overlap of Whitman's "half-hid warp" of homoerotic masculine friendship and the *Georgekreis's* "secret Germany," despite the former's rough populist democratic expansiveness and the latter's exclusive, quasi-mystical purism lay in their mutual devotion to masculine homoeroticism as "the real behind the real," subtending a fierce nationalism. Although both Kantorowicz and Spicer, as employees of the University of California, refused to take the requisite McCarthyite loyalty oath to the U.S. government (which refusal led to Kantorowicz's departure to Princeton and to Spicer's dropping out of his doctoral program in linguistics at the ABD stage); despite Blaser's (and other poets and artists of the movement, including Stan Persky, Russell FitzGerald, and George Stanley) later departure for Canada, where he spent the remainder of his life; and despite the decades-long critique Robert Duncan launched against the Vietnam War and other U.S. imperialisms in his "Passages" series, spanning the publication of *Bending the Bow* (1968), *Ground Work I: Before the War* (1984), and *Ground Work II: In the Dark* (1986), the complex and often internally contradictory nationalisms of these dissenting communities of poets deserves nuanced critical attention. The San Francisco Renaissance poets were "older" Americans than the Beats, many of whom were first-generation immigrants whose parents had come through Ellis Island or other points of entry in then-recent history: Italians, Jews, Greeks, and so forth, with a far more fraught relationship to both the Europe of World War II (David Meltzer in particular, in the retrospective *Beat Thing*, has stressed the Jewish genocide in Europe as a backdrop for Beat emergence) and to the New World. The Berkeley/San Francisco Renaissance poets as a whole were far less invested in African-American culture and in the vernacular of the street, and more attuned to issues of sexuality and gender. Women were not excluded from participation as equals as they tended to be, with very few exceptions (mostly just Diane di Prima), in Beat circles. (Ginsberg very explicitly and uncritically, in later years, identified the Beats as a "boy gang.") Joanne Kyger, Helen Adam, and Madeline Gleason experimented with gendered forms of silence-breaking and myth, expanding the possibilities of contemporary poetry into koan-as-poem, traditional balladry, and performance. In addition to the University of California, Berkeley, the Six Gallery, and City Lights Bookstore – whose press inaugurated the concept of high-end literary paperbacks designed to be carried in the back pocket of the wayfaring bohemian poet – the Poetry Center at San Francisco State University also became a focal institution, which, through workshops featuring local poets and lecture/reading series bringing out-of-towners to the Bay Area, helped to establish San Francisco as a leading literary center for writing. Although City Lights had a relationship to the academy, it was certainly not dependent on academia for either aesthetics or social infrastructure and in fact thrived on an ethos resistant to what Duncan referred to in one of his letters to Spicer as the "campiss" atmosphere that encouraged that rotting "English Department of the soul" (Spicer 1975). Other tactical institutions that sprang up in response to the need for a spontaneous literature included a number of mimeographed literary magazines, such as *Beatitude* (co-founded by Kaufman, Bill Margolis and Ginsberg), *Measure* (Wieners), *J* (Spicer), and small presses like White Rabbit (Joe Dunn, a protégé of Spicer's), Black Sparrow Press (John Martin and Graham Mackintosh, the latter also a pro-tégé of Spicer's), Enkidu Surrogate (Duncan), and Oyez (Robert Hawley, an alumnus of Black Mountain College).

And San Francisco was not the sole site of Beat literary activity, though New York was the only other city of comparable intensity for the key poets. One could identify Columbia University, where Ginsberg met Kerouac and Lucien Carr, who in turn introduced him to Neal Cassady and William Burroughs, in the mid-1940s as the Beat counterpart to the San Francisco Renaissance's Berkeley, the latter so significant that Jack Spicer once gave his birthdate/place as 1946, Berkeley, CA. The Times Square underworld of hustlers and addicts complemented Harlem uptown and Greenwich Village further downtown as sites of alternative literary and cultural production as well as a greater tolerance for non-normative domestic relations whether same-sex, cross-racial, open, polyamorous, or transient. Although figures like Allen Ginsberg moved from coast to coast frequently enough to warrant status as both a San Francisco presence and a New York figure, others were fairly rooted despite occasional forays.

Associated with New York were Gregory Corso, an autodidactic ex-con urchin whom Ginsberg met and befriended in a Village lesbian bar; Diane di Prima, descendant of Italian anarchists and labor activists; LeRoi Jones/ Amiri Baraka (who could be productively considered to participate in mul-tiple categories and communities of U.S. poetry across his many decades of creative activity), like Ted Joans, Stephen Jonas, and Bob Kaufman, among the few African-American writers who are now recognized to have actively participated in the scene, although others, like James Baldwin (who became well known) were present either through publication, socializing, or both; self-taught literary ex-con Ray Bremser, his college-educated wife Bonnie Bremser (Brenda Frazer); and of course all the lesser-known writers and literary activists who helped to produce broadsides, collate journals and bulk-mail them, cook dinners, host readings, and so forth. Among the key presses of the East Coast scene were Totem (LeRoi Jones and Hettie Jones), Grove (Barney Rossett and Richard Seaver) with its Evergreen imprint, New Directions (James Laughlin), the periodicals *Yugen* (LeRoi Jones and

Hettie Jones), *The Floating Bear* (LeRoi Jones and di Prima), *SET* (Gerrit Lansing), *Origin* (Cid Corman), *Kulchur* (Lita Hornick), and many others. Boston (Stephen Jonas, Cid Corman, John Wieners again, along with the Spicer/Duncan/Blaser trio, who spent a few significant months there), Denver (as a site for inspiration through Neal Cassady's and Lucien Carr's roots rather than through a fully articulated writing community, though the Jack Kerouac School of Disembodied Poetics, the poetics department of Naropa University in Boulder, Colorado, was founded in 1974 by Ginsberg and Anne Waldman and has continued to flourish, as has its Manhattan counterpart, the Poetry Project at St. Mark's Church); Los Angeles (Stuart Perchick, et al.); and Chicago (*Big Table, The Chicago Review*) helped to create a national web of beat activity.

Although the Beat poets are better known to the general public than the San Francisco/Berkeley Renaissance poets, the latter have been far more easily assimilated into serious scholarship and analysis. Starting in the early to mid-1990s, a major push in academic interest in the beats was initiated through a series of conferences, a traveling art exhibit sponsored by the Whitney Museum, and eventually the formation of a Beat Studies Association, now an academic subdivision of the relatively conservative American Literature Association. There is reason to be dubious about the continued hagiographic strand of beat scholarship, but pressure that exposes the limits of the beats' own claims while understanding in critical detail the value of an exuberant literature that counters the mainstream, and "high IQ, low-virtuosity" (Ratliff 2013) creative practice is most welcome.

WORKS CITED

Bernstein, Charles. 2001. "The Academy in Peril." *Content's Dream: Essays 1974–1985*. Evanston, IL: Northwestern University Press.

Blake, William. 1793. *The Marriage of Heaven and Hell.*

Blaser, Robin. 2009. "Cups 1." *The Holy Forest: Collected Poems of Robin Blaser.* Berkeley: University of California Press.

Cándida Smith, Richard. 1996. *Utopia and Dissent.* Berkeley: University of California Press.

Damon, Maria. 2012. "Beat Poetry." *Princeton Encyclopedia of Poetry and Poetics.* Ed. Roland Greene et al. Princeton, NJ: Princeton University Press. 130–1.

Duncan, Robert. 1968. *Bending the Bow.* New York: New Directions Press.

 1984. *Ground Work I: Before the War.* New York: New Directions Press.

 1986. *Ground Work II: In the Dark.* New York: New Directions Press.

 2011. *The H.D. Book.* Berkeley: University of California Press.

Ehrenreich, Barbara. 1987. *The Hearts of Men: American Dreams and the Flight from Commitment.* New York: Anchor.

Ginsberg, Allen. 1965. "Kral Majales." In Ginsberg, Allen, *Selected Poems 1947–1995.* New York: Harper Collins, 2001, p. 147.

Kaufman, Bob. 1965. "Bagel Shop Jazz." *Solitudes Crowded with Loneliness*. New York: New Directions Press. 15.

1967. "October 5, 1963, Letter to the San Francisco Chronicle," *Golden Sardine*. San Francisco: City Lights Books. 80–1.

Lipton, Lawrence. 1959. *Holy Barbarians*. New York: Grove.

Mailer, Norman. 1992. "Hipsters." *Advertisements for Myself*. Cambridge, MA: Harvard University Press.

May, Elaine Tyler. 1990. *Homeward Bound: American Families In The Cold War Era*. New York: Basic.

Meltzer, David. 2004. *Beat Thing*. Albuquerque, NM: La Alameda Press.

Podhoretz, Norman. "The Know-Nothing Bohemians." *Partisan Review* 2: 25 (Spring), 1958: 305–18.

Ratliff, Ben. October 27, 2013. "Lou Reed Dies at 71: Outsider Whose Dark, Lyrical Vision Helped Shape Rock n' Roll." *New York Times*. http://www.nytimes.com/2013/10/28/arts/music/lou-reed-dies-at-71.html?_r=0

Sutherland, Keston. "The World and John Wieners." *World Picture* 7, Autumn 2012. http://worldpicturejournal.com/WP_7/Sutherland.html

Spicer, Jack. 1975. *The Collected Books of Jack Spicer*. Ed. Robin Blaser. Santa Barbara, CA: Black Sparrow.

"Letter to Gary Bottone." c. 1951–2. *Poetry*. July-August 2008.

"Last Hokku." 1980. *One Night Stand and Other Poems*. Bolinas, CA: Grey Fox. 84.

1975. "Ten Poems for Downbeat." *The Collected Books of Jack Spicer*. Ed. Robin Blaser. Santa Barbara, CA: Black Sparrow. 263–7.

Wieners, John. 1986. *Selected Poems 1958–1964*. Ed. Raymond Foye. Santa Rosa, CA: Black Sparrow.

Whitman, Walt. 1982. "Democratic Vistas." *Whitman: Poetry and Prose*. Ed. Justin Kaplan. New York: Library of America. 929–94.

14

EVIE SHOCKLEY

The Black Arts Movement
and Black Aesthetics

The title poem of Sonia Sanchez's 1969 debut collection, *Home Coming*, like other oft-cited poems by her Black Arts Movement (BAM) contemporaries, stages a confrontation between two world views. One is implicitly "white," picked up in "college," and brought with the speaker in a "tourist"-style visit to the neighborhood in which she grew up, where it leads her to look unfeelingly upon "all / the niggers killing / themselves with" illegal drugs (Sanchez 1978, 3). The other world view, explicitly "black," is constructed as mature, authentic, and wise (rather than educated), giving voice to the true homecoming:

> now woman
> i have returned
> leaving behind me
> all those hide and
> seek faces peeling
> with freudian dreams.
> this is for real.
> black
> niggers
> my beauty.
> (Sanchez 1978, 3)

Rejecting the world view urged on her by her college education and "the newspapers," which is deemed unreliable and disconnected from reality, the speaker is now equipped to revise her view of her neighbors. She repeats the racial epithet deployed dismissively in the poem's opening, but this time lovingly envelopes it within lines that value who and what she sees, visually and conceptually aligning "black" with "my beauty" – the "my" claiming not only her own "blackness," but also theirs, and them.

What Sanchez and some of her contemporaries theorized in poetry, Addison Gayle theorized in prose. In his 1971 essay, "Cultural Strangulation: Black Literature and the White Aesthetic," Gayle counters the "expected opposition to the concept of a 'Black Aesthetic'" with a telling recitation of the history of "the white aesthetic" (Gayle 1994, 207). Beginning with Platonic philosophy and running through the English literary tradition, Gayle traces the idealization of the color white as symbolizing purity, goodness, and beauty and the demonization of the color black as taint, evil, and ugliness, across centuries of European thought. His point – neither strictly racial nor unconnected to the racial politics of his era – focuses on the realm of culture, which cannot be understood, in the context of circum-atlantic modernity, without reference to race. In the wake of the 1968 Kerner Commission Report, which studied the mid-sixties urban riots, one could not act on the flawed assumption that there was a single America with "a common cultural heredity," he argues (ibid.). Recognition of the cultural specificity of aesthetic standards was for Gayle a crucial first step in relieving African American writers from the burden of external (and internalized) aesthetic criteria that consistently degraded the experiences and subjectivity of black people. The cultural nationalist mantra "Black is beautiful" was a starting point, in Gayle's analysis, for the long, hard work of developing a criticism – an aesthetics – that, taking black culture as the primary frame of reference, could do justice to African American artistry.

This mid-twentieth-century moment was not the first time that the relationship of race and culture to the evaluation of work by black U.S. artists had been interrogated. W. E. B. Du Bois's 1926 essay "Criteria of Negro Art" proposed that the use of art as "positive propaganda" in the struggle of "black folk" to gain recognition of their full humanity and citizenship rights was a necessary counter to the racist propaganda found in much white American art (Du Bois 1986, 1000). The "black public," he asserted, "must come to the place where the work of art when it appears is reviewed and acclaimed by our own free and unfettered judgment," which required them to "make [them]selves free of mind, proud of body and just of soul" (Du Bois 1986, 1001–2). His words resonated with Langston Hughes's own 1926 essay, "The Negro Artist and the Racial Mountain," in which Hughes defended his generation's intent to dance to the beat of their own "tom-tom" as part of their right as artists to fully utilize their cultural inheritance ("Negro Artist").

From the vantage point of the mid-1960s, these New Negro Renaissance-era declarations appeared inefficacious, if they were remembered at all. After three decades during which barely a handful of African American writers were recognized by the American literary establishment (primarily Richard Wright, James Baldwin, Gwendolyn Brooks, and Ralph Ellison), the time was ripe for establishing their own "Black Aesthetic" standards.[1] Not only did literary-critical conditions call for it; the racial politics and the socioeconomic situation of African Americans demanded it. The Civil Rights Movement's successes and failures had enabled the wide dissemination of a new political program: Black Power. Notwithstanding rhetorical and visual cues to the contrary, Black Power was less about separatism than independence and self-determination, less about destruction and violence than immediate and dramatic sociopolitical change. Black Power politics spoke to African Americans, particularly younger ones, who had grown up outside the South in unprecedented numbers and were impatient with the slow gains made through nonviolent protest, judicial campaigns, and legislative lobbying. Civil Rights organizations that had employed these relatively conservative strategies, sometimes with notable success, were being compared negatively to organizations with more radical, less conciliatory politics, such as the Oakland-based Black Panther Party for Self-Defense and the Stokely Carmichael-led Student Nonviolent Coordinating Committee (SNCC), by then an exclusively black group. The riots that punctured the years following Malcolm X's assassination, flaming up in cities from Newark to Detroit to Los Angeles, manifested evolving attitudes and energies that Black Power politics sought to guide into liberatory channels (Collins and Crawford 2006, 1–8).

Where Black Power offered a political program, Black Arts – "the aesthetic and spiritual sister of the Black Power concept" (Neal 1994, 184) – engaged the political stakes of the cultural arena. Among the earliest, most powerful and influential of the voices calling for a Black Aesthetic were poets LeRoi Jones (Amiri Baraka) and Larry Neal. Part of Jones/Baraka's power stemmed from his visibility; he had already made a name for himself among a cross-section of variously counterculture poets (Beat, New York School, Black Mountain, and surrealist). Living in Greenwich Village, Jones voraciously read and created poetry, publishing such associates as Allen Ginsberg, Jack Kerouac, Diane di Prima, A. B. Spellman, Frank O'Hara, Barbara Guest, Ted Joans, Phillip Lamantia, Charles Olson, and Ed Dorn.[2] His first play, *Dutchman*, produced off-Broadway in early 1964, had earned him an Obie Award and the approval of the critical establishment. Thus, his decision to act on his growing disillusionment with American society by cutting ties with white bohemia and relocating to Harlem – not instigated but cemented by Malcolm X's assassination – reverberated widely. The Black Arts Repertory Theater and School (BARTS), which he founded upon his arrival uptown, was a vibrant, culturally significant institution; although short-lived, it has had a long afterlife.

In this new context, Jones/Baraka worked to make the aesthetics announced in his prose and his poetry a lived practice. Calling for a "Revolutionary Theatre," he invoked an aesthetic that "should force change" – indeed, "should be change" (Jones 1966, 210). This art "should stagger through our universe correcting, insulting, preaching, spitting craziness – but a craziness taught to us in our most rational moments" (Jones 1966, 211). Jones conceived of an art that, informed by Wittgenstein's insight that "ethics and aesthetics are one," would value the real: "We will talk about the world, and the preciseness with which we are able to summon the world will be our art" (Jones 1966, 212). His unforgettable poem "Black Art" opens with such a summoning – "Poems are bullshit unless they are / teeth or trees or lemons piled / on a step. Or black ladies dying / of men leaving nickel hearts / beating them down" (Baraka 1995, 142) – which renders even abstractions, like nurture or heartbreak, in concrete, organic terms. "Black Art," in other words, would provide African Americans with what Neal called "a new synthesis; a new sense of literature as a *living* reality" connected to their own experiences (Neal 2007, 654).

Neal, a poet more widely known as a theorist, looked to black speech and music as models for poetry seeking to embody a Black Aesthetic. In "And Shine Swam On," the essay that closes the signal anthology *Black Fire* that he and Jones/Baraka coedited, Neal held up "the cadences of Malcolm's speeches" and the "James Brown scream" as that which the black poet should learn from and emulate (Neal 2007, 653). Only by refusing to approach themselves by way of "Western culture" would African Americans be able to write without the internal "tension" Du Bois identified as "double-consciousness," he argued (Neal 2007, 647, 640). The search for elements of black culture that were arguably less mediated by Eurocentric values led to the emphasis on oral and aural expression – cultural forms that could have best survived the rupture of the Middle Passage and conditions of enslavement. BAM poets thus frequently repudiated standard modes of capitalization, spelling, punctuation, and syntax in favor of typography and orthography meant to represent a *written* vernacular speech and other sonic forms of black culture. Profanity and other provocative or shocking "street" language regularly peppered BAM poetry, to signal racial "authenticity" and commitment to BAM ideology. BAM poets often used such diction to critique the racism and classism of American society and to call for radical change. We see these goals in Nikki Giovanni's oft-cited poem "The True Import of Present Dialogue, Black vs. Negro," in which she notes that "they sent us to kill / Japan and Africa," then asks: "Can you kill a white man / Can you kill the nigger / in you" (Giovanni 1970, 20). Giovanni's spare, unadorned style relies primarily on repetition, rhythm, and the unapologetic use of brusque language for its energy.

But these same investments, in various hands, produced a range of results. One could not confuse Don L. Lee's (Haki Madhubuti's) sharp-tongued incorporation of "the dozens" with Mari Evans's witty or melancholic sketches of black life, or want to conflate Giovanni's direct invocation of armed resistance in the poem mentioned earlier with the spiraling odes penned by Askia Touré (Rolland Snellings), even if Touré's work emphasized the value and significance of black culture inherently and as a foundation for radical (potentially militant) sociopolitical change. BAM poets used everything from historical knowledge to stylistic excess, as in Henry Dumas's "mosaic harlem," a potentially blasphemous riff on the coexistence of Islam and Christianity:

> *what news from James' bastard bible?*
>   al-Mahdi kneels in the mosque,
>   Melchizedek, Moses, Marcus, Muhammad, Malcolm!
>   marshaling words, mobilizing swords
> the message is mixed and masticated with Martin
> the good news of the gospel is crossing a crescent
>   (Baraka and Neal 2007, 346)

Pushing alliteration to the limit, Dumas sonically replicates Harlem's blend of respect for the political and religious leadership of Martin Luther King, Jr. and Malcolm X. The Movement's embrace of various kinds of poetic innovation intended to signal and promote sociopolitical change aligns it with other twentieth-century artistic avant-gardes, from Dada to surrealism to the Beats.[3]

New York and the Northeast have been central in BAM scholarship, but to fully grasp the Movement's national scope, we must account for other regional hotspots, as James Smethurst's work has demonstrated. The Midwest (particularly Chicago and Detroit) was a significant site of BAM activity, not least because of the influential and long-lived cultural institutions based there, including the Organization of Black American Culture (OBAC) and the African Commune of Bad Relevant Artists (AFRI-COBRA), both collectives of writers and visual artists; the Association for the Advancement of Creative Musicians (AACM); and such crucial publishing operations as Dudley Randall's Broadside Press, Madhubuti's Third World Press, Naomi Long Madgett's Lotus Press, and the Hoyt Fuller-edited periodical *Negro Digest* (later *Black World*). These black institutions had a major impact on the shape of the Movement and the careers of individual poets (Rambsy 2011). Broadside Press, for example, brought out Sanchez's first books; succeeded Harper & Row as Brooks's publisher after she embraced the Movement and its call for racial solidarity; and published one of the Movement's most visible anthologies, the elegiac *For Malcolm*. The consistent engagement of Broadside Press and *Negro Digest/Black World*, for example, with "veteran" poets as well as the writers who came of age in the Movement, fostered more encompassing black aesthetics than those featured in the rather personality-driven BAM of the Northeast (Rambsy 2011, 94–100; Smethurst 2005, 100–1). This intergenerational mix was also reflected in the close relationship young Chicago poets like Carolyn Rodgers, Johari Amini, and Madhubuti had with Brooks. That she, a nationally recognized Pulitzer Prize winner, would experience a cultural rebirth at the 1967 Fisk Writers Conference, walk away from her influential white publisher, and foreswear her formal wizardry in search of the compelling energy she admired in the lines of Jones/Baraka and even younger poets just starting their careers was a powerful testament to the Movement.

The West Coast and South had their own regional imperatives. The Movement in California was shaped by the relatively recent establishment of significant black communities; alliances with Chicano, Latino, and Asian American anti-racist movements under a "Third World" or "people of color" heading; and sometimes violent intraracial disputes between the Oakland-based Black Panther Party and the Los Angeles-based Us Organization. Artistically, California poets absorbed important surrealist influences from Bob Kaufman and such jazz musicians as Ornette Coleman and Eric Dolphy, all of whom started or ended their careers on the West Coast. Although Jayne Cortez spent most of her career based in the Northeast (and Ghana), she began writing and performing in the BAM of Los Angeles. Before heading to New York in 1967, she helped found the Studio Watts and Watts Repertory Theatre collectives, where early collaborations with jazz musicians fostered her signature mode of surrealist yet biting social criticism, frequently performed with her jazz band, The Firespitters (Smethurst 2005, 298–9). BAM artists in the South reckoned with that region's historical significance for African Americans without the disdain sometimes shown by those who had never or no longer lived there. Also important to black aesthetics in the South was the deep-rootedness of local cultures, especially the unique New Orleans culture that Tom Dent (of the Umbra poets) and Kalamu ya Salaam (Val Ferdinand) drew upon. The HBCUs, so prevalent in the South, played a key role in disseminating new black aesthetic possibilities, hiring Movement-affiliated or BAM-era poets as visiting or permanent faculty (Smethurst 2005, 336).

These regional divergences further evidence the Movement's range. Close attention to the writing of even the BAM's most central figures demonstrates that while there was some consensus among these poets and theorists about the potential for poetry and other arts to advance the Black Power struggle, there was no particular agreement about *how* that potential might be realized or what other roles African American poetry might play. Some BAM-era artists and thinkers advocated a highly prescriptive Black Aesthetic, insisting that African American poets "should" create "black" poems – a demand for a black nationalist political commitment that ironically contradicted the concomitant contention that this Black Aesthetic was "natural" to African American poets. This prescriptive, racially essentialist aspect of the BAM – along with its sexism, homophobia, and most militant, invective-filled artic-ulations of black nationalist ideology – stood for over three decades as the prevailing characterization of the Movement. The past 5–10 years, how-ever, have seen a critical reassessment, in which scholars are beginning to redress and complicate the reductive understanding of the Movement that has dominated the criticism since its heyday.[4] Building on a significant, once underutilized line of prior scholarship,[5] these recent studies have challenged and reevaluated the established thinking about BAM periodization; its geo-graphical scope; the extent to which racial essentialism, sexism, and homo-phobia over-determined its politics and discredited its artistic production; and the rigidity and reach of a prescriptive conceptualization of the Black Aesthetic.

This new scholarship – and the earlier work it amplifies – is of signal importance to our understanding of African American poetry. As I have argued elsewhere, the impact of a narrow and prescriptive Black Aesthetic has been both overstated and underestimated. The powerful articulation of aesthetics as culturally specific (rather than universal) values, the insights into why oral and aural cultural production have been vital to understand-ings of African American culture, and the recognition of the inextricability of politics and art: these elements of BAM-era theories of the Black Aesthetic have continued to influence and guide African American literary theory and criticism to the present moment. This influence has to some degree affected all scholars of African American literature trained in the wake of the Movement's ascendancy – even those who have repudiated or distanced themselves from the Movement's critical and creative work (whether on formal, political, or intellectual grounds) – and thus informs their schol-arship on literature produced *before and after* the 1960s (Shockley 2011, 8–9). Some of the impact of this influence has impoverished the African American literary tradition, as it has led to the marginalization of authors and works that do not conform to or fit easily within the narrower Black Aesthetic boundaries (Mullen 2012a, 79–80; Mullen 2012b, 173). But while a prescriptive Black Aesthetic has sometimes weighed heavily on late-twentieth-century African American scholars and poets, there is an increas-ingly lively discussion – carried out in the criticism, theory, and creative writing – of the idea that, rather than a singular Black Aesthetic, there have been many various *black aesthetics*.[6]

The remainder of this essay will engage some of the implications of an expansive approach to black aesthetics for thinking about African American poetry just before, during, and since the BAM, into the twenty-first century. To begin with, it brings into clearer focus the poets and collectives Lorenzo Thomas has called the "Roots of the Black Arts Movement." Early to mid-1960s New York saw the experimentation of the Umbra Workshop and their journal; Thomas himself, David Henderson, Ishmael Reed, Calvin Hernton, Snellings/Touré, N.H. Pritchard, Tom Dent, and Steve Cannon, among others, met regularly to debate poetics and share work (Thomas 2000, 119–20). Their innovations, including explorations of "Black English," adventurous typography, recourse to black musical traditions for rhythmic and lyrical cues, and the incorporation of political critique, anticipated and directly fed the BAM's innovative aesthetics: half of the poets just named contributed work to *Black Fire*, for instance (Thomas 2000, 120–9; Nielsen 1997, 13–14). Also noteworthy was the assemblage of poets associated with *The Liberator* magazine, including Neal. Poetry by members of these groups, which tended to be more abstract and less readily paraphrased, extends the range of work in *Black Fire* and troubles the notion that BAM commitments to Black Art's "accessibility" constrained poets to produce uniformly "easy" work.

Some critics have charged BAM poetry with a sameness of style and rhetoric that eliminates the need to read widely or deeply in the work of that period, but this charge relies on the exclusion of work by Thomas, Henderson, and others with similar aesthetic concerns from the literary history of the 1960s and '70s. Similarly marginalized are BAM-era poetry's African, diasporic, and multiethnic voices. An only recently studied but quite active participant in the Movement was Keorapetse "Willie" Kgositsile, a member of South Africa's African National Congress (ANC) who was in exile in the United States from 1962 to 1975. His poetry in that period drew on not only the cultures and politics of his native land but also his experiences as a member of a revolutionary organization with a military wing. Kgositsile's contributions to *Black Fire* include "Ivory Masks in Orbit," which connects African American culture to Africa via Nina Simone's piano playing ("moves / over 300 mississippies" that "rock the village / gate with future memory") (Baraka and Neal 2007, 224). His "Towards a Walk in the Sun," by contrast, references armed revolution with an energy perhaps derived from his country's proximity to ongoing African independence movements – "WHEN THE MOMENT HATCHES IN TIME'S WOMB THERE WILL BE NO ART TALK. THE ONLY POEM YOU WILL HEAR WILL BE THE SPEARPOINT PIVOTED IN THE PUNCTURED MARROW OF THE VILLAIN" – his plosive *p*'s piercing the fearful ear (Baraka and Neal 2007, 229). Diasporic influences within BAM

aesthetics are also reflected in the anthology's inclusion of Puerto Rican/
Nuyorican poet Victor Hernández Cruz. His poem "white powder!," also in
Black Fire, indicts the "gringos & their grey men" for filling the "project[s]"
with mind-numbing drugs, endorses the call for "black power" with its
playful title, and implicitly acknowledges that a common African ancestry
makes U.S. blacks and Puerto Ricans "brothers" (Baraka and Neal 2007,
437). And, as previously noted, West Coast demographics meant that black
aesthetics there shaped and were shaped by Asian American and Chicano
politics and cultural production (Smethurst 2005, 285–90).

This more expansive conception of black aesthetics diminishes the appeal
and potency of drawing a bright line between the most visible Movement
participants – those actively placing their poetry in the service of black
nationalist politics – and other African American poets writing during this
era. We need to better account for the Movement's influence on poets who
were not BAM-affiliated but nonetheless seriously engaged with the *aesthetic possibilities* the Movement engendered.[7] Rejecting the dichotomy of
full embrace or total repudiation of the Movement, we find in the middle ground such poets as Audre Lorde, Ishmael Reed, Jay Wright, Lucille
Clifton, Etheridge Knight, Ed Roberson, Michael Harper, Clarence Major,
and June Jordan. While these poets may have been uncommitted or even
sharply opposed to black nationalist politics, their interest in the cultures,
histories, or lived experiences of Africans and African-descended people has
drawn all of them, at times, to wrangle productively with questions of black
aesthetics. Certainly rifts developed between Movement poets and particular writers who vehemently disavowed the more programmatic aspects of
its ideology (*the* Black Aesthetic, so to speak) – Robert Hayden famously
drew a line in the sand against giving primacy to his black identity over his
identity as a poet, for instance – and I would not downplay the undeniable
pressure many African American poets have felt, then and since, to produce
"recognizably black" writing (Nielsen 2001, 539). But to create a rigid separation between these poets' work and that of their BAM counterparts would
be to reify black nationalist politics as the only recognizable anti-racist politics and to perpetuate the notion of *a* Black Aesthetic in the face of the wide
variety of ways in which poets explore matters of race and "blackness."

With a view toward a broad range of black aesthetics, we do not find Jay
Wright's appearance in *Black Fire* incongruous. The mode in which his early
career poem "The End of Ethnic Dream" evokes "[Albert] Ayler's screams"
and "African chant[s]" intersected neatly with Baraka's and Neal's editorial
commitment to present "a surging new sound," "a tone, your own" (Baraka
and Neal 2007, 365, 653, xxiv). By not expecting black aesthetics to manifest predictably as black vernacular language and depictions of an African

American social real, we make space for Wright's continuing engagement with black aesthetics in later poetry treating African cultures (such as Dogon cosmology). Similarly, we remember that Audre Lorde, whose political commitment to an intersectional analysis of oppression and identity as an out lesbian placed her at odds with the Movement's black nationalist stance, nonetheless published her second, third, and fourth poetry collections with Broadside Press. This work encompassed the overtly political critique and the celebration of black identity – "Speak proudly to your children / where ever you may find them / tell them / you are the offspring of slaves / and your mother was / a princess / in darkness" (Lorde 1997, 60) – that accorded with other Broadside Press offerings, despite Randall's discomfort with her sexuality (De Veaux 2004, 129–31).

From the 1980s onward, we see an explosion of black aesthetics, the range and complexity of which speaks to the increasingly varied experiences of African-descended people and the constantly changing forms racism takes in the United States. With room only to gesture toward this multiplicity, we might begin by considering the development of a few key poets whose active careers spanned the decades from the late-1960s through the twenty-first century. Poets like Sanchez and Clifton, who began writing in the male-dominated Movement, deepened an always present exploration of womanhood and racially inflected questions of gender as they subsequently absorbed and contributed to a generative period of black (lesbian) feminist thought. Both poets retain BAM-era stylistics, like exclusively lowercase typography and an inclination toward plain diction and vernacular. Yet Sanchez has grown increasingly open about her poetry's feminist and anti-homophobic amendments to black nationalist ideology and her interest in traditional forms (such as haiku, tanka, and rhyme royal). And Clifton trained her eye with greater intensity on the body – black, female, and powerful, but also ill, aging, and vulnerable – as a sign and source of our common humanity, even in its raced and gendered specificity. Baraka's career also diverged from and exceeded the narrower contours of his BAM-era nationalism and writing, in poetry that moved through Marxism toward what is perhaps best described as a fluidly and fiercely anti-capitalist stance. Readings of his and Brooks's oeuvres have been similarly over-determined by attention to their renunciation of their pre-BAM aesthetics. While Brooks did jettison the formalist poetics for which she had become famous, her poetry after the 1960s remained unmistakably her own: elliptical, alliterative, dense, strongly rhythmic, and devoted to depicting the lives of black people. Brooks's and Baraka's aesthetic shifts have been overemphasized; still, the influence of each on later poets tends to differ depending on whether early or later work served as model. Baraka's poetry, of course, was consistent in its search within jazz and other African American musical forms for sources of exemplary rhythmic and lyrical energy. Jayne Cortez's black aesthetics were similarly dedicated to decrying injustice – economic, racial, gendered – through poems grounded sonically, structurally, and thematically in music that stems from African cultural roots. Her unusual approach to language – increasingly surrealist-informed, drenched in African diaspora cultures, and using repetition to play words like notes – has been influential yet inimitable.

The forces that inspired movement and growth within these poets' individual careers have encouraged younger African American poets to draw their black aesthetics from a widening range of experiences and with decreasing pressure to exhibit loyalty to a single set of aesthetic choices. Those forces include new patterns of (im)migration among people of African descent; broader educational and employment opportunities available to African Americans thanks to the Civil Rights and Black Power movements; steps toward residential desegregation; new or revitalized social movements among women, the LGBTQ community, Chicanos and Latinos more broadly (and later, the backlash against identity politics); Reagan era political losses and the rise of hip hop culture; and the technological advances that have facilitated networking, information sharing, and dissemination of cultural products. With somewhat greater access to powerful cultural institutions and positions, and greater diversity of experience than ever, African American poets are reimagining black aesthetics in rich, complicated, and exciting ways. Again, a few key examples will have to stand in for a small universe of poets and poetics.

Rita Dove, a former Poet Laureate and Pulitzer Prize-winning poet, rose meteorically to these heights on a poetics of delicate yet icy precision, poems that play language as lightly as a grace note and make free verse seem almost formalist in its careful structure. Generous in its use of the German language and cultural references she absorbed while studying abroad, Dove's poetry quite consciously rejects the Black Aesthetic mode in which she felt she was expected to write. But this determined resistance to racialized expectations for her work, like Hayden's before her, was an expression of her own black aesthetics. For Dove, whose most celebrated book, *Thomas and Beulah*, told the lives of her grandparents in poetry, there was no contradiction between her fine-tuned lines and the Great Migration-content of their working-class lives. Her black aesthetic describes a day laborer's impatient courtship as a "waiting – for what? A / magnolia breeze, someone / to trot out the stars?" (Dove 1993, 146). Uninterested in making political statements, she seeks to let the lives, the images, speak for themselves.

Yusef Komunyakaa, another poet in the small circle of African American Pulitzer Prize winners, creates a language in which to treat his experience and concerns as a man raised in the overtly racist climate of Bogalusa, Louisiana, and as a Vietnam veteran. His subjects – black manhood, jazz and blues, war and other kinds of conflict – reveal connections between Baraka's black aesthetics and his, although Komunyakaa, like Dove, shies away from direct political critique. Energizing his lines with a gumbo of strong nouns, adjectives, and verbs, he invites our cultural knowledge to inform images of a young boy's quest for muscadines:

> A silence
> Coaxed me up into oak branches
> Woodpeckers had weakened.
> But they held there, braced
> By a hundred years of vines
> Strong & thick
> Enough to hang a man.
> (Komunyakaa 1993, 14)

We recognize the same taste for alliteration and consonance that appeared in Dumas's poem and that characterizes Brooks's poetry, early and late. Komunyakaa's black aesthetics echoes these earlier poets, as the shadow of lynching looms over the discovery of a cache of sweet fruit.

Harryette Mullen, noted for her poetic innovation, wrote her first book very deeply influenced by the Movement's prescriptive emphasis on "authentic" black vernacular. But finding it ironically unauthentic to write in the "nonstandard" English that her schoolteacher mother forbade in their house, Mullen developed a poetics of subversive wordplay that mixed dazzling and elliptical Brooksian lines with investigations into the sentence à la Gertrude Stein. In her second book, *Trimmings*, she works through the gendered (and racial) politics of clothing (here, bracelets) in a shower of rhyme and consonance: "Akimbo bimbos, all of a jangle. Tricked out trinkets, aloud galore. Gimcracks, a stack. Bang and a whimper. Two to tangle. It's a jungle" (Mullen 2006, 41). Without saying "bangles," Mullen uses sonically adjacent language to suggest the accessory and its ethnic baggage. Similarly, Kevin Young, an early member of the Dark Room Collective, began his oeuvre with a poetic chronicle of Southern black family life, but has gone on to generate his own brand of poetry that features popular culture references and takes up subjects and contexts as varied as film noir, the blues, Jean-Michel Basquiat's graffiti art, and the historical *Amistad* rebellion. Steeped in African American music from the field holler to hip hop, as well as black film and literature, Young is as irreverent as many of the Movement-era poets in his "post-soul" black aesthetics. In a poem playfully titled "Tune," he jumbles syntax and mixes metaphors to create the spoken equivalent to singing off-key: "In the Africa / of your eyes – my // lost tribe – / I am safari

// this stumbling / shooting off // foolishly. Apologies – / you are no country // Hottentot to trot // you are not" (Young 2003, 42). Young plays the dozens not with a rival, but with himself and the cultures he taps and mingles.

Natasha Trethewey, U.S. Poet Laureate (as of this writing), may be a fitting poet with whom to close a sampling that could extend for many pages. Also a member of the Dark Room Collective, winner of the first Cave Canem Book Prize for her debut collection, *Domestic Work*, and winner of the Pulitzer Prize for her third book of poetry, *Native Guard*, Trethewey stands at the crossroads of many paths through the contemporary (African) American poetry landscape. She is not unique in this but representative, although her honors certainly distinguish her. Trethewey's black aesthetics, unlike Dove's, calls for an overt commitment to social justice, which permeates her work. She gives voice to a specific black experience – that of the biracial child of black and white parents – that was cast as tragedy by the writers of the New Negro Renaissance era and was little heard of during the BAM, when a darker, "purer" blackness was finally being celebrated. Adopting what we might call the "first-person political" voice and a diction that mixes Clifton's simplicity and Hayden's lexical flourish, Trethewey calls the nation to task for the politics – historical and present; raced, gendered, and classed – that ripped her parents apart and haunt her even into one of poetry's most honored offices. Her poem "Miscegenation," a ghazal, begins: "In 1965 my parents broke two laws of Mississippi; / they went to Ohio to marry, returned to Mississippi" (Trethewey 2007, 36). The piece recalls the discriminatory laws that constructed her birth as a product of crime and evidence of "sin" and points to the importance ascribed to *place*, in terms of geography and (racial) status. The homecoming Trethewey stages in her poem, like the Sanchez poem about Harlem with which we began, involves the clash of two world views, one implicitly "black," the other "white." Almost forty years after Sanchez's poem was published, another African American poet brings a contemporary black aesthetic to a concern with the way race inscribes a black woman's relationship to her home. Baraka once called this kind of thing "the changing same" (Baraka 1991, 203).

NOTES

1 Louis Simpson's assessment, in a 1963 review of Brooks's *Selected Poems*, suggests the kind of attitudes black writers were up against: "I am not sure it is possible for a Negro to write well without making us aware that he is a Negro; on the other hand, if being a Negro is the only subject, the writing is not important" (quoted in Kent 1990, 163).
2 Jones edited the journal *Yugen* (with his then-wife Hettie Cohen Jones), the affiliated Totem Press, and the literary magazine *The Floating Bear* (with di Prima) during this period.

3 For further reading on the BAM as an avant-garde, see Nielsen 1997, Frost 2003, and Yu 2010.
4 See works cited in this essay's bibliography by James Smethurst, Cheryl Clarke, Lisa Gail Collins and Margo Natalie Crawford, Amy Abugo Ongiri, Howard Rambsy, and Carter Mathes.
5 See works cited in this essay's bibliography by Erica Hunt, Nathaniel Mackey, Fred Moten, Harryette Mullen, Aldon Nielsen, and Lorenzo Thomas.
6 For an elaboration of my argument that black aesthetics are not constituted by a specific set of ("black") themes, tropes, stylistics, or structures but by the racialized subjectivity of African American poets and the whole range of strategies they devise as artists for negotiating the terrain of a white supremacist society, see Shockley 2011.
7 As poet Ed Roberson notes: "People forget about how broad and deep the Black Arts Movement went. People were changed. I know I was changed by it, and I didn't look like the movement at all to some folks.... It felt that I was really being given a whole new layer of places of myself to work from.... The movement began to open up ways to put names to things and feelings that were more accurate, in terms of how deeply and powerfully they were felt" (Roberson 2010, 765). My thanks to Aldon Nielsen for conversations that also illuminated this point for me.

WORKS CITED

Baraka, Amiri. 1991. "The Changing Same (R&B and the New Black Music)." In *The LeRoi Jones / Amiri Baraka Reader*. Ed. William J. Harris, 186–209. New York: Thunder's Mouth Press.

——— 1995. *Transbluesency: The Selected Poems of Amiri Baraka/LeRoi Jones (1961–1995)*. New York: Marsilio Publishers.

Baraka, Amiri, and Larry Neal. 2007. *Black Fire: An Anthology of Afro-American Writing*. Baltimore: Black Classic Press. Originally published 1968.

Clarke, Cheryl. 2005. *"After Mecca": Women Poets and the Black Arts Movement*. New Brunswick, NJ: Rutgers University Press.

Collins, Lisa Gail, and Margo Natalie Crawford. 2006. *New Thoughts on the Black Arts Movement*. New Brunswick, NJ: Rutgers University Press.

De Veaux, Alexis. 2004. *Warrior Poet: A Biography of Audre Lorde*. New York: Norton.

Dove, Rita. 1993. *Selected Poems*. New York: Vintage/Pantheon.

Du Bois, W. E. B. 1986. "The Criteria of Negro Art." In *W. E. B. Du Bois: Writings*. Ed. Nathan Huggins, 993–1002. New York: Library of America.

Frost, Elisabeth. 2003. *The Feminist Avant Garde in American Poetry*. Iowa City: University of Iowa Press.

Gayle, Addison. 1994. "Cultural Strangulation: Black Literature and the White Aesthetic." In *Within the Circle: An Anthology of African American Literary Criticism from the Harlem Renaissance to the Present*. Ed. Angelyn Mitchell, 207–12. Durham, NC: Duke University Press. Originally published in Addison Gayle, ed., *The Black Aesthetic*, 1971. New York: Doubleday.

Giovanni, Nikki. 1970. *Black Feeling, Black Talk / Black Judgement*. New York: Morrow.

Hughes, Langston. "The Negro Artist and the Racial Mountain." *The Nation*, March 11, 2002, accessed November 23, 2013, http://www.thenation.com/article/negro-artist-and-racial-mountain. Originally published June 23, 1926.

Hunt, Erica. 1990. "Notes for an Oppositional Poetics." In *The Politics of Poetic Form*. Ed. Charles Bernstein, 197–212. New York: Roof Books.

Jones, LeRoi. 1966. *Home: Social Essays*. New York: Morrow.

Kent, George. 1990. *A Life of Gwendolyn Brooks*. Lexington: University of Kentucky Press.

Komunyakaa, Yusef. 1993. *Neon Vernacular: New and Selected Poems*. Middletown, CT: Wesleyan University Press.

Lorde, Audre. 1997. *The Collected Poems of Audre Lorde*. New York: Norton.

Mackey, Nathaniel. 1993. *Discrepant Engagement: Dissonance, Cross-Culturality, and Experimental Writing*. Tuscaloosa: University of Alabama Press.

Mathes, Carter. Forthcoming, 2014. *Imagine the Sound: Experimental African American Literature After Civil Rights*. Minneapolis: University of Minnesota Press.

Moten, Fred. 2003. *In the Break: The Aesthetics of the Black Radical Tradition*. Minneapolis: University of Minnesota Press.

Mullen, Harryette. 2006. *Trimmings*. In *Recyclopedia*, 1–62. Saint Paul, MN: Graywolf Press.

2012a. "African Signs and Spirit Writing." In *The Cracks Between What We Are and What We Are Supposed to Be: Essays and Interviews*. Tuscaloosa: University of Alabama Press, 79–101. Originally published in *Callaloo*, 19.3 (1996).

2012b. "Incessant Elusives: The Oppositional Poetics of Erica Hunt and Will Alexander." In *The Cracks Between What We Are and What We Are Supposed to Be: Essays and Interviews*. Tuscaloosa: University of Alabama Press, 173–81. Originally published in *Holding Their Own: Perspectives on the Multi-Ethnic Literatures of the United States*. Eds. Dorothea Fischer-Hornung and Heike Raphael-Hernandez. Tübingen: Stauffenburg Verlag, 2000.

Neal, Larry. 1994. "The Black Arts Movement." In *Within the Circle: An Anthology of African American Literary Criticism from the Harlem Renaissance to the Present*. Ed. Angelyn Mitchell, 184–98. Durham, NC: Duke University Press. Originally published in *The Drama Review*, 12.4 (1968).

2007. "And Shine Swam On." In *Black Fire: An Anthology of Afro-American Writing*. Eds. Amiri Baraka and Larry Neal, 638–56. Baltimore: Black Classic Press, 638–56. Originally published 1968.

Nielsen, Aldon. 1997. *The Calligraphy of Black Chant: Languages of African-American Postmodernism*. New York: Cambridge University Press.

2001. "This Ain't No Disco." In *The World in Time and Space: Towards a History of American Innovative Poetry in Our Time*. Eds. Edward Foster and Joseph Donahue, 536–46. Jersey City, NJ: Talisman House, 536–46.

Ongiri, Amy Abugo. 2010. *Spectacular Blackness: The Cultural Politics of the Black Power Movement and the Search for a Black Aesthetic*. Charlottesville: University of Virginia Press.

Rambsy, Howard, II. 2011. *The Black Arts Enterprise and the Production of African American Poetry*. Ann Arbor: University of Michigan Press.

Roberson, Ed. 2010. "The Structure, Then the Music: An Interview with Ed Roberson." By Randall Horton. *Callaloo*, 33.3: 762–9.

Sanchez, Sonia. 1978. *I've Been a Woman: New and Selected Poems*. Chicago: Third World.

Shockley, Evie. 2011. *Renegade Poetics: Black Aesthetics and Formal Innovation in African American Poetry*. Iowa City: University of Iowa Press.

Smethurst, James. 2005. *The Black Arts Movement: Literary Nationalism in the 1960s and 1970s*. Chapel Hill: University of North Carolina Press.

Thomas, Lorenzo. 2000. *Extraordinary Measures: Afrocentric Modernism and Twentieth-Century American Poetry*. Tuscaloosa: University of Alabama Press.

Trethewey, Natasha. 2007. *Native Guard*. New York: Mariner/Houghton Mifflin.

Young, Kevin. 2003. *Jelly Roll: A Blues*. New York: Knopf.

Yu, Timothy. 2010. *Race and the Avant Garde: Experimental and Asian American Poetry Since 1965*. Stanford, CA: Stanford University Press.

15

EDWARD BRUNNER

New York School and American Surrealist Poetics

A handful of poets in New York interacting with visual artists who extended Surrealist principles to invent action painting produced new work that grew exponentially, revolutionizing the texture, scope, and tone of American poetry. Their poetic lines captured the flush and surge of city life, cultivated the chance opportunity, and looked ironically on social forms. Against the mid-century poetry that trumpeted major themes (Robert Lowell's *Mills of the Kavanaughs*, 1951) or wove tapestries of multiple meanings (Richard Wilbur's *Ceremony*, 1950) their work was less about describing than performing, more process than product. This innovative writing, moreover, emerged in relation to everyday experience. The irrational was inescapably folded into modern life, a Surrealistic view embraced by John Ashbery and Frank O'Hara, although each unfolded that irrationality in different ways. Ashbery's meditative lyrics followed the ruminative speculations of late Wallace Stevens and W. H. Auden, while O'Hara's free verse mixed irony with the observational improvisations of William Carlos Williams. Two so different approaches established wide perimeters within which others found work.

City living made collaboration attractive; coterie behavior was one response to urban anonymity, sheltering queer lifestyles, bringing painters and playwrights together with ongoing projects. Out of a mid-century core group that included Barbara Guest, Kenneth Koch, and James Schuyler, second-generation newcomers arrived in the late 1960s. Ted Berrigan, Diane Wakoski, Ron Padgett, Alice Notley, and Anne Waldman expanded the tenets of the first generation, incorporating a politics inflamed by Vietnam, women's issues, and working-class perspectives. Other poets in New York resisted the Surrealism of an urban everyday, pursuing a Surrealism rooted in mythic awareness, using subterranean insights that challenged regimes of order. This "Deep Image" poetics sought out highly charged moments that Robert Bly and James Wright first located in translation projects. This transnational, transcultural, and transhistorical vision reoriented poetry toward an ethics of responsibility attuned to the natural world as a complex system especially in the non-anthropocentric writings of W. S. Merwin and A. R. Ammons, that developed a related but divergent set of poetics in which deep image led to deep ecology with global overtones.

American Surrealism: Homegrown Garden Variety

The Surrealism in André Breton's 1924 manifesto insisted on "the superior reality of certain forms of association hitherto neglected, in the omnipotence of dream, in the disinterested play of thought" to challenge the ideological underpinnings of society (Breton 1969, 26). So broad a project lent itself to export, even as other cultures would suit the Surreal to them. *View* (1940–7), edited in America by Charles Henri Ford and Parker Tyler, "paralleled rather than represented" Surrealism, according to Catrina Neiman, with Ford and Tyler reaching back to the artists who had influenced the Surrealists, fostering "the eccentric or irrational elements" that flourished in-country, as in their "American Fantastica" issue of 1943 featuring Joseph Cornell (Neiman 1982, xii). When Surrealists were not homegrown, they were repurposed into garden varieties by American painters such as Robert Motherwell, who theorized in 1944 that "automatic writing" could be transposed into "plastic automatism" so brush strokes on canvas were a "primary conduit for channeling unconscious ideas" (Hobbs 2005, 58). Recalling the 1940–8 art world, Impresario John Bernard Myers remembered Jackson Pollock using similar words, embracing the Surrealist "belief in an 'automatism' or making a picture without 'conscious' control of what would happen on the canvas before beginning one" (Myers 1977, 56). When Marjorie Perloff, describing O'Hara's poetry circa 1953, declared "Surrealism has now been assimilated into an American idiom," that assimilation had been long under way (Perloff 1977, 74).

For Ashbery and O'Hara, that assimilation process went back to college days centered on the tiny stage of the Poets' Theatre in Cambridge, Massachusetts, as authors of and actors in experimental plays wrought by Violet Lang and others, productions that were "shot with old-fashioned surrealism," in Nora Sayre's words, with "echoes of Cocteau or whiffs of Ionesco" (Sayre 1995, 196). When Ashbery and O'Hara became New York poets, they retained their interest in theater. John Bernard Myers, an all-weather Impresario, not only directed the Tibor de Nagy gallery but in 1953 established the "Artists' Theater" that featured plays by O'Hara, Ashbery, Koch, and Guest, with sets designed by artists Larry Rivers, Nell Blaine, and Grace Hartigan. Collaborations invited crossover experiments and coterie behavior. Schuyler's "The Mystery Chef Mystery (A Play for Two Pianos)"

(1953) in which Ashbery acted with a bewigged Koch, included a reference to "Drank Dzohara" and alluded to a current love interest, one half of a piano duo. If this camp sensibility was coded to enable queer sensibilities, it also purveyed an aesthetic that invited second looks at neglected material, encouraged flippancy, and upended judgment (Sontag 1999, 53–65).

This unlikely mix of elements – free-form writing, collaborative borrowings, and camp attitudes – became hallmarks of New York poetry. No poet activated these traits as subtly as Ashbery. In a 1989 lecture, he distinguished between a helpless Surrealism that proceeded by "abandoning itself to the unconscious" and a helpful Surrealism that tried to "accurately reflect experience in which both the conscious and the unconscious play a role" (Ashbery 2000, 134). The fractured texture of Ashbery's poetic lines evokes the unconscious pressing upon the conscious, producing "a discursive or meditative poet of a new kind," in David Perkins's description: "disorienting, comic, and profound" (Perkins 1987, 531). The closing couplet of a 1956 poem resonates across Ashbery's career – "And only in the light of lost words / Can we imagine our rewards" (Ashbery 1970, 29). But what "our rewards" might be and how we use "lost words" as a resource is up to us. Yet moments of clarity emerge from a verbal texture whose markers for distinguishing surface from depth are always shifting. "The Skaters" (1966) confers stability by self-reflexively describing the writing underway – the wheeling circles of figure eights in ice standardize that early poem's extravagant modulations, recasting digressive forays as exploratory tropes. The poem that advanced Ashbery's cause most spectacularly was "Self-Portrait in a Convex Mirror," a response to the Renaissance painter Parmigianino's self-portrait, itself skewed by the painter's examining himself within a distorting surface that bends the figure into it. That poem revealed a multi-layered method of attending to an attentive subject's attentiveness.

Ashbery's poems regarding painting are themselves "painterly," as Michael Davidson has shown: The poet is not describing a painting but taking the artwork's sign-system, the artwork's perspective, into the poem (Davidson 1983, 69–79). Yet Ashbery's interests coalesced around not high-art performance but Surrealistic permissiveness: "The possibility of using your dreams, your average thoughts, things you overhear people saying in the street – anything that comes into your mind – as a raw material for poetry" (Poulin 1981, 249). What began as a capacious style borrowing from late Stevens and late Auden steadily unmoored itself from high art to peer with a mix of curiosity, dread, and delight into the culture of advanced capitalism, with its sloganeering, its media emblems, its contradictory gestures. "Daffy Duck in Hollywood" (1970) is based on a 1938 cartoon that ends with a cartoon director reacting in horror to the product we get to watch, a mélange stitched by Daffy from throwaway shots from stock film (Avery 2005, DVD). *Girls on the Run* (1999) is a homage to outsider artist Henry Darger whose epic tales of the "Vivian Girls" assaulted by vengeful combatants appropriates adventure serials, comic strips, and pulp mysteries. Ashbery's appropriation of Darger's appropriations, with its figures under siege, hints at disasters we may have taught ourselves not to see but that are visible to outsiders like Darger. Ashbery's aesthetic is intent on responding to, even redeeming, the detritus of mass culture, much as Surrealism regarded items that appeared to be valueless as, however implausibly, the bearers of powerful secrets.

As the New York poets began their careers, the 1950s art world was looking past the enormous canvases of action painting toward the figural realism and degraded icons of Pop Art. Frank O'Hara's poetry unfolds across this shift, with a poem in O'Hara's 1959 monograph on Jackson Pollock admiring the channeling force of the hand: "There is the Pollock, white, harm / will not fall, his perfect hand" (O'Hara 1959, 23). But the painting closest to O'Hara's own method is the one whose title places him right before it: "On Seeing Larry Rivers' *Washington Crossing the Delaware* at the Museum of Modern Art" (1955).

Rivers's painting was an affront to the art world as well as to historical memory. The figural representations in Rivers's partly erased version of an iconic moment of heroism (first painted by Emmanuel Leutze) ventured far from abstract expressionism, although Philip Auslander points out that the subject that "seemed distastefully hackneyed was soon paralleled by [Jasper] Johns's use of the flag, and [Robert] Rauschenberg's use of found images" (1989, 21–2). Like Rivers's painting, O'Hara's poem encourages strange associations ("here are your bones crossed / on my breast like a rusty flintlock / pirate's flag, bravely specific") and, in a parallel act of revisionist historiography, imparts hesitancy and even fear to its iconic figure: "our hero has come back to us / in his white pants" but we now know "his nose / trembling like a flag under fire" (O'Hara 1971, 233–4).

Escaping the categorical is O'Hara's signature, most evident in "I do this, I do that" poems that reproduce the flare and swagger of New York shop windows, advertising, and fashion. These poems look with the eye of a Rivers, attentive to suggestive swatches, erased visions, and even imposing absences. In "A Step Away from Them" (1956), a meandering walk defined by haphazard glances – "I look / at bargains in wristwatches. There / are cats playing in sawdust" – is unexpectedly interrupted with a memory of those recently deceased, beginning with Violet Lang: "First / Bunny died, then John Latouche, / then Jackson Pollock. But is the / earth as full as life was full, of them?" (O'Hara 1971, 258). The title of O'Hara's *Lunch Poems* (1964) records how intensely time passes outside the workday's authoritarian spaces. "The Day Lady Died" is a quintessential poem of the unofficial, ending its array of African and African American artistic references with O'Hara listening to Billie Holiday "in the 5 SPOT / while she whispered a song along the keyboard / to Mal Waldron and everyone and I stopped breathing" (O'Hara 1971, 325). O'Hara may have known that Holiday, her cabaret license lifted, was barred from singing at a club serving alcohol, so this moment was spontaneous and illegal, a "whisper" in every respect. But what matters is that the moment belongs to "everyone and I," a powerful occurrence in a racist country. And it is an unexpected gift, like the jazz that no one is ever wholly prepared for, including those who produce it. This poem's widespread circulation is the highest mark of the success of the New York poetry aesthetic.

Lunch hour poetry is a fugitive art, escaping inhospitable confines, and companion-poets Kenneth Koch and James Schuyler are equally adept, though in disparate modes, at serial verse that unspools itself against an inimical authoritarianism. Koch locates oppressive environments whose stiffness demands rules should be bent. Koch's *Ko, or a Season on Earth* (1959) proffers an increasingly outrageous mock epic that drills into baseball as a national sport by intercutting the story of a Japanese baseball player with unlikely digressions, including a stunt in which women in Kansas express themselves by going nude and an interlude in which a talking dolphin rescues a drowning man. Koch's mechanism is the *ottava rima* devised for heroic verse:

> "I have
> No pitchers left!" he cries, while on Ritzitznikov's
> Left shoulder a canary lands who's rav-
> Ished by the tree-like sturdiness and hits it off, 's
> Contented, and he sings. ...
>
> (Koch 2007, 108)

Koch's sallies broaden out from O'Hara's divagations; Schuyler's vignettes chart in detail the verbal flow that Ashbery floats within. "The Morning of the Poem" (1980) is a suite of recollections emerging out of and against (most are reveries of same-sex attraction) the slow-paced routine to which Schuyler cannot adjust during a visit to his hometown. Earlier works by gay New York poets proclaimed same-sex affiliations in camp postures and queer stylings, but this poem becomes Schuyler's occasion for revisiting what he can't say or do in his hometown. In the process, he records particulars of a lifestyle that would otherwise remain secret: "I have never been / Sure about sin: wrong yes, but sin and evil, it all gets too (/) glib, too easy" (Schuyler 1988, 221). Alternating lyrical description with dramatic confession, Schuyler retrieves luminous anecdotes from the day's routines. As he illuminates the ordinary ("An August morning, cool and cloudless, / Maple leaves lightly moving, conifers perfectly still" (Schuyler 1988, 223) so the erotic adventures that he recalls arise out of casual meetings, familiar occasions, and regular events; they lack the aura of the dangerous risk. The visual field of his poetry notices the missing, the absent, the lost; describing what is there through what is not-there occurs regularly in Schuyler's "reviews" of artwork in gallery openings: "the thrown-up edge of the knifed pigment casts fine, fast-traveling shadows that keep the action spinning like the murmur of a lightly-brushed snare" (Schuyler 1998, 219).

New York poets examine art with the intensity that Rilke brought to Cézanne "*so that he might apply Cézanne's discoveries to his own work*," as Barbara Guest recalled (italics hers) in a 1986 talk, "The Shadow of Surrealism" (Guest 2003, 53). Her earliest poems inhabit sites by repeating phrases to mark out spheres of meaning. "Belgravia" (1962) states "I am in love with a man" four times in a forty-two-line poem that describes the "many interiors" of "his own house" experienced metaphorically, emotionally, aesthetically – an "open house of windows, / locks and balconies" (Guest 1995, 14). Geographical sweep in Guest's impressive sequence, "A Handbook for Surfing" (1972), folds an anti-Vietnam war message into a manual offering mock-advice to surfers. The forty-two poems in *The Countess from Minneapolis* (1976) feature anecdotes from a fantastic history, depict a "countess" surviving under challenging conditions, and register an urban Midwest that attracts mysterious brand names. It transforms boxcars crossing a Mississippi River bridge into a moment of beauty, foreshadowing the industrial-scale steel angles in Tony Smith's minimalist sculpture on the Walker Art Center roof garden, whose description concludes the sequence. Because Guest works spatially herself, she readies us to envision an art object like Smith's that plausibly alters even resistant space.

Enhancing the Surreal: The New York School, a Second Generation

If Guest prospered outside the New York settings that energized her work, a second generation of young poets found what they needed in a city where the arts flourished, where communities emerged within public performance venues, and where publishing was enabled by inexpensive photocopying. This generation arrived after the zenith of Abstract Expressionism, when the hard bop of 1950s jazz had been superseded by rock and as the war in Vietnam escalated. Missing out on postwar prosperity and lacking Ivy League pedigrees, they scrabbled to find work, sharing tiny apartments with the families they might also be raising. Their writing centered on the quotidian but never burnished it to dazzle.

Alice Notley's *165 Meeting House Lane* (1971) develops a crystalline voice that emerges from an agitated domesticity, disruptive and productive at once, in which an exact tone elevates the simplest words. A domestic disturbance in "But He Says I Misunderstood" turns on money issues, but the exactness with which Notley speaks – "I'm a slave, well mildly, to a baby" (Notley 1993, 7) – generates her triumphant finale: "This poem is in the Mainstream American Tradition." Domestic space is inadequate to women's needs. "The De Carlo Lots" in Anne Waldman's 1966 multi-part poem refers to an Atlantic City site subdivided into lots so small no house can be built on one. In poetry, though, memories are sometimes best fragmented: "You are allotted a childhood as wood / splinters right under your thumbs" (Waldman 1989, 10). In a space cleared of expectation, women poets find speech unlimited in its ambition, as in Waldman's shaman-like incantations in the twenty-three page "Fast-Speaking Woman": "I get on the airplane and fly away / know how to work the machines!" (Waldman 1989, 42).

Women in carnivalesque mode also undermine the prevailing ideology. Koch revisited the George Washington figure in a travesty written as a pageant play for his son's school; garbling basic facts, the play burlesqued institutional anxiety about imparting life-values to the young (Koch 1966, 43–66). But Diane Wakoski, in *The George Washington Poems* (1967), took a national icon as a symbol of male stolidity to be targeted ad infinitum. Wakoski found in Washington an array of burdensome negatives, confronting him in one poem as father-figure, in another as mystifying footnote in history, then as fussy surveyor, as politically incorrect slaveholder, as failed lover, as military man, and even as estranged companion to a black Uncle Sam. In poems scored for oral delivery, Wakoski's feminist voice turned playful and sharp, witty and defiant. The Surreal in such verse lay in its insouciant behavior as it sustained a politics of ideological critique (Wakoski 1967).

One text that would define second generation New York poetry was not designed to be delivered as clear talk but constructed as a cut-up, to muddle communication. Ted Berrigan's *The Sonnets* (1964) deployed word-games across a cluster of poems driven by conversational buzz, peppered with repeating phrases, sometimes outrageously jumbled with lines shuffled out of sequence, needing reconstitution. Berrigan adored O'Hara's "I do this" poems and imitated several, but his best impulse was to begin outrageously, stepping into a verbal thicket that might lead anywhere: "Joyful ants rest on the roof on my tree" (XLIX), or "Ou sont les neiges des neiges?" (XXXIII) or "my dream a drink with Lonnie Johnson we discuss the code of the west" (LXXXII) (Berrigan 2000, 46, 30, 73). (Discussing "the code of the west" with various figures is a thread running through the sonnets.) The bravado of such unlikely beginnings carries Berrigan far. By contrast, Ron Padgett's *Great Balls of Fire* (1969) extends the concept of the doodle in a collection that alludes to cartoons; sketching verse sparsely, producing maximum effect with minimal effort, the poetic tradition becomes an archive to be irreverently absorbed and replayed subversively while burlesquing everyone (even O'Hara, in "Strawberries in Mexico" [Padgett 1969, 83–5]), celebrating poetry as an art with no borders, with rules that can always be revised.

Extending the Surreal: "Deep Image" Poets

As second-generation poets expanded the New York school, they made common cause with such Beat writers as Diane di Prima, who published in *Angel Hair* (1966–9, coedited by Waldman with Lewis Warsh), just as Waldman would appear in *Women of the Beat Generation*. Others in New York, however, declared common cause with West Coast and Black Mountain poets interested in myth. Their engagement with the Surreal tradition turned on the literary, with translation serving them as painting had once challenged conventional expectations. Editing *From the Floating World* (1959–63), Jerome Rothenberg invoked a "deep image" with roots in dream-like Spanish Surrealism as "the content of the vision emerging in the poem" (Rothenberg 1998, 117). Robert Bly's poem in the first issue blended the mechanical and the fantastic, imagining cars in an automobile graveyard eerily revived: "The ghosts of the dead motors are singing / And birds are rising from undiscovered lakes" (Bly 1959, 4). He would pursue the significance of "undiscovered lakes" in later poems in *Silence in the Snowy Fields* (1962). Within a bare and vast Minnesota setting these find the "strange and dark features" that are the "true / Gift, beneath the pale lakes of Minnesota" (Bly 1961, 56).

The "deep image" sensibility, Bly writes in the important essay "Looking for Dragon Smoke" (1967), rests on a "freedom of association" that opens "corridors to the unconscious" that permit a "leaping – really about the psyche" (Bly 1967, 10). But Spanish Surrealists, Bly wrote, differed from French surrealists whose associational leaps were dry, rational ("many believe that the unconscious does not *have* emotions"); in contrast, Spanish Surrealists enter a poem "excited, with the emotions alive … angry or ecstatic, or disgusted" (Bly 1975, 40). "The Teeth-Mother Naked at Last" (1970), exposing the short-range strategies of military success, introduces a cruel aesthetics in its opening – "Massive engines lift beautifully from the deck. / Wings appear over the trees, wings with eight hundred rivets" – that it counters in its closing with visionary longing: "let us drive cars / up / the light beams / to the stars ..." with its Whitmanian ellipsis that elicits assent (Bly 1973, 18, 26). Bly's poetry readings present his works alongside others; an admirer of tiny poems, he would gift his audiences with pamphlets featuring the eighteenth century Japanese poet Issa that situate humans in the natural world: "Insects, why cry? / We all go / that way" (Bly 2004, 222). Deep image in such poems moves associationally to reveal affiliating networks.

James Wright's apprenticeship with Theodore Roethke at the University of Washington prepared him for a friendship with Bly, as Roethke's "regressive" verse that dabbled in word-sounds, especially when aligned with descriptions of the natural world, enabled Wright to shift from tidy rhymed pentameters to free verse in *The Branch Will Not Break* (1963) with leaps that reveal networks both destructive and supportive. Two widely acclaimed poems resist the summary gesture featured in the well-made poems Wright had been trained to produce. In "Lying in a Hammock in William Duffy's Farm," Wright follows exquisite observations in which the ordinary is enriched with the startling but apt pronouncement: "I have wasted my life" (Wright 1971, 114). In a similar way, the realization that concludes "A Blessing" – "if I stepped out of my body I would break / into blossom" – culminates a description of two ponies who approach with a welcome delicacy (Wright 1971, 135). The finale-effect in both poems is not, however, a compressed moment that drives us back into the poem but the opposite: It imagines a stepping away from the poem's field to escape elsewhere. The Surrealist impulse to make art within the everyday is here wrought literally to a breaking pitch, and in the remarkably flat yet vivid poems of *Shall We Gather at the River* (1968), Wright rejects even the "leap" Bly had championed, moving toward a figure addressed as "Jenny," who occupies the book's final poem, "To the Muse." Poised with her on the bank of the Ohio River, where the lives of the lost succumb to time's flow, Wright again ends dramatically: "Come up to me, love, / Out of the river, or I will / Come down to you" (Wright 1971, 169). Jenny is never a fully drawn presence. Barely casting a shadow – a girl driven to prostitution, victim of a botched abortion or a possible suicide – she represents the impossibility of recording the forgotten, neglected, and discarded even as they call out to be remembered.

Wright and Bly operated in a setting dominated by natural forces, different from the urban reality of the New York poets. Drawn to such "third world" surrealists as Neruda and Vallejo, immersed in a "soft surrealism" of dreamlike moments, Bly and Wright's attendance on the uncanny imagined art whose profound desires countered repressive social regimes. That release began, for W. S. Merwin, a contemporary of Bly and Wright returning to America in 1956 on a fellowship to the Poets' Theatre after seven years in

Europe, when he began rewriting his play "Favor Island," replacing its conversational exchanges with nightmarish inklings of disaster (Merwin 1957, 122–54). Working with the *greguería*, the fractured aphorism that short-circuits expectations and recharges understanding ("And the hands of the clock still knock without entering") and translating Neruda's poems of city violence, Merwin assembled an archive of resistance in *The Moving Target* (1963), in which he bid farewell to compromise attitudes and embraced the pain of leave-taking as itself empowering: "Tell me what you see vanishing and I / Will tell you who you are / To Whom I say Goodbye" (Merwin 1963, 33, 93). Merwin built on his negatives in *The Lice* (1967) to associate war in Asia with environmental catastrophe. The same authority that extinguishes entire species unthinkingly, because "it is we who are important" cannot understand "There is no season / That requires us" (Merwin 1988, 139, 125). He tracks evasions, distractions, omissions, examining habitual acts in a searing light in *The Carrier of Ladders* (1970), then reveals possible beginnings in *Writings to an Unfinished Accompaniment* (1973) with a language that promises a new clarity: "before me stones begin to go out like candles / guiding me" (Merwin 1988, 223). Supporting Merwin are natural events almost unnoticed – "shadows of leaves slip along me / crossing my face" (Merwin 1988, 208) – and phrases worn smooth by centuries of poets, a community of ancestors sending messages across time, even anonymously in texts from the Crow tribe ("Your way / is turning bad // and nobody but you / is there" (Merwin 1979, 1965).

Thinking within deep imagery prepares for a "deep ecology" whose anti-anthropocentrism takes scope from a "biospheric perspective on all living and nonliving parts of the earth" that, in Elizabeth A. Povinelli's words, calls attention to "the deforming nature of the human perspective" (Povinelli 2011, 104). A. R. Ammons's engagements with natural events question the extent of that "deforming nature" without denying it, in which the poem is a human effort to work as a complex system to honor its surroundings as a complex system. Ammons wants to think at the micro- and the macro-level: "the universe comes / to bear / on a willow-slip and / you cannot unwind / a pebble / from its constellations" (Ammons 1968, 104). As descriptive detail comports with generalizing tendency, the poem becomes a system dependent on modification, gathering new information into sets of feedback loops shaping the work away from the improbable. Anticipating Niklas Luhmann's *Art as a Social System* (2000), in which the poem streams "contextual dependencies, ironic references, and paradoxes, all of which refer back to the text that generates these effects" (Luhmann 2000, 125), Ammons depicts a world, as in the title poem of *Corson's Inlet* (1965), that dynamically clusters words across the page, inviting puzzlement, resolving dilemmas temporarily, in line with a setting without boundaries that features "manifold events," that offers "the possibility of rule as the sum of rulelessness" and that has "no finality of vision" because "tomorrow a new walk is a new walk" (Ammons 1968, 137, 139, 140).

Each small poem Ammons produces generates its own set of self-correcting forms that make up an open system. In *Garbage* (1993), Ammons (age sixty-three) writes about dying friends ("if you are not gone at a certain // age, your world is,") and a planet buried under "Styrofoam verbiage: since words were // introduced here things have gone poorly for the / planet." (Ammons 1993, 93, 74). Still, Ammons insists on continuing: "poems / that give up the ideal of making sense do not // give up the ideal of not making sense" (Ammons 1993, 89). *Garbage* is digressive, verbose, and diffuse, but for all the detritus it bears, it refuses to be refuse.

"Where Ammons veers between centers and peripheries," Willard Spiegelman observes, "for Ashbery there is no center, no substance, only discrete particulars" (Spiegelmann 2005, 154). Yet both these poets – writing as one century closed and another began – reveal that Surrealist influence, that intrusion of inconvenient and even incompatible elements troubling a system but in the process actually testing its durability and extending its range. As O'Hara described Surrealism in 1959, it was not simply a call for "idiosyncratic experimentation.... Surrealism enjoined the duty, along with the liberation, of saying what you mean and meaning what you say, above and beyond any fondness for saying or meaning" (O'Hara 1959, 15, 16). For poets who took up this prompt, it was the radical adjustment that both clarifies and transforms. This important strain in American poetry moves into the twenty-first century with exemplary texts – the meditative sequence reconceived by Ashbery and Ammons, the ecological lyric in all its modes from the urban to the pastoral from O'Hara to Bly and Merwin, and innovations by Guest that redefine the expanse of poetic space and that continue in the work of Notley, Waldman, and others.

BIBLIOGRAPHY

Ammons, A. R. 1968. *Selected Poems*. Ithaca, NY: Cornell University Press.
    Garbage. 1993. New York: W. W. Norton.
Ashbery, John. 1970. *Some Trees*. New York: Corinth.
    1991. *Reported Sightings: Art Chronicles 1957–1987*. Ed. David Bergman. Cambridge, MA: Harvard University Press.
    2000. *Other Traditions*. Charles Eliot Norton Lectures, 1989–90. Cambridge, MA: Harvard University Press.
Auslander, Philip. 1989. *The New York School Poets as Playwrights: O'Hara, Ashbery, Koch, Schuyler and the Visual Arts*. New York: Lang.

Berrigan, Ted. 2000. *The Sonnets*. Introduction by Alice Notley. New York: Penguin.

Bly, Robert. 1959. "The Inner Life Has Its Own Joy (I)." *Poems from the Floating World* 1: 4.

— 1961. *Silence in the Snowy Fields*. Middletown, CT: Wesleyan University Press.

— 1967. "Searching for Dragon Smoke." *Stand: A Quarterly of the Arts* 9: 10–12.

— 1973. *Sleepers Joining Hands*. New York: Harper & Row.

— 1975. *Leaping Poetry: An Idea with Poems and Translations*. Pittsburgh: University of Pittsburgh Press.

— 2004. *The Winged Energy of Delight: Selected Translations*. New York: HarperCollins.

Breton, André. 1969. "Manifesto of Surrealism." *Manifestoes of Surrealism*. Translated by Richard Seaver and Helen Lane. Ann Arbor: University of Michigan Press.

Daffy Duck in Hollywood. 1938. Directed by Fred Avery. Burbank, CA: Warner Home Video. DVD.

Davidson, Michael. 1983. "Ekphrasis and the Postmodern Painter Poem." *Journal of Aesthetics and Art Criticism* 42: 69–79.

Guest, Barbara. 1976. *The Countess from Minneapolis*. Providence, RI: Burning Deck.

— 1995. *Selected Poems*. Los Angeles: Sun and Moon Press.

— 2003. *Forces of Imagination: Writing on Writing*. Berkeley, CA: Kelsey St. Press.

Hobbs, Robert. 2005. "Surrealism and Abstract Expressionism: From Psychic to Plastic Automatism." In *Surrealism USA*. Ed. Isabelle Dervaux, 56–65. New York: National Academy Museum.

Koch, Kenneth. 1966. *Bertha and Other Plays*. New York: Grove Press.

— 2007. "Ko, or a Season on Earth." In *On the Edge: Collected Longer Poems*. New York: Knopf.

Luhmann, Niklas. 2000. *Art as a Social System*. Translated by Eva M. Knodt. Stanford, CA: Stanford University Press.

Merwin, W. S. 1957. *Favor Island*. In *New World Writing* 12: 122–54.

— 1963. *The Moving Target*. New York: Atheneum.

— 1979. *Selected Translations 1948–1968*. New York: Atheneum.

— 1988. *Selected Poems*. New York: Knopf.

Myers, John Bernard. 1977. "Surrealism and New York Painting, 1940–1948: A Reminiscence." *ArtForum* 15: 55–8.

Neiman, Catrina. 1992. *Introduction to View: Parade of the Avant-Garde, 1940–1947*. Eds. Catrina Neiman and Paul Nathan, xi-xvi. New York: Thunder's Mouth Press.

Nelson, Maggie. 2007. *Women, the New York School and Other Abstractions*. Iowa City: University of Iowa Press.

Notley, Alice. 1993. *Selected Poems*. Hoboken, NJ: Talisman House.

O'Hara, Frank. 1959. *Jackson Pollock*, New York: Braziller.

— 1971. *The Collected Poems of Frank O'Hara*. Ed. Donald Allen. New York: Knopf.

Padgett, Ron. 1969. *Great Balls of Fire*. Chicago: Holt, Rinehart and Winston.

Perkins, David. 1987. *A History of Modern Poetry: Modernism and After*. Cambridge, MA: Harvard University Press.

Perloff, Marjorie. 1977. *Frank O'Hara: Poet Among Painters*. New York: Braziller.

Poulin Jr., A. 1981. "The Experience of Experiencing: A Conversation with John Ashbery." 1972. In *Michigan Quarterly Review* 20: 242–52

Povinelli, Elizabeth A. 2011. *Economies of Abandonment: Social Belonging and Endurance in Late Liberalism.* Durham, NC: Duke University Press.

Rothenberg, Jerome. 1961. Statement. *Poems from the Floating World* 3: inside cover.

Sayre, Nora. 1995. *Previous Convictions: A Journey through the 1950s.* New Brunswick, NJ: Rutgers University Press.

Schuyler, James. 1988. *Selected Poems.* New York: Farrar, Straus, Giroux.

   1998. *Selected Art Writings.* Ed. Simon Pettet. Santa Rosa, CA: Black Sparrow.

Sontag, Susan. 1999. "Notes on 'Camp.'" In *Camp: Queer Aesthetics and the Performing Subject: A Reader.* Ed. Fabio Cleto, 53–65. Ann Arbor: University of Michigan Press.

Spiegelman, Willard. 2005. *How Poets See the World: The Art of Description in Contemporary Poetry.* New York: Oxford University Press.

Wakoski, Diane. 1967. *The George Washington Poems.* New York: Rivverrun press.

Waldman, Anne. 1989. *Helping the Dreamer: New and Selected Poems 1966–1988.* Minneapolis: Coffee House Press.

Wright, James. 1971. *Collected Poems.* Middletown, CT: Wesleyan University Press.

16

JANET MCADAMS

Land, Place, and Nation: Toward an Indigenous American Poetics

> The space between things is as much as the things space separates.
> – Diane Glancy
>
> Where we come from is also who we are.
> – Gladys Cardiff

Published in 1993, poet and critic Kimberly Blaeser's "Native Literature: Seeking a Critical Center" issued a "call for an 'organic' native critical language" (56). Blaeser sought to reclaim Native literary studies from extrinsic literary interpretation; her essay marked the shift away from the focus on individual identity that dominated the field in response to the so-called Native American Renaissance of the 1970s and '80s, as she argued for a critical intervention

> alert for critical methods and voices that seem to arise out of the literature itself (this as opposed to critical approaches applied from an already established critical language or attempts to make the literature fit already established genres and categories of meaning).   (Blaeser 1993, 53–4)

Named by Kenneth Lincoln in his 1983 eponymous critical study, the Native American Renaissance referred especially to a handful of novels that each featured a mixed-blood protagonist struggling to discover his place in the world. The first of these, N. Scott Momaday's *House Made of Dawn* won the Pulitzer Prize in 1969; it was followed by James Welch's *Winter in the Blood* (1974), Leslie Marmon Silko's *Ceremony* (1977), and Louise Erdrich's *Love Medicine* (1984). The critical response to these works focused on the genre of the novel and identity, attending in particular to the image of the mixed-blood as a symbol for the vexed relationship between tradition and modernity in the lives of the contemporary American Indian characters who populated these Renaissance-era works. As such, it dovetailed beautifully with Cold War narrative frames about individual struggle and triumph.

Blaeser's article was followed by a handful of critical monographs, chief among them Robert Warrior's influential 1994 study *Tribal Secrets,* which made the case for reading Indigenous writing within tribal frameworks rather than bringing to bear upon them more cosmopolitan and universalizing theoretical paradigms. Warrior drew upon Simon J. Ortiz's 1981 essay, "Towards a National Indian Literature: Cultural Authenticity in Nationalism," which noted that "The struggle to maintain life and the resistance against loss ... illustrate a theme, national in character and scope, common to all American native people and to all people indigenous to lands which have suffered imperialism and colonialism" (Warrior 2005, 259). Literary nationalism, the rubric under which these newer theoretical interests accrue, thus holds that questions of sovereignty must figure in the way we read, define, contextualize, and understand Indigenous American writing.

At the center of literary nationalism, land abides as both key material concern and trope – land manifested as national boundary, as sovereign struggle, as well as a broader signifier of space, place, and location. Because nationalist readings – given the emphasis on the ways texts speak from, for, and back to tribal nations – have tended to be thematically driven, I am interested in the ways a nationalist reading methodology can be extended to accommodate poetry's special concerns,[1] among them its formal patterns and the lyric voice, which might seem to offer a reader unmediated access to the Indigenous subject. I am not suggesting that pan-Indian themes or formal strategies unite the widely diverse projects of the poets from six different Indigenous nations I discuss in the following pages: Simon Ortiz (Acoma Pueblo), Diane Glancy (Cherokee), Linda Hogan (Chickasaw), Deborah Miranda (Esselen-Chumash), Gladys Cardiff (Eastern Band Cherokee), and Layli Long Soldier (Oglala Lakota).[2] Rather, I consider how land – and specifically land theft as an historical constant – contextualizes the way absence and presence signify on the page, both thematically and formally. Given the history of more than two centuries of land theft, it is not surprising that place remains a persistent and immutable issue in Native-authored poetry. Writing about her own nation, Jodi Byrd explains: "There is a difference between recovered and having never lost in the first place that stands in breach still for those of us attempting to theorize the legacies of colonialism within indigenous worlds" (Byrd 2011, xi). Thus, Native poets bear witness in multiple ways to "what stands in breach"; they produce an array of what Hank Lazer calls "opposing poetries," that is, "poetries that critique and contest assumptions and practices of more mainstream poetries" (Lazer 1996, 1–2). Dean Rader calls these practices "compositional resistance," which is "an intentional reluctance to make a text conform to the formulaic expectations of its genre," and he notes, "Almost every Native poet produces some sort of compositional resistance, either through line breaks, capitalization, closure, fragmentation, play with poetic traditions, bilingualism, and even genre shifting"(Rader 2011, 129).[3]

Cherokee author Diane Glancy exemplifies this "compositional resistance" throughout her work, which includes poetry, fiction, memoir, essays, plays, and films. Glancy, the daughter of an Indigenous father and a white mother, frequently attends to questions of mixed heritage, and her poems might seem ideal candidates for a retrograde, Renaissance-era critique focused on hybrid subjects trapped between worlds. But the borders that preoccupy Glancy are equally – if not more so – of language and form, and her subjects are not merely acted upon: They exercise agency, not just to "drift" passively but to "redrift," to regain old ground. She writes:

> In the dryings after a flood, there are revisions. In new versions, there are redrifts and "transveillances" across cultures. There are reconstructions of the sentence. Which I hit when writing. Because the sentence constructs a way of thinking which does not include the transpositions, the fragmentations, the interjections, the disjunctions.   (Glancy 1999, 114)

Glancy, who is perhaps best known for her formally innovative work, is a master of the fragmentary; she crosses borders between and among literary genres. I begin, however, with one of her more formally conventional poems, "Without Title," which is written in the form of a personal lyric and driven by a conceit: The speaking subject's dispossessed Indian father, because he can no longer follow Cherokee hunting traditions, has been relegated to mere figurative hunting, that is, as a day worker in a meatpacking house:

> Without Title
> *for my father who lived without ceremony*
>
> It's hard you know without the buffalo,
> the shaman, the arrow,
> but my father went out each day to hunt
> as though he had them.
> He worked in the stockyards.
> All his life he brought us meat.
> No one marked his first kill,
> no one sang his buffalo song.
> Without a vision he had migrated to the city
> and went to work in the packing house.
> When he brought home his horns and hides
> my mother said, *get rid of them.*
> I remember the animal tracks of his car
> backing out the drive in snow and mud,
> the aerial on his old car waving like a bow string.

I remember the silence of his lost power,
the red buffalo painted on his chest.
Oh, I couldn't see it
but it was there, and in the night I heard
his buffalo grunts like a snore.

(Glancy 2005, 107)

Thematically, the father lives without title to homelands in the South taken away by the removals of the 1830s, and without the title accorded to someone, especially an elder, who lives *with* ceremony. This absence, this "withoutness," pervades the poem. His disenfranchisement is layered and multiple. In addition to the historical weight of his nation's removal from the South, he is displaced from the present-day nation in Oklahoma, living, as he does, "without ceremony." The father's work is defined by what it is not; not hunting, but killing and annihilation – negation, absence, negative space as it were – constitute the poem's subject.

The poem's title is a joke so bluntly obvious that its more subtle unfolding throughout the poem provides surprise after surprise. The place where the title should appear – at the head of the poem as well as in the book's table of contents – is a figurative blank: The poem is "without title." Indeed, the poem is constructed as a series of dislocations; it continually points not to *what* it isn't but to *where* it isn't, until it comes to its ultimate dislocation, the reversal of the poem's conceit. There, the father is transformed from the already lamented state of not-hunter to the entity equally diminished in this life "without ceremony," the hunted, whose "buffalo grunts" are "like a snore."

In other poems, such as her short lyric "Tuning," Glancy does not merely describe the dislocations of Indigenous experience, but renders them spatially on the page:

My father's Cherokee heritage tucked under
some sort of shame. The past _____
What was it?   (Glancy 2005, 31)

Similarly, her "Christopher" deploys language conspicuously poised to unsettle and dislocate. In it, she uses an invented pidgin, a mixture (but not a creole) of English and Spanish to disrupt colonialist narratives of simple Natives greeting Columbus's arrival in the Americas:

Hey Yndias. He say. HEY ERMERICA.
He brang glaz beads & bells.
Luego se ayunto alli mucha gente dla Isla.
We think he god from skie. Yup. Yup. Wedu.

(Glancy 2005, 17)

In his description of the "compositional resistance" of Native poetry, Dean Rader refers to the "bilingualism" increasingly to be found in the works of certain Native poets who code switch between English and their tribal language. While Glancy speaks neither Spanish nor Cherokee, I would yet argue that she has effected a complex *multi*lingualism in "Columbus." This is Glancy's radically imaginative and layered version of what Gloria Bird and Joy Harjo call "reinventing the enemy's language" (1998); what has been reinvented – and thrown back in the face of the enemy – is the infantilizing "Tonto-speak" (Hilden 1995, 55) accorded to the newly colonized Indigenous speaker. Glancy extends the joke even further, switching between Tonto-speak Spanish and Tonto-speak English and throwing in a handful of nonsense syllables, thus subverting the colonialist logic of Columbus's "discovery of the New World" with wild silliness. She does not write back to the empire; she ridicules it.

In his book-length poem, *from Sand Creek*, Simon J. Ortiz (Acoma Pueblo) also reckons with the ways empire and its damages might be written down and written back to. Published in 1981 by Thunder's Mouth Press and reprinted in 1999 by Arizona, *from Sand Creek* links the historical trauma of the 1864 Sand Creek Massacre to the lives of the veterans in the nearby Fort Lyon, Colorado, Veterans Administration hospital, where Ortiz was hospitalized for alcoholism in 1974–5. *from Sand Creek* has an intricate and complicated structure; it is both a collection of closely tied verses and a book-length poem. It comprises extremely terse lyrics on each of the forty-two recto pages juxtaposed with prose epigraphs on each of the verso pages.

The first of these epigraphs sets up the situation of the project: "Passing through, one gets caught into things: this time it was the Veterans Administration Hospital, Ft. Lyons, Colorado, 1974–1975" (10). The epigraph not only frames the poem facing it, but locates the entire project: Fort Lyon – where Ortiz spent time as a veteran in recovery – and Sand Creek, site of the 1864 massacre of Southern Cheyenne and Arapaho people. "How to deal with history – that is the question," Ortiz explains in a note to the new edition. These prose epigraphs are likewise arguably epigrams; the poem is both expansive and economical, both, as Dean Rader argues, lyric and epic (2003, 135–6).

The book's frames are marked typographically: The lyrics appear in roman text, the epigraphs appear in italics, and there is front matter including an historical note and what I call the two "America verses," which are printed in a weighty, sans serif boldface. That is to say, in addition to the book's actual covers, there are two additional sets of frames enclosing the interior, the juxtaposed prose and verse sections that make up the heart of the book. Just as the language of *from Sand Creek* is intent upon delimiting Sand Creek through boundaries of historical trauma, pinning down in sharp and exacting detail what happened in this particular place, so do the typographical frames of the book's material presence serve to enclose and delimit its interior. The effect is twofold: Not only is it necessary to cross through instructive boundaries to enter the poem fully, these boundaries make the poem into a reliquary, a version of a monument that can be wrought on paper. There is a striking visual impact to the layout of this and each pair of pages. The carefully placed juxtaposition of prose epigraph and verse (which recurs forty-two times) is reminiscent of a vitrine, a display case for objects of significance.

> [verso page]
> Passing through, one gets caught into things: this time it was the
> Veterans Administration Hospital, Ft. Lyons, Colorado, 1974–75.
>
> [recto page]
> Grief
> memorizes this grass.
> Raw
> courage,
>   believe it,
> red-eyed and urgent,
> stalking Denver.
> Like stone,
> like steel,
> the hone and sheer gone,
> just the brute
> and perceptive angle left.
>
> Like courage,
>   believe it,
>
> left still;
> the words from then
> talk like that.
>
> Believe it.   (Ortiz 1999, 10–11)

The poem takes as self-evident that place and land are deeply connected to historical trauma. The first verse – with what Robert Warrior has called its "incredibly focused first image" (2009, 393) – subtly unsettles the more expected notion of trauma attaching to place. Rather, Ortiz constructs the inverse; it is not the grass bearing witness to grief, but grief itself encoding this place in its memory. His terse lineation, particularly as it is set in relief against its prose epigraph, and framing strategies draw our gaze uncomfortably and intimately into the book's heart. It is difficult to look away. The use of present tense here –"memorizes" – points to the site's unique temporality. His refrain – "Believe it" – is insistent: Ortiz refuses to relegate to the past the events of Sand Creek, as so many things Indian are relegated to the past, closed off and over with, fit only as a locus for imperialist nostalgia.[4]

These essential and historical connections between land and Indigenous body are also crucial in Linda Hogan's 1993 collection, *The Book of Medicines*. In the opening poem, "The History of Red," red is a multifaceted force connecting the flesh of the body with the flesh of the land. Red is blood; it is also "this yielding land / turned inside out" (1993, 9). The poem works its way through the various interconnected elements: earth, water, and finally fire. I have noted elsewhere that Hogan's lineation is deceptively plain in style (2010, 226–35), suggesting that the relentlessly short line that drives *The Book of Medicines* has a cumulative effect, exacerbating the sense of witness borne to genocide and environmental wreckage. This effect seems evident in the penultimate stanza. Hogan writes:

> Red is the human house
> I come back to at night
> swimming inside the cave of skin
> that remembers bison.
> In that round nation of blood
> we are all burning,
> red, inseparable fires
> the living have crawled
> and climbed through
> in order to live
> so nothing will be left
> for death at the end.   (Hogan 1993, 11)

Lineation wrought from phrases already designated by the syntax tends to produce language that is fluid and untroubling. Hogan builds upon this effect, moving from the seemingly straightforward "In that round nation of blood / we are all burning," to the subtle friction in "red, inseparable fires" with its polysyllabic, slightly thorny adjective to the deeply unsettling "the living have crawled / and climbed through / in order to live." These lines unsettle not only for the images they conjure – the desperation implicit in the verb "crawled" – but also for the way the first line break works on the line retroactively: In the first reading, the living have *crawled* the fires, the intransitive verb becomes transitive; in the second, the meaning shifts, not dramatically, but abruptly – "have crawled / and climbed *through*" (my emphasis). The following line – "in order to live" – registers as afterthought, its position a casual aside belying the significance of the words.

Thematically, this stanza not only points to the remarkable chain of transformations that links body with home, nation, and the essential energy of the universe, but also, through the key image of the "cave of skin," Hogan's verse simultaneously articulates the earth's bodily presence even as it makes the body into a part of an energized and fluid landscape. Skin figures as a site of exchange between earth and body, and this seeming permeability is essential to the functioning of the world she documents. It is what precludes separation, what enables full connection. Loss, grief, joy – all are experienced as shared phenomena. When violence is waged against the Indigenous body, it is also waged against the land. When land is broken open, the Indigenous body is broken.

In the prefatory author's note to her 1999 collection, *Indian Cartography*, Esselen-Chumash poet Deborah Miranda writes: "The worst legacy of all for California Indians whose ancestry emerged from the Missions was the basic loss of familial connections through a diasporic, desperate scattering of tribes without a landbase" (xii). Published six years after Hogan's *The Book of Medicines*, *Indian Cartography* is also deeply informed by the lived and essential relationship between place and Native body, in particular the moving poem "I Dreamt Your True Name," an erotically charged love letter from the land to the Indigenous body (or bodies) displaced from it. Here Miranda mines an eros that is as maternal and fecund as it is sensual:

> Our past
>
> evolved in my belly:
> centuries of rain
> gave way to ripening.
> Between my legs valleys
> deepened into rivers
> where you bathed
> in early mornings.
> (Miranda 1999, 94)

The poem is left-justified, with the first two stanzas written in an easeful plain style, its line breaks corresponding to the syntax. The suspension of the phrase "our past" over the break between stanzas one and two highlights and emphasizes that this is a poem about history. The restful quality of the language is enhanced by the long vowels toward the end of the stanza: "milkweed," "weaving," "flowed." The poem's first significant turn occurs in stanza three, when the land and its people are colonized:

> We did not see
> evil coming in masks of
> disease, murder, displacement.
> We became separated from
> one another.
> I could not find you.
> (Miranda 1999, 94–5)

The "We" that marks this turn is simultaneously lover and loved, moth-erland and Indigene. The line that follows, with its abrupt break after the preposition "of," disrupts the easeful – I would argue even *loving* – cadences that have come before. Miranda unsettles the language further by ratcheting up the consonance:

> Your bones
> came back to me unbroken,
> scattered without ceremony.
> My body bore bright scars.
> (Miranda 1999, 95)

Ending with a plea for the lost one to return, the poem deploys a language that is both loving and fiercely insistent:

> Follow it back to me.
> I want to feel your handprints
> on my skin, your teeth in my hair.
> I want the dark cloud of
> memory to open –
> release the perfect syllables
> of your birth.
> (Miranda 1999, 95)

Following the abrupt break after "dark cloud of," the word "memory" is deeply resonant, an emphasis paralleling the phrase "Our past" earlier in the poem. But where "Our past" is actual, literal, to be acknowledged, the loom-ing, to-be-shared "dark cloud of memory" is considerably more powerful, promising rain, storm, change.

Like Miranda, Gladys Cardiff deploys the erotic as a way both to investigate colonization and to resist it. Her 1999 collection, *A Bare, Unpainted Table*, opens with an epigraph from a sixteenth century English traveler to the Americas: "These simple gentiles lyvinge only after the lawe of nature, may well bee lykened to a smoothe and bare table unpainted, or a white paper unwritten upon" (5). This coloniz-ing conception of the Indigenous body as "unpainted" or "unwritten upon" is the subject of "Prelude to Love," an ekphrastic poem based on a "Victorian postcard [of a]

> photo, a portrait. Long hair, black eyes –
> my gaze skips the rest.
> Whose wouldn't? Except for a necklace, no,
> not a necklace, except for her earrings, she's naked.
> (Cardiff 1999, 7)

Although they approach the colonizing of Indigenous erotics from different perspectives, both Miranda and Cardiff deploy the erotic as a potent force for resisting colonization. While Miranda's focus is on the essential and abiding bond between homeland and Indigenous body, Cardiff shows how tenaciously unsettling the seemingly captured Native body can be. Her subject is

> standing under the arch of a mission window, looking out.
> Almost courtly, the arousals, almost Spenserian, to be so framed,
> > *her neather parts*
> concealed *in secret shadow farre from all men's sight,*
> space pulled up like a high-waisted Empire gown.   (Cardiff 1999, 8)

It is, of course, not the gown itself that covers the subject's "neather parts," but imperial space writ large, covering the land and culture it finds with language and laws, and with missions. But the body is persistently unsettling, disruptive to the colonial logic that attempts to pose and fix it. Because the photograph and its frame are insufficient to contain their subject, it must be made "archival," filed under the "legend: / Dangers of the Indian Country" (1999, 8).

Of the thirty-seven lines in "Prelude to Love," six are indented, four strikingly so. Because so much of the poem appears in the more conventional left-justified lineation, the poem's dispersed lines[5] are particularly conspicuous and disruptive, especially the four indented all the way to the poem's right boundary: "do they match?" – referring to the subject's "black eyes" and "hoped-for, pleasurable, reassuring mouth" – "cropped" to mark the portion of the body left out of the photograph – "*her neather parts*" and "Dangers of the Indian Country," as ultimate disruptors, the eroticized, dangerous Indigenous body, the one the colonizer looks to both for pleasure and reassurance against its dangers.

"Prelude to Love," along with the epigraph about "unwritten upon" Natives, opens the first part of Cardiff's two-part collection; the epigraph of its second half introduces poems characterized by subtle yet important formal differences from the first. Cited as a "Cherokee Sacred Formula," the epigraph states: "May the paths from every direction recognize each other" (1999, 33). No dispersed lines appear in any of the Part II poems, and, while an array of subjects populate the book's second half, themes of homecoming are especially visible, particularly in the handful of poems that close the volume. The final poem, "Two Plots: Qualla Boundary, Cherokee," is set on the Eastern Band's Reservation in Cherokee, North Carolina, as the speaker returns for a funeral and ponders "the two little cemeteries [that] are fitted on either side of the road" (1999, 60). While there are literally two cemetery plots in the poem, "plot" is also a pun that points to two different stories, the one where "space allotted is carved and fitted" and the other where space

> dissembles, yellow and overgrown.
> In the shadows, crosses and headstones, dull bronze plaques,
>
> and inconspicuous flowers strewn like afterthoughts.
> (Cardiff 1999, 60)

As well, the two plots allude to the volume's two stories, the rupture of colonization documented in the first half and the possibility of return driving the second – the "paths from every direction [that] recognize each other." "Some things won't fit in a photograph," the speaker of "Two Plots" tells us, as she surveys the rich and familiar landscape around her, bringing the volume full circle, back to the opening poem, with its cropped photograph, its concealments, and its dangers. Stories that circulate out of context are necessarily incomplete, like a portrait of a table, which, from the wrong perspective, only seems bare and unpainted.

Finally, I come to the poet who, among the six I discuss, has most recently come into print, Layli Long Soldier (Oglala Lakota) whose chapbook, *Chromosomory*, appeared in 2010. Describing her discovery of the long poem after "labor[ing] over small poems and cautious line breaks," Long Soldier says,

> I learned I could write one single poem and extend it to its furthest outer limits, I could take it as far as I wanted and exhaust myself. How beautiful. Long poems allowed me to really explore and grow into a subject, to write in sections and experiment with form.   (Long Soldier 2013, 4)

Her poem "Hˆe Sapa" is a long, formally complex poetic work engaged with language play, visual poetry, and field composition. It is also an extended meditation that begins with the mountain of the title, part of the contested Lakota homeland occupied by the United States, and "not a black hill, not Paha Sapa, by any name you call it" (2012), then moves through a series of linguistic associations – English and Lakota. Long Soldier literally extends the poem to "its furthest outer limits" on the page. Sections one and two sprawl from left to right margin. Four is right-justified, and five is left-justified, with a single line unfurling across the page. Poised in the poem's center – section three – is a field of white space, boxed in by four lines of poetry, each of which is a variation on the line, "This is how you see me the space in which to place me."

Three

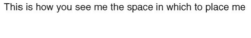

This is how you see me the space in which to place me

This is how to place you in the space in which to see

The space in me you see   is this place

To see this space   see how you place me in you

"Hˆe Sapa," a poem that visually claims – aggressively so – the full space of the page, is both a poem *about* resistance and a poem that perpetually resists through key syntactical and lexical strategies. Through a gaze that is both exacting and intimate, meaning is approached but never resolved: "Because **drag** changes when spoken of in the past i.e. he was **dragged**, or they **drug** him down the long road, the pale rock and brown" (2012). Even as the poem seems poised to settle into narrative, into a particular story of violence – "Then begins a yank / and slide, begins his skin and scalp" – it is irrupted by the enclosed white space of section three. Arguably, the poem's crucial turn occurs in the final section when the speaker discovers that the earlier images of violence have changed, "not one word sounds as before." The brutalized head of section one is now "each born to our own crown – a single power, our distinction" and "dragging" is a gesture toward wholeness: "I'm dragging myself, the other me, every strand up to the surface." Location is crucial here; these are discoveries that can only be made – and it is the poem's most marvelous surprise – in "the hairline light of kitchen and home."

Localities – material and textual – I would argue, figure in the work of many Native poets, where they are charged with the historical condition of land theft and its varied implications: diaspora and removal, but also reclamation and resilience. If we posit the text itself as *locale* – the quintessential site at which Native studies and literary studies meet – we make possible "critical methods … that seem to arise from the literature itself" (Blaeser

53–4) and enable a full accounting of the historical and cultural currents – including the intricacies of literary form – that circulate through and around this fluid and heterogeneous *locale*,[6] the poem.

NOTES

1 In a longer essay – or one intended for a different venue – I could also make the argument for a greater attention to formal concerns in all genres. Generic categories are meaningful but unstable, and larger claims about what poems *are* or *do* break down in the face of the particular. For the purposes of this chapter, I wish to make a space-clearing gesture and acknowledge the heightened attention given to a poem's formal design, both by its maker and its reader.

2 This chapter in no way attempts to survey the amazing array of Native poets writing and publishing in 2014. My very small sample shows some generational range – Ortiz published his first book in 1971; Long Soldier's first chapbook appeared in 2010 – and the poets hail from ancestral lands in the Southeast, Southwest, West Coast, and the Dakotas. A notable absence is the Mvskoke Creek poet Joy Harjo, whose prophetic recastings of space infuse much of her poetry. In a more extensive treatment of this topic, I would also likely include work by Carter Revard (Osage), Luci Tapahonso (Diné), Kimberly Blaeser (Anishinaabe), Sherwin Bitsui (Diné), James Thomas Stevens (Akwesasne Mohawk), Allison Adele Hedge Coke (Huron/Eastern Tsalagi), and Karenne Wood (Monacan).

3 Eric Gary Anderson's work on Native literature and genre (2003) is also useful here.

4 Imperialist nostalgia is a term coined by Renato Rosaldo in his essay of the same name to indicate "a particular kind of nostalgia, often found under imperialism, where people mourn the passing of what they themselves have transformed" (1989, 108).

5 This term was coined by poet-critic Jerry Harp who adapted it from "Mallarmé's commentary on his 'Un coup de dés,' which employs this kind of spacing. In the commentary he writes, 'I do not transgress the measure, only disperse it'" (e-mail message to author, October 9, 2013).

6 My use of "heterogeneous" is inflected by Chadwick Allen's term "the heterogeneous local" (2002).

WORKS CITED

Allen, Chadwick. 2002. *Blood Narrative: Indigenous Identity in American Indian and Maori Literary and Activist Texts*. Durham, NC: Duke University Press.

Anderson, Eric Gary. 2003. "Situating American Indian Poetry: Place, Community, and the Question of Genre." In *Speak to Me Words: Essays on Contemporary American Indian Poetry*. Eds. Dean Rader and Janice Gould, 34–55. Tucson: University of Arizona Press.

Byrd, Jodi A. 2011. *The Transit of Empire: Indigenous Critiques of Colonialism*. Minneapolis: University of Minnesota Press.

Blaeser, Kimberly. 1993. "Native Literature: Seeking a Critical Center." In *Looking at the Words of Our People: First Nation Analysis of Literature*. Ed. Jeannette Armstrong, 51–62. Penticton: Theytus Books, Ltd.

Cardiff, Gladys. 1999. *A Bare, Unpainted Table*. Kalamazoo, MI: New Issues Press.
Glancy, Diane. 1999. "Give Me Land Lots of Land." *Modern Fiction Studies* 45 (1): 114–19.
2005. *Rooms: New and Selected Poems*. Earthworks Series. Ed. Janet McAdams. Cambridge: Salt Publishing.
Harjo, Joy, and Gloria Bird. 1998. *Reinventing the Enemy's Language*. New York: Norton.
Hilden, Patricia Penn. 1995. *When Nickels Were Indians*. Washington, DC: Smithsonian Institution Press).
Hogan, Linda. 1993. *The Book of Medicines*. Minneapolis: Coffee House Press.
Lazer, Hank. 1996. *Opposing Poetries Volume One: Issues and Institutions*. Evanston, IL: Northwestern University Press.
Long Soldier, Layli. 2012. "Hˊe Sapa." *Kenyon Review Online*, May.
2013. "Profiles in Poetics: Layli Long Soldier." WomensQuarterlyConversation. com, http://womensquarterlyconversation.com/2013/03/06/profiles-in-poetics-layli-long-soldier/
Lincoln, Kenneth. 1983. *Native American Renaissance*. Berkeley: University of California Press.
McAdams, Janet. 2010. "'Ways in the World': Formal Poetics in Linda Hogan's *Rounding the Human Corners*." *Kenyon Review* 32 (1): 226–35.
Miranda, Deborah. 1999. *Indian Cartography*. Greenfield Center, NY: Greenfield Review Press.
Ortiz, Simon. 1999. *from Sand Creek*. Tucson: University of Arizona Press.
2005. "Towards a National Indian Literature: Cultural Authenticity in Nationalism." In *American Indian Literary Nationalism*. Eds. Jace Weaver, Craig S. Womack, and Robert Warrior, 253–60. Albuquerque: University of New Mexico Press.
Rader, Dean. 2003. "The Epic Lyric: Genre and Contemporary American Indian Poetry." In *Speak to Me Words: Essays on Contemporary American Indian Poetry*. Eds. Dean Rader and Janice Gould, 123–42. Tucson: University of Arizona Press.
2011. *Engaged Resistance: American Indian Art, Literature, and Film from Alcatrez to the NMAI*. Austin: University of Texas Press.
Rosaldo, Renato. 1989. "Imperialist Nostalgia." *Representations*, No. 26 (Special Issue: Memory and Counter-Memory): 107–22.
Warrior, Robert. 2009. "Simon J. Ortiz – Wali wathon pa-ke pai." In *Simon J. Ortiz: A Poetic Legacy of Indigenous Continuance*. Eds. Susan Berry Brill de Ramirez and Evelina Zuni Lucero, 389–94. Albuquerque: University of New Mexico Press.

17

YUNTE HUANG

Transpacific and Asian American Counterpoetics

In my earlier work, *Transpacific Imaginations: History, Literature, Counterpoetics*, I define counterpoetics as "poetic resistance to imperial, national, and other forms of homogeneous narratives" (Huang 2008, 9). In the context of the transpacific, poetic imagination "departs from its Romanticist, transcendentalist origin and spreads new roots in 'articulation' as a situated and contested social imaginary" (ibid.). In the current essay, I continue this line of thinking while trying to delineate a brief history of Asian American poetry.

Writing such a history with a focus on poets of Asian descent, it is easy but erroneous for us to forget the long Orientalist legacy in American poetry and its deep impact on Asian American writings. From Walt Whitman's Asia-themed poems to the Imagism of Ezra Pound and Amy Lowell, from Emerson's fascination with Hindu religion to the mysticism of the Beat poets, the Orient has long haunted the American imagination. In this genealogy, perhaps no one can surpass Ernest Fenollosa in his seminal role of bridging the poetics of the East and the West. His posthumous essay, "The Chinese Written Character as a Medium for Poetry," edited and published by Pound, became a foundational text for American modernism. An avid follower of Emersonian Transcendentalism, Fenollosa claims that the Chinese character is so close to nature that one can see the magical workings of the universal grammar in the language. Inspired by Fenollosa, Pound proposed to treat things directly in poetry and "to use absolutely no word that does not contribute to the presentation" (Pound 1954, 3). These principles of Imagism as much lie at the heart of poetic modernism as they smack of Orientalism, an ethnographic view of the East. This legacy, as Josephine Park shrewdly puts it, will influence Asian American poetry both as a burden and an opportunity (Park 2008, 4).

While these "blossoms from the East" were sweeping through the landscape of American modernism, Asian American poets had already appeared on the horizon. Among the earliest were Sadakichi Hartmann, who once served as a secretary to Whitman, and Yone Noguchi, who was published by Harriet Monroe in *Poetry*. But these two were more followers of the American canon than trailblazers of Asian American poetry. For the latter, we need to turn to those Chinese poems carved on the walls of Angel Island, those revolutionary articulations of Carlos Bulosan, and those radical experiments of José García Villa.

From 1910 to 1940, immigrants from Asia had to pass through the immigration station on Angel Island near San Francisco. Chinese were the main target of detention because of the draconian 1882 Chinese Immigration Act, which banned labor immigration from China. Many of these detainees were the so-called paper sons, who claimed to be descendants of a native-born U.S. citizen. Armed with secret coaching notes, Chinese detainees would face immigration officers who interrogated them on family history, relationships, village life, and a wealth of legally irrelevant minutiae. The length of their stay inside the barracks ranged from a few weeks to as long as a year. Frustrated, fearful, anxious, bored, many of them doodled on the walls, writing curses, slogans, and very often, poems. Today more than 135 calligraphic poems, all in classical Chinese style, have been recovered from the walls. Edited and translated, they are now collected in *Island: Poetry and History of Chinese Immigrants on Angel Island, 1910–1940*, as well as appearing in canonical venues, such as the *Heath Anthology of American Literature*. Canonization has surely elevated the status of these poems, many of which are anonymous, but it is no guarantee that they have been understood sufficiently. In fact, many works of American literature written in languages other than English – French, German, Yiddish, Spanish, Japanese, etc. – have fallen victim to the limitations of English-only monolingualism we practice in American literary studies. In English translation, these Angel Island poems, deemed "artlessly direct" by some critics, are as easy to consume as cheap Made-in-China products crowding the shelves of American supermarkets today. These critics insist that the significance of these poems derives from their contents alone, from the ideological imperative of reading a body of ethnic writing that has been historically underrepresented – call that literary affirmative action, if you will.

I propose, however, that we pay attention to the politics of the poetic form. Just as the black slaves who survived the "Middle Passages" carried with them African music, myths, and beliefs upon their arrival in the New World, these transpacific immigrants also brought with them specimens of Chinese culture. *Tibishi* (writing on the wall) is one such example of transpacific migration of literary traditions, a migration set in motion by the global circulation of capital. For thousands of years, tibishi, literally "poetry inscribed on the wall," was an important form of composing and disseminating poems in China. Akin to modern-day urban graffiti, tibishi provided an outlet for the poetically inspired, regardless of their status in society. Knowing the historical and geographical origin of the literary practice will not only enrich what we know as American Literature but also help us appreciate how these anonymous authors, as soon as they set foot in America, were transforming themselves from mere imitators of the educated elite to graffiti artists waging protests. Read as tibishi, these Angel Island poems become another example of how the powerless take advantage of the power of writing and inscribe themselves into history.

"If you want to know what we are," writes Carlos Bulosan in a poem, "WE ARE REVOLUTION!" (Bulosan 1995, 168). Born in the Philippines in 1911 and coming to the United States in 1930, Bulosan is largely known today for his classic autobiographical novel, *America Is in the Heart* (1943). Active in the labor movement on the West Coast, Bulosan took up the pen to write for the dispossessed, exploited working class. Like the Angel Island poets, Bulosan explored in his Whitmanesque-style lyrics the full potential of poetry as protest and propaganda, as he acknowledged in his autobiography: "I did not stop to analyze why my thoughts and feelings found expression in poetry. It was enough that I was creating.... I could fight the world now with my mind, not merely with my hands. My weapon could not be taken away from me any more"(Bulosan 1973, 224). In poetry, Bulosan sings lullabies for poor children dying in tenements, dedicates hymns to luckless men betrayed by the sinful "fabulous city," and declares solidarity with the working class.

In contrast, Bulosan's fellow Philippines-born poet, José Villa, sought a very different path in writing. Garnering top awards and honors, including a Shelley Memorial Award, American Academy of Arts and Letters Award, and Guggenheim Fellowship, Villa was a consummate artist who turned English as a colonial language inside out. Foreshadowing the future generation of Asian American poetic experimenters, such as John Yau, Theresa Cha, and Myung Mi Kim, Villa shied away from overt racial, ethnic themes and mined the resources of a second language for effects of defamiliarization. Two of his most famous innovations are what he called "reversed consonance" and "comma poems." The former involves reversing the last sounded consonants of the last syllable of a line to create the corresponding rhyme. Thus a rhyme for *near* would be *run*, for *light, tell, tall, tale*, etc. For instance, in the lead poem of his major book, *Have Come, Am Here*, published by Viking in 1942, the first four lines read:

It is what I never said,
What I will always sing –

It's not found in days,
It's what always begins
(Villa 1999, 3)

Applying the principle of reversed consonance, we find that here *said* rhymes with *days*, and *sing* with the *-gins* in *begins*. Similarly, Villa's comma poems also create a sense of strangeness in English, like this stanza from a sequence called "Divine Poems":

As,much,as,I,perceive,the,Future,
Lo:the,future,perceives,me:
A,Mutuality,of,Eyes.   (45)

Like Emily Dickinson sewing together her metaphysical musings with dashes, hyphens, and other unconventional textual markers, Villa sought to integrate commas as an essential part of the poetic medium in order to regulate verbal density and temporality, enable each word to attain a fuller tonal and sonic value, and facilitate meditative pauses throughout a poem.

The outbreak of World War II turned a new page for Asian Americans. China became an ally of the United States, which promptly ended the racist practice of detaining Chinese immigrants on Angel Island and soon repealed the 1882 Chinese Exclusion Act. The attacks on Pearl Harbor, however, threw the lives of Japanese Americans into chaos. On February 19, 1942, President Franklin D. Roosevelt signed an executive order removing about 110,000 people of Japanese ancestry from the Pacific coast, relocating them to ten internment camps in seven states. Having lost their homes, businesses, and freedom, the internees tried to cope with hard life circumscribed by barbed wire. "It was hell," recalled one internee who had to stay in a horse stable. "Everybody felt lonely and anxious about the future" (Okihiro and Myers 1996, 190). Under harsh circumstances, however, arts flourished: haiku, *bon-kei* (miniature landscape), flower arranging, tea ceremony, sewing, and newspaper publishing. Many internees wrote diaries and poems. Violet Kazue Matsuda de Cristoforo, for instance, penned hundreds of haiku in Tule Lake concentration camp. Just as tibishi provided an emotional outlet for the Chinese detainees on Angle Island, haiku, tanka, and other forms of traditional Japanese poetry sustained the internees spiritually. But the wound cut deep, and poetical reflections continued well after WWII.

In this regard, Lawson Fusao Inada, who was sent to the camp with his family at the tender age of four, has given us one of the most profound meditations on the tragedy befallen Japanese Americans. In a long poetic sequence entitled "Legends from Camp," Inada explores the inadequacy of history: "There's a remoteness to history, and to simply know the facts is not always satisfactory. There's more to life than that" (Inada 1993, 3). The gap between history as lived experience and history as the account of such experience is what the poet intends to fill, and he does so through a deliberate, ingenious choice of genre: legend. As a nonhistorical, unverifiable story often handed down by tradition and through oral narrative, legend stays alive and vibrant outside the realm of official discourse. Most of the poems in this sequence describe the daily lives of ordinary internees, "Lost Boy," "Hakujin Woman," "Bad Boy," and so on. These are people who would otherwise appear in our official account of the camp experience merely as numbers: "10 camps, 7 states, / 120,113 residents" (7). Besides resisting numerical, statistical abstraction exercised by historical narrative, Inada also refuses to romanticize the past. The word "legend" in the title turns out to be a decoy, an intentionally empty promise meant to frustrate our desire for hermeneutical containment. Inada's legends contain nothing legendary: in "The Legend of the Great Escape," there was no escape; "The Legend of the Jerome Smokestack" describes an old smokestack with absolutely no story behind it: "There is no legend / It just stands there / in a grassy field" (16). Anticipating that some may try to monumentalize the past, erecting shrines and crowning heroes at the cost of the ordinary, the poet warns, "Some might say it's / a tribute, a monument, / a memorial to something. / But no, not really" (16). Just like Theresa Cha later in her work denies readers' ability to know past events happening elsewhere, Inada also tries to undermine, unsettle our desire to know history from a comfortably historical distance. His persistent use of the word "just," as in "It just stands there" (16), "It's just the tallest" (16), and "It's just a pile of past" (17), not only serves the poetics of the ordinary, but also invites us to do *justice* to the past.

Inada is one of the many poets coming of age during the storm of Asian American protests sweeping through the United States in the 1960s and '70s, when college students formed political alliances, occupied administrative buildings, and demanded curriculum reforms to include Asian American studies. This movement gave birth to the term "Asian American," which replaced "Oriental," an old label that carried a long association with racism and prejudice. It also brought about the renaissance of Asian American poetry. In 1974, Inada and his fellow writers Frank Chin, Jeffery Chan, and Shawn Wong published *Aiiieeeee!*, the first anthology of Asian American literature, in which the editors declare that "Asian America, so long ignored and forcibly excluded from creative participation in American culture, is wounded, sad, angry, swearing, and wondering, and this is his AIIIEEEEE!!! It is more than a whine, shout, or scream. It is fifty years of our whole voice" (Chan et al. 1991, xi). The same year also saw the publication of *Asian-American Heritage: An Anthology of Prose and Poetry*, edited by David Hsin-Fu Wand, who had turned from a protégé of Pound to an

Asian American activist. In the ensuing years, especially in the 1990s, when Asian American studies became a hot field of academic pursuit, indicating that the new political and social consciousness born in the crucible of the 1960s had now borne fruit, anthologies devoted exclusively to poetry mushroomed, including *The Open Boat: Poems from Asian America* (1993), edited by Garrett Hongo; *Premonitions: The Kaya Anthology of Asian North American Poetry* (1995), edited by Walter Lew; *Quiet Fire: A Historical Anthology of Asian American Poetry, 1892–1972* (1996), edited by Juliana Chang; and *Asian American Poetry: The Next Generation* (2004), edited by Victoria Chang. Individual poets also gained more recognition by the mainstream, winning major prizes and awards. Cathy Song's *Picture Bride* was selected by the Yale Series of Younger Poets in 1982. John Yau's *Corpse and Mirror* was chosen by the National Poetry Series in 1983, as was David Mura's *After We Lost Our Way* in 1989. Ai, Garrett Hongo, and Li-Young Lee won the Lamont Poetry award from the Academy of American Poets in 1978, 1987, and 1990 respectively.

Acceptance by the mainstream, however, could be a mixed blessing. As Timothy Yu has cogently argued in *Race and the Avant-Garde: Experimental and Asian American Poetry Since 1965*, when Asian American poetry drew more attention, it became detached from its original social context and came to be perceived through more conventional categories, creating "an image of Asian American poetry as a body of work that diverged from mainstream writing only in its overt themes, not in its politics or style" (Yu 2009, 102). Such a skewed image may not be a mischaracterization of the kind of conventional lyrical poetry by Song, Lee, and Mura, poetry that conforms to the norms of mainstream aesthetics, but it distorts the achievements of poets who continue to write against the grain of normalizing, totalizing narratives, poets such as Theresa Cha, Frances Chung, Jessica Hagedorn, Mei-mei Berssenbrugge, Kimiko Hahn, Lois-Ann Yamanaka, Walter Lew, and Myung Mi Kim.

Among these poets, Cha has undoubtedly drawn the most critical energy from scholars of Asian American literature. For a while it was impossible to attend a conference on American literature without hearing at least one paper about Cha's *DICTEE*. A collage of poetry, memoir, quotes, translations, and images, *DICTEE* is to Asian American poetry what Maxine Hong Kingston's *The Woman Warrior* is to Asian American prose. What in part makes this single volume of poetry so enticing is perhaps its engagement with the readers on the very question of textual intelligibility and historical responsibility. *DICTEE* is built on quicksand, engulfing sure-footed trespassers unaware of the hidden perils: An opening graffito supposedly left behind by Korean laborers enslaved by the Japanese turns out to be of dubious provenance; an epigraph that reads like vintage Sappho, as it claims to be, is pure fabrication; and the list of Nine Muses contains an inconspicuous, but nonetheless undeniable, alteration. Why all these glaring textual "errors"?

The answer may be found in Cha's persistent interrogation of history as written by the winners and her bold indictment against readers of such history as conspirators of crime. "To the other nations who are not witnesses, who are not subject to the same oppressions," she insists, "they cannot know" (Cha 2001, 32). To Cha, the readers' inability to know is a lesser offense than the way they claim to know. "Unfathomable the words, the terminology: enemy, atrocities, conquest, betrayal, invasion, destruction" (32). Through these abstract words, we make a generalized claim to knowledge, that "one enemy nation has disregarded the humanity of another" (32). In this way, historical knowledge is "neutralized," made "bland and mundane," "not physical enough," "not to the very flesh and bone, to the core, to the mark, to the point where it is necessary to intervene" (32–3). Modern-day TV viewers or newspaper readers who learn about atrocities happening in faraway places and then go on with their lives as usual – to Cha, these are merely consumers of information who conspire with the oppressors, colonizers, and war criminals through their inertia. To challenge our complacent habits of reading, the poet builds her book around discomfort, putting us at unease as we try to move ahead in an unfamiliar textual landscape. More than once, we are directed by the poet to turn back and revisit previous pages, re-witnessing sites of atrocity and trauma. The circularity and repetition disrupt our otherwise habitually linear, mindlessly teleological mode of reading. To read *DICTEE*, as Naoki Sakai usefully reminds us, "requires a different kind of labor" (Sakai 1997, 25). It is the kind of labor that would transform the reader as a passive consumer of information into one that accepts responsibility. To this end, the poet is willing to do anything, "even if to invent anew" (Cha 2001, 32), to forge, to mimic, to speak in a forked tongue. After all, the title word *dictee* is an anagram of *deceit*. If, as Cha believes, we have been deceived by history, been dictated to (like a dictee vs. dictator), then reading a book like *DICTEE* would be a step, however small, in the right direction of transcending what Cha condemns as our "conspirator method" of relating to history (33).

Writing in the wake of *DICTEE*, Cha's fellow Korean-American poet Myung Mi Kim also challenges us to move out of our own comfort zone of intelligibility and to counter, in her own words, "the potential totalizing power of language that serves the prevailing systems and demands of coherence" (Kim 2002, 110). Her book *Dura* (1998) is a discrete series of musings, articulations, and reconfigurations, variably syncopated to the pulse and rhythm of migrating between nations, languages, and temporalities. Like Cha's neologism *dictee*, Kim's coined title word *dura* is also suggestive and rhizomatic, like a root or tissue that carries a generative power. The immediate reference of *dura* is obvious, to "duration," a word that springs up in the book everywhere: "speed and duration" (Kim 1998, 14), "no movement independent of time" (17), and "the year's duration" (40). Echoing Villa's "comma poems," Kim adopts idiosyncratic punctuation marks such as double colons "::" to take the measure of temporality, to mark time experienced by those who must dislocate, move, and translate. Whereas in totalizing narratives, "the unremarkable become the stuff of dust" (55), in *Dura* the poet negotiates for a pause, a trajectory that requires "constant translation" (78): "When there is a pause, pause. / Duration that a pair of starlings' participation magnetized" (58). Like a bird's line of flight in the air that is as swift as it is still, the migrant dwells in the duration of the voyage, "due west directly west" (32), and is caught in a zone that Kim calls "placement between *l* and *r*" (33). In the Korean language there is no differentiation between the phonemes of l and r. Any semantic traffic between Korean and English will therefore be only "a provisional translation" (44). "Is that accurate?" Kim asks over and over again (63–4). Across the Pacific, the 38th parallel, and other deadly spaces charted by power and violence, roaming fragments, scattered phonemes, and obdurate sounds all *endure* the toll of time, "cross their limits cut a sloping way" (56).

Words cut a sloping way – that may be an apt description of the work of Lois-Ann Yamanaka, who adopts Hawaiian pidgin in her performance poetry. Many of the poets I discuss in this essay have toyed with the English language, twisting, torqueing, and turning it inside out: Villa's reverse consonance, Cha's mimicry, and Kim's provisional translation. Yamanaka adds a new, colorful element: code-switching. In the multiracial universe of Hawaii, parallel to the socioeconomic hierarchy, there is a linguistic pyramid, a scale that descends variously from standard English to pidgin, from standard Japanese or Chinese to pidgin Japanese or Chinese, and so on. But such stratification is by no means stable, enabling writers to explore the cracks and to mine the richness of linguistic soil. In a series of poems about a teenage girl named Tita, who lives in a world of abuse, violence, exploitation, and sexual awakening, the poet tests the limit of standard English. She uses street slang to describe the street, violent lingo to portray the violence, and abusive language to depict the abuse. More importantly, Yamanaka turns the linguistic pyramid upside down, as in "Tita: Boyfriends":

> Richard wen' call me around 9:05 last night.
> Nah, I talk *real* nice to him.

> Tink I talk to him the way I talk to you?
> You cannot let boys know your true self.
> Here, this how I talk.
> *Hello, Richard. How are you?*
> *Oh, I'm just fine. How's school?*
> (Yamanaka 1993, 35)

Here we can hear the teenage speaker switching from Hawaiian pidgin to what might be called standard American California Valley Girl English. The creole and the standard languages are juxtaposed against each other, the latter sounding as artificial and pale as the former appearing lively and colorful.

The comic effect induced by Yamanaka's code-switching points us to one of the staple features of transpacific, Asian American counterpoetics: parody. As I have argued elsewhere, racial parody has been the driving force of the American imagination. From blackface to redface, Jewface, and yellowface, characters such as Nigger Jim, Al Jolson's Jazz Singer, Charlie Chan, and Ah Sin are all born in the toxic soil of racial parody, without which American literature and culture would be penurious (Huang 2010, 286–7). In poetry, John Yau is the best example of the complicated relationship between the legacy of racial parody and Asian American spit-back. As Yau once acknowledged, he learned how to write poetry from figures such as Pound and other Imagists (Yau 1990, 43). In an odd way, the faraway world of the Orient that Yau depicts in his work derives as much from his China-born father's tales as from high modernism's transpacific imagination and popular culture's racial ventriloquism. Double irony and countermockery abound in Yau's work, as in these haiku-like pithy lines from a poem entitled "Genghis Chan: Private Eye":

> I posed
> as a cookie
> fortune smeller.
> (Yau 1989, 87)

The title conflates the legendary Mongolian king, Genghis Khan, with the aphorism-spouting Charlie Chan. And "cookie fortune smeller" muddles two common phrases, fortune cookie and fortune teller. As the crown jewel of American Orientalism, the fortune cookie actually cannot tell one's fortune; hence "teller" is phonetically transformed into "smeller." One word slides toward, puns on, and parodies the other, creating sonic and orthographical approximations that fill Yau's lines: grab/grub, sum/some (dim sum), treat/feet (pig feet), chow lane/chow mein, and so on. If the Orientalist imagination and racial stereotype often feed on mimicry and parody, Yau spits back and turns the table around, as does Frances Chung in *Crazy Melon and Chinese Apple* and Jessica Hagedorn in *Danger and Beauty*.

Charlie Chan says, "Door of opportunity swing both ways." While the U.S. literary Orientalism has been an onerous burden for Asian Americans and racial stereotype has equally been a hurdle, they have also offered a fertile ground for counterpoetics, for poetic writings against colonial violence, historical traumas, and narrative closures. When we hear Whitman sing America and Langston Hughes proclaims that "I, too, am America," we can also hear the Cantonese lyric, the undying Chinatown blues: "I roam America undocumented / I am all ready."

WORKS CITED

Bulosan, Carlos. 1973. *America Is in the Heart*. Seattle: University of Washington Press.

    1995. *Selected Writings of Carlos Bulosan*. Ed. E. San Juan, Jr. Philadelphia: Temple University Press.

Chang, Juliana, ed. 1996. *Quiet Fire: A Historical Anthology of Asian American Poetry, 1892–1970*. New York: Asian American Writers' Workshop.

Chan, Jeffery, et al, ed. 1991. *The Big AIIIEEEEE!: An Anthology of Chinese American and Japanese American Literature*. New York: Meridian.

Cha, Theresa Hak Kyung. 2001. *DICTEE*. Berkeley: University of California Press.

Huang, Yunte. 2002. *Transpacific Displacement: Ethnography, Translation, and Intertextual Travel in Twentieth-Century American Literature*. Berkeley: University of California Press.

    2008. *Transpacific Imaginations: History, Literature, Counterpoetics*. Cambridge, MA: Harvard University Press.

    2010. *Charlie Chan: The Untold Story of the Honorable Detective and His Rendezvous with American History*. New York: W. W. Norton.

Inada, Lawson Fusao. 1993. *Legends from Camp*. Minneapolis: Coffee House Press.

Kim, Myung Mi. *Dura*. 1998. Los Angeles: Sun & Moon Press.

    2002. *Commons*. Berkeley: University of California Press.

Lai, Him Mark, et al., eds. and trans. 1991. *Island: Poetry and History of Chinese Immigrants on Angel Island, 1910–1940*. Seattle: University of Washington Press.

Okihiro, Gary, and Joan Myers. 1996. *Whispered Silences: Japanese Americans and World War II*. Seattle: University of Washington Press.

Park, Josephine. 2008. *Apparitions of Asia: Modernist Form and Asian American Poetics*. New York: Oxford University Press.

Pound, Ezra. 1954. *Literary Essays of Ezra Pound*. Ed. T. S. Eliot. London: Faber and Faber.

Sakai, Naoki. 1997. *Translation and Subjectivity: On "Japan" and Cultural Nationalism*. Minneapolis: University of Minnesota Press.

Villa, José García. 1999. *The Anchored Angel: Selected Writings by José García Villa*. Ed. Eileen Tablios. New York: Kaya Press.

Yamanaka, Lois-Ann. 1993. *Saturday Night at the Pahala Theatre*. Honolulu: Bamboo Ridge Press.

Yau, John. 1989. *Edificio Sayonara*. Santa Rosa, CA: Black Sparrow Press.

1990. "Interview with Edward Foster." *Talisman* 5: 31–50.

Yu, Timothy. 2009. *Race and the Avant-Garde: Experimental and Asian American Poetry Since 1965*. Stanford, CA: Stanford University Press.

18

BARRETT WATTEN

Language Writing

Language writing emerged as a distinct social formation of American poetry in the 1970s, primarily in metropolitan areas such as New York and San Francisco, and developed new forms of experimental verse practice marked as much by its politics as its formal procedures. Like the movement itself, nearly every component of the preceding sentence is open to debate; even its name is controversial. "Language writing" exists at the center of a field of terms that includes "language poetry" and "language-centered writing," as well as the name of the journal $L=A=N=G=U=A=G=E$, with which it is at times confused. As a movement, Language writing emerged in the 1970s as a distinct break from prior verse traditions, but it also saw itself in relation to experimental writing from the modernist and postmodern periods. Primary influences included Russian futurism and American imagism; dada and French surrealism; Gertrude Stein, William Carlos Williams, and Louis Zukofsky among modernist precursors; and New American, New York school, and chance-generated poetries among post-1945 movements. At the same time, Language writing developed alongside alternative art practices of the 1970s, including site-specific, performance, conceptual art; experimental cinema; and improvised music. It articulated its turn to language and critique of the self in relation to the rise of identity politics and second-wave feminism. Language writing was in its origins a social formation: a phenomenon of groups of poets, small presses, ephemeral journals, public readings, and talk series, resulting in a mutual understanding of its social construction among dozens of writers who knew each other's work and variously identified with its collective project. It gained momentum particularly through a series of little magazines and presses, whose names provide a virtual index of the movement's history: *Tottel's* (ed. Ron Silliman); *This* (eds. Barrett Watten and Robert Grenier); *Hills* (ed. Bob Perelman); *Roof* (ed. James Sherry); *A Hundred Posters* (ed. Alan Davies); *Dog City* (ed. Doug Lang); *Là Bas* (ed. Douglas Messerli); and $L=A=N=G=U=A=G=E$ (eds. Bruce Andrews and Charles Bernstein). These in turn influenced a proliferation of new journals in the 1980s and 1990s: *HOW(ever)* (ed. Kathleen Fraser et al.); *Boxcar* and *Temblor* (ed. Leland Hickman, Jr.); *Acts* (ed. David Levi Strauss); *The Difficulties* (ed. Tom Beckett); *Jimmy and Lucy's House of "K"* (ed. Benjamin Friedlander et al.); and *Chain* (ed. Juliana Spahr and Jena Osman).

Language writing is at its origins specific to the politics and culture of the 1970s, a distressed or reparative period after the liberationist upsurge of the 1960s and the debacle of Vietnam. The historical sequence marked by 1968, as utopian and liberatory; 1973, as a crisis of multinational capital; 1975, as the American political defeat; and the neoconservative takeovers of the 1980s with Reagan and Thatcher offer a timeline for the political unconscious of Language writing. We may again notice the constructed claims of the preceding sentence, which depends on a periodizing account of the 1970s that is still undeveloped, and on the concept of a political unconscious that led Fredric Jameson to identify Language writing (citing Bob Perelman's poem "China") as symptomatic of the depthless simulacra of the postmodern in an influential essay. Language writing was at the same time a metropolitan and largely bicoastal phenomenon, reflecting the relocation of well-educated, politicized, but underemployed graduates of major universities and programs (Berkeley, Harvard, Chicago, Yale, and Iowa among them) to cities like New York and San Francisco, both of which were undergoing a period of economic and political turbulence (Washington, DC, is an important third site for Language writing). San Francisco in the 1970s witnessed not only the struggles between neighborhood groups and developers that lead to its "Manhattanization" in the 1980s but also the rise of district politics that elected an openly gay supervisor, Harvey Milk (and led to his assassination, along with that of Mayor George Moscone). New York in the 1970s saw the development of an art district in SoHo that paralleled the progressive gentrification of the city in the West Village and Lower East Side, framed by financial bankruptcy and general anxiety over the rise of class antagonisms (reflected in the visibility of graffiti in non-art locations). The rise of alternative exhibition and literary spaces in both cities aided the development of Language writing, at the Poetry Center at San Francisco State University and at alternative sites, such as 80 Langton Street (New Langton Arts), Southern Exposure, The Lab, and The Farm in San Francisco; and the Poetry Project at St. Mark's Church and the Ear Inn, along with art spaces such as The Kitchen and P.S. 1, in New York. Also important for its development was federal support for the arts in urban environments, particularly the CETA (Comprehensive Education and Training Act) program and NEA (National Endowment for the Arts), which targeted alternative arts projects as a jobs program; and the small press networks supported by the West Coast Print

Center and Small Press Distribution, located in Berkeley. As the progressive, recession-prone 1970s becomes understood as a hybrid decade that combines aspects of the depressed 1930s and the liberationist 1960s, the material history of its emergent social networks may be better appreciated.

Language writing has been so identified with the foregrounding of language itself as a poetic strategy, a precedence of signifier over the signified in structuralist terms, that it has for some amounted to a contextless formalism divorced from any specific political, cultural, or even personal claims. It is important for this reason to stress the highly constructed social networks and political frameworks that marked its development as a literary school (taken in a broadly descriptive, rather than narrowly exclusionary sense). Language writing, however, distinguishes itself from other movements by the relation of its literary forms to theoretical claims developed from them, by which it extends the formal construction of the work to a larger politics. The movement is marked by its parallel innovation of radical forms of writing (in a range of genres and styles) and a discourse of poetics that accounts for them. The radicalness of its turn to language, in formal terms, necessitated immediate justification as a poetics over the run of publications such as *L=A=N=G=U=A=G=E* (1978–82) and *Poetics Journal* (1982–98), and the two genres – poetry and poetics – developed side by side. As an autonomous literary development, aware of but taking place far from the reception of poststructuralist or neo-Marxist theory in the 1970s and 1980s, Language writing participated in, even anticipated, the turn to language and decentered subjectivity that became hallmarks of postmodern theory. Its radical textual forms can be easily read with the deconstruction of Jacques Derrida (for his critique of presence associated with structuralist accounts of language and the "play" of the signifier) or the psychoanalysis of Jacques Lacan (for the importance of "speech chain" for subjectivity, as well as the identification of language with the Symbolic Order). But Language writing also responded to, and may be read in relation to, other theoretical movements: the development of a structuralist post-Marxism for its critiques of commodity, ideology, and class; the anti-foundationalism of American neo-pragmatism, with its suspension of truth claims for an inquiry into the adequacy of terms (in the 1970s reception of Ludwig Wittgenstein, J. L. Austin, W. V. O. Quine); the development of post-generativist semantics, particularly after Berkeley linguists George Lakoff and Charles Fillmore; the critique of language and gender in French and second-wave feminisms, after Julia Kristeva and Luce Irigaray; and the foregrounding of language in conceptual and site-specific art. As Language writing developed in the 1980s, it variously engaged with numerous other theoretical schools, many of which would profoundly change its original relation of theory and practice: cultural studies, critical theory, New Historicism, narrative theory, performance studies, and gender/queer theory among them. Language writing should be read in its development as engaged with and open to but not determined by one or another set of theoretical perspectives.

Specific to Language writing is its innovation of radical forms of poetry and prose that foreground the language of which they are made. For some readers, even some Language writers, the foregrounding of language renders entirely opaque any transparency of language as a form of communication, as it eliminates reference to content outside the text. But even from the beginnings of Language writing, such a narrow definition is inadequate, even as the goal of making language itself a basis for poetics had its polemical effect. More accurately, at the outset of Language writing, there is a sliding scale between language "as such" and other levels of language use: reference, narrative, rhetoric, or expression. Ron Silliman's combinatorial poetics in his serial poem "2197" provides a good example of one pole of language-centered writing, in which meaning can only be seen as a constructed effect:

> We calm perfectly with never.
> A people who run
> front by the bus catch.
> Boys asks up of the small.
> Longer of the language to thought.
> By this I meet
> a poem in the progressions and its remorseful.
> Order is our form as to what might have strewn.
> (Silliman 2007, 203)

Here, Silliman explores the constructivist potential of grammatical relations within a poetic framework of phrases, sentences, and lines. Contesting Noam Chomsky's separation of linguistic levels in the nonsensical but grammatical sentence "Colorful green ideas sleep furiously," Silliman shows grammar and meaning are interwoven, even when the propositional content of the sentence is not determinable. At the same time, the poem makes a metalinguistic comment on its own (lack of) organization, connecting the particular to the entire form in a nonorganic, rhizomic manner. While the poem was originally published in discrete sections, Silliman eventually saw it as part of a poetic cycle (*The Age of Huts*) in which higher levels of meaning were generated by language in each of its parts, starting with the work that first demonstrated the open construction of the New Sentence, *Ketjak*. In this text, and in his articles on poetics, Silliman theorized the linguistic unit of the New Sentence as a formal device among Language writers, in which the grammatical form of the sentence creates a kind of linguistic autonomy apart from and rising "above" the level of component parts, independent of subordination to any narrative or discursive context. Silliman first discerned this device in the hybrid prose of Carla Harryman, and it became a stylistic hallmark of early Language writing that connected linguistic elements "below" the level of sentence to larger propositional, nonnarrative, and hybrid narrative forms, uniting form and content:

> The earth is as narrow as the sky is full: a postulation, on a rudimentary level. Clouds protrude to the point of abandoning context. Ducks fly across teasing the edges of clouds with their wings. Reason tells us not to make anything out of these events. Birds fall into the sea. The sea swells, pushing the land under. A seeming eternity, by force. So all that's left is a narrative concealing an error. Contentment is sediment below this image. Passivity has been accomplished through the descriptive process, a mechanism which devours objects, subjecting them to the decay of inner life. Perfection is a disease. Each rock, each sentence suppresses an embryo, elevated as they are to the status of isolated objects to be regarded unto themselves.
>
> ("Property," in Harryman 1989, 19)

While Language writing in these two examples clearly cannot be reduced to a single effect, the constructive potential of language is open and does not seek closure in a singular determination of meaning. At the same time, specific aesthetic, ethical, gendered, and political agendas may be built at the site of language: in Silliman's poem, possibilities of grammatical play preceding the determination of meaning, even at a linguistic level; in Harryman's prose, a high degree of self-consciousness of the framing assumptions of narrative as it is being both created and dismantled. While Language writing is generally thought to be constructivist and anti-expressive (and thus to be clearly separated from the expressiveness of identity poetries being developed in the same period), a nascent ground of expression is evident in many Language writers, often combined with a tendency to question the stable location of the expressive subject. For Charles Bernstein, the expressive subject may be distorted or impeded to the point of noncommunication, resulting in a rhetoric of opacity that reveals and conceals the speaking subject's difference from conventional norms of address:

> Impossible outside you want always the other. A continual
> recapitulation, & capture all that, against which our redaction
> of sundry, promise, another person, fills all the
> conversion of that into, which intersects a continual
> revulsion of, against, concepts, encounter,
> in which I hold you, a passion made of cups, amidst
> frowns. Crayons of immaculate warmth ensnare our
> somnambulance to this purpose alone.
>
> ("Live Acts," in Bernstein 1980, 28)

Bernstein's rhetoric may be termed a skeptical expressivism, willfully interfering with the construction of any thirdness (after C. S. Peirce's "interpretant") between speaker and hearer. Typical of early Language writing, this skepticism precludes the consolations of confessional poetry: an ethical attitude in which a common ground of identification is impossible. Such a skepticism has a gendered politics in this language-centered poem by Jean Day:

> If you leave your body,
> you will live in the hall.
>
> I can't shoot
> from far away.
>
> This is an easy ring
> of caution toxin.
>
> From welfare
> to this insistent hazard.
>
> I'm king of exits;
> you're hiring railroads.
>
> Can you do it
> mirror? ...
>
> ("Beverage Napkin," in Day 1983, n.p.)

The space between speaker and hearer, like the space between strophes within each stanza, is charged with undecidability, creating an interpersonal dynamic that suspends any outcome. The turn to language, as attitude, stems from "the rejection of closure" in Hejinian's sense, amounting to a gendered poetics of indeterminacy. Such an effect, and its larger motivation, is widely deployed among the lyric practitioners of Language writing like Rae Armantrout, Beverly Dahlen, and Erica Hunt, whose work refuses a central, organizing subject position while preserving the affect of lyric suspension.

Moving from the devices of language to the motivations for their use arrives at the horizon of the author, whose poststructuralist theory death seems confirmed by Language writing. Language writing, so it has been thought, removes the subject from poetry and proceeds from work to text, in Roland Barthes's formulation. Just as Language writing is not reducible to a single set of formal devices, nor even the turn to language as autonomous form, it should not be restricted to a canon of representative authors. Going beyond its origins as a historical avant-garde, Language writing is now widely dispersed, multi-generational, and culturally diverse – to the point of having overturned previous paradigms for poetry, particularly the workshop style developed after confessional poetry but also the romance of presence of the New Americans' poetry. But the relation of author, language, text, and work in the Language school is much more complex than a simple moment of negation of previous verse conventions. The early, most recognizable figures, often associated with its key journals and presses, have moved beyond their formal similarity to their contemporaries and established authorship with the publication of major works or collections. Of the West Coast writers, Ron Silliman has produced a cycle of experimental texts (*The Age of Huts*) and a 1000-page language-centered abecedary (*The Alphabet*). Lyn Hejinian's language-centered autobiography *My Life* continues in updated editions (each containing as many sections as her age), along with a series of book-length poems: *The Cell*, *A Border Comedy*, and *The Book of a Thousand Eyes*. The present author's long poems, which explore a poetics of historical non/narration, include *Progress*, *Under Erasure*, and *Bad History*; a collected shorter poems appeared as *Frame*; and two multi-authored projects: *Leningrad* and the just completed *Grand Piano*. Rae Armantrout received the Pulitzer Prize in 2010 for her collection *Versed* and publishes new volumes of her acerbic lyric poetry every other year from a university press. Career-spanning collections have appeared (or will appear) from Bob Perelman (*Ten to One*); Kit Robinson (*The Messianic Trees*); Leslie Scalapino (*It's go in horizontal*); Beverly Dahlen (*A Reading*); and Ted Pearson (*Extant Glyphs* and *An Intermittent Music*). Carla Harryman has pioneered a unique form of hybrid writing, between poetry, narrative, essay, and performance, in *The Words*, *Gardener of Stars*, and *Adorno's Noise*, and her twin-authored novella with Hejinian, *The Wide Road*. She is also a major innovator of language-centered Poets Theater, along with Robinson and Scalapino. Steve Benson, a practicing psychotherapist, is known for performance texts that are both transactional and procedural; his work, and the philosophically acute verse of Alan Bernheimer, Jean Day, and Tom Mandel await a collected edition. Of the East Coast figures, Charles Bernstein is widely recognized for his transgressive verse strategies and mesmerizing performances, published as *All the Whiskey in Heaven* from a major publisher, and has written the libretto for a staged opera based on Walter Benjamin's writings (*Shadowtime*). Bruce Andrews has produced two book-length poems (*I Don't Have Any Paper So Shut Up* and *Lip Service*) as well as numerous volumes of socially constructed, materially opaque Language writing, written "below" the level of the sentence. Susan Howe is known for her deformative encounters with historical texts, often the sites of patriarchal misrecognition, beginning with *My Emily Dickinson* and continuing with *The Birth-Mark*, *Pierce-Arrow*, and *Souls of the Labadie Tract*. Hannah Weiner's psychotropic Language writing (in which she "sees" words) has been edited and published, after her death in 1997, as *Hannah Weiner's Open House*. Ted Greenwald's improvisatory lyrics (*The Licorice Chronicles* and *Common Sense*) and long poems (*You Bet!*

and *Word of Mouth*) are notable New York/Language hybrids, as are the works of Michael Gottlieb, Alan Davies, Peter Seaton, and Nick Piombino, each of whom continues to publish language-centered writing that is both ironic and meditative, performative and philosophical. Poets emerging from the Washington, DC, scene in the 1970s, often involved with visual culture, include Tina Darragh, Lynne Dreyer, p. inman, Doug Lang, Joan Retallack, Phyllis Rosenzweig, and Diane Ward. Of Canadian figures, Steve McCaffery is represented by a collected writings and *The Black Debt*, a book-length enactment of textual opacity; Christopher Dewdney publishes experimental writing influenced by science studies (neurology and geology); and Jeff Derkson pushes Language writing toward global horizons. Tom Raworth, who published often in Language venues, has become the UK's best-known innovative poet; Fluxus-influenced writer Allen Fisher and performance poet cris cheek are also key early figures. Finally, Robert Grenier, whose serial poems *A Day at the Beach* and *Sentences* (500 index cards in a box) are unquestioned origins of Language writing, went on to produce a unique form of hand-drawn visual poetry that is widely exhibited and reproduced online. In each case, Language writing developed at the intersection of new forms, genres, and contexts that are irreducible to language "as such" as a poetics.

The concept of social formation (after Raymond Williams) intersects with innovative form in the genealogy of Language writing. As a literary avant-garde, Language writing is both urban and decentered, produced and consumed among a self-conscious collective through its journals and presses. As such, it continues the social momentum of post-1945 countercultural literary movements (the Beats, Black Mountain, and New York schools), while interpreting their formal innovations in the context of increasingly less open social and political horizons. Language writing is perhaps the most numerous avant-garde in American literary history; its capacity for social reproduction, and influence on successive generations of writers, is more akin to dada, surrealism, and Oulipo (which proliferated on the basis of their new poetic forms) than the coterie poetics of Anglo-American modernism – including imagism and objectivism. As a moment of interpretation and renewal, Language writing has a critical relation to its immediate predecessors and the more distant tradition, exercising a revisionist hermeneutics that extends to Whitman and Dickinson, Pound and Williams, Stein and Zukofsky – influences shared by the majority of Language writers. But relations of proximity, affiliation, and influence – more spatial and horizontal than linear and vertical – better account for its relation to literary history than any single tradition. Language writing developed, for instance, in relation to a number of highly individualistic poets, each notable for radical forms, who did not adhere to any form of collective understanding: among them, Clark Coolidge, whose long poems *The Maintains* and recently published *A Book Beginning What and Ending Away* inspired several early Language writers; Bernadette Mayer, who incorporated strategies of documentary and performance art in *Studying Hunger* and *Memory*; Michael Palmer, whose terse, analytic lyrics worked to reconfigure poetic subjectivity; Bill Berkson, who combined New York school values of abstraction and personism; and Joanne Kyger, who gendered the ecstatic impulses of the Beats in her open, improvisatory poetry. The most immediate influence of New American poetry on Language writing was Robert Creeley, whose intensification of poetic form and pressure on poetic language, especially in *Words*, *Pieces*, and *A Day Book*, led to an emphasis on fragmentation and seriality, a breakdown of poetry into words and phrases, in Language writing. Equally important was the projectivist verse of disabled poet Larry Eigner, who spent the 1970s housebound in Massachusetts but who carried on a wide correspondence with Language writers, resulting in frequent publication of his work; his four-volume collected poems has been published by a major university press. Of the New American poets who propounded a "Muthologos" as a metaphysics of speech and presence, Charles Olson and Robert Duncan authored and theorized a univocal, expressive poetics that was often at odds with Language writing's emphasis on the materiality of writing. The aleatorical methods of John Cage and Jackson Mac Low, on the other hand, were positive models for the compositional strategies of Language writing, as was the lyric self-consciousness of George Oppen and Denise Levertov. Of the New York school, John Ashbery's *Tennis Court Oath*, Frank O'Hara's *Second Avenue*, and Ted Berrigan's *The Sonnets* were immediate touchstones for Language writing. Of African-American poets, Lorenzo Thomas and, later, Nathaniel Mackey, and Harryette Mullen were engaged with Language writers, while the development of Black Arts poetry in the 1960s and 1970s did not, as a general rule, connect with Language writing due to their differing relations to persona, orality, and expression, even as 1970s avant-garde jazz improvisers – Cecil Taylor, Anthony Braxton, Leroy Jenkins, and the AACM – were esteemed by both. A significant debate over Language writing and minority identity between Silliman and Scalapino (1992) anticipated the emergence of a number of poets of color using language-centered forms: Harryette Mullen, Rodrigo Toscano, Pamela Lu, Renee Gladman, Hung Q. Tu, and others.

Language writing is intersectional; it exists at the boundary of multiple determinations, of which the turn to language, the critique of the subject, and its social formation are the most significant. A kind of centrifugal/centripetal movement describes its development: drawing in multiple influences in the formation of its representative poetic and hybrid forms, extending outward through multiple sites of reception. As a social literary feedback system, Language writing understood itself collectively through its many readings and talks, performances and publications, which focused the movement's collective identity. This was reflected in the first essays on poetics that attended Language writing, particularly in the journals *Alcheringa* ("The Dwelling Place," ed. Silliman, 1975); *Open Letter* ("The Politics of the Referent," ed. McCaffery, 1977); *A Hundred Posters* (ed. Davies, 1976–79); the Talks issue of *Hills* (ed. Perelman, 1980); *HOW(ever)* (eds. Fraser et al., 1983–92); *Code of Signals* (ed. Palmer, 1983); as well as the two major publications devoted entirely to Language poetics: *L=A=N=G=U=A=G=E* (eds. Andrews and Bernstein, 1978–82); and *Poetics Journal* (eds. Hejinian and Watten, 1982–98). Language writing's reception thus began as a discourse between and among participants, in its own style of critical practice and its literary affiliations and influences. As Alan Golding writes in *From Outlaw to Classic*, the self-forming construction of a group of writers is one of many legitimate models for literary reception and canon formation. Language writing established itself not only through forms of innovative writing but by means of its self-generated reception, in terms of literary history and theory.

The polemical aspects of Language writing's claims for poetry were immediately noticed and reacted to, at first in the many "language-baiting" articles in poetry and academic journals (among them, *Poetry Flash*, *Georgia Review*, *Partisan Review*, and *New Criterion*). By the mid-1980s, Language writing was at the center of "the poetry wars," a psychologically charged debate between avant-garde, workshop, confessional, populist, and New American poets, many of whom saw Language writing as hostile to central tenets of their poetics (such as persona, expression, identity, spontaneity, narrative, or convention). A more principled and less reactive debate occurred with San Francisco partisans of New Narrative writing, a competing tendency that focused on gender, sexuality, and narrative. Meanwhile, Language writers moved to consolidate their literary formation through the publication of anthologies and essay collections: *The L=A=N=G=U=A=G=E Book* (eds. Andrews and Bernstein, 1984); *Writing/Talks* (ed. Perelman, 1985); *Total Syntax* (Watten, 1985); *In the American Tree* (ed. Silliman, 1986); *The New Sentence* (Silliman, 1987); and *"Language" Poetries* (ed. Messerli, 1987). This first wave of Language writing's reception culminated in three essays by critics who became known as promulgators of Language writing, at least initially, in academia: Marjorie Perloff, in "The Word as Such: L=A=N=G=U=A=G=E Poetry in the Eighties" (1985), read Language writing in terms of the historical avant-garde's foregrounding of language (particularly in Russian futurism), albeit to the exclusion of its Left politics;

Jerome McGann, in "Contemporary Poetry/Alternate Routes" (1987), saw Language writing as both an anti-establishment romanticism and a contemporary Marxism; and Andrew Ross, in "The New Sentence and Commodity Form," interpreted Language writing as a Marxist structuralist critique of the commodity and ideology. These led to continued discussion in academic journals and were followed by a wave of book-length studies: George Hartley's *Textual Politics and the Language Poets* (1989) extended a Marxist structuralist approach to a range of writers; Linda Reinfeld's *Language Poetry: Writing as Rescue* (1992) gave a reader-centered account of three individual poets; Perelman's *The Marginalization of Poetry* (1996) focused on the plurality and materiality of its textual forms; while Ann Vickery's *Leaving Lines of Gender* (2000) questioned its gendering of authorship. The reception of Language writing was in no sense univocal or fixed; later assessments of Language writing have understood it through critical methods or theoretical frameworks that were either underemphasized at its origins or overlooked since then, such as political economy (Christopher Nealon); collectivity (Oren Izenberg); social formations (Friedlander); feminism (Rachel Blau DuPlessis); queer theory (Kaplan Harris); race (Aldon Lynn Nielsen); ethnicity (Timothy Yu); affect theory (Sianne Ngai); ethics (Grant Jenkins); psychoanalysis (Alex Blaser); material textuality (Craig Dworkin); technology (Davidson); media theory (Adalaide Morris); avant-garde theory (Paul Mann), and language philosophy (Perloff). Language writing's intersectionality has been generative not only in formal or social terms but for how it has been read and received.

The key term is "generative": because Language writing broke with literary predecessors and contemporary verse conventions, it established a criticality that has not rested in easy summary or paraphrase. At the same time, it has, through stylistic or formal innovations, affiliation or aversion, and public literary debates, directly influenced new tendencies. In the early 1980s, the controversy over New Narrative was decisive for a generation of experimental prose writers that included Kathy Acker, Robert Glück, Bruce Boone, Kevin Killian, Dodie Bellamy, Camille Roy, Gail Scott, and others. Also important was the development of Poets Theater, with numerous productions, particularly in San Francisco. Second and third waves of poets influenced by Language writing, too numerous to name, emerged in the 1980s and 1990s, many associated with the Poetics program at SUNY Buffalo and publishing in *Chain* (eds. Spahr and Osman), *Ob/lek* (ed. Peter Gizzi), and *Writing from the New Coast* (eds. Gizzi and Connel McGrath). The geographical, gendered, ethnic, and even linguistic identities of these emergent writers, particularly in the United States, United Kingdom, and Canada, had become pluralized. During these decades, as well, Language writing made contact with like-minded movements in the UK, France (with several anthologies featuring Language writing in French translation), and the former Soviet Union (site of the 1989 poetics conference chronicled in *Leningrad*). Representative authors have been translated into Swedish, Danish, Finnish, Dutch, German, Polish, Czech, French, Italian, Spanish, Russian, Serbian, Hebrew, Japanese, and other languages. Since 2001, however, the focus of experimental writing has shifted from stylistic or formal questions to the formation of new groups of writers who position themselves, either positively or negatively, in relation to Language writing. Most prominent of these have been the self-defined groupings of Flarf, which writes highly performative poems using the results of internet searches; and Conceptual writing, which appropriates material from nonaesthetic sources as part of their "uncreative" writing. The structure of these recent literary groupings has been highly influenced by Web 2.0 social media, along with the construction of substantial online archives of experimental writing at *UbuWeb*, *PennSound*, *Eclipse*, and other sites. The importance of two online phenomena – the Poetics Listserv and Silliman's Blog – cannot be overstressed for their remediation of poetics. During the 2000s, as well, ten poets associated with San Francisco Language writing published a ten-volume "experiment in collective autobiography," *The Grand Piano*, that chronicled the origins of Language writing and used online media as part of its writing process. Despite overstated narratives of succession put forward by Perloff and others, Language writing is both highly active and in productive contact with numerous new literary movements, among them: disability poetries, ecopoetry, gurlesque, hybrid narrative, multi-languaged poetry, the New Essay, the New Lyric, new media writing, and Occupy poetry. These nascent groups, again too numerous to name, give ample evidence of the generative formal and social dynamics of Language writing in its emergence, influence, and continued productivity.

SELECTED BIBLIOGRAPHY

Andrews, Bruce. 1996. *Paradise & Method*. Evanston, IL: Northwestern University Press.
Andrews, Bruce, and Charles Bernstein, eds. 1984. *The L=A=N=G=U=A=G=E Book*. Carbondale: Southern Illinois University Press.
Armantrout, Rae, Steve Benson, Carla Harryman, Lyn Hejinian, Tom Mandel, Ted Pearson, Bob Perelman, Kit Robinson, Ron Silliman, and Barrett Watten. 2006–10. *The Grand Piano: An Experiment in Collective Autobiography, San Francisco, 1975–1980*. 10 vols. Detroit: Mode A/This Press.
Beach, Christopher, ed. 1998. *Artifice & Indeterminacy: An Anthology of New Poetics*. Tuscaloosa: University of Alabama Press.

Benson, Steve, Carla Harryman, Lyn Hejinian, Bob Perelman, Ron Silliman, and Barrett Watten. 1998. "Aesthetic Tendency and the Politics of Poetry." *Social Text* 19/20: 261–75.

Bernstein, Charles. 1980. *Controlling Interests*. New York: Roof Books.

　1992. *A Poetics*. Cambridge, MA: Harvard University Press.

Clay, Stephen and Rodney Phillips, eds. 1998. *A Secret Location on the Lower East Side: Adventures in Writing, 1960–1980*. New York: New York Public Library/ Granary Books.

Davidson, Michael. 1997. *Ghostlier Demarcations: Modern Poetry and the Material Word*. Berkeley: University of California Press.

Davidson, Michael, Lyn Hejinian, Ron Silliman, and Barrett Watten. 1991. *Leningrad: American Writers in the Soviet Union*. San Francisco: Mercury House.

Day, Jean. *Linear C*. 1983. Berkeley, CA: Tuumba Press.

DuPlessis, Rachel Blau. 1990. *The Pink Guitar: Writing as Feminist Practice*. London: Routledge.

Golding, Alan. 1995. *From Outlaw to Classic: Canons in American Poetry*. Madison: University of Wisconsin Press.

Harryman, Carla. 1989. *Animal Instincts: Prose, Plays, Essays*. San Francisco: This.

Hartley, George. 1989. *Textual Politics and the Language Poets*. Bloomington: Indiana University Press.

Hejinian, Lyn. 2000. *The Language of Inquiry*. Berkeley: University of California Press.

Hejinian, Lyn, and Barrett Watten, eds. 2013. *A Guide to Poetics Journal: Writing in the Expanded Field, 1982–1998*. Middletown, CT: Wesleyan University Press.

Jameson, Fredric. 1991. *Postmodernism; or, the Cultural Logic of Late Capitalism*. Durham, NC: Duke University Press.

Mann, Paul. 1991. *The Theory Death of the Avant-Garde*. Bloomington: Indiana University Press.

McCaffery, Steve, ed. 1977. "The Politics of the Referent." *Open Letter*. 3rd ser., no. 7:60–107.

McGann, Jerome. 1987. "Contemporary Poetry, Alternate Routes." In *Politics and Poetic Value*. Ed. Robert von Hallberg, 253–76. Chicago: University of Chicago Press.

Messerli, Douglas, ed. 1994. *From the Other Side of the Century: A New American Poetry, 1960–1990*. Los Angeles: Sun & Moon Press.

　ed. 1987. *"Language" Poetries*. New York: New Directions.

Noland, Carrie, and Barrett Watten, eds. 2009. *Diasporic Avant-Gardes: Experimental Poetics and Cultural Displacement*. New York: Palgrave MacMillan.

Perelman, Bob. 1996. *The Marginalization of Poetry: Language Writing and Literary History*. Princeton, NJ: Princeton University Press.

　ed. 1985. *Writing/Talks*. Carbondale: Southern Illinois University Press.

Perloff, Marjorie. 1996. "The Word as Such: L=A=N=G=U=A=G=E Poetry in the 1980s." In *The Dance of the Intellect: Studies in the Poetry of the Pound Tradition*. Evanston, IL: Northwestern University Press, 215–38.

Reinfeld, Linda. 1992. *Language Poetry: Writing as Rescue*. Baton Rouge: Louisiana State University Press.

Ross, Andrew. 1988. "The New Sentence and the Commodity Form: Recent American Writing." In *Marxism and the Interpretation of Culture*. Ed. Cary Nelson and Lawrence Grossberg, 361–80. Urbana: University of Illinois Press.

Silliman, Ron. 1987. *The New Sentence*. New York: Roof.

　2007. *The Age of Huts (compleat)*. Berkeley: University of California Press.

　ed. 1986. *In the American Tree: Language, Realism, Poetry*. Orono, ME: National Poetry Foundation.

Vickery, Ann. 2000. *Leaving Lines of Gender: A Feminist Genealogy of Language Writing*. Middletown, CT: Wesleyan University Press.

Watten, Barrett. 1984. *Total Syntax*. Carbondale: Southern Illinois University Press.

　2003. *The Constructivist Moment: From Material Text to Cultural Poetics*. Middletown, CT: Wesleyan University Press.

19

EVAN KINDLEY

Poet-Critics and Bureaucratic Administration

Village Explainers: Poet-Critics and Modernism

In *The Autobiography of Alice B. Toklas*, Gertrude Stein describes Ezra Pound as "a village explainer, excellent if you were a village, but if you were not, not" (Stein 1990, 200). This quip is justly famous, and it zeroes in on exactly the question that will concern me in the following pages: the need for public explanation and justification of art and literature, for socially acceptable "explanations" of practices that are presumed, by their very nature, to be autonomous, mysterious, and fundamentally unaccountable. The implication of Stein's remark is that modernist writers themselves have little need of criticism or of the productions of critics; these serve a primarily didactic function, helping to indoctrinate the philistine public into the mysteries of poetry, and to clarify the practice for "villagers" who might otherwise misunderstand or distrust it. In Stein's time, these concerns were embodied in a figure that is not unique to the twentieth century, but that takes on an unprecedented amount of social power and importance in the last hundred years of literary history: the poet-critic.

Notwithstanding Stein's jab, the modernists – not only the helplessly didactic Pound, but everyone from T. S. Eliot and William Carlos Williams to Marianne Moore and even Stein herself – were inveterate and passionate explainers, and it is largely thanks to historical developments of the modernist era that we now expect poets – and, increasingly, other types of creative artists as well – to explain and justify their art to us as well as produce it. To a certain extent, this activity of reflexive self-explanation can be seen as part of the "routine autopoiesis" that Mark McGurl sees as essential to modernism. "In the modernist tradition," McGurl writes, "the portrait of the artist is not only an important single book and an important genre, but also a name for one of the routine operations of literary modernism. For the modernist artist, that is, the reflexive production of the 'modernist artist' – i.e., job description itself – is a large part of the job" (McGurl 2009, 48). In much the same spirit, we might say that the reflexive production of justifications, analyses, defenses, and critiques of modernism form a crucial part of the modernist project. What would modernism be without its explanations?

That poet-critics have been important to the definition and promulgation of modernism should be an uncontroversial claim. Pound and Eliot, after all, are exemplary figures in both traditions; the critical prose of Stevens, Williams, Moore, and others are frequently consulted by scholars of those poets' work; and university-based poet-critics like John Crowe Ransom, Allen Tate, and R. P. Blackmur played a crucial and acknowledged role in the institutionalization of the twentieth-century academic literary curriculum under the auspices of the New Criticism. It is important to stress, however, that the poet-critic is hardly a modernist invention. There exists a long tradition of poets who have written critical prose (what John Milton memorably called "the work of the left hand"), a lineage that includes Sidney, Milton, Johnson, Pope, Wordsworth, Emerson, Arnold, and many others. Nevertheless, the poet-critics of the modernist era do play a role in literary history distinct from their predecessors, and this is a function not only of their number – no other period, with the possible exception of our own, can compete with the twentieth century for sheer density of poet-critics – but also of their role in the administration of large bureaucratic institutions. The importance of the modernist era is not that it produced a new kind of literary figure, but that it found a new kind of work for that figure to do.

As scholars like McGurl, Langdon Hammer, Gerald Graff, and others have noted, the research university is, by a wide margin, the dominant bureaucratic institution in Anglo-American postwar literary life. Literary historians have commonly associated poet-critics with the New Criticism and the institutionalization of literary study as an academic discipline in the mid twentieth century. Indeed, the litany of important modernist poet-critics who held posts at American universities in the first half of the century is extensive, and includes Ransom, Tate, Blackmur, Robert Penn Warren, Yvor Winters, Delmore Schwartz, and Randall Jarrell, among others.

Preeminent though it may be, the university is not the only bureaucratic institution that found a use for the poet-critic. A fuller account of the poet-critic as administrator would venture beyond the university and include those poet-critics who worked in tandem with government and philanthropic foundations. None of these administrative commitments were merely "second jobs": the rubric that sociologist Bernard Lahire uses to refer to work undertaken by writers to finance less profitable artistic activities (Lahire 2010). Rather, they were all positions that drew on the specific symbolic capital these poet-critics had acquired in the literary sphere, and that allowed them to advance ambitious administrative aims consistent with their practical interests as writers. We are dealing here not with the poet-critic as teacher or researcher – activities which, while supported by bureaucracy, are not intrinsic to its functioning – but with the poet-critic as *administrator*: as the deviser and facilitator of systems for organizing productive activity on a very large scale. Rather than continue the oppositional anti-institutional project of the historical avant-garde as described by Peter Bürger and others, modernist poet-critics adopted an alternative strategy, taking on a different but no less ambitious political project: to justify the ways of poetry to bureaucracy, and vice versa.

Interrupting the Muse: Poet-Critics and Government

One major bureaucratic institution that found a use for the talents of poet-critics was the federal government. Michael Szalay, in his *New Deal Modernism*, has argued for the imbrication of American modernism with the Rooseveltian welfare state, and indeed the Roosevelt administration showed a surprising interest in the talents of poet-critics. Consider the career of Sterling A. Brown, who worked for the Federal Writers Project as "Editor of Negro Affairs" from 1936 to 1940. By this point, Brown had already established himself as both poet and critic, though he was already better known as the latter. As Lawrence Jackson puts it in *The Indignant Generation*, his magisterial study of Brown's cohort of African American intellectuals, "Brown's early success as a poet seemed nearly secondary to his career as a professional advocate of black arts" (Jackson 2011, 37). Although many of Brown's peers, after the 1927 publication of his first collection, *Southern Road*, expected him to be one of the great poets of his generation, his role in the collective project of African American literature would prove, in the event, to be primarily critical and administrative rather than creative.

Much of Brown's literary inspiration came from African American folk culture; *Southern Road* was widely hailed for its rehabilitation of the "dialect" tradition, which had become unfashionable among middle-class black audiences. As fate would have it, in the 1930s, these interests dovetailed with the interests of the American government, which sought to provide relief to rural areas in part by making them the subject of ethnographic research programs. In 1935, the Federal Writers' Project launched an ambitious series of state-by-state Field Guides focusing on the celebration and preservation of American folk culture, and director Harry Alsberg tapped Brown, at the suggestion of prominent African American intellectuals like Alain Locke and James Weldon Johnson, as "Editor of Negro Affairs" for the entire project.

Brown felt considerable hesitation about accepting the administrative position. Still, he recognized the historic opportunity that the program, which would collect and archive the testimonies of many former slaves, represented. He also felt that he had an opportunity to dispel certain deeply entrenched misunderstandings about African American life and culture; in effect, to instrumentalize the social critique he had been advancing in the pages of little magazines, such as The Crisis and Opportunity, about the corrosive effects of negative racial stereotypes. Finally, working for the Federal Writers Project allowed him to employ many out-of-work friends, students, and colleagues who had been suffering under the Depression and to help bring legitimacy and financial support to the underfunded black academic institutions that had made his career to date possible.

Brown was not the only modernist poet-critic courted for a high-profile administrative position by the Roosevelt administration. Three years after Brown's appointment, Archibald MacLeish, an editor at *Fortune* who had made his literary reputation as the author of modernist works, including *Einstein* (1929) and *Conquistador* (1932), was tapped to replace Herbert Putnam as Librarian of Congress. Although MacLeish, who had no degree in library science or previous experience in government, was an unlikely choice, Judge Felix Frankfurter's letter of recommendation for MacLeish gives some idea of his attractiveness as a candidate:

> He unites in himself qualities seldom found in combination – those of the hardheaded lawyer with the sympathetic imagination of the poet, the independent thinker, and the charming "mixer." He would bring to the Librarianship intellectual distinction, cultural recognition the world over, a persuasive personality and a delicacy of touch in dealing with others, and creative energy in making the Library of Congress the great center of the cultural resource of the Nation in the technological setting of our time.   (Winnick 1983, 291)

Frankfurter's letter limns the collection of traits that poet-critics like MacLeish were thought, by some forward-thinking members of the mid-century U.S. establishment, to possess: "sympathetic imagination" along with both social and cultural capital; a combination of charismatic creativity, practical *savoir faire*, and social distinction. Writing to Frankfurter in May 1939, MacLeish agreed that he "unite[d] in himself qualities seldom found in combination," although he characterized this as a liability rather than a strength: "From the beginning of my more or less adult life I have been plagued by the fact that I seem to be able to do more or less well things which don't commonly go together" (Winnick 299). But he, too, was anxious about the prospect of accepting a governmental position: "It may be that I have now come to the place in my life where I should stop writing poetry and turn to the public service. But if I thought so, I am afraid I should not be of much use to the public service, because the one thing I have ever wanted to do with all my heart was to write poetry and the one thing I have ever wanted to be was a poet" (Winnick 300).

Nevertheless, MacLeish eventually agreed to accept the librarianship on the condition that he be given time to complete his long poem *America was Promises*. (President Roosevelt wrote MacLeish personally to "guarantee that I will not interrupt the Muse when she is flirting with you" [Winnick 294].) He held the position of Librarian of Congress until 1944 and also served as director of the War Department's Office of Facts and Figures and assistant director of the Office of War Information. During his tenure, MacLeish not only oversaw an immense reorganization of the Library's organizational structure and revised its acquisition and cataloguing practices but also provided support to modernist writers like Saint-John Perse, W. H. Auden, Thomas Mann, Allen Tate, and Robert Penn Warren.

The Foundations of Criticism: Poet-Critics and Philanthropy

The employment of poet-critics like MacLeish and Brown in bureaucratic capacities was a phenomenon of the 1930s and '40s. But as the war effort began to consume more and more resources and attention, the federal government's role in sustaining a certain "New Deal" modernism gradually declined. In the postwar era, then, modernism's village explainers began to look to new bureaucratic institutions for support. In 1945, R. P. Blackmur published a short essay in the *Sewanee Review* entitled "The Economy of the American Writer." The piece was something of a departure for him, in that up to that point he was primarily known as a close reader of texts, not as a social critic. Nonetheless, here we have Blackmur trying his hand at cultural criticism, beginning by quoting no less a past master of the form than Alexis de Tocqueville: "Democracy not only infuses a taste for letters among the trading classes, but introduces a trading spirit into literature" (Blackmur 1945, 175). This "trading spirit," in Blackmur's estimation, had never been stronger in the United States than it was at the dawn of the post–World War II era, nor had there ever been more men and women of letters looking to trade their wares. Blackmur argued that the growth in what he elsewhere called "the new literacies" had had powerful transformative effects on the world of literature, but these effects had never been checked by any institutional oversight: "The trade of writing is the chief positive obstacle, in our world, to the preservation and creation of the art of literature," he wrote,

> and it is an obstacle all the harder to overcome because there is a greater and negative obstacle, which goes with it, in the absence, through all our societies, of any social, public, or quasi-public institution which consistently and continuously encourages the serious writer to do his best work.
>
> (Blackmur 1945, 176)

In the postwar period, Blackmur realized, "the art of literature" – which, for him and his cohort, meant first and foremost the under-recognized, unfinished project of modernism – would require institutional support on a scale unprecedented in American literary history.

The precedent of Roosevelt's Works Progress Administration – for which Blackmur and his wife Helen, like many other literary intellectuals of the time, both worked – had emboldened modernists to feel that they could finally make the case for the deliberate perpetuation of the support of "serious literature" as a social good. But Blackmur is conspicuously silent on the subject of state support for the arts in "The Economy of the American Writer," and goes out of his way to disparage the Soviet system, which he finds no more conducive to aesthetic values than the American one. What institution, then, would allow for literary administration of the art of literature on the enormous scale that Blackmur has in mind? He puts forward two "existing institutions which show potential aesthetic bias – the universities and the Foundations." Although he had, at the time of the publication of "The Economy of the American Writer," already been teaching at Princeton for five years, Blackmur voices important reservations about academia:

> In this country writers and artists have for some years been penetrating the universities; but it is too soon to tell with what results. The risk in the experiment is that the universities are themselves increasingly becoming social and technical service stations – are increasingly, that is, attracted into the orbit of the market system. (Blackmur 1945, 185)

Whereas other modernist poet-critics like John Crowe Ransom tended (as we will see) to see the academy as the safest bet for the future of the modernist project, Blackmur the autodidact keenly perceived the university's crucial relation to the national labor market as a whole. The risk was that universities, while employing poets and critics as teachers and thus keeping them from having to debase their work by adjusting its value to the fluctuations of the market, would reintroduce market values into literature by virtue of the university's unacknowledged function as a "social and technical service station" – that is, a training ground for the professional-managerial class. This, for Blackmur, would be missing the point of the academy's sponsorship of modernism, protecting literature from one market (the market for literary commodities) by yoking it to another (the market for skilled labor). Blackmur concludes the essay with a stern warning that "the universities will need the courage as well as the judgment to see how vitally implicated are their own standards in the experiment. All's Alexandrian else" (Blackmur 1945, 185).

The philanthropic foundation, on the other hand, did appear to present a real alternative to the market system, and though Blackmur does not take up the theme in "The Economy of the American Writer," his faith in the foundations is borne out by his subsequent administrative activities. Blackmur's philanthropic career grew out of his close friendship with John Marshall, the associate director of the Rockefeller Foundation's Humanities Division, whom he had known since their adolescent years in Cambridge, Massachusetts. In 1946, Blackmur participated in a Rockefeller-funded initiative, spearheaded by Marshall, to provide funding to little magazines.[1] The Rockefeller little magazines project shows Blackmur's commitment to the possibilities of administration by committee and his developing sense of the role that the loose cadre of poet-critics to which he belonged might be able to play in shaping postwar American literary culture.

It was not difficult for Blackmur to determine which individuals were best equipped to administer the necessary dose of intelligence and imagination. The cohort of modernist poet-critics who had been attending to questions of aesthetic value and autonomy since the late 1910s were ready and, for the most part, willing to take their turn at the managerial wheel. Poet-critics appealed to mid-century foundation officers like Marshall for the same reason MacLeish had appealed to Frankfurter and Roosevelt: In the unique compromise they embodied between the apparently antithetical values of charisma and bureaucracy, they were perfect management material. (Remember MacLeish's "qualities seldom found in combination.") Furthermore, as self-interested agents worried about the decline and even disappearance of literary culture, they had strong incentives to align themselves with institutions that sought, in Blackmur's words, to "remove their values from the market." Finally, as moral actors with access to sophisticated discourses of justification and explanation, disposed to view the furtherance of poetic and literary culture as a common good, they were extremely convincing in their defense of those values. As unlikely as the union might seem on paper, in practice, poet-critics and bureaucracy were a perfect match.

With the Program: Poet-Critics and Academia

Although he was right to perceive the central importance of criticism to the future of literary modernism in the United States, Blackmur's dream of a robust public culture supported by the largesse of philanthropic foundations did not quite come to pass. Instead, the work of poet-critics continued to be supported by the already existing institutional structures of the universities, with philanthropic organizations lending the occasional infusion of capital but not advancing initiatives of their own. Two years after the Rockefeller survey, John Crowe Ransom received a three-year grant from the foundation to fund the Kenyon School of English, a summer program dedicated to training undergraduate teachers in criticism and critical theory; the same year, Blackmur received similar support to establish the Christian Gauss Seminars in Criticism at Princeton. It would be projects like these, rather than the work of critical little magazines, that would provide the way forward for the kind of discourse that modernist poet-critics had inaugurated.

It is thus possible to see the immediate postwar period as a contest between two rival visions of modernism's institutionalization, one stressing philanthropic support of public culture (Blackmur), the other higher education and academic research (Ransom). If this admittedly schematic historical perspective is adopted, then Ransom was the clear victor. "If there was a single critical career whose personal trajectory perfectly coincided with the institutional fortunes of criticism," Gerald Graff writes in *Professing Literature*, "it was that of John Crowe Ransom" (Graff 1987, 155). Of all the poet-critics of the modernist era, it was Ransom who invested most deeply in the institution of the university, an investment motivated not only by humanist piety but also by his awareness of a looming crisis within the professoriate. "I have an idea," he wrote to Allen Tate in 1937, à propos his move from Vanderbilt to Kenyon and the creation of the *Kenyon Review*, "that we could really found criticism if we could get together on it.... The professors are in an awful dither trying to reform themselves and there's a big stroke possible for a small group that knows what it wants in giving them ideas and definitions and showing the way" (Graff 1987, 157). Ransom, like Blackmur, sought to "found" criticism by giving it a solid grounding in the practical and financial as well as the theoretical and intellectual sense. By the mid-1940s, the high-minded ethical talk of "principles" that Eliot had inaugurated with "The Function of Criticism" (1923) and that I. A. Richards had subsequently developed in *The Principles of Literary Criticism* (1925) and other theoretical texts, had given way to the archaeological discourse of "foundation"; the concern is not so much for an ethics, or methodology, as it is the establishment of an institutional headquarters or home base.

Nor was Ransom's call for institutionalization expressed only in private correspondence. "It is strange," he writes in "Criticism, Inc.," first published in the *Virginia Quarterly Review* in autumn 1937 and reprinted the next year in his collection *The World's Body* (1938), "but nobody seems to have told us what exactly is the proper business of criticism." Those currently writing criticism "have not been trained to criticism so much as they have simply undertaken a job for which no specific qualifications were required. It is far too likely that what they call criticism when they produce it is not the real thing." So far, this is close to T. S. Eliot's early calls for criticism by poets in essays like "The Perfect Critic," especially considered alongside the opinion that "probably the best critics of poetry we can now have are the poets." But Ransom insists far more strongly than Eliot ever did on the limits of the artist's pragmatic approach to criticism. "The artist himself ... should know good art when he sees it," Ransom writes, "but his understanding is intuitive rather than dialectical – he cannot very well explain his theory of the thing" (Ransom 1938, 327). The need for theory, as much as the need for institutional financial support, undergirds Ransom's decisive call for a university-based culture of criticism:

> It is from the professors of literature, in this country the professors of English for the most part, that I should hope eventually for the erection of intelligent standards of criticism. It is their business. Criticism must become more scientific, or precise and systematic, and this means that it must be developed by the collective and sustained effort of learned persons – which means that its proper seat is in the universities.... Rather than occasional criticism by amateurs, I should think the whole enterprise might be seriously taken in hand by professionals. Perhaps I use a distasteful figure, but I have the idea that what we need is Criticism, Inc., or Criticism, Ltd. (Ransom 1938, 329)

Ransom was not the first to call for a professionalized academic criticism, but the fact that he did so *as a poet*, with the full force of his literary prestige behind him – making the leap that Eliot, for all of his academic leanings, never quite had – had an immense symbolic significance, and not only for other poets but for ambitious administrators as well.

Poet-critics such as Brown, MacLeish, Blackmur, and Ransom all made deliberate decisions about the relation of their work to postwar bureaucratic institutions, and these decisions – alongside, of course, a multitude of other determining factors – led to significant changes in the Anglo-American literary field. In the light of subsequent literary and institutional history, and from within the disciplinary matrix that the New Criticism helped to initiate, Ransom's governing idea – that the "proper seat" of criticism was in the universities – has come to seem self-evident, but it was only one of many possible outcomes. The role of modernist poet-critics was, as I have suggested, to provide explanations, justifications, and defenses of poetry, and, if the university ultimately proved the most receptive audience, it may not be so forever. This is why it may be useful to revisit the alternative visions of poet-critics like Blackmur, MacLeish, and Brown and to imagine other institutions for the support of literary and intellectual culture. All's Alexandrian else.

NOTES

1 For further details of the Rockefeller survey, see my "Big Criticism."

WORKS CITED

Blackmur, R. P. 1945. "The Economy of the American Writer: Preliminary Notes." *Sewanee Review* 53:12, 175–85.

Bürger, Peter. 1984. *Theory of the Avant-Garde.* Trans. Michael Shaw. Minneapolis: University of Minnesota Press.

Graff, Gerald. 1987. *Professing Literature: An Institutional History.* Chicago: University of Chicago Press.

Hammer, Langdon. 1993. *Hart Crane & Allen Tate: Janus-Faced Modernism.* Princeton, NJ: Princeton University Press.

Jackson, Lawrence P. 2011. *The Indignant Generation: A Narrative History of African American Writers and Critics, 1934–1960.* Princeton, NJ: Princeton University Press.

Kindley, Evan. 2011. "Big Criticism." *Critical Inquiry* 38.1: 71–95.

Lahire, Bernard. 2010. "The Double Life of Writers." Trans. Gwendolyn Wells. *New Literary History* 41:2: 443–65.

McGurl, Mark. 2009. *The Program Era: Postwar Fiction and the Rise of Creative Writing.* Cambridge, MA: Harvard University Press.

Ransom, John Crowe. 1938. *The World's Body.* New York: C. Scribner's Sons.

Stein, Gertrude. 1990. *The Autobiography of Alice B. Toklas.* New York: Vintage.

Szalay, Michael. 2000. *New Deal Modernism: American Literature and the Invention of the Welfare State.* Durham, NC: Duke University Press.

Winnick, R. H. ed. 1983. *Letters of Archibald MacLeish, 1907 to 1982.* New York: Houghton Mifflin.

GUIDE TO FURTHER READING

The Emergence of "The New Poetry"

Cahill, Daniel J. 1973. *Harriet Monroe*. New York: Twayne Publishers.

Carlin, T. Kindilien. 1956. *American Poetry in the Eighteen Nineties: A Study of American Verse, 1890–1899*. Brown University Studies, vol. xx. Providence, RI: Brown University Press.

Duffey, Bernard I. 1978. *Poetry in America: Expression and Its Values in the Times of Bryant, Whitman, and Pound*. Durham, NC: Duke University Press.

Egan, Ken, Jr. 1995. "The Machine in the Poem: Nineteenth-Century American Poetry and Technology." *Weber Studies: An Interdisciplinary Humanities Journal* 12.1: 70–81.

Hagenbüchle, Roland, ed. 1984. *American Poetry Between Tradition and Modernism, 1865–1914*. Regensburg: Pustet.

Lee, Maurice. 2002. "Re-Canonizing Nineteenth-Century American Poetry." *Minnesota Review* 55–7: 327–30.

Monroe, Harriet. 1938. *A Poet's Life: Seventy Years in a Changing World*. New York: Macmillan.

Monroe, Harriet and Alice Corbin Henderson, eds. 1917. *The New Poetry: An Anthology*. New York: Macmillan.

Rubin, Joan Shelley. 2007. *Songs of Ourselves: The Uses of Poetry*. Cambridge, MA: Harvard University Press.

Sorby, Angela. 2005. *Schoolroom Poets: Childhood, Performance, and the Place of American Poetry, 1865–1917*. Hanover, NH: University Press of New England.

Tomsich, John. 1971. *A Genteel Endeavor: American Politics and Culture in the Gilded Age*. Stanford, CA: Stanford University Press.

Waggoner, Hyatt H. 1968. *American Poets from the Puritans to the Present*. Boston: Houghton Mifflin & Co.

Williams, Ellen. 1977. *Harriet Monroe and the Poetry of the Renaissance: The First Ten Years of Poetry, 1912–22*. Urbana: University of Illinois Press.

Modern American Archives and Scrapbook Modernism

Andrews, Bruce. 1996. *Paradise and Method: Poetics and Praxis*. Evanston, IL: Northwestern University Press.

Benjamin, Walter. 1999. "Unpacking My Library: A Talk About Collecting." Trans. Harry Zohn. *Selected Writings*. Vol. 2, 1927–34. Eds. Michael W. Jennings,

Howard Eiland, and Gary Smith, 486–93. Cambridge, MA: Belknap/Harvard University Press.

1999. "The Work of Art in the Age of Its Technological Reproducibility." Trans. Edmund Jephcott and Harry Zohn. In *Selected Writings*. Vol. 3, 1935–8. Eds. Howard Eiland and Michael W. Jennings, 101–33. Cambridge, MA: Belknap/ Harvard University Press.

Bornstein, George. 2001. *Material Modernism: The Politics of the Page*. Cambridge: Cambridge University Press.

Bourdieu, Pierre. 1990. *The Logic of Practice*. Trans. Richard Nice. Stanford, CA: Stanford University Press.

Braddock, Jeremy. 2012. *Collecting as Modernist Practice*. Baltimore: Johns Hopkins University Press.

Brinkman, Bartholomew. 2011. "Scrapping Modernism: Marianne Moore and the Making of the Modern Collage Poem." *Modernism/modernity* 18.1: 43–66.

Chasar, Mike. 2012. *Everyday Reading: Poetry and Popular Culture in Modern America*. New York: Columbia University Press.

Derrida, Jacques. 1998. *Archive Fever: A Freudian Impression*. Trans. Eric Prenowitz. Chicago: University of Chicago Press.

Garvey, Ellen Gruber. 2013. *Writing with Scissors: American Scrapbooks from the Civil War to the Harlem Renaissance*. New York: Oxford University Press.

Helfand, Jessica. 2008. *Scrapbooks: An American History*. New Haven, CT: Yale University Press.

Morrison, Mark. 2001. *The Public Face of Modernism: Little Magazines, Audiences, and Reception, 1905–1920*. Madison: University of Wisconsin Press.

Munich, Adrienne and Melissa Bradshaw, eds. 2004. *Amy Lowell, American Modern*. New Brunswick, NJ: Rutgers University Press.

Schreiber, Maeera and Keith Tuma, eds. 1998. *Mina Loy: Woman and Poet*. Orono, ME: National Poetry Foundation.

Teitelbaum, Matthew, ed. 1992. *Montage and Modern Life 1919–1942*. Cambridge, MA: MIT Press.

Experimental Modernisms

Burke, Carolyn. 1985. "Without Commas: Gertrude Stein and Mina Loy." In *Coming to Light: American Women Poets in the Twentieth Century*. Eds. Diane Wood Middlebrook and Marilyn Yalom, 37–57. Ann Arbor: University of Michigan Press.

Bürger, Peter. 1984. *Theory of the Avant-Garde*. Trans. Michael Shaw. Minneapolis: University of Minnesota Press.

Churchill, Suzanne W. 2006. *The Little Magazine Others and the Renovation of Modern American Poetry*. Aldershot: Ashgate.

Crunden, Robert M. 1993. *American Salons: Encounters with European Modernism, 1885–1917*. New York: Oxford University Press.

DeKoven, Marianne. 1983. *A Different Language: Gertrude Stein's Experimental Writing*. Madison: University of Wisconsin Press.

Diepeveen, Leonard. 2003. *The Difficulties of Modernism*. New York: Routledge.

Dijkstra, Bram. 1969. *The Hieroglyphics of a New Speech: Cubism, Stieglitz and the Early Poetry of William Carlos Williams*. Princeton, NJ: Princeton University Press.

DuPlessis, Rachel Blau. 2001. *Genders, Races, and Religious Culture in Modern American Poetry, 1908–1934*. New York: Cambridge University Press.

Pound, Ezra. 1934. *ABC of Reading*. New Haven, CT: Yale University Press.

Krauss, Rosalind. 1985. *The Originality of the Avant-Garde and Other Modernist Myths*. Cambridge, MA: MIT Press.

Rainey, Lawrence. 1998. *Institutions of Modernism: Literary Elites and Public Culture*. New Haven, CT: Yale University Press.

Schwartz, Sanford. 1985. *The Matrix of Modernism: Pound, Eliot and Early Twentieth-Century Thought*. Princeton, NJ: Princeton University Press.

Smith, Terry. 1993. *Making the Modern: Industry, Art, and Design in America*. Chicago: University of Chicago Press.

Stein, Gertrude. 1935. *Lectures in America*. New York: Modern Library.

The Legacy of New York

Churchill, Allen. 1959. *The Improper Bohemians: A Recreation of Greenwich Village in Its Heyday*. New York: Dutton.

Dickie, Margaret and Thomas Travisano. 1996. *Gendered Modernisms: American Women Poets and Their Readers*. Philadelphia: University of Pennsylvania Press.

Douglas, Ann. 1995. *Terrible Honesty: Mongrel Manhattan in the 1920s*. New York: Farrar, Straus & Giroux.

Kantor, Sybil Gordon. 2002. *Alfred H. Barr, Jr. and the Intellectual Origins of the Museum of Modern Art*. Cambridge, MA: MIT Press.

Kushner, Marilyn Satin and Kimberly Orcutt, eds. 2013. *The Armory Show at 100: Modernism and Revolution*. New York: Giles.

Miller, Christanne. 2005. *Cultures of Modernism: Marianne Moore, Mina Loy, and Else Lasker-Schüler: Gender and Community in New York and Berlin*. Ann Arbor: University of Michigan Press.

Naumann, Francis M. with Beth Venn. 1996. *Making Mischief: Dada Invades New York*. New York: Whitney Museum of American Art.

Nelson, Cary. 2001. *Revolutionary Memory: Recovering the Poetry of the American Left*. New York: Routledge.

Sawelson-Gorse, Naomi, ed. 1998. *Women in Dada: Essays on Sex, Gender, and Identity*. Cambridge, MA: MIT Press.

Stansell, Christine. 2000. *American Moderns: Bohemian New York and the Creation of a New Century*. New York: Metropolitan Books.

Tashjian, Dickran. 1975. *Skyscraper Primitives: Dada and the American Avant-Garde 1910–1925*. Middletown, CT: Wesleyan University Press.

The Modern American Long Poem

Bakhtin, M. M. 1981. *The Dialogic Imagination: Four Essays*. Ed. Michael Holquist. Trans. Caryl Emerson and Michael Holquist. Austin: University of Texas Press.

Bernstein, Michael André. 1980. *The Tale of the Tribe: Ezra Pound and the Modern Verse Epic*. Princeton, NJ: Princeton University Press.

Davies, Catherine A. 2012. *Whitman's Queer Children: America's Homosexual Epics*. New York: Continuum.

Dickie, Margaret. 1986. *On the Modernist Long Poem*. Iowa City: University of Iowa Press.

Gabriel, Daniel. 2007. *Hart Crane and the Modernist Epic*. Basingstoke: Palgrave Macmillan.

McHale, Brian. 2004. *The Obligation toward the Difficult Whole: Postmodernist Long Poems*. Tuscaloosa: University of Alabama Press.

McWilliams, John P., Jr. 1989. *The American Epic: Transforming a Genre, 1770–1860*. Cambridge: Cambridge University Press.

Rosenthal, M. L. and Sally M. Gall. 1983. *The Modern Poetic Sequence: The Genius of Modern Poetry*. New York: Oxford University Press.

Schweitzer, Bernard. 2006. *Approaches to the Anglo and American Female Epic, 1621–1982*. Aldershot: Ashgate.

American Modernism and the Harlem Renaissance

Baker, Houston A., Jr. 1987. *Modernism and the Harlem Renaissance*. Chicago: University of Chicago Press.

Brown, Sterling A. 1931. *Outline for the Study of the Poetry of the American Negroes*. New York: Harcourt Brace.

1955. "The New Negro in Literature (1925–1955)." In *The New Negro Thirty Years Afterward*. Ed. Rayford L. Logan. 57–72. Washington, DC: Howard University Press.

1990. *Jean Toomer's Years with Gurdjieff: Portrait of an Artist, 1923–1936*. Athens: University of Georgia Press.

Calo, Mary Ann. 2007. *Distinction and Denial: Race, Nation, and the Critical Construction of the African American Artist, 1920–40*. Ann Arbor: University of Michigan Press.

Cruden, Robert M. 2000. *Body and Soul: The Making of American Modernism*. New York: Basic Books.

De Long, James. 1990. *Vicious Modernism: Black Harlem and the Literary Imagination*. Cambridge: Cambridge University Press.

DuBois, W. E. B. 1989. *The Souls of Black Folk*. New York: Penguin Books.

Gabbin, Joanne V. 1985. *Sterling Brown: Building the Black Aesthetic Tradition*. Westport, CT: Greenwood Press.

Goeser, Carolyn. 2007. *Picturing the New Negro: Harlem Renaissance Print Culture and Modern Black Identity*. Lawrence: University of Kansas Press.

Hutchinson, George. 1995. *The Harlem Renaissance in Black and White*. Cambridge, MA: Belknap/Harvard University Press.

Johnson, James Weldon. 1991. *Black Manhattan*. New York: Da Capo Press, 1991.

Levine, Lawrence W. 1977. *Black Culture and Black Consciousness: Afro-American Folk Thought from Slavery to Freedom*. New York: Oxford University Press.

Lewis, David Levering. 1981. *When Harlem Was in Vogue*. New York: Oxford University Press.

Locke, Alain, ed. 1925. *The New Negro: An Interpretation*. New York: Albert and Charles Boni.

Maxwell, William J. 1999. *New Negro, Old Left: African American Writing and Communism Between the Wars*. New York: Columbia University Press.

Moses, Wilson. 1987. "The Lost World of the Negro, 1895–1919: Black Intellectual Life before the 'Renaissance.'" *Black American Literature Forum* 21: 61–4.

Sanders, Mark A. 1999. *Afro-Modernist Aesthetics and the Poetry of Sterling A. Brown*. Athens: University of Georgia Press.

Sollors, Werner. 2008. *Ethnic Modernism*. Cambridge, MA: Harvard University Press.

Objectivist Poetry and Poetics

Bremen, Brian A. 1993. *William Carlos Williams and the Diagnostics of Culture*. New York: Oxford University Press.

Dettmar, Kevin J. H. and Stephen Watt, eds. 1996. *Marketing Modernisms: Self-Promotion, Canonization, Rereading*. Ann Arbor: University of Michigan Press.

DuPlessis, Rachel Blau and Peter Quartermain, eds. 1999. *The Objectivist Nexus: Essays in Cultural Poetics*. Tuscaloosa: University of Alabama Press.

Hatlen, Burton, ed. 1981. *George Oppen: Man and Poet*. Orono, ME: National Poetry Foundation.

Quartermain, Peter. 1992. *Disjunctive Poetics: From Gertrude Stein and Louis Zukofsky to Susan Howe*. Cambridge: Cambridge University Press.

Nicholls, Peter. 2007. *George Oppen and the Fate of Modernism*. Oxford: Oxford University Press.

Izenberg, Oren. 2010. *Being Numerous: Poetry and the Ground of Social Life*. Princeton, NJ: Princeton University Press.

Ridell, Joseph N. 1974. *The Inverted Bell: Modernism and the Counterpoetics of William Carlos Williams*. Baton Rouge: Louisiana State University Press.

Rifkin, Libbie. 2000. *Career Moves: Olson, Creeley, Zukofsky, Berrigan, and the American Avant-Garde*. Madison: University of Wisconsin Press.

Scroggins, Mark. 1998. *Louis Zukofsky and the Poetry of Knowledge*. Tuscaloosa: University of Alabama Pres.

American Poetry and the Popular Front

Barnard, Rita. 1995. *The Great Depression and the Culture of Abundance*. Cambridge: Cambridge University Press.

Berke, Nancy. 2001. *Women Poets on the Left: Lola Ridge, Genevieve Taggard, Margaret Walker*. Gainesville: University Press of Florida.

Browder, Earl. 1938. *The Popular Front*. New York: International Publishers.

Conlin, Joseph R., ed. 1974. *The American Radical Press 1880–1960*. Westport, CT: Greenwood.

Diggins, John P. 1973. *The American Left in the Twentieth Century*. New York: Harcourt Brace Jovanovich.

Fishbein, Leslie. 1982. *Rebels in Bohemia: The Radicals of the Masses, 1911–1917*. Chapel Hill: University of North Carolina Press.

Kalaidjian, Walter. 1993. *American Culture Between the Wars: Revisionary Modernism and Postmodern Critique*. New York: Columbia University Press.

Nelson, Cary. 1989. *Repression and Recovery: Modern American Poetry and the Politics of Cultural Memory*. Madison: University of Wisconsin Press.

Sinclair, Upton, ed. 1915. *The Cry for Justice: An Anthology of the Literature of Social Protest*. Philadelphia: John C. Winston.

Smethurst, James Edward. 1999. *The New Red Negro: The Literary Left and African American Poetry, 1930–1946*. New York: Oxford University Press.

Szalay, Michael. 2000. *New Deal Modernism: American Literature and the Invention of the Welfare State*. Durham, NC: Duke University Press.

Tracking the Fugitive Poets

Beck, Charlotte H., ed. 2001. *The Fugitive Legacy: A Critical History*. Baton Rouge: Louisiana State University Press.

Conkin, Paul. 2001. *The Southern Agrarians*. Nashville, TN: Vanderbilt University Press.

Duncan, Christopher. 2000. *Fugitive Theory: Political Theory, the Southern Agrarians, and America*. Lanham, MD: Lexington Books.

Malvasi, Mark G. 1997. *The Unregenerate South: The Agrarian Thought of John Crowe Ransom, Allen Tate, and Donald Davidson*. Baton Rouge: Louisiana State University Press.

Murphy, Paul V. 2001. *The Rebuke of History: The Southern Agrarians and American Conservative Thought*. Chapel Hill: University of North Carolina Press.

Jancovich, Mark. 1993. *The Cultural Politics of the New Criticism*. Cambridge: Cambridge University Press.

Pratt, William, ed. 1991. *The Fugitive Poets: Modern Southern Poetry in Perspective*. Nashville, TN: J. S. Sanders.

Twelve Southerners. 1930. *I'll Take My Stand: The South and the Agrarian Tradition*. New York: Harper Brothers.

Mid-Century Modernism

Breslin, James. 1984. *From Modern to Contemporary: American Poetry, 1945–1965*. Chicago: University of Chicago Press.

Damon, Maria. 2011. *Postliterary America: From Bagel Shop Jazz to Micropoetries*. Iowa City: University of Iowa Press.

Filreis, Alan. 2007. *Counter-Revolution of the Word: The Conservative Attack on Modern Poetry, 1945–1960*. Chapel Hill: University of North Carolina Press.

Gery, John. 1996. *Nuclear Annihilation and Contemporary American Poetry*. Gainesville: University Press of Florida.

Kalstone, David. 1989. *Becoming a Poet: Elizabeth Bishop with Marianne Moore and Robert Lowell*. Ed. Robert Hemenway. London: Hogarth Press.

Keller, Lynn. 2009. *Re-making it New: Contemporary American Poetry and the Modernist Tradition*. Cambridge: Cambridge University Press.

Kenner, Hugh. 1971. *The Pound Era*. Berkeley: University of California Press.

Longenbach, James. 1997. *Modern Poetry after Modernism*. New York: Oxford University Press.

Wald, Alan M. 2001. *Exiles from a Future Time: The Forging of the Mid-Twentieth Century Left*. Chapel Hill: University of North Carolina Press.

Wasley, Aidan. 2011. *The Age of Auden: Postwar Poetry and the American Scene*. Princeton, NJ: Princeton University Press.

Psychotherapy and Confessional Poetry

Breslin, Paul. 1987. *The Psycho-Political Muse: American Poetry since the Fifties*. Chicago: University of Chicago Press.

Brunner, Edward. 2001. *Cold War Poetry: The Social Text in the Fifties Poem*. Urbana: University of Illinois Press.

Davidson, Michael. 2003. *Guys Like Us: Citing Masculinity in Cold War Poetics*. Chicago: University of Chicago Press.

Gill, Jo, ed. 2006. *Modern Confessional Writing: New Critical Essays*. New York: Routledge Press.

Nelson, Deborah. 2002. *Pursuing Privacy in Cold War America*. New York: Columbia University Press.

Rosenthal, M. L. 1967. *The New Poets: American and British Poetry Since World War II*. New York: Oxford University Press.

Sherwin, Miranda. 2011. *"Confessional" Writing and the Twentieth-Century Literary Imagination*. Houndmills, Basingstoke: Palgrave Macmillan.

Rose, Jacqueline. 1992. *The Haunting of Sylvia Plath*. Cambridge, MA: Harvard University Press.

Vendler, Helen. 1995. *The Given and the Made: Strategies of Poetic Redefinition*. Cambridge, MA: Harvard University Press.

Black Mountain Poetry

Clark, Tom. 1991. *Charles Olson: The Allegory of a Poet's Life*. New York: W. W. Norton & Co.

1993. *Robert Creeley and the Genius of the American Commonplace*. New York: New Directions.

Conte, Joseph M. 1991. *Unending Design: The Forms of Postmodern Poetry*. Ithaca, NY: Cornell University Press.

Dawson, Fielding. 1991. *The Black Mountain Book*. Expanded and revised edition. Rocky Mount, NC: Wesleyan College Press.

Duberman, Martin. 1972. *Black Mountain: An Exploration in Community*. New York: Dutton.

Katz, Vincent, ed. 2003. *Black Mountain College: An Experiment in Art*. Cambridge, MA: MIT Press.

Paul, Sherman. 1981. *The Lost America of Love: Rereading Robert Creeley, Robert Duncan, and Ed Dorn*. Baton Rouge: Louisiana State University Press.

Rodgers, Audrey T. 1993. *Denise Levertov: The Poetry of Engagement*. Rutherford, NJ: Fairleigh Dickinson Press.

Seelye, Catherine, ed. 1975. *Charles Olson & Ezra Pound: An Encounter at St. Elizabeth's*. New York: Grossman Publishers.

Beat Poetry: HeavenHell USA, 1946–1965

Belgrade, Daniel. 1998. *The Culture of Spontaneity: Improvisation and the Arts in Postwar America*. Chicago: University of Chicago Press.

Davidson, Michael. 1989. *The San Francisco Renaissance: Poetics and Community at Mid-Century*. Cambridge: Cambridge University Press.

Ehrenreich, Barbara. 1993. *The Hearts of Men: American Dreams and the Flight from Commitment*. New York: Anchor.

Johnson, Ronna C. and Nancy M. Grace, eds. 2002. *Girls Who Wore Black: Women Writing the Beat Generation*. New Brunswick, NJ: Rutgers University Press.

Knight, Brenda, ed. 1996. *Women of the Beat Generation: The Writers, Artists and Muses at the Heart of a Revolution*. Berkeley, CA: Conari Press.

Meltzer, David. 2001. *San Francisco Beat: Talking with the Poets*. San Francisco: City Lights.

Parkinson, Thomas, ed. 1961. *Casebook on the Beat*. New York: Crowell.

Skerl, Jennie, ed. 2004. *Reconstructing the Beats*. New York: Palgrave/St. Martin's Press.

Smith, Richard Candida. 1995. *Utopia and Dissent: Art, Poetry, and Politics in California*. Berkeley: University of California Press.

Sternitt, David. 2013. *The Beats: A Very Short Introduction*. New York: Oxford University Press.

The Black Arts Movement and Black Aesthetics

Baker, Houston A. 1988. *Afro-American Poetics: Revisions of Harlem and the Black Aesthetic*. Madison: University of Wisconsin Press.

Clarke, Cheryl. 2005. *"After Mecca": Women Poets and the Black Arts Movement*. New Brunswick, NJ: Rutgers University Press.

Edwards, Brent Hayes. 2003. *The Practice of Diaspora: Literature, Translation, and the Rise of Black Internationalism*. Cambridge, MA: Harvard University Press.

Gates, Henry Louis, Jr. 1986. *The Signifying Monkey: A Theory of Afro-American Literary Criticism*. New York: Oxford University Press.

1987. *Figures in Black: Words, Signs, and the "Racial" Self*. New York: Oxford University Press.

Gayle, Addison, ed. 1971. *The Black Aesthetic*. Garden City, NY: Doubleday.

Moten, Fred. 2003. *In the Break: The Aesthetics of the Black Radical Tradition*. Minneapolis: University of Minnesota Press.

Nielson, Alden Lynn. 1988. *Reading Race: White American Poets and the Racial Discourse of the Twentieth Century*. Athens: University of Georgia Press.

North, Michael. 1994. *The Dialect of Modernism: Race, Language, and Twentieth-Century Literature*. New York: Oxford University Press.

Ongiri, Amy Abugo. 2010. *Spectacular Blackness: The Cultural Politics of the Black Power Movement and the Search for a Black Aesthetic*. Charlottesville: University of Virginia Press.

Smethurst, James Edward. 2005. *The Black Arts Movement: Literary Nationalism in the 1960s*. Chapel Hill: University of North Carolina Press.

Thomas, Lorenzo. 2000. *Extraordinary Measures: Afrocentric Modernism and Twentieth-Century American Poetry*. Tuscaloosa: University of Alabama Press.

Winkiel, Laura. 2008. *Modernism, Race, and Manifestos.* Cambridge: Cambridge University Press.

New York School and American Surrealist Poetics

Ashbery, John. 1999. *Reported Sightings: Art Chronicles 1957–1987.* Ed. David Bergman. Cambridge, MA: Harvard University Press.
2000. *Other Traditions.* Charles Eliot Norton Lectures, 1989–90. Cambridge, MA: Harvard University Press.
Breton, André. 1969. *Manifestoes of Surrealism.* Trans. Helen R. Land and Richard Seaver. Ann Arbor: University of Michigan Press.
Diggory, Terence and Stephen Paul Miller, eds. 2001. *The Scenes of My Selves: New Work on the New York School Poets.* Orono, ME: National Poetry Foundation.
DuPlessis, Rachel Blau. 2006. "The Gendered Marvelous: Barbara Guest, Surrealism, and Feminist Reception." In *Blue Studios,* 162–85. Tuscaloosa: University of Alabama Press.
Epstein, Andrew. 2006. *Beautiful Enemies: Friendship and Postwar American Poetry.* New York: Oxford University Press.
Guest, Barbara. 2003. *Forces of Imagination: Writing on Writing.* Berkeley, CA: Kelsey Street Press.
Lehman, David. 1998. *The Last Avant-Garde: The Making of the New York School of Poets.* New York: Doubleday.
O'Hara, Frank. 1975. *Art Chronicles 1954–1966.* New York: Braziller.
Nelson, Maggie. 2007. *Women, the New York School, and Other True Abstractions.* Iowa City: University of Iowa Press.
Perloff, Marjorie. 1977. *Frank O'Hara: Poet among Painters.* New York: Braziller.
Sawin, Martica. 1995. *Surrealism in Exile and the Beginning of the New York School.* Cambridge, MA: MIT Press.
Schuyler, James. 1998. *Selected Art Writings.* Ed. Simon Pettet. Santa Rosa, CA: Black Sparrow Press.
Watkin, William. 2001. *In the Process of Poetry: The New York School and the Avant Garde.* Lewisburg, PA: Bucknell University Press.

Land, Place, and Nation: Toward an Indigenous American Poetics

Armstrong, Jeannette, ed. 1993. *Looking at the Words of Our People: First Nations Analysis of Literature.* Penticton, Theytus Books.
Lincoln, Kenneth. 1983. *Native American Renaissance.* Berkeley: University of California Press.
Lundquist, Suzanne Eversten. 2004. *Native American Literatures: An Introduction.* New York: Continuum.
Nelson, Robert. 1993. *Place and Vision: The Function of Landscape in Native American Fiction.* New York: Peter Lang.
Pulitano, Elvira. 2003. *Toward a Native American Critical Theory.* Lincoln: University of Nebraska Press.
Rader, Dean and Janice Gould, eds. 2003. *Speak to Me Words: Essays on Contemporary American Indian Poetry.* Tucson: University of Arizona Press.

Swann, Brian and Arnold Krupat, eds. 1987. *Recovering the Word: Essays on Native American Literature*. Berkeley: University of California Press.

Velie, Allan R., ed. 1995. *Native American Perspectives on Literature and History*. Norman: University of Oklahoma Press.

Warrior, Robert Allen. 1994. *Tribal Secrets: Recovering American Indian Traditions*. Minneapolis: University of Minnesota Press.

Weaver, Jace, Craig S. Womack, and Robert Warrior, eds. 2005. *American Indian Nationalism*. Albuquerque: University of New Mexico Press.

Wiget, Andrew O., ed. 1985. *Critical Essays on Native American Literature*. New York: G. K. Hall.

Transpacific and Asian American Counterpoetics

Kern, Robert. 1996. *Orientalism, Modernism, and the American Poem*. Cambridge: Cambridge University Press.

Miller, Joshua L. 2010. *Accented America: The Cultural Politics of Multilingual Modernism*. Oxford: Oxford University Press.

Ong, Aihwa. 1999. *Flexible Citizenship: The Cultural Logics of Transnationality*. Durham, NC: Duke University Press.

Park, Josephine. 2008. *Apparitions of Asia: Modernist Form and Asian American Poetics*. New York: Oxford University Press.

Qian, Zhaoming. 1995. *Orientalism and Modernism: The Legacy of China in Pound and Williams*. Durham, NC: Duke University Press.

Ramazani, Jahan. 1994. *A Transnational Poetics*. Chicago: University of Chicago Press.

Yu, Timothy. 2009. *Race and the Avant-Garde: Experimental and Asian American Poetry Since 1965*. Stanford, CA: Stanford University Press.

Walkowitz, Rebecca. 2007. *Cosmopolitan Style: Modernism Beyond the Nation*. New York: Columbia University Press.

Language Writing

Andrews, Bruce and Charles Bernstein, eds. 1984. *The L=A=N=G=U=A=G=E Book*. Carbondale: Southern Illinois University Press.

Davidson, Michael. 1997. *Ghostlier Demarcations: Modern Poetry and the Material Word*. Berkeley: University of California Press.

Hartley, George. 1989. *Textual Politics and the Language Poets*. Bloomington: Indiana University Press.

Hejinian, Lyn. 2000. *The Language of Inquiry*. Berkeley: University of California Press.

Ma, Ming-Qian. 2008. *Poetry as Re-Reading: American Avant-Garde Poetry and the Poetics of Counter-Method*. Evanston, IL: Northwestern University Press.

McGann, Jerome. 2007. *The Point is to Change It: Poetry and Criticism in the Continuing Present*. Tuscaloosa: University of Alabama Press.

Perelman, Bob. 1996. *The Marginalization of Poetry: Language Writing and Literary History*. Princeton, NJ: Princeton University Press.

Reinfeld, Linda. 1992. *Language Poetry: Writing as Rescue*. Baton Rouge: Louisiana State University Press.

Silliman, Ron, ed. 1986. *In the American Tree: Language, Realism, Poetry.* Orono, ME: National Poetry Foundation.

Poet-Critics and Bureaucratic Administration

Golding, Alan. 1995. *From Outlaw to Classic: Canons in American Poetry.* Madison: University of Wisconsin Press.

Graff, Gerald. 1987. *Professing Literature: An Institutional History.* Chicago: University of Chicago Press.

Graff, Gerald and Michael Warner, eds. 1989. *The Origins of Literary Studies in America: A Documentary Anthology.* New York: Routledge.

Guillory, John. 1993. *Cultural Capital: The Problem of Literary Canon Formation.* Chicago: University of Chicago Press.

Jackson, Lawrence P. 2011. *The Indignant Generation: A Narrative History of African American Writers and Critics, 1934–1960.* Princeton, NJ: Princeton University Press.

Lazer, Hank. 1996. *Opposing Poetries: Volume One: Issues and Institutions.* Evanston, IL: Northwestern University Press.

McGurl, Mark. 2009. *The Program Era: Postwar Fiction and the Rise of Creative Writing.* Cambridge, MA: Harvard University Press.

INDEX

Abbott, Charles, 31–32, 33
academia, poet-critics and, 255–57
academic libraries, 30–31
Acker, Kathy, 244
aesthetics. *See* black aesthetics
African American poetry/poets. *See* Harlem
  Renaissance; New Negro Renaissance
Agrarian project, 120–21
Albers, Anni, 157
Albers, Josef, 157
Aldington, Richard, 38
Allen, Donald, 162–63
Alsberg, Harry, 250–51
American New Critics, 1, 2–3
American poetry, modern. *See also* Native
  American poetry
  Communist presence and, 107–10
  communist presence in, 5–6
  crisis in, at turn of twentieth century,
    11–12, 15
  divide between popular and avant-garde
    in, 21
  Great Depression and, 5–6
  importance of scrapbooks for study
    of, 26–27
  landscape of, in 1930s, 102–4
  legacy of Popular Front and, 111–13
  narrative accounts of, 50
  Orientalist legacy in, 8–9
  proletarianism and modernism in, 104–7
  reading and teaching of, 2
  rebuilding of institutional infrastructured
    of, 15–16
American poets, mid-century, 130,
  See also poet-critics
  trademarks of, 139–40
American poets, modern. *See also* poet-critics
  first two waves of, 15
  reading of, 2

American Surrealism. *See* Surrealism
Amerrican Literary History, 1
Ammons, A. R., 205–6
Anderson, Margaret, 19
Anderson, Sherwood, 79
Andrews, Bruce, 98–99, 240
Angel Island, Chinese immigrants and, 224
archival preservation, 3
archives
  reconstructing modern poetry, 33–35
  rise of modern poetry, 30–33
Arensberg, Walter and Louise, 46–47, 58
Armantrout, Rae, 98–99, 239, 240
Armory Show, opening of, 50, 58
Ashbery, John, 74, 196, 197–99, 241–42
Asian American poetry, 223
  renaissance of, 227–32
Auden, W. H., 70, 105, 129–30, 133–34

Baker, Houston, 77–78
Baldwin, James, 177–78, 181
BAM. *See* Black Arts Movement (BAM)
Baraka, Amiri (*See* LeRoi Jones), 98,
  162, 177–78, 182–83
Barnard, Rita, 2
Barney, Natalie, 46–47
Beardsworth, Adam, 146–47
Beat poetry, 98
Beat poets, 167–68
  French existentialism and, 173–74
  New York City and, 177
  postwar US and, 168–70
  reaction of, to academically sanctioned
    poetry, 171–73
  Walt Whitman and, 174
Becker, Florence, 108
Bellamy, Dodie, 244
Benet, Stephen Vincent, 103
Bennett, Gwendolyn, 85, 86

Cambridge Companions to...

AUTHORS